快感 Sensual Phrase

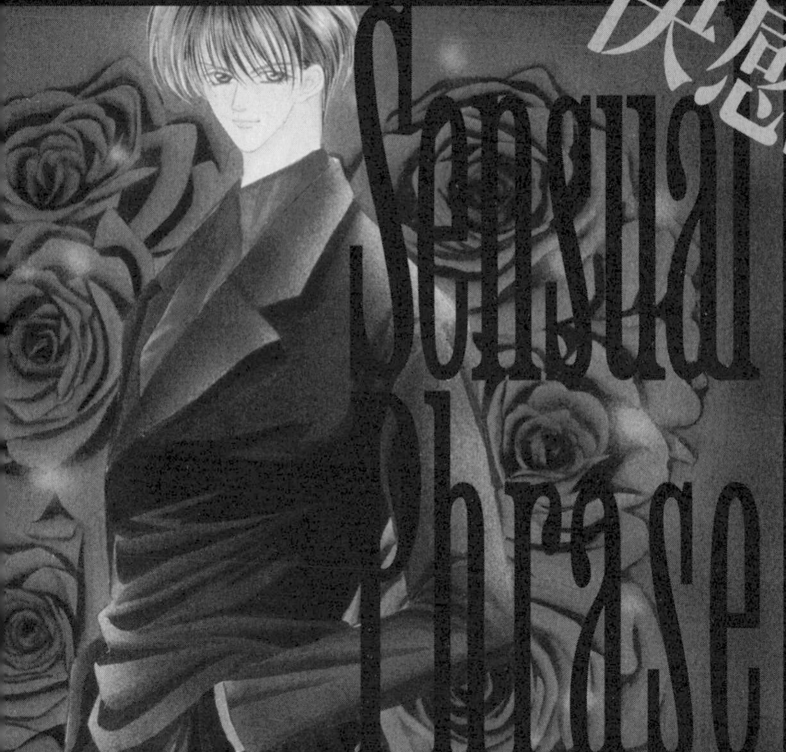

Story and Art by Mayu Shinjo

vol.4

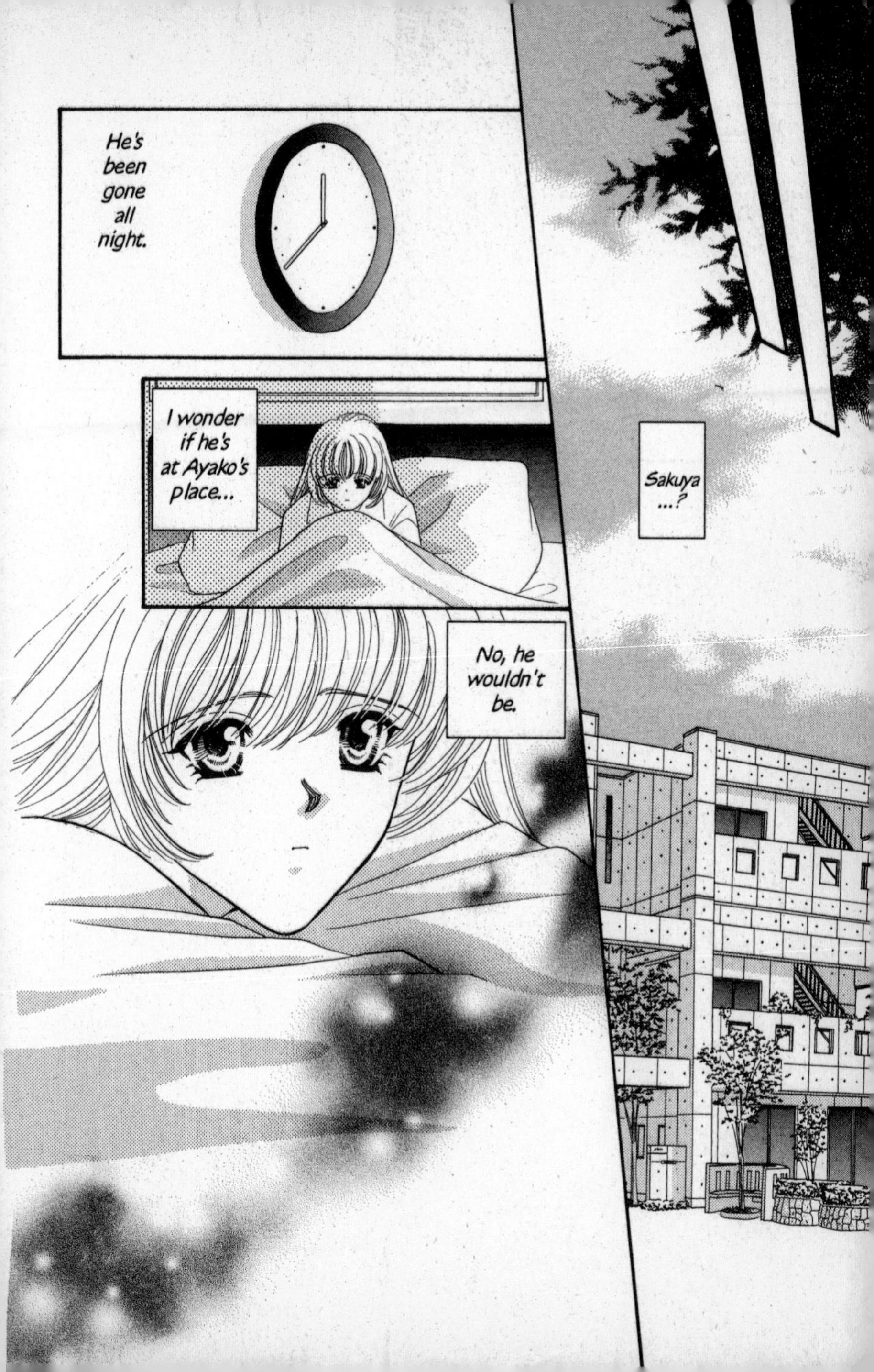
Sakuya ...?
He's been gone all night.
I wonder if he's at Ayako's place...
No, he wouldn't be.

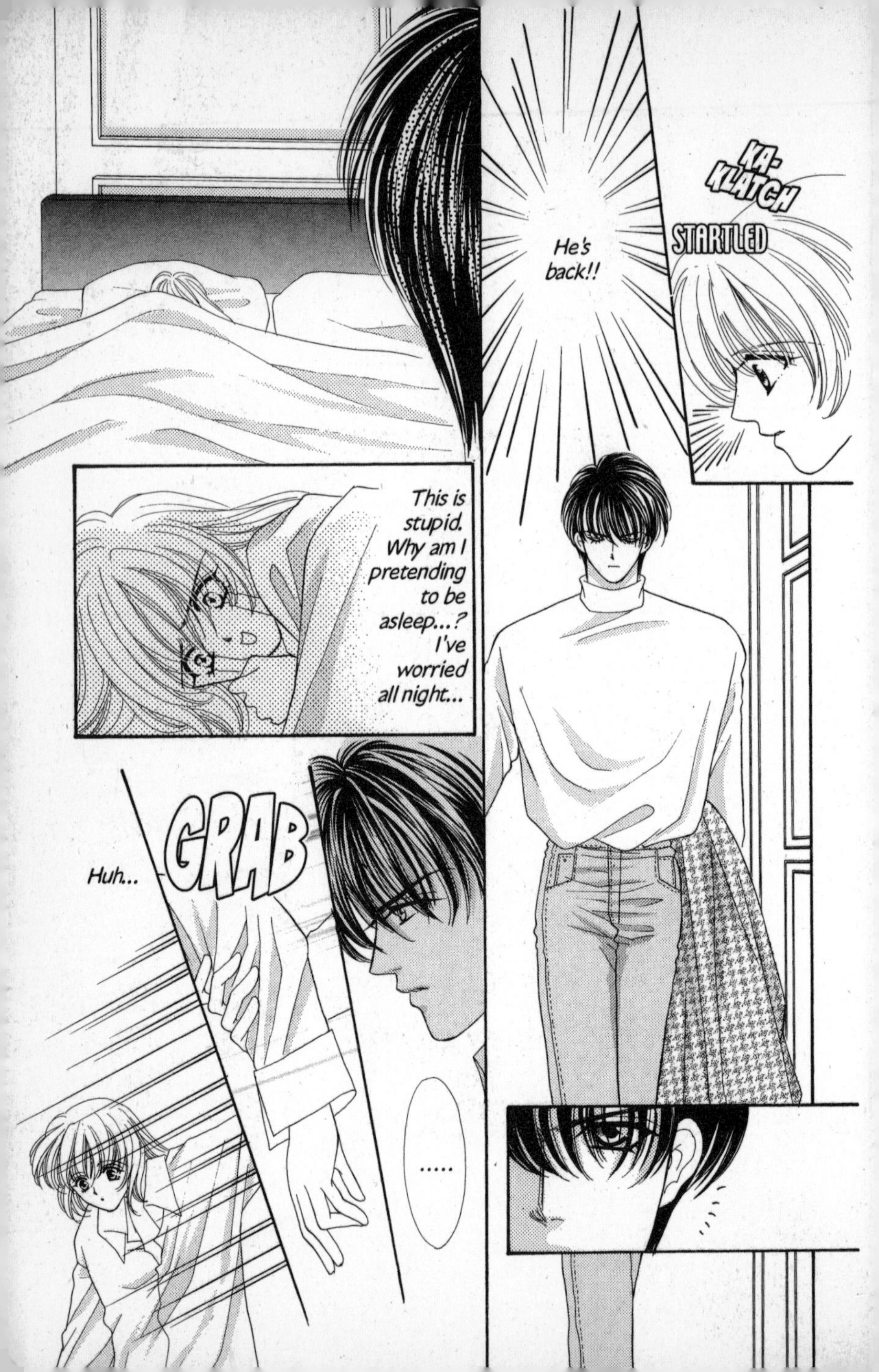
KA-KLATCH
STARTLED
He's back!!
This is stupid. Why am I pretending to be asleep...? I've worried all night...
GRAB
Huh...
.....

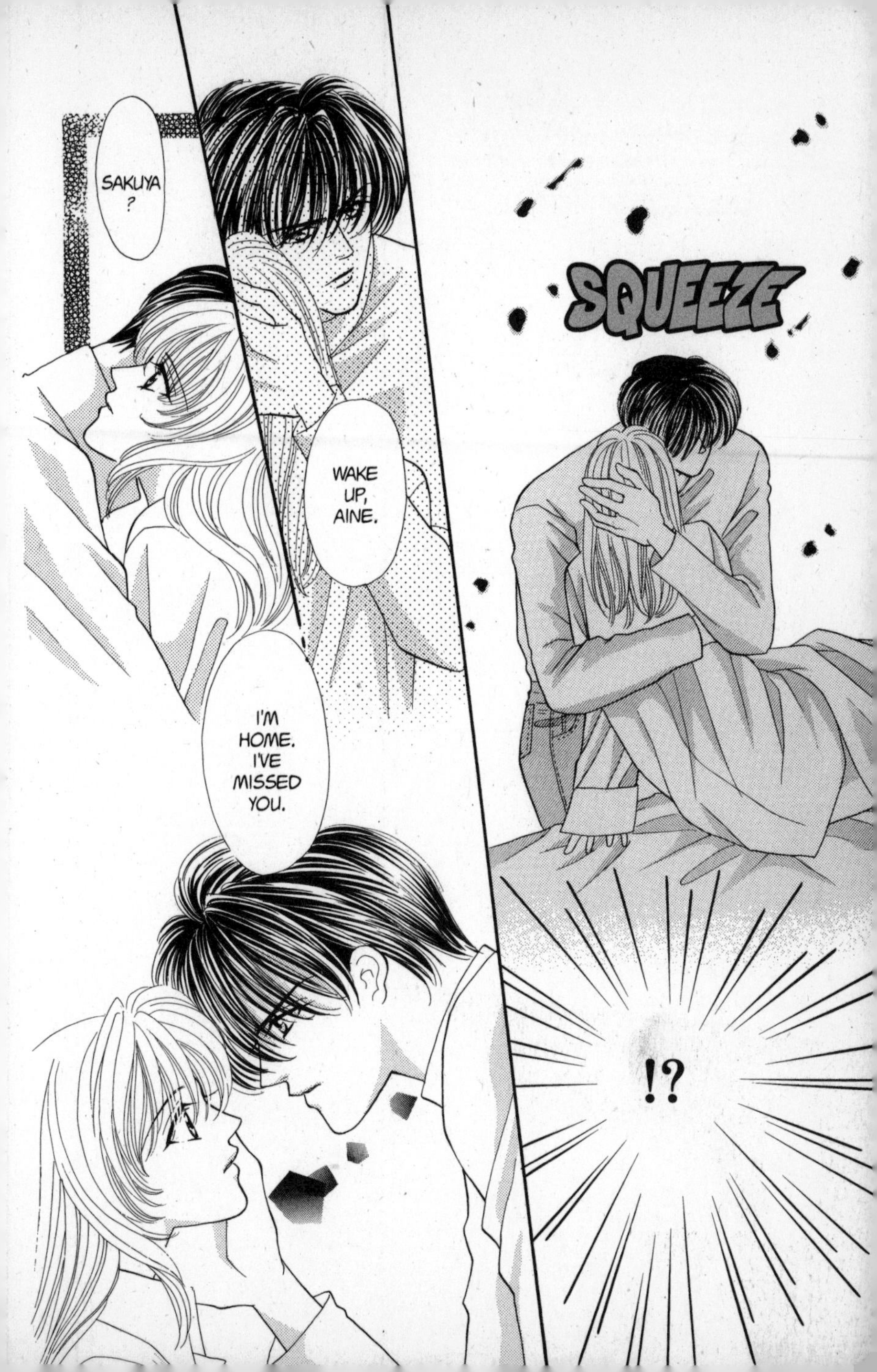
SQUEEZE
!?
WAKE UP, AINE.
SAKUYA?
I'M HOME. I'VE MISSED YOU.

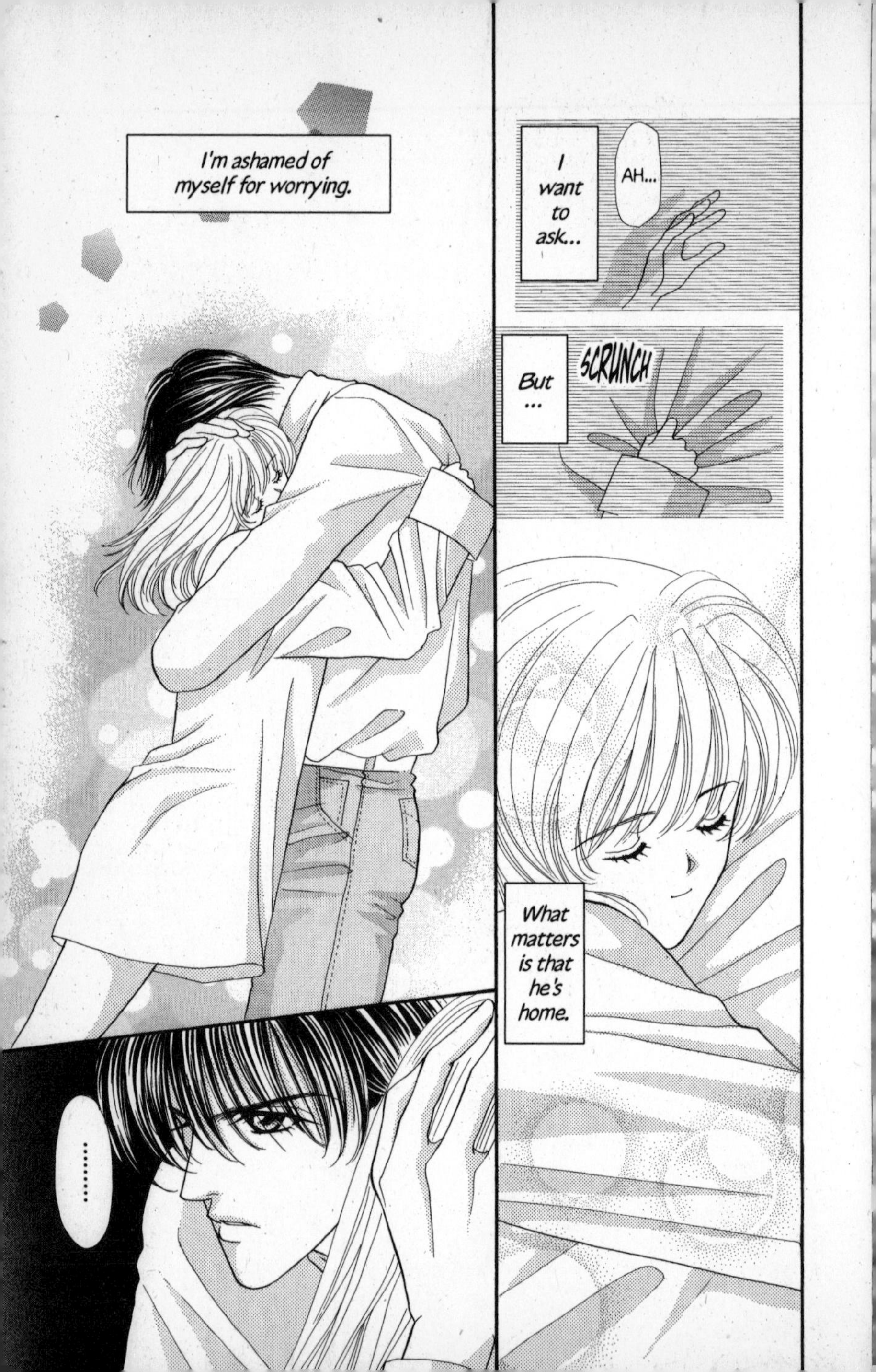
AH...
I want to ask...
SCRUNCH
But...
What matters is that he's home.
I'm ashamed of myself for worrying.
....

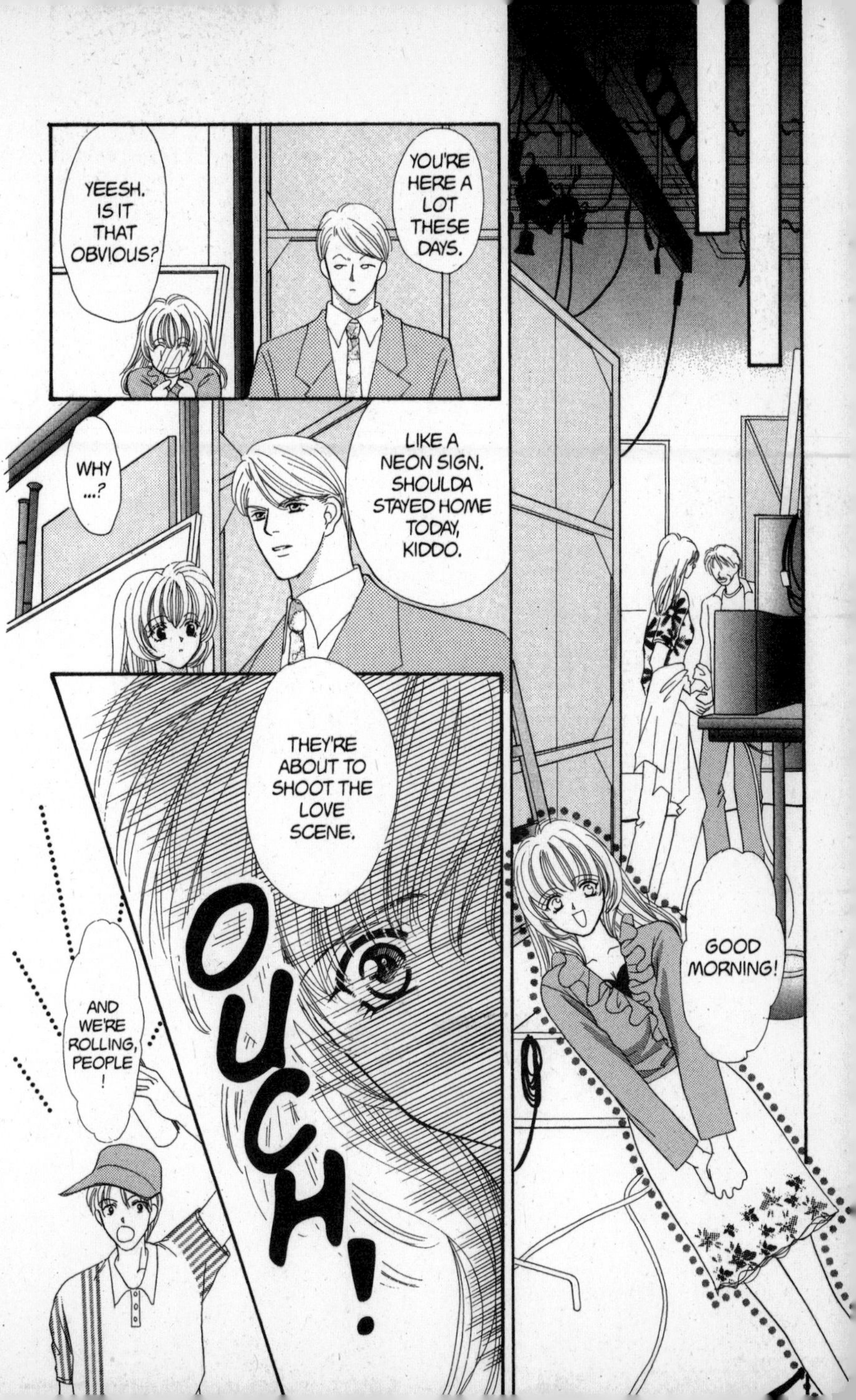
GOOD MORNING!
YOU'RE HERE A LOT THESE DAYS.
YEESH. IS IT THAT OBVIOUS?
LIKE A NEON SIGN. SHOULDA STAYED HOME TODAY, KIDDO.
WHY ...?
THEY'RE ABOUT TO SHOOT THE LOVE SCENE.
OUCH!
AND WE'RE ROLLING, PEOPLE !

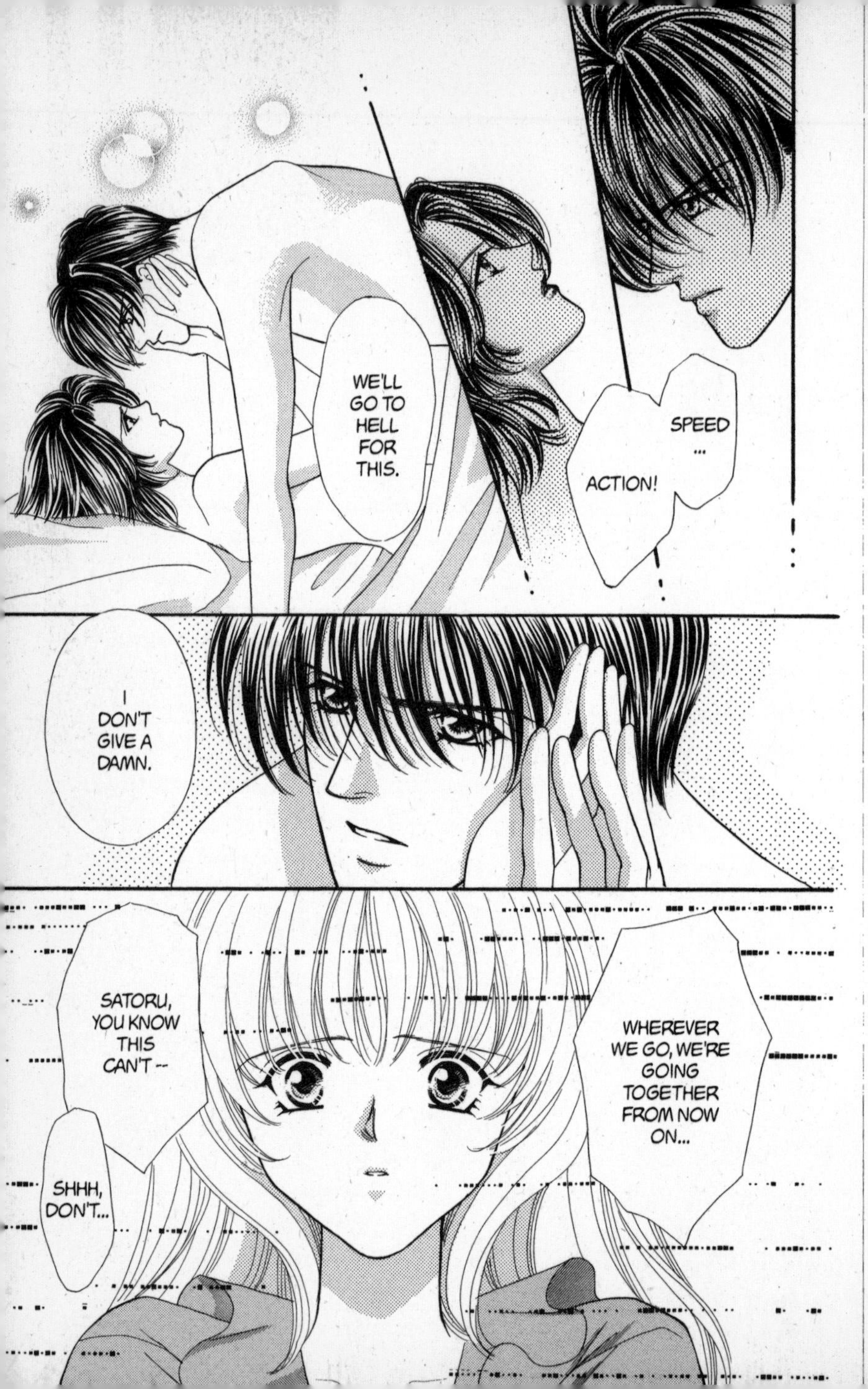
SPEED ... ACTION!
WE'LL GO TO HELL FOR THIS.
I DON'T GIVE A DAMN.
SATORU, YOU KNOW THIS CAN'T --
SHHH, DON'T...
WHEREVER WE GO, WE'RE GOING TOGETHER FROM NOW ON...

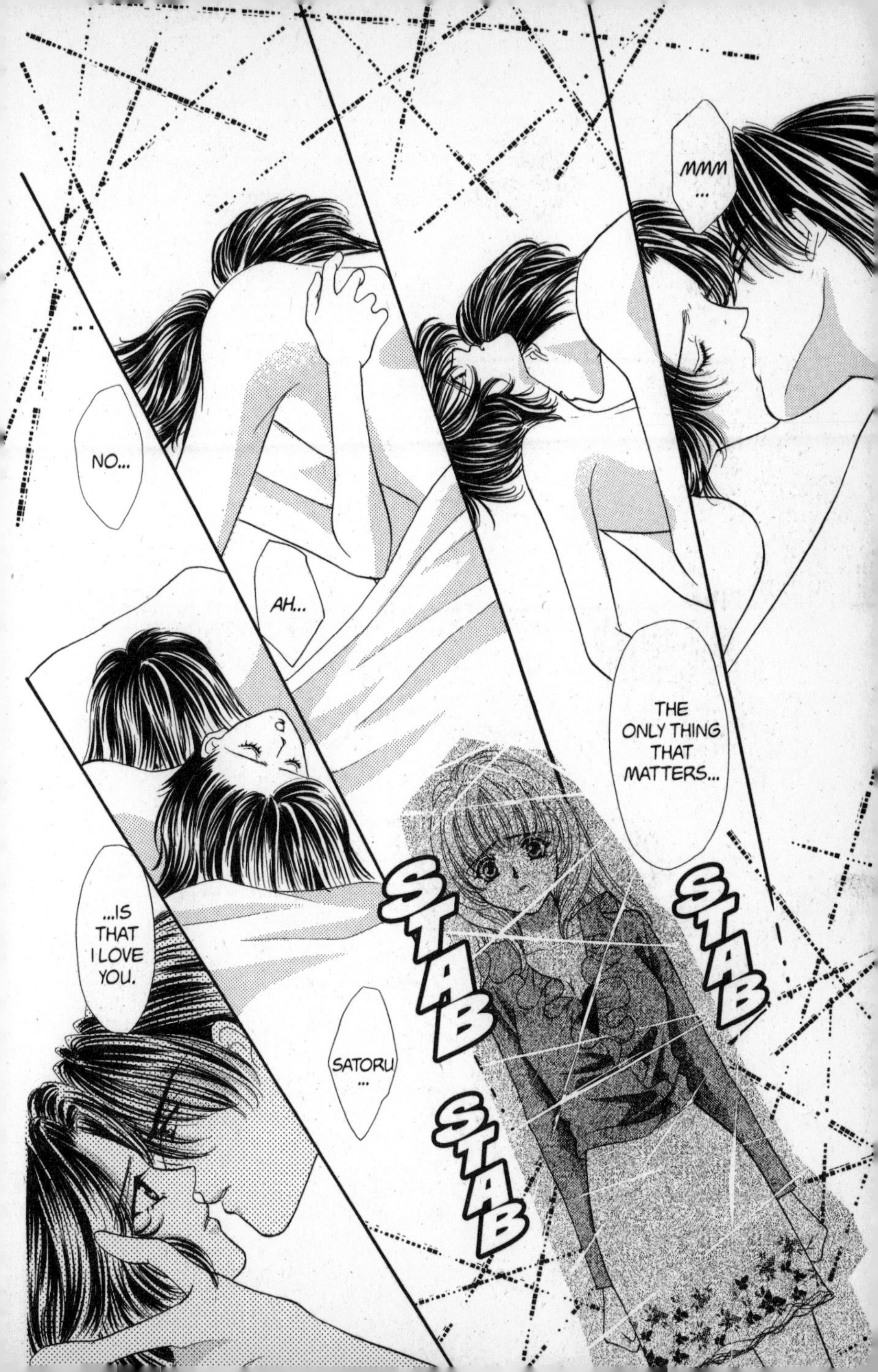
MMM...
THE ONLY THING THAT MATTERS...
STAB
STAB
AH...
NO...
...IS THAT I LOVE YOU.
SATORU...
STAB
STAB

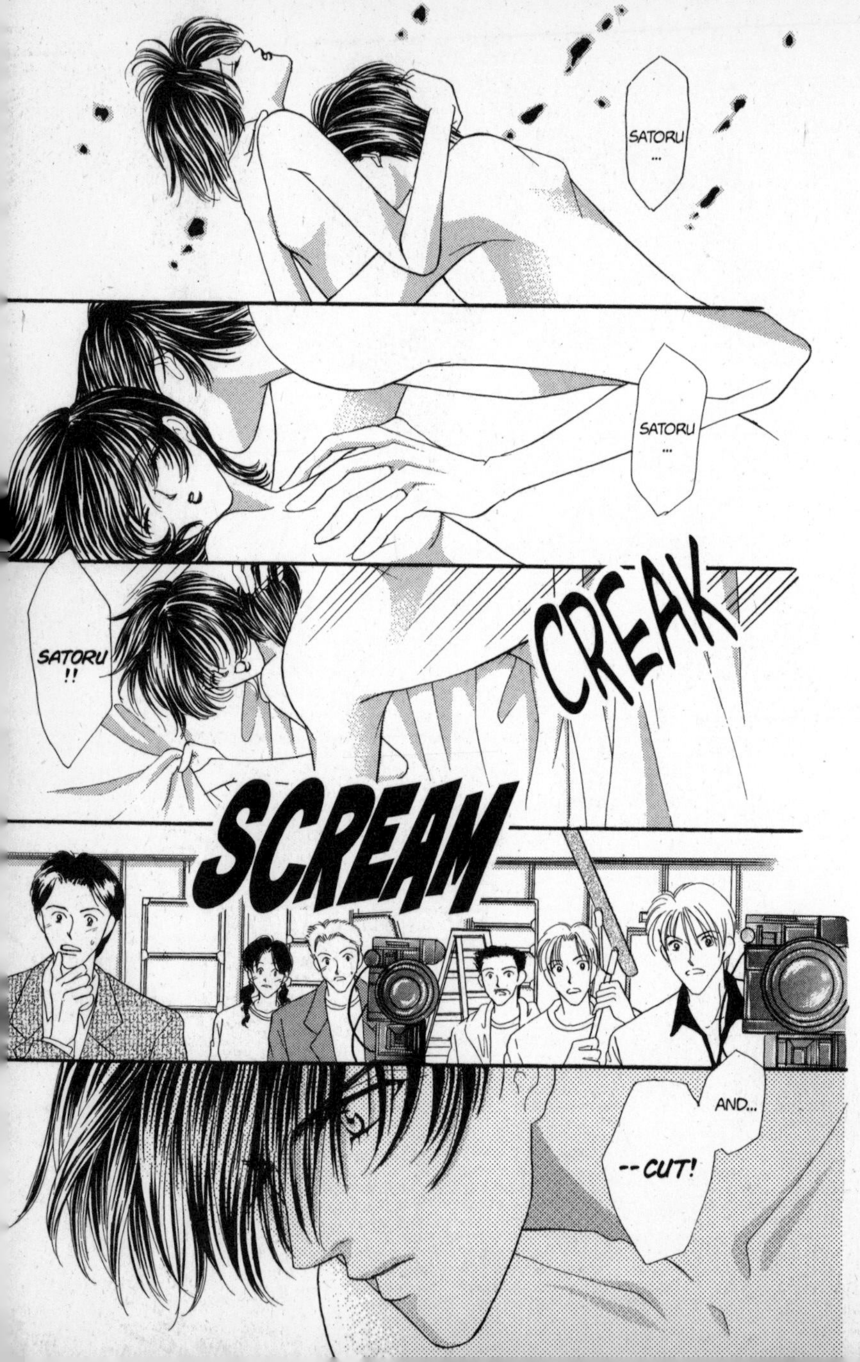
SATORU...
SATORU...
CREAK
SATORU!!
SCREAM
AND...
--CUT!

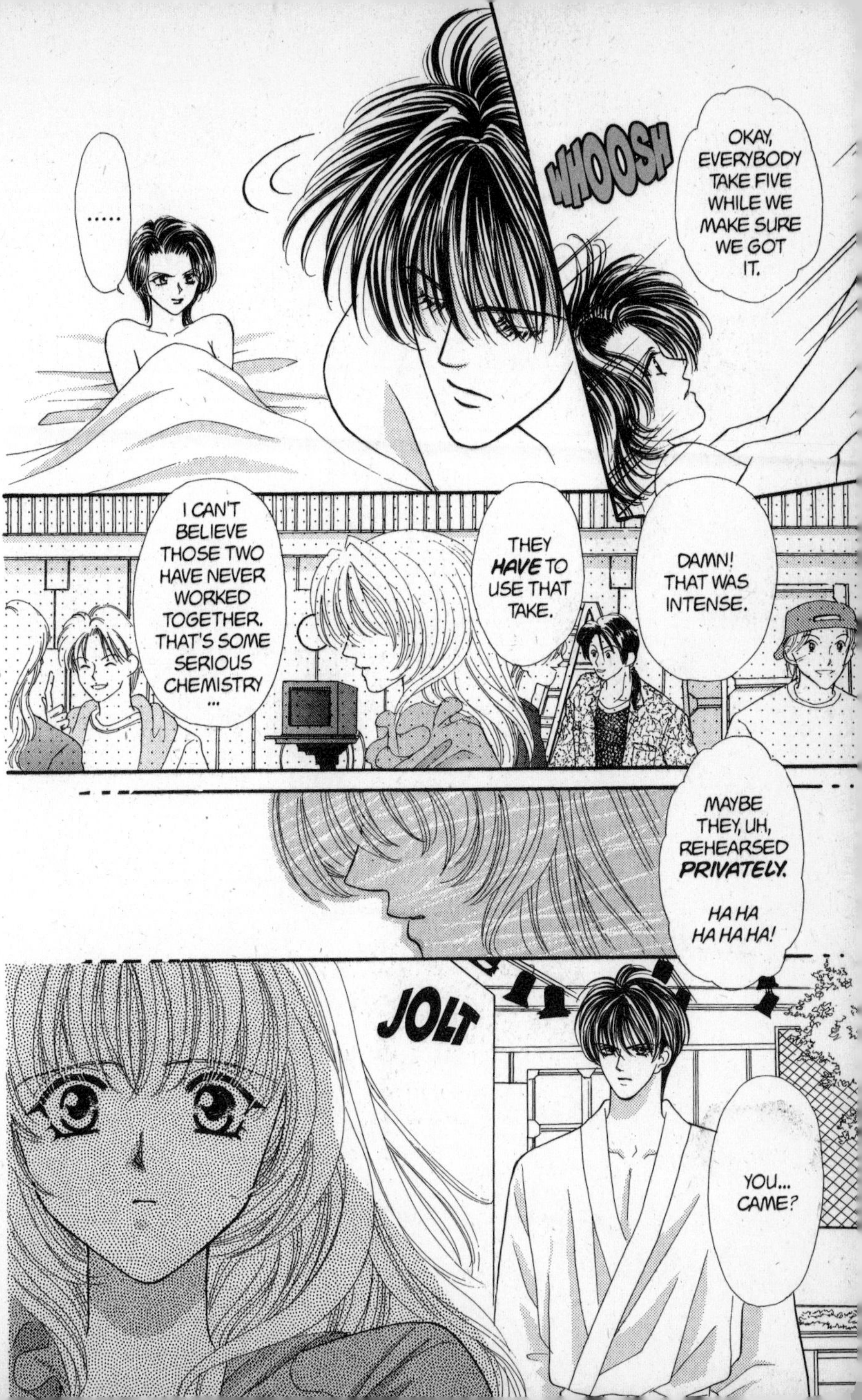
WHOOSH
OKAY, EVERYBODY TAKE FIVE WHILE WE MAKE SURE WE GOT IT.
......
DAMN! THAT WAS INTENSE.
THEY HAVE TO USE THAT TAKE.
I CAN'T BELIEVE THOSE TWO HAVE NEVER WORKED TOGETHER. THAT'S SOME SERIOUS CHEMISTRY ...
MAYBE THEY, UH, REHEARSED PRIVATELY.
HA HA HA HA HA!
YOU... CAME?
JOLT

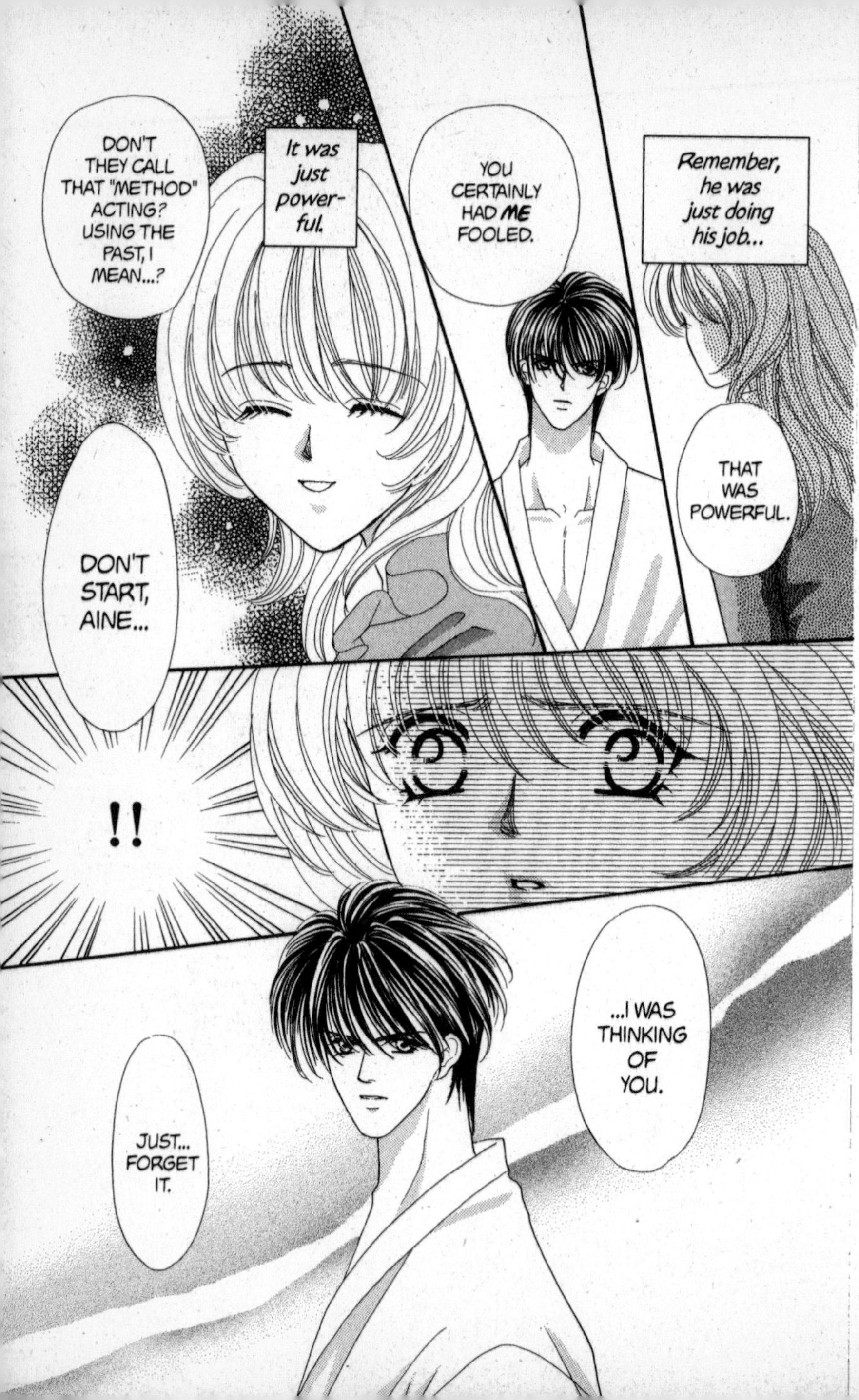
Remember, he was just doing his job...
THAT WAS POWERFUL.
YOU CERTAINLY HAD ME FOOLED.
It was just power-ful.
DON'T THEY CALL THAT "METHOD" ACTING? USING THE PAST, I MEAN...?
DON'T START, AINE...
!!
...I WAS THINKING OF YOU.
JUST... FORGET IT.

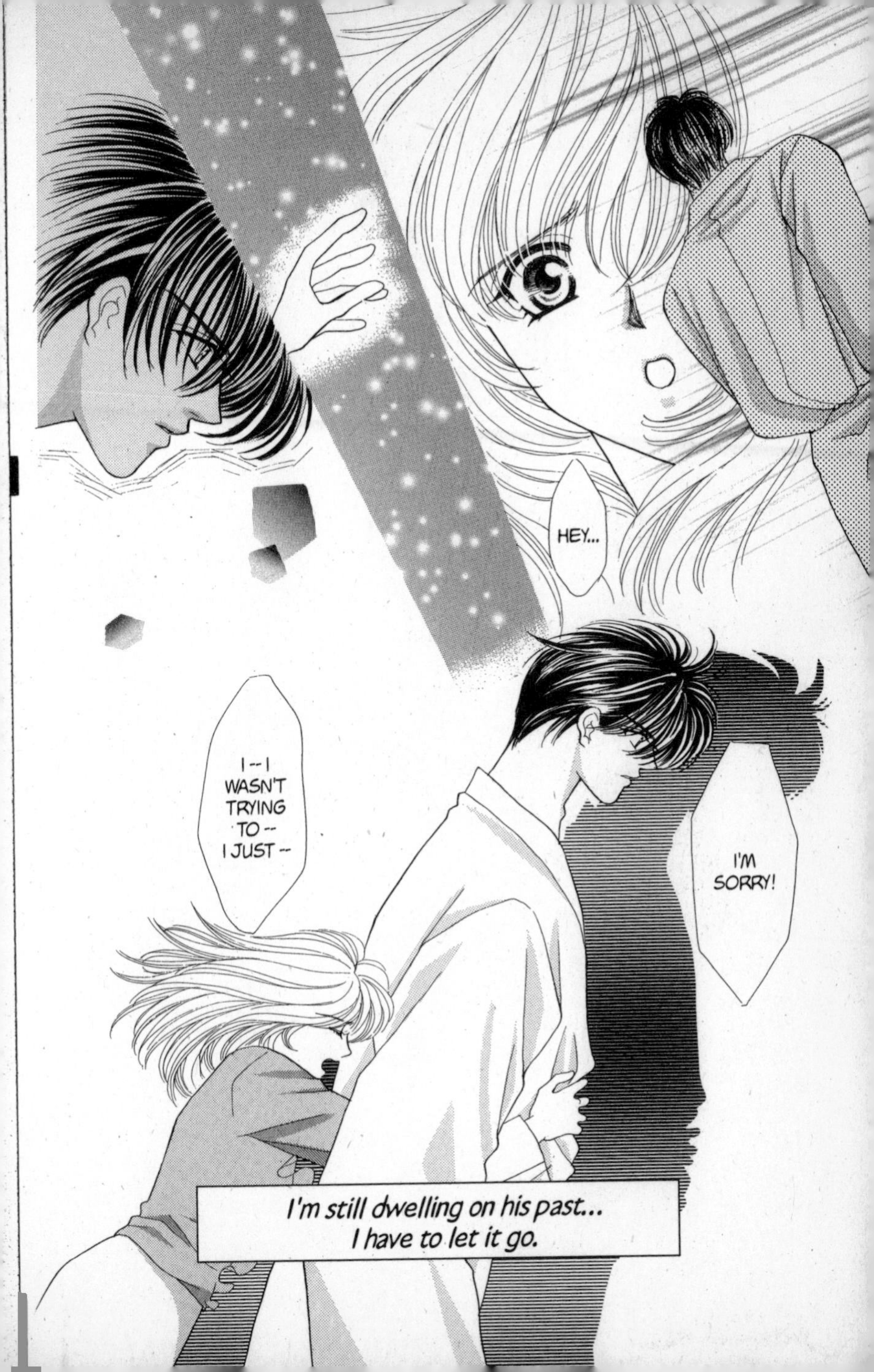
HEY...
I'M SORRY!
I -- I WASN'T TRYING TO -- I JUST --
I'm still dwelling on his past... I have to let it go.

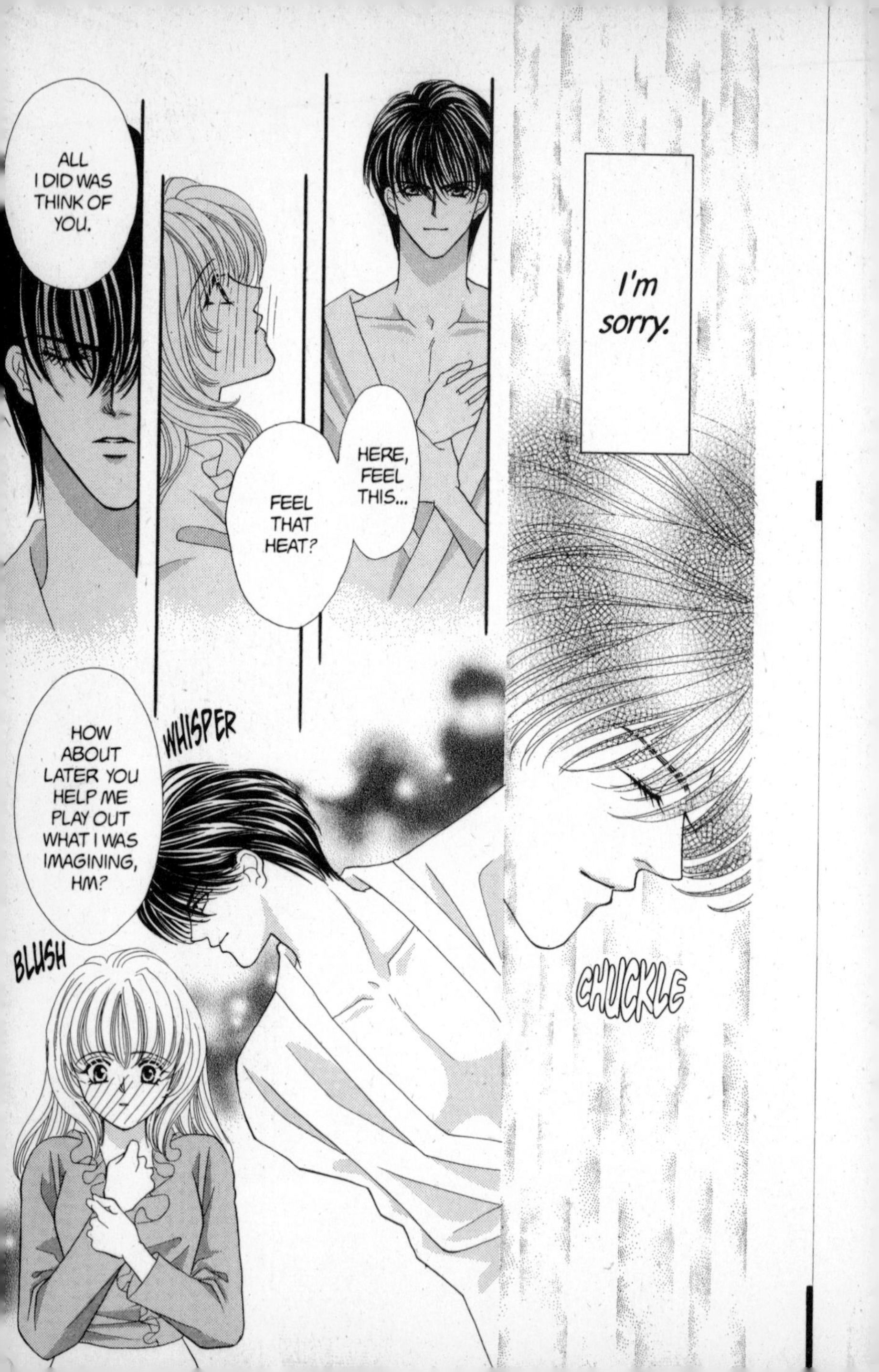
I'm sorry.
CHUCKLE
HERE, FEEL THIS...
FEEL THAT HEAT?
ALL I DID WAS THINK OF YOU.
WHISPER
HOW ABOUT LATER YOU HELP ME PLAY OUT WHAT I WAS IMAGINING, HM?
BLUSH

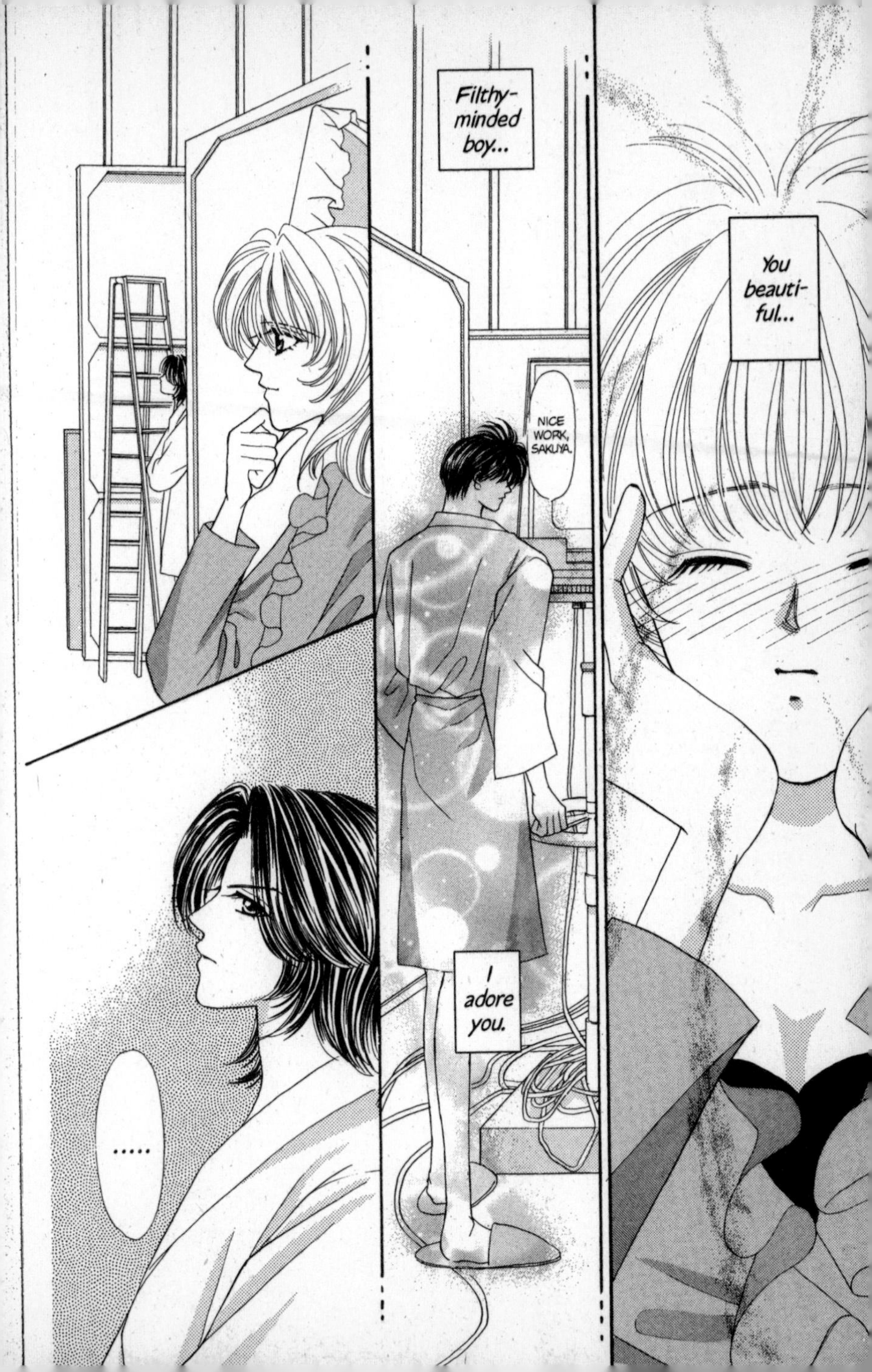
You beautiful...
Filthy-minded boy...
NICE WORK, SAKUYA.
I adore you.
.....

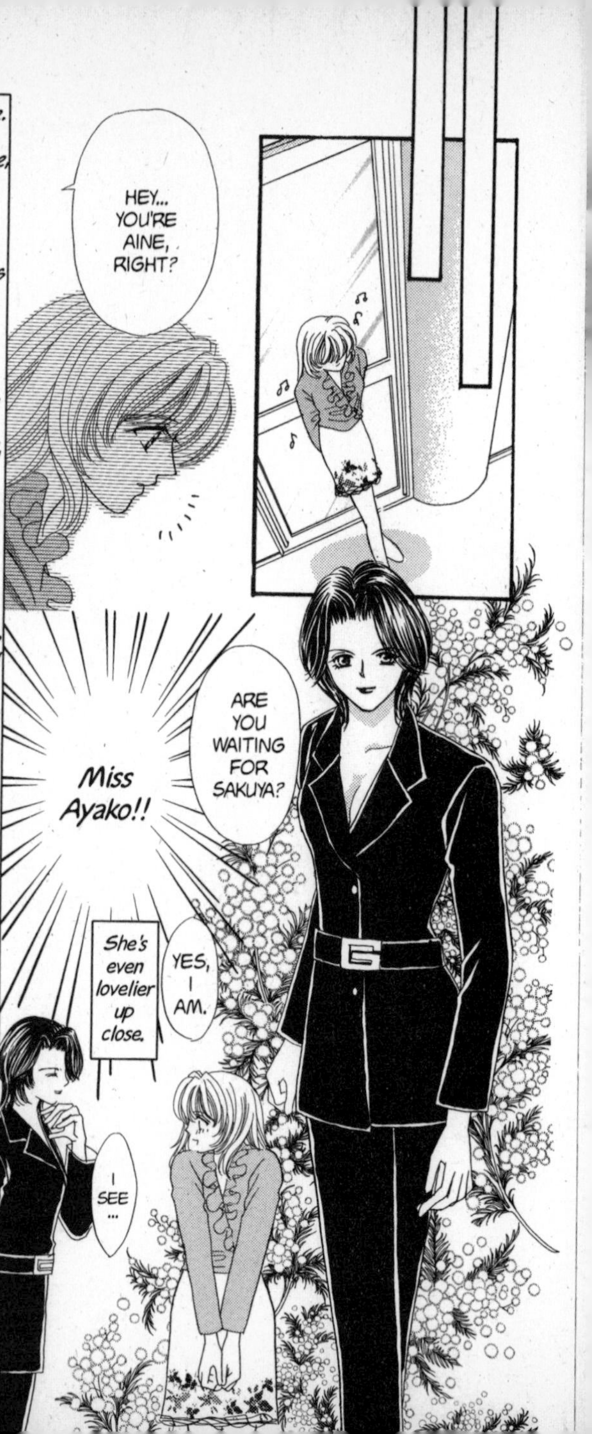
HEY... YOU'RE AINE, RIGHT?
ARE YOU WAITING FOR SAKUYA?
Miss Ayako!!
YES, I AM.
She's even lovelier up close.
I SEE ...

Hello again! Mayu Shinjo here. Welcome to Vol. 4. What's happened since we last spoke, hm? Well, the band Siam Shade has finally received some recognition and I couldn't be happier for them. I interviewed them when I was researching this comic and I've been quietly keeping my eye on them ever since. They're kind of like a Japanese version of Metallica. If metal's your thing, you should check them out. In addition to rocking, they're funny enough to make a girl bust a gut. And cool. Funny and cool. Is there a better combination than that?!

Speaking of up-and-coming success stories, Michy aka Mitsuharu Oikawa is great!! The title track "Will You Dance With Me?" was so good I had to buy the video. Prince Michy...he's so swarthy-hot.

By the way, I know I'm the last person to catch this fever, but I'm finally getting into Glay. So many of you wrote to compare Teru to Sakuya that I had to check them out. The thing that's great about Glay is that when I set out to record a mix of just their good songs, I realized ALL their songs were good. Usually, no matter how much I like the artist, there are songs that I just skip over. What? Like you don't?! Well, I do! Except with Glay. Oh - and I got my hair cut to look like Jiro's. I walk around town in Glay cosplay mode -- ha ha! But seriously, Glay wasn't the inspiration for Lucifer, I didn't get into Glay until way later. Of course, if it makes you happy to think of Lucifer as Glay, you go right ahead. I want my readers to be happy.

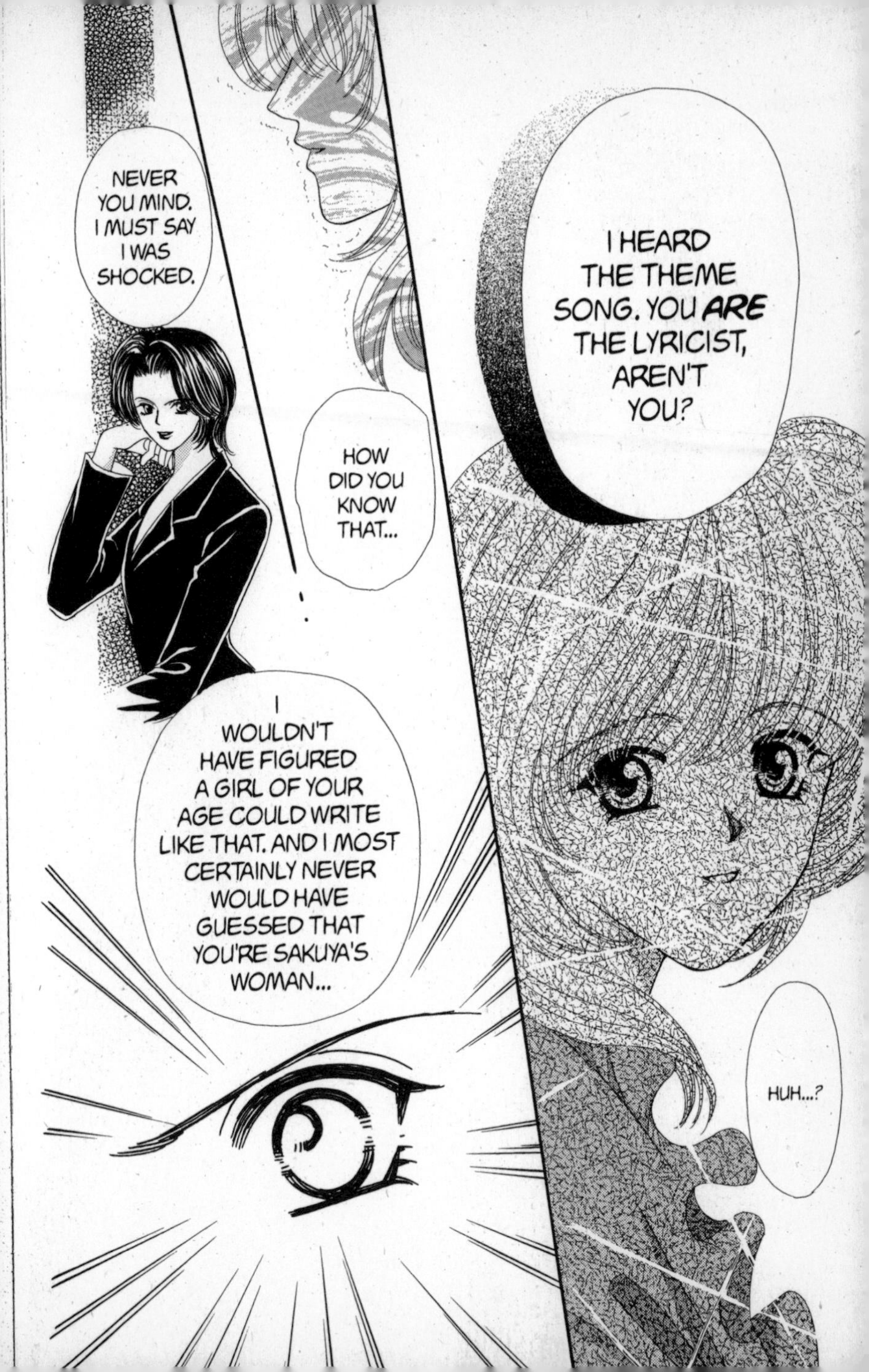
I HEARD THE THEME SONG. YOU **ARE** THE LYRICIST, AREN'T YOU?
HUH...?
HOW DID YOU KNOW THAT...
NEVER YOU MIND. I MUST SAY I WAS SHOCKED.
I WOULDN'T HAVE FIGURED A GIRL OF YOUR AGE COULD WRITE LIKE THAT. AND I MOST CERTAINLY NEVER WOULD HAVE GUESSED THAT YOU'RE SAKUYA'S WOMAN...

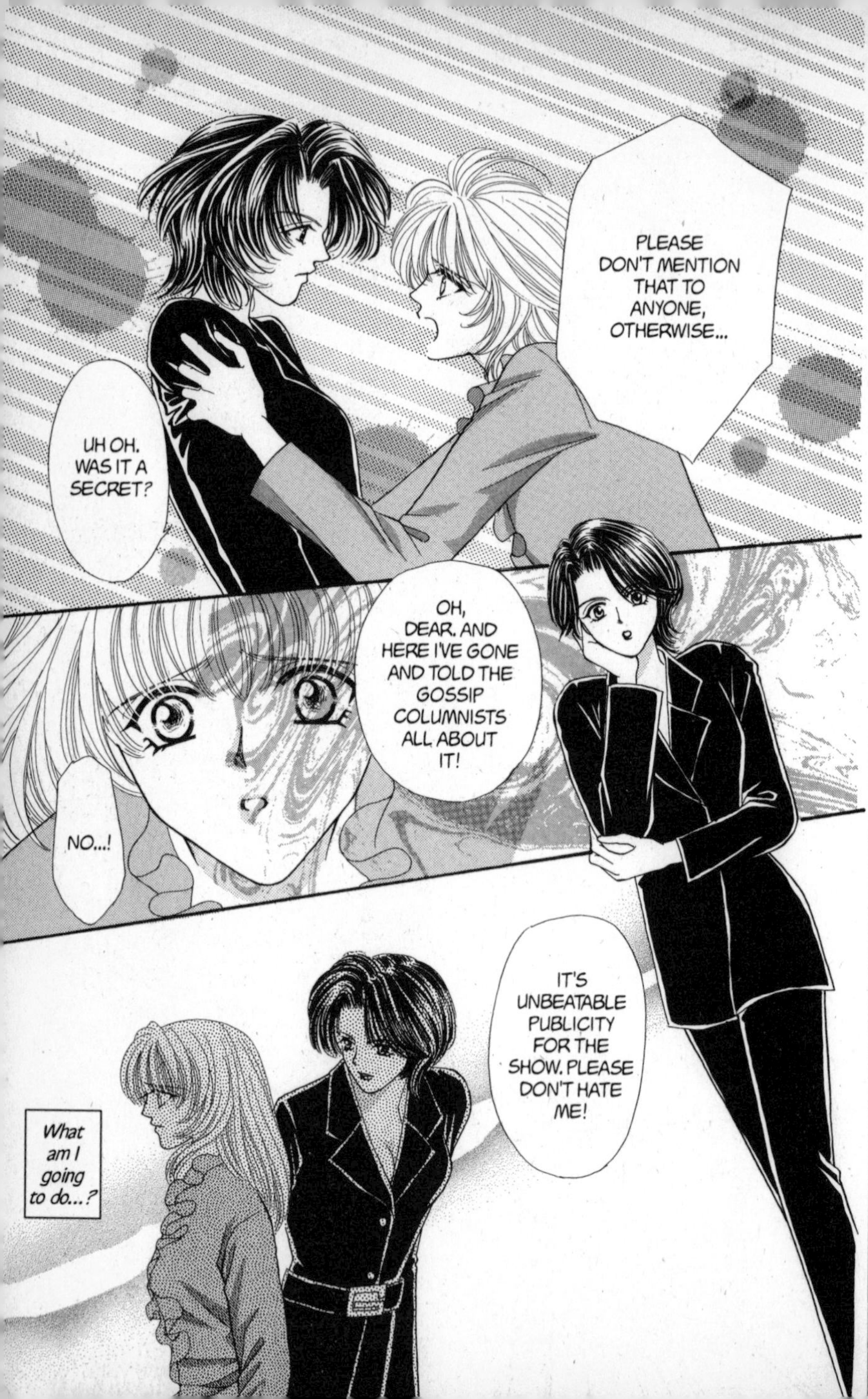
PLEASE DON'T MENTION THAT TO ANYONE, OTHERWISE...
UH OH. WAS IT A SECRET?
OH, DEAR. AND HERE I'VE GONE AND TOLD THE GOSSIP COLUMNISTS ALL ABOUT IT!
NO...!
IT'S UNBEATABLE PUBLICITY FOR THE SHOW. PLEASE DON'T HATE ME!
What am I going to do...?

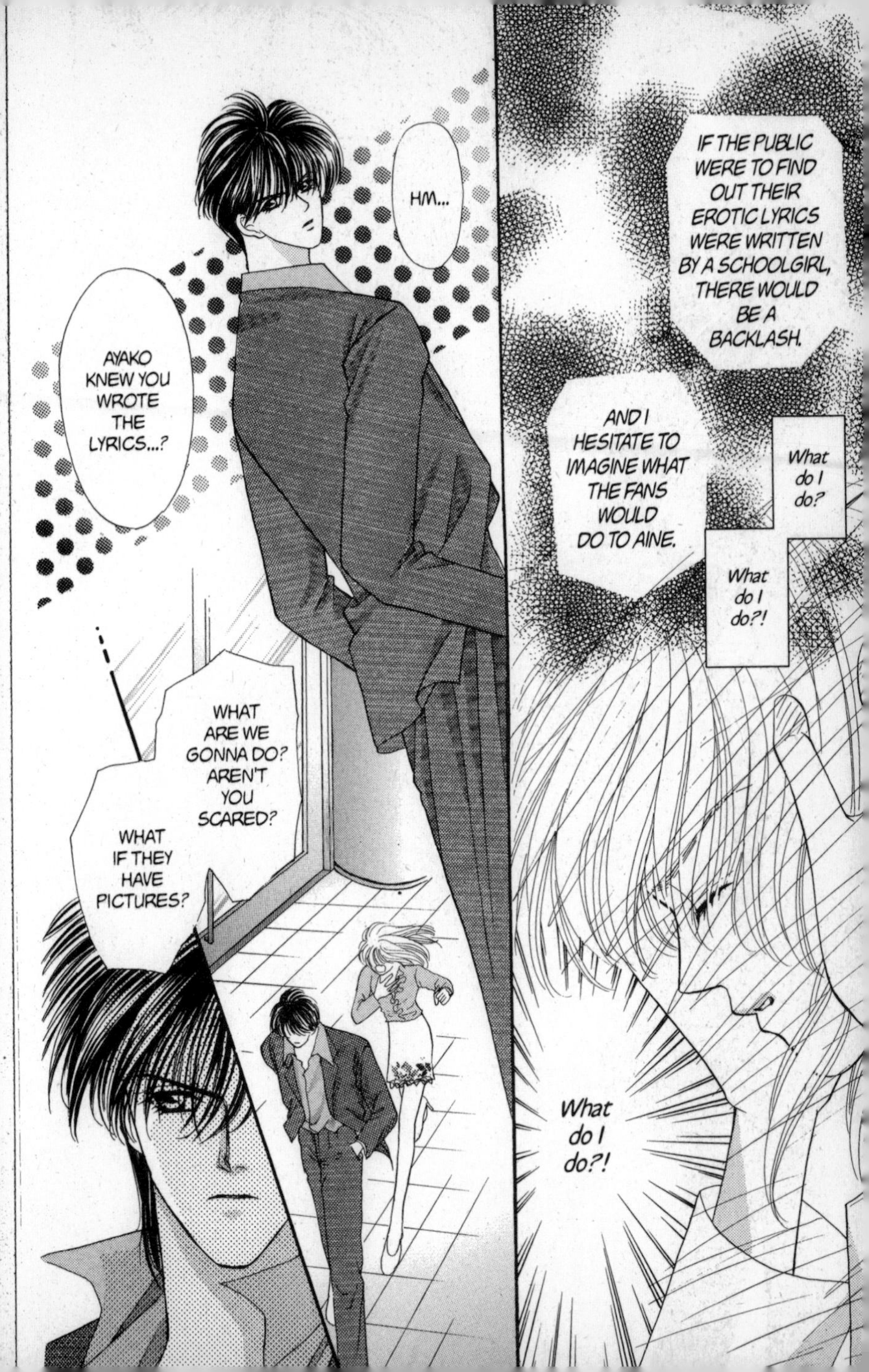
IF THE PUBLIC WERE TO FIND OUT THEIR EROTIC LYRICS WERE WRITTEN BY A SCHOOLGIRL, THERE WOULD BE A BACKLASH.
AND I HESITATE TO IMAGINE WHAT THE FANS WOULD DO TO AINE.
What do I do?
What do I do?!
What do I do?!
HM...
AYAKO KNEW YOU WROTE THE LYRICS...?
...
WHAT ARE WE GONNA DO? AREN'T YOU SCARED?
WHAT IF THEY HAVE PICTURES?

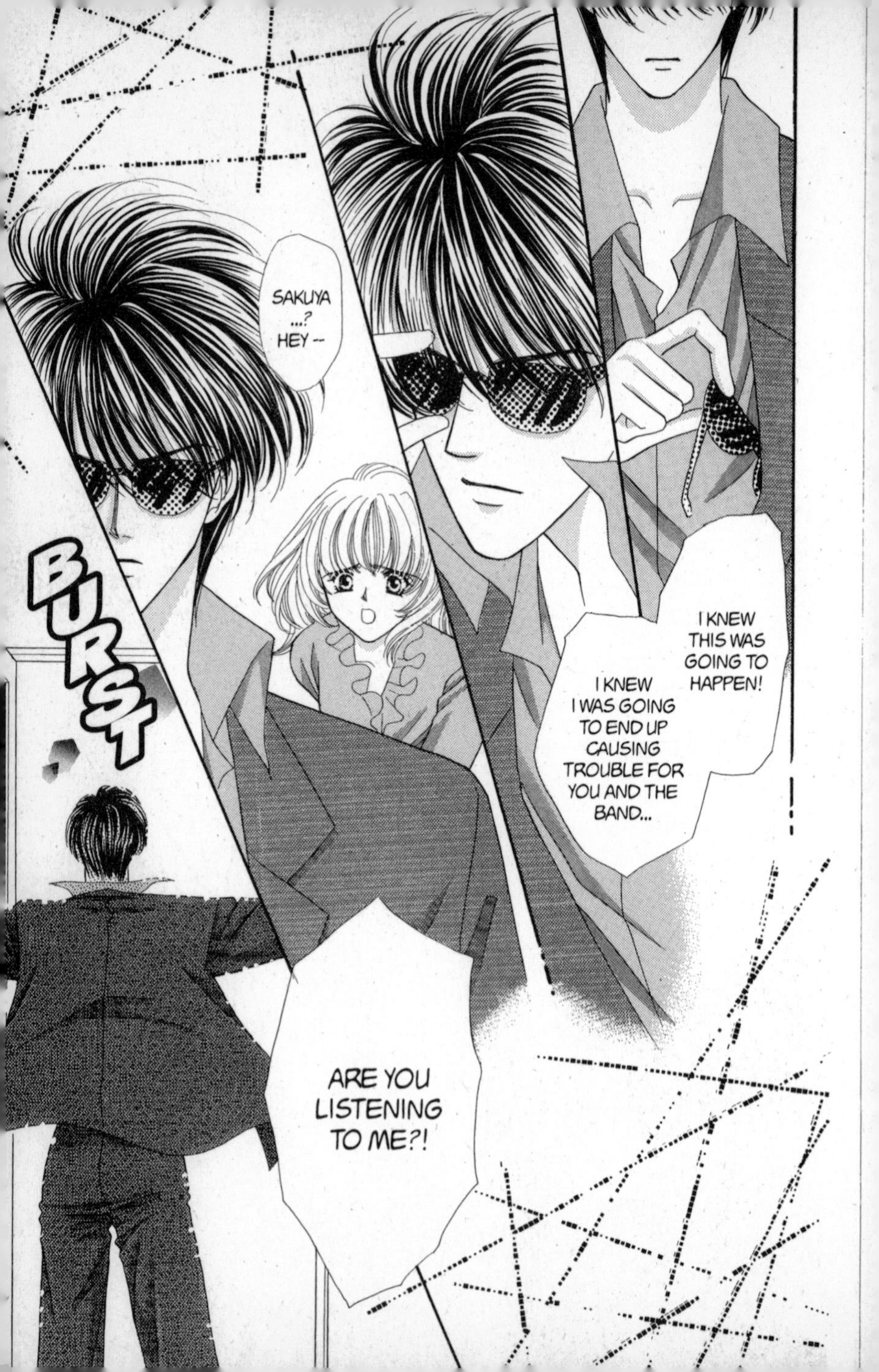
I KNEW THIS WAS GOING TO HAPPEN!
I KNEW I WAS GOING TO END UP CAUSING TROUBLE FOR YOU AND THE BAND...
SAKUYA ...? HEY --
BURST
ARE YOU LISTENING TO ME?!

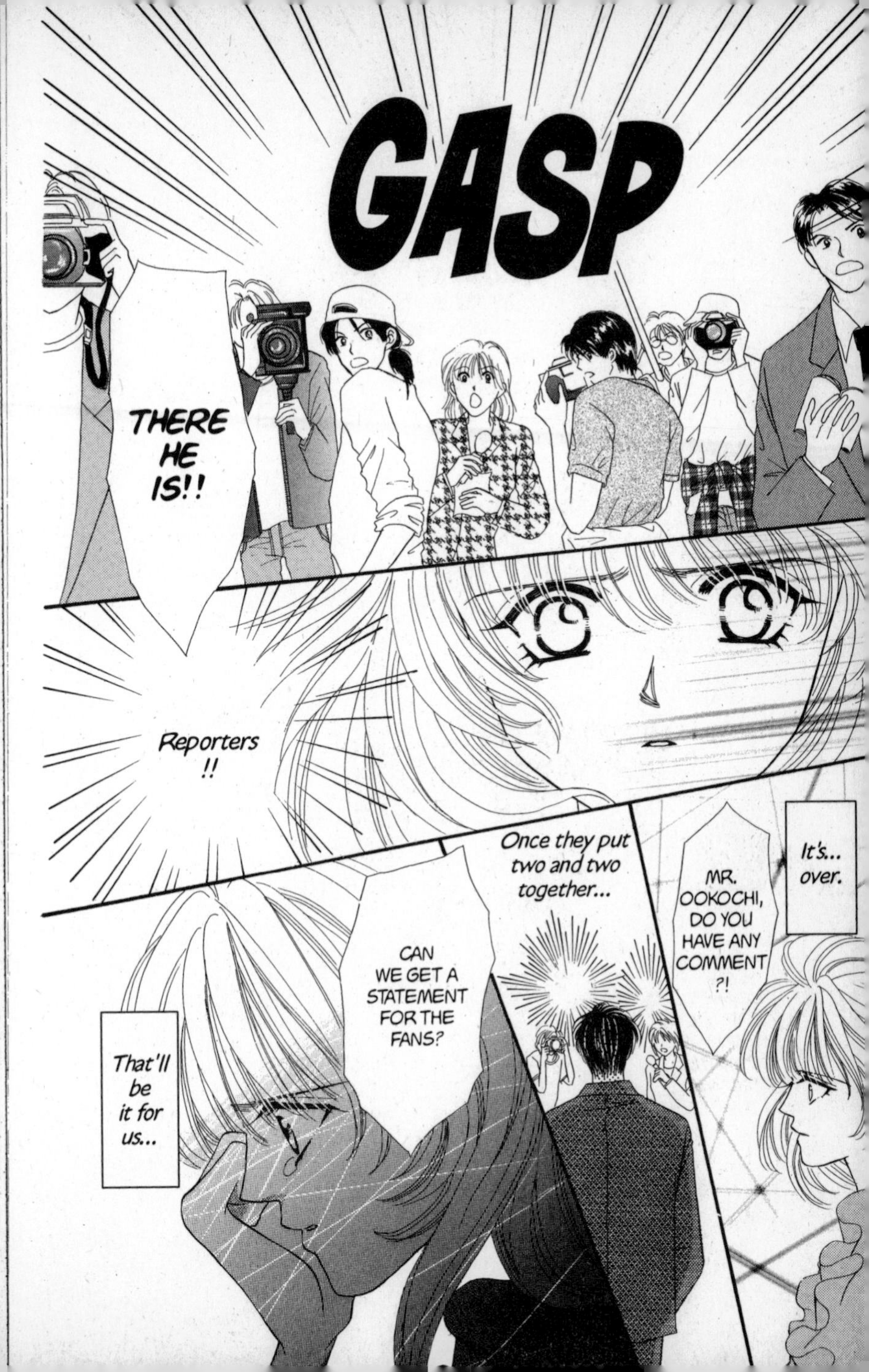
GASP
THERE HE IS!!
Reporters !!
It's... over.
MR. OOKOCHI, DO YOU HAVE ANY COMMENT ?!
Once they put two and two together...
CAN WE GET A STATEMENT FOR THE FANS?
That'll be it for us...

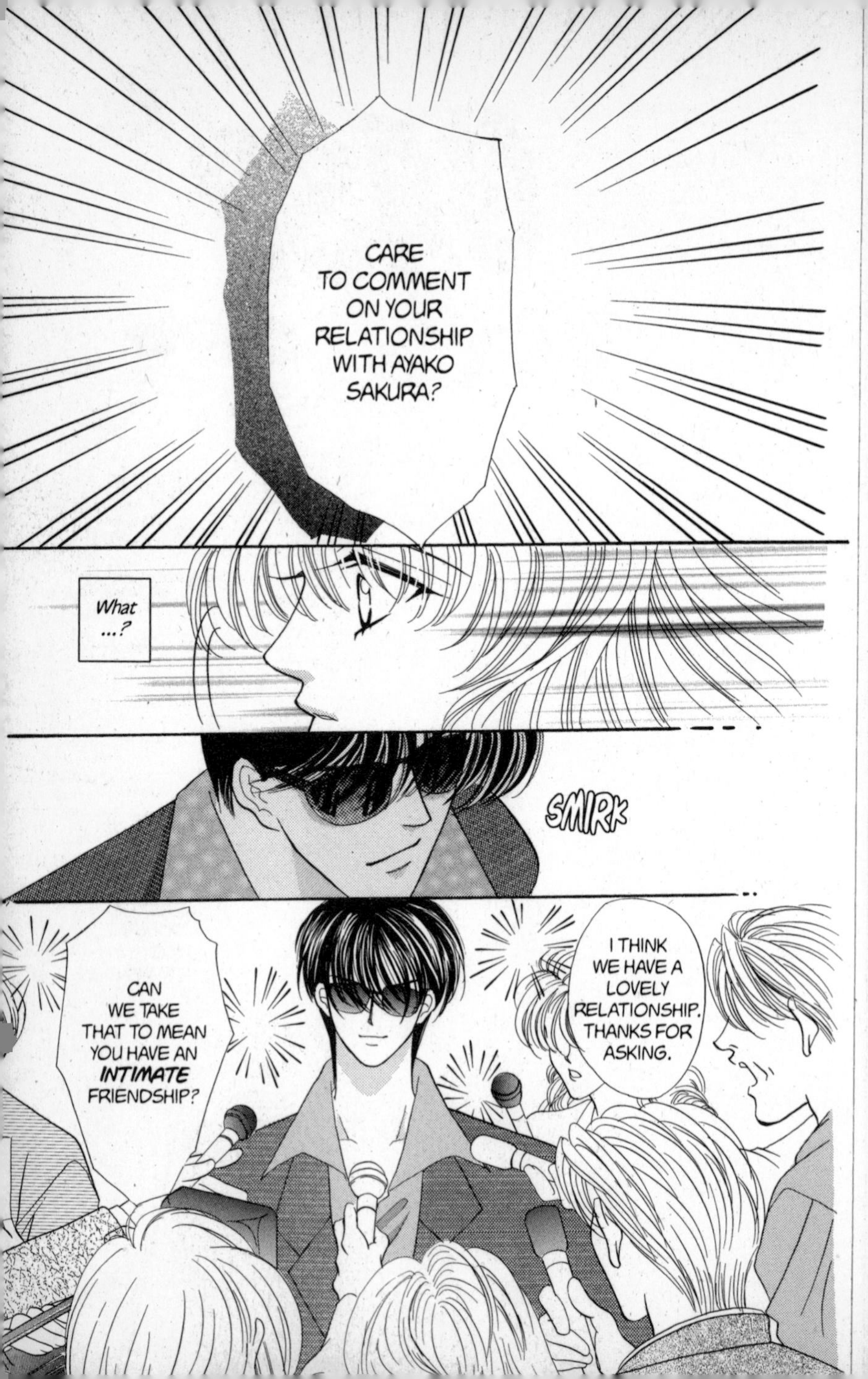
CARE TO COMMENT ON YOUR RELATIONSHIP WITH AYAKO SAKURA?
What ...?
SMIRK
I THINK WE HAVE A LOVELY RELATIONSHIP. THANKS FOR ASKING.
CAN WE TAKE THAT TO MEAN YOU HAVE AN *INTIMATE* FRIENDSHIP?

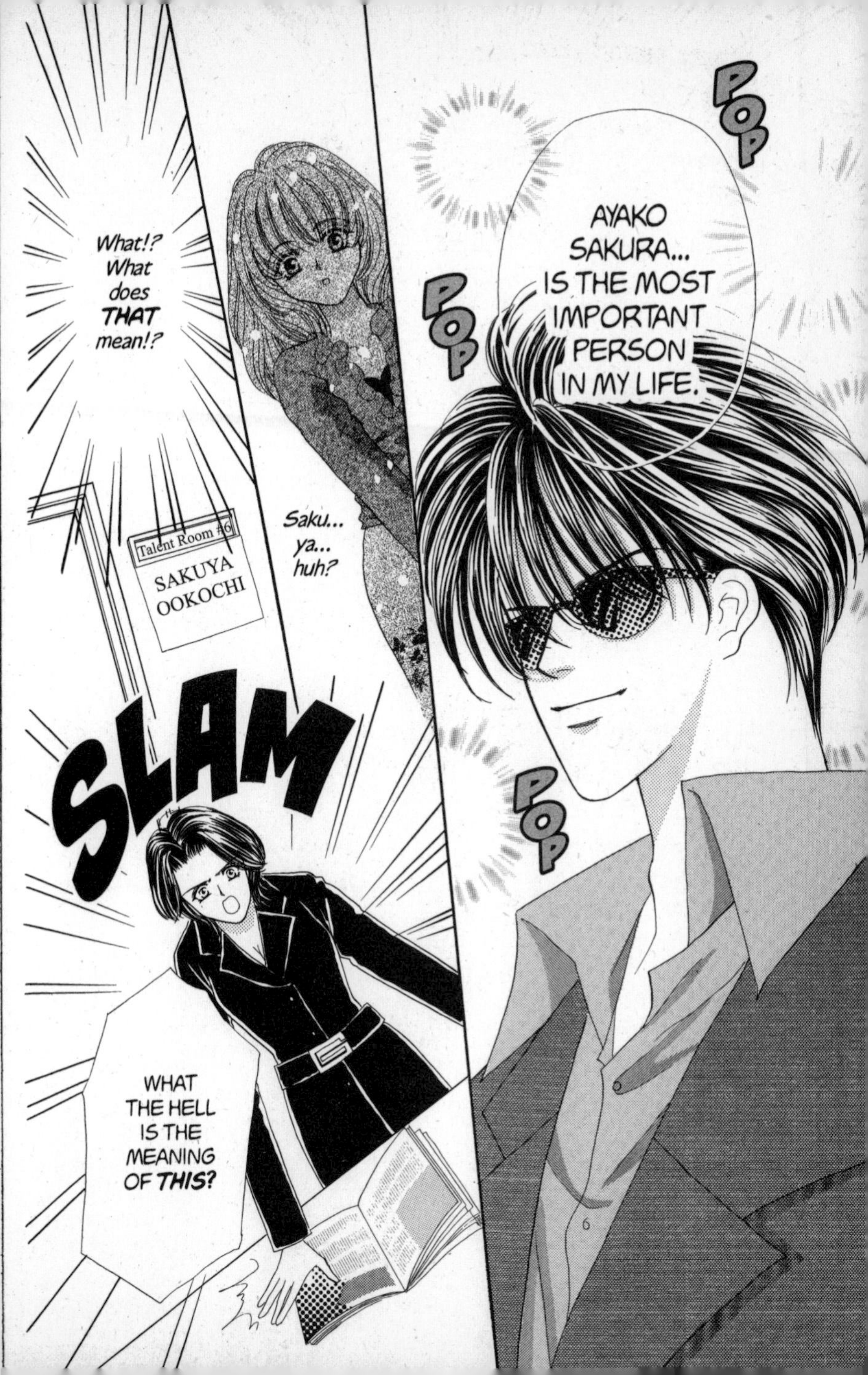
POP
AYAKO SAKURA... IS THE MOST IMPORTANT PERSON IN MY LIFE.
POP
POP
Saku... ya... huh?
What!? What does THAT mean!?
Talent Room #6
SAKUYA OOKOCHI
SLAM
WHAT THE HELL IS THE MEANING OF THIS?

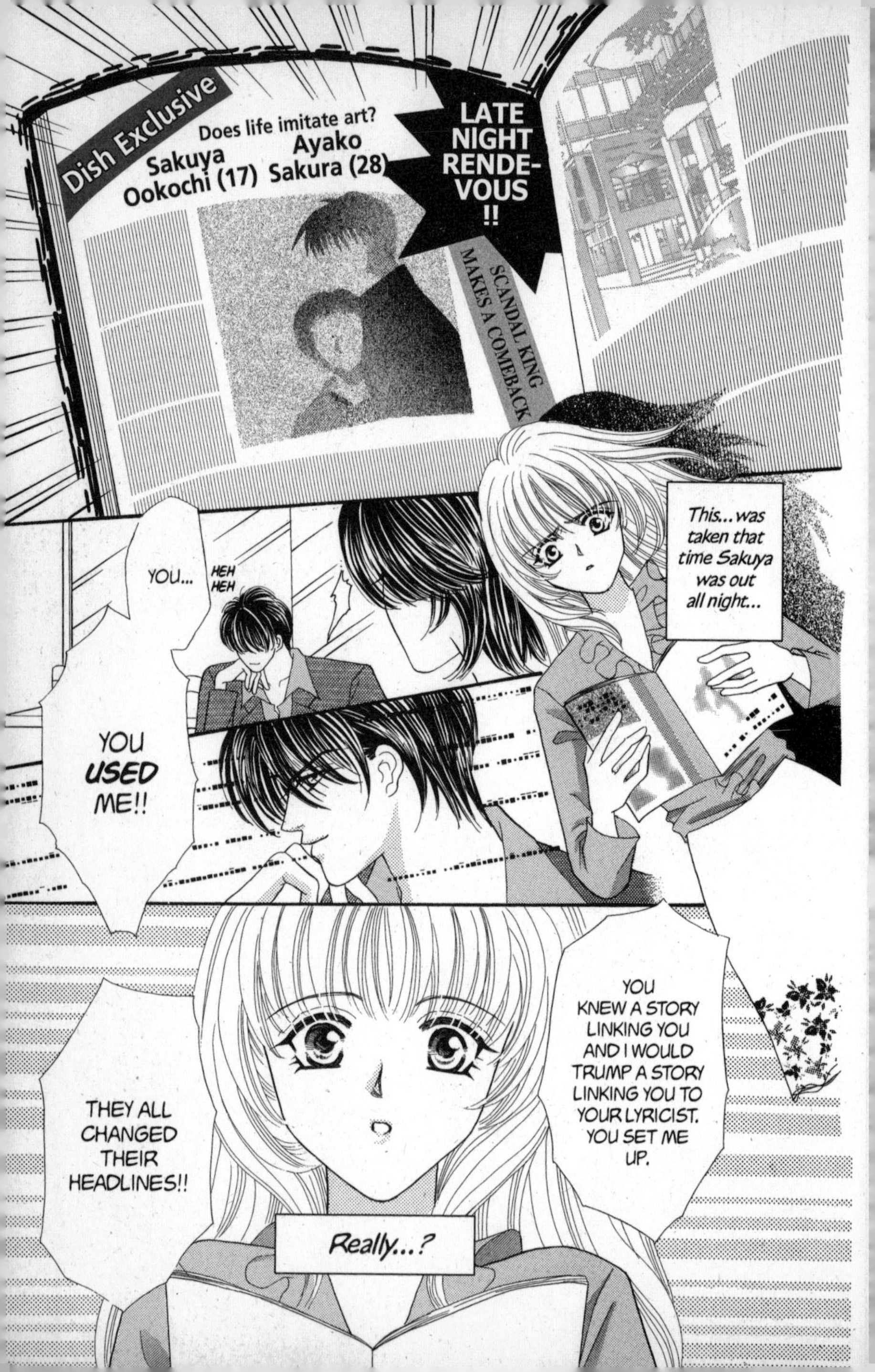
Dish Exclusive
Does life imitate art?
Sakuya Ookochi (17)
Ayako Sakura (28)
LATE NIGHT RENDE-VOUS!!
SCANDAL KING MAKES A COMEBACK
This...was taken that time Sakuya was out all night...
YOU...
HEH HEH
YOU USED ME!!
YOU KNEW A STORY LINKING YOU AND I WOULD TRUMP A STORY LINKING YOU TO YOUR LYRICIST. YOU SET ME UP.
THEY ALL CHANGED THEIR HEADLINES!!
Really...?

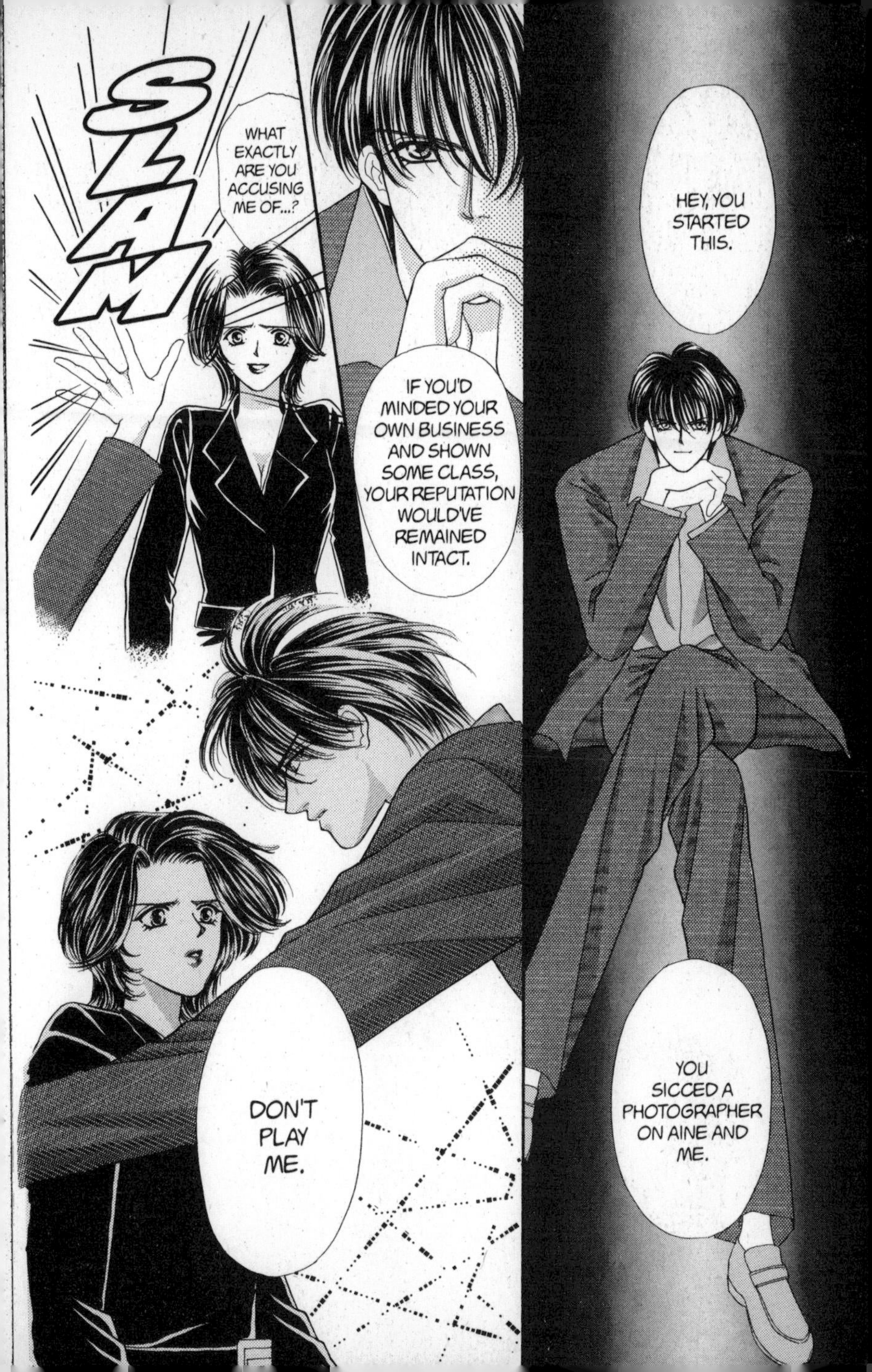
HEY, YOU STARTED THIS.
YOU SICCED A PHOTOGRAPHER ON AINE AND ME.
SLAM
WHAT EXACTLY ARE YOU ACCUSING ME OF...?
IF YOU'D MINDED YOUR OWN BUSINESS AND SHOWN SOME CLASS, YOUR REPUTATION WOULD'VE REMAINED INTACT.
DON'T PLAY ME.

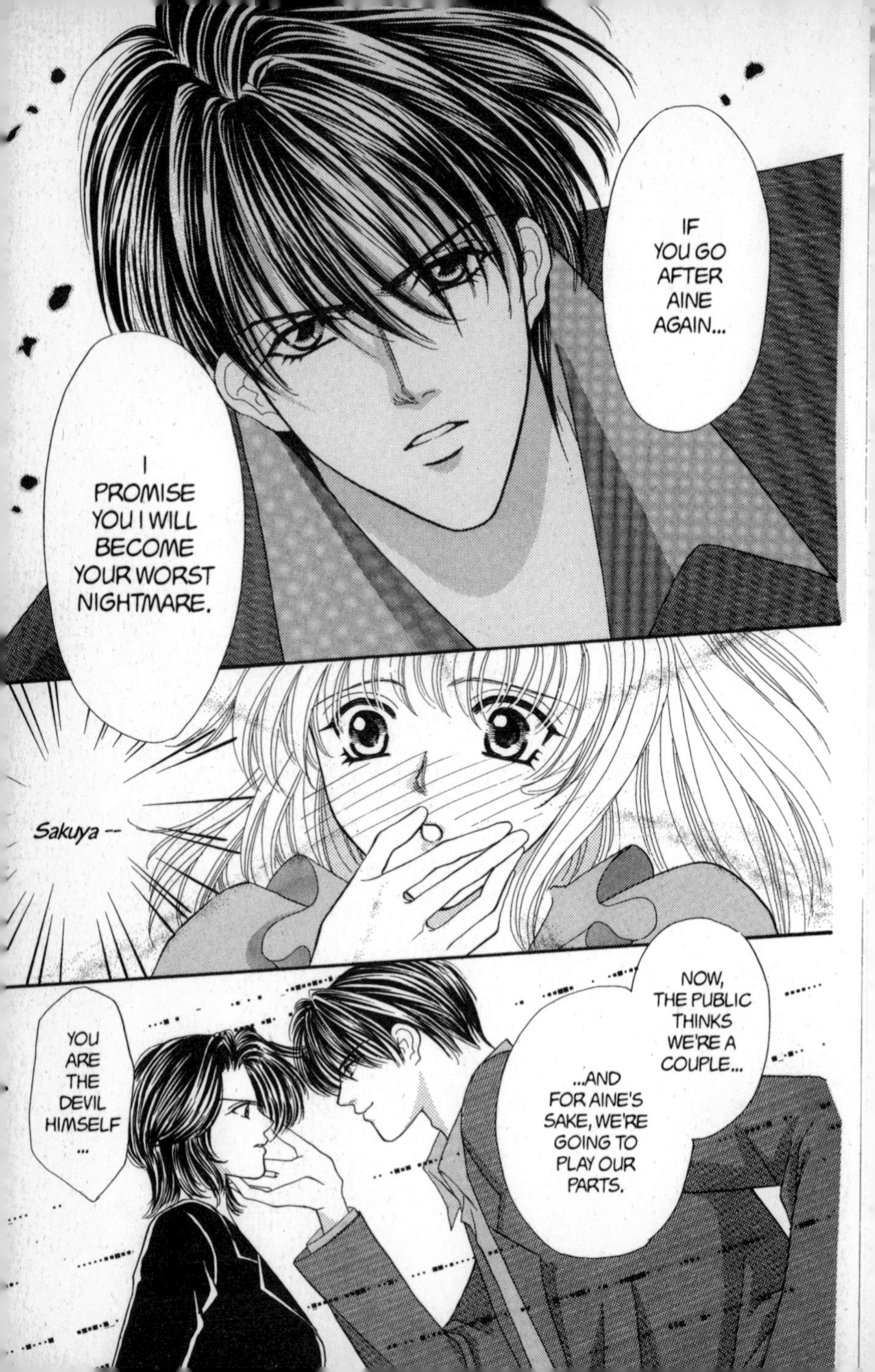
IF YOU GO AFTER AINE AGAIN...
I PROMISE YOU I WILL BECOME YOUR WORST NIGHTMARE.
Sakuya --
NOW, THE PUBLIC THINKS WE'RE A COUPLE...
...AND FOR AINE'S SAKE, WE'RE GOING TO PLAY OUR PARTS.
YOU ARE THE DEVIL HIMSELF ...

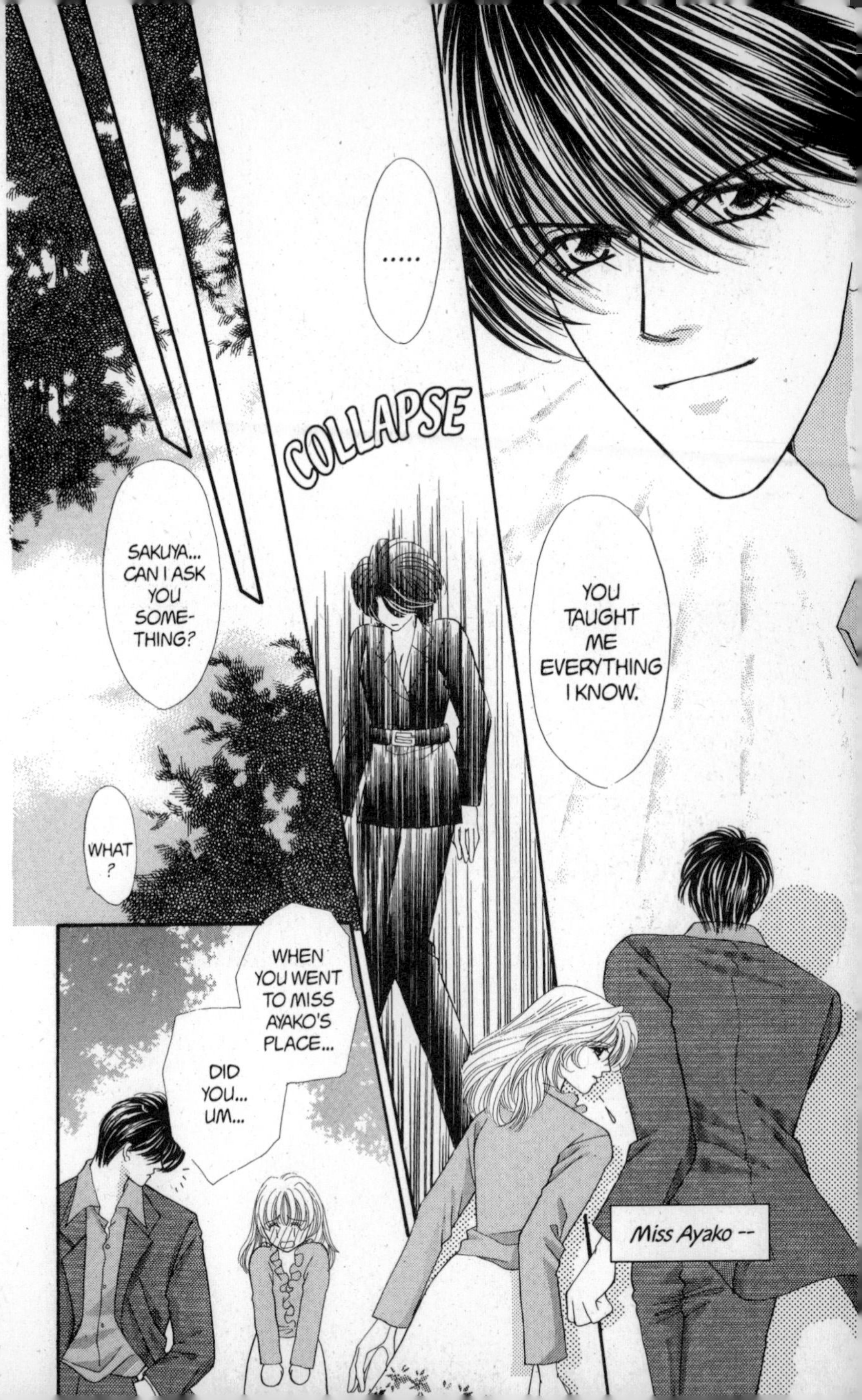
YOU TAUGHT ME EVERYTHING I KNOW.
Miss Ayako --
.....
COLLAPSE
SAKUYA... CAN I ASK YOU SOME-THING?
WHAT?
WHEN YOU WENT TO MISS AYAKO'S PLACE...
DID YOU... UM...

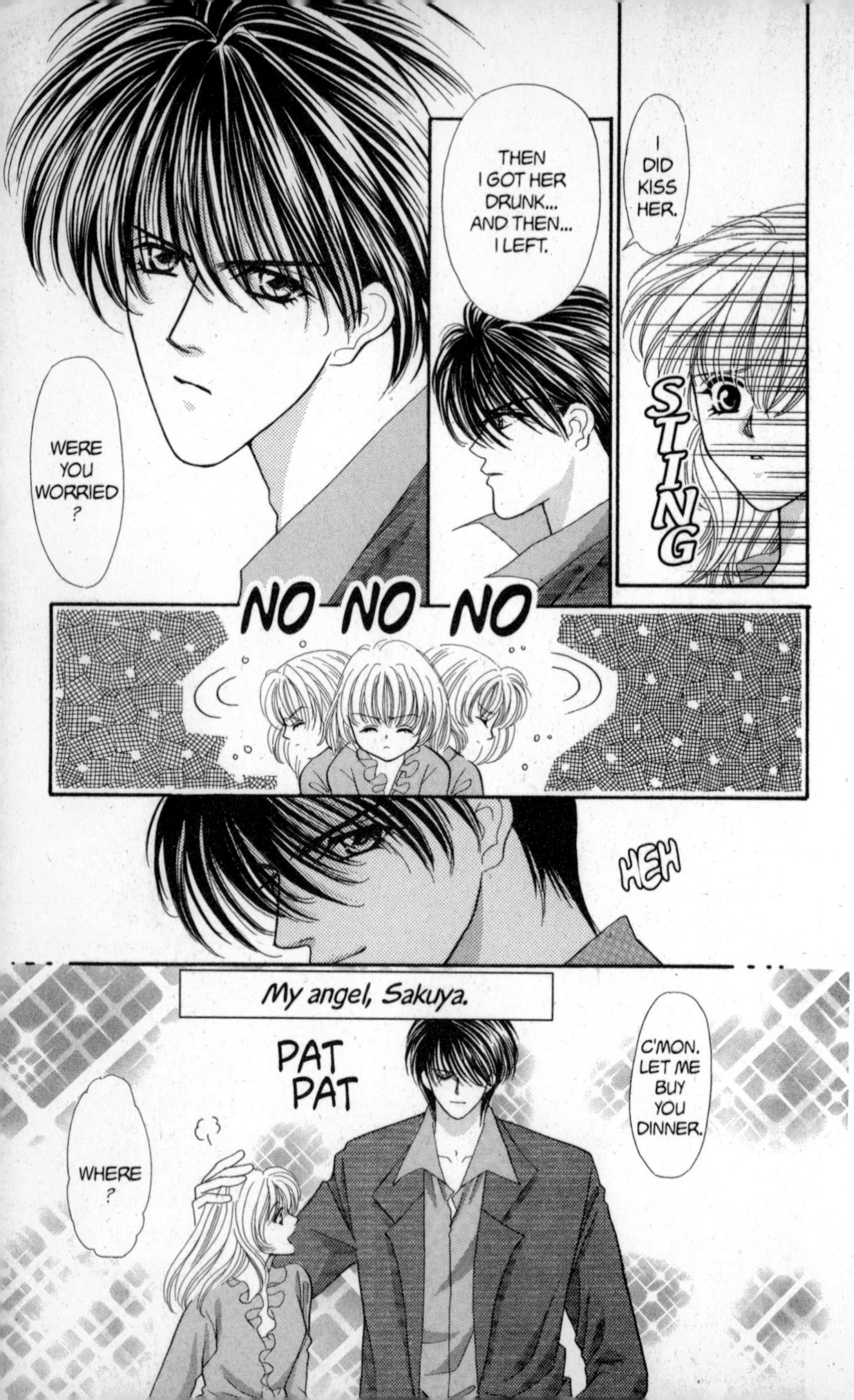
I DID KISS HER.
STING
THEN I GOT HER DRUNK... AND THEN... I LEFT.
WERE YOU WORRIED?
NO NO NO
HEH
My angel, Sakuya.
C'MON. LET ME BUY YOU DINNER.
PAT PAT
WHERE?

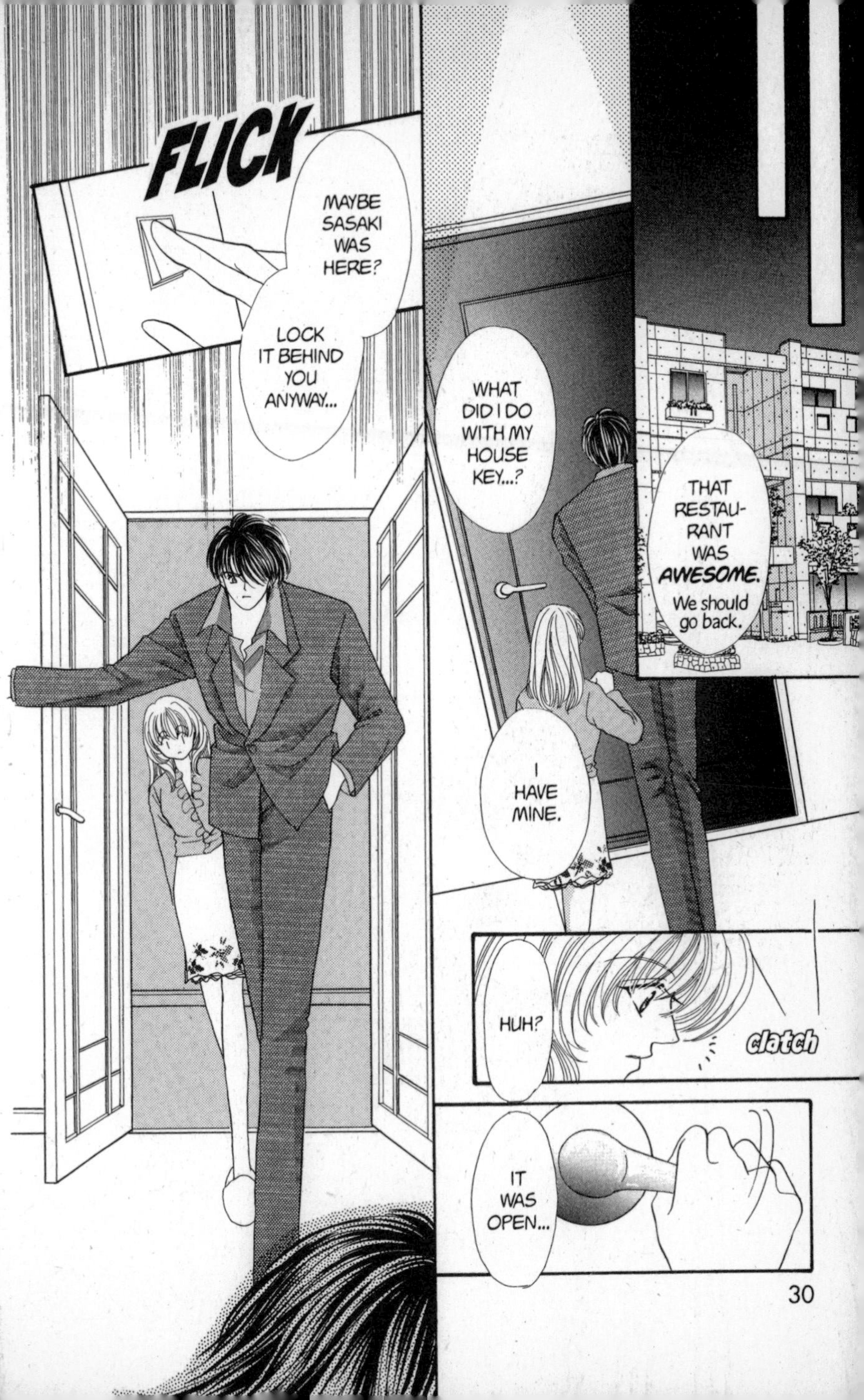
THAT RESTAU-RANT WAS AWESOME. We should go back.
WHAT DID I DO WITH MY HOUSE KEY...?
I HAVE MINE.
clatch
HUH?
IT WAS OPEN...
FLICK
MAYBE SASAKI WAS HERE?
LOCK IT BEHIND YOU ANYWAY...

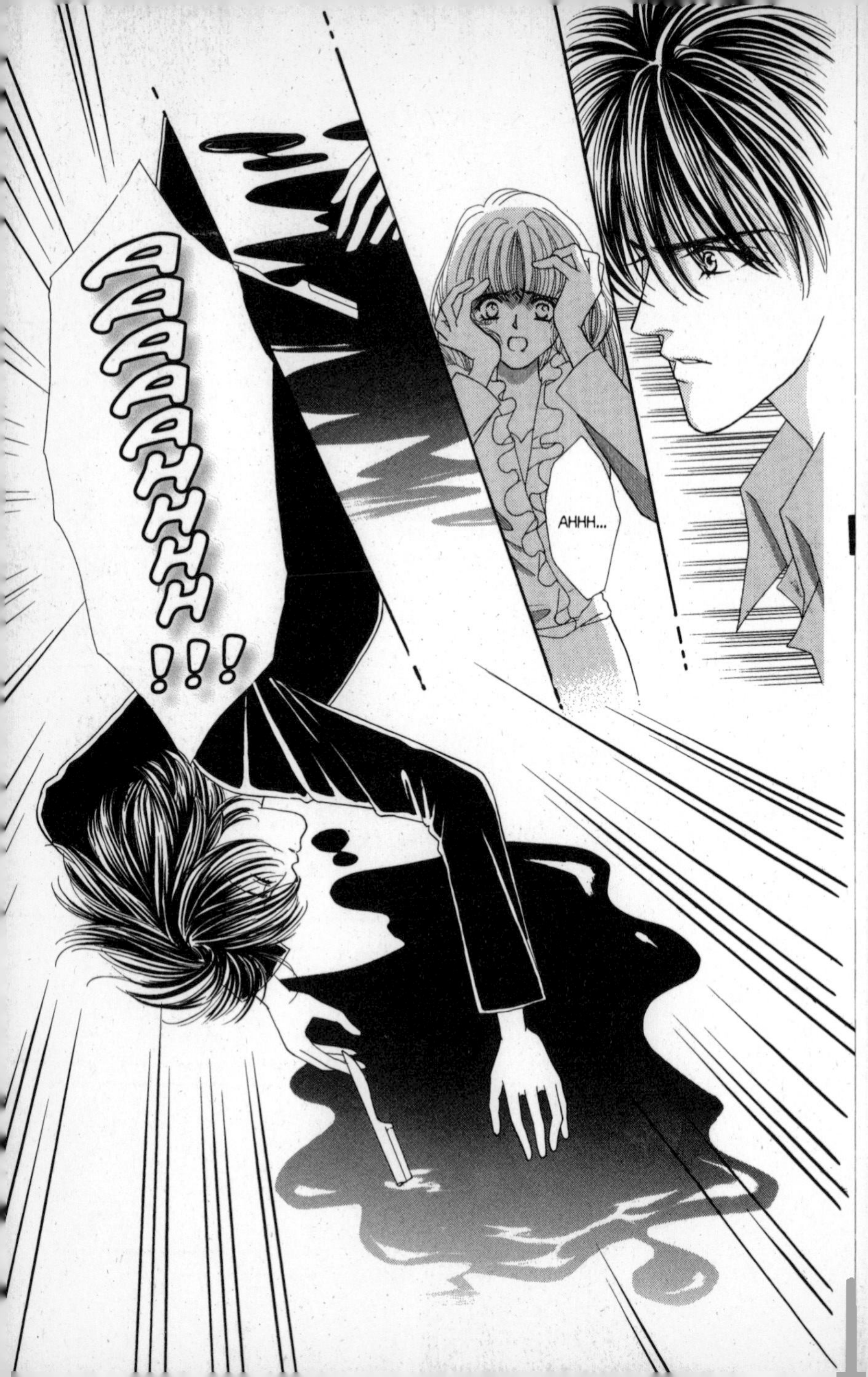
AHHH...
AAAAAHHHH!!!

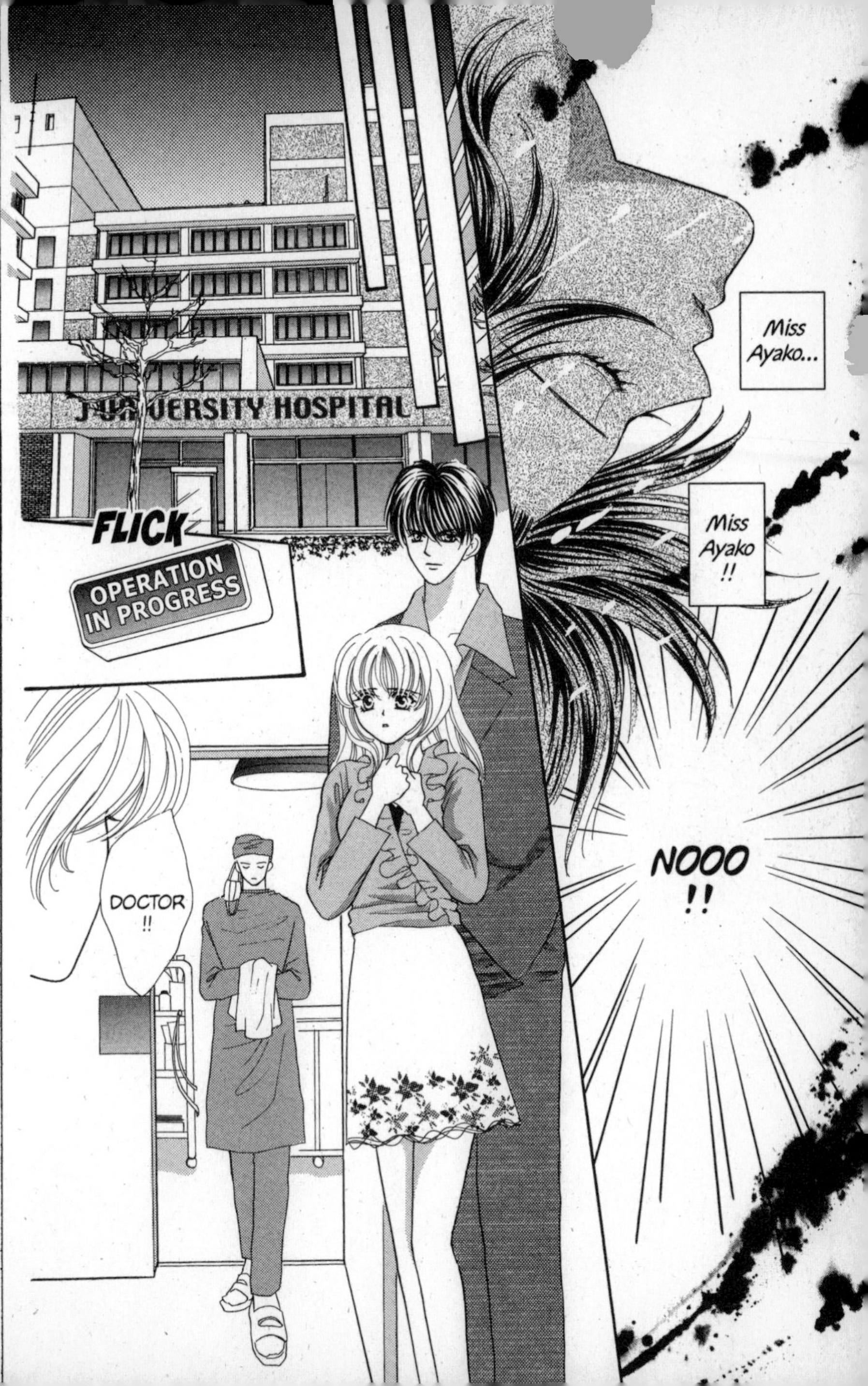
Miss Ayako...
Miss Ayako !!
NOOO !!
HOSPITAL
FLICK
OPERATION IN PROGRESS
DOCTOR !!

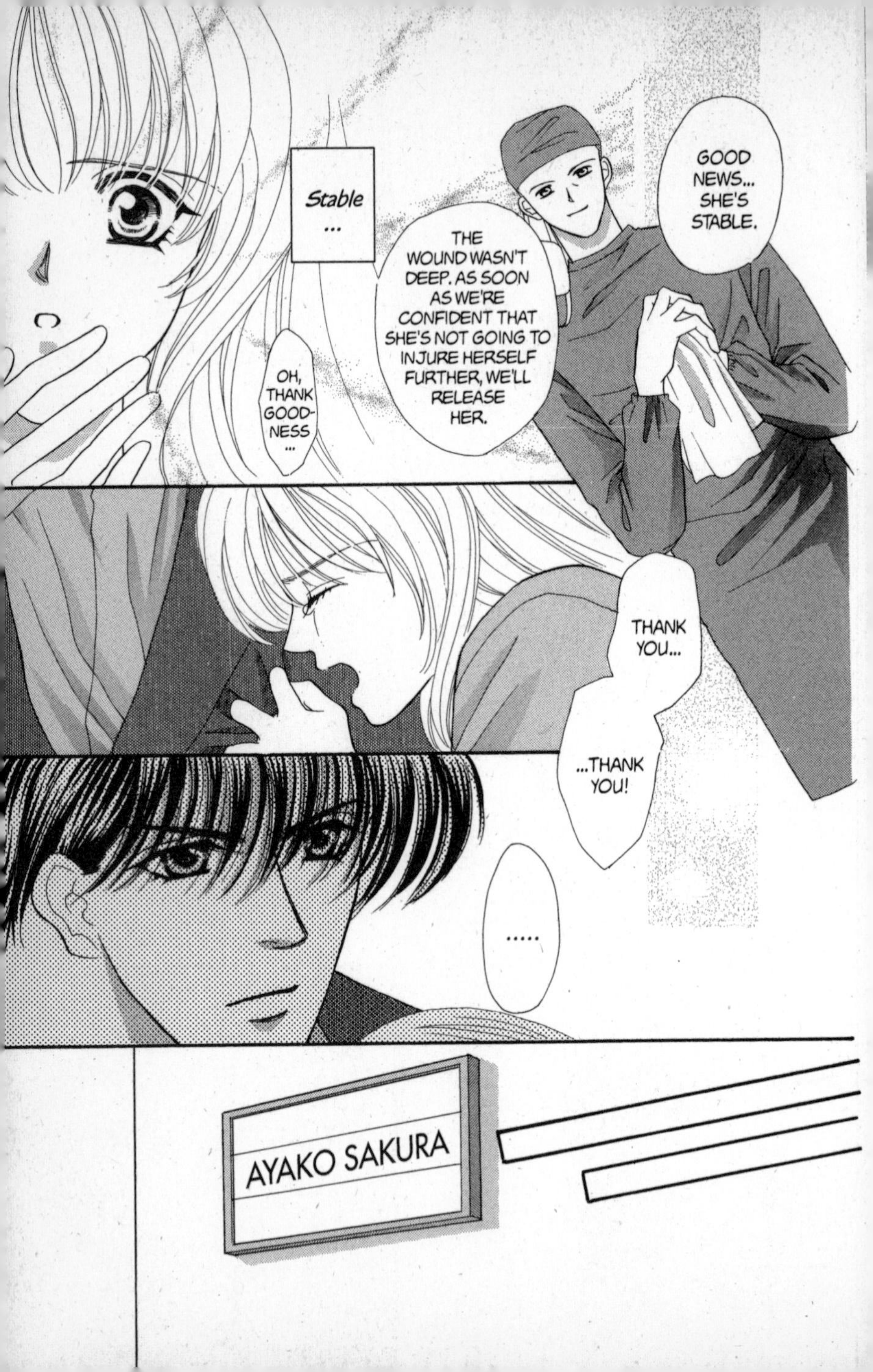
GOOD NEWS... SHE'S STABLE.
Stable ...
THE WOUND WASN'T DEEP. AS SOON AS WE'RE CONFIDENT THAT SHE'S NOT GOING TO INJURE HERSELF FURTHER, WE'LL RELEASE HER.
OH, THANK GOOD-NESS ...
THANK YOU...
...THANK YOU!
.....
AYAKO SAKURA

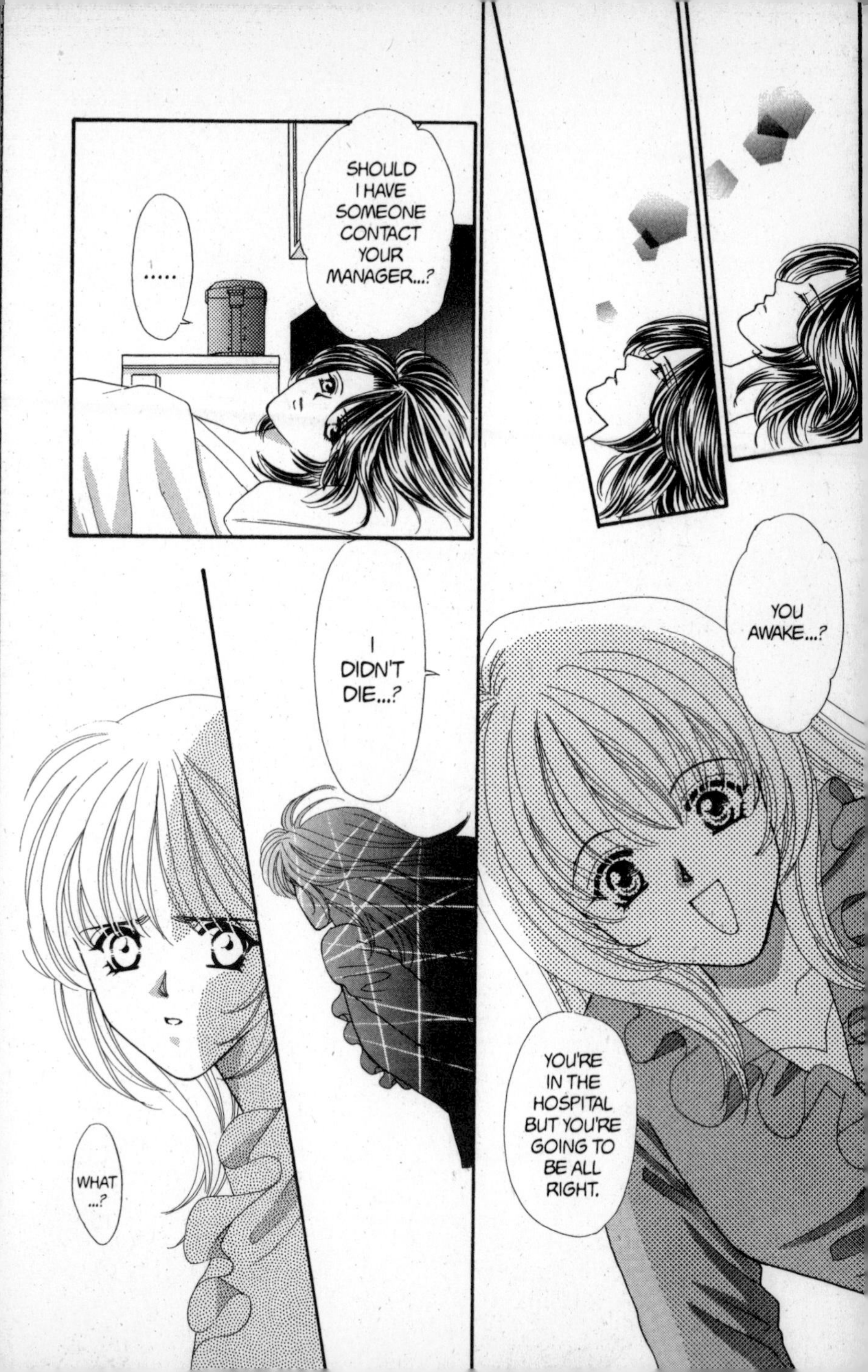
SHOULD I HAVE SOMEONE CONTACT YOUR MANAGER...?
.....
YOU AWAKE...?
YOU'RE IN THE HOSPITAL BUT YOU'RE GOING TO BE ALL RIGHT.
I DIDN'T DIE...?
WHAT...?

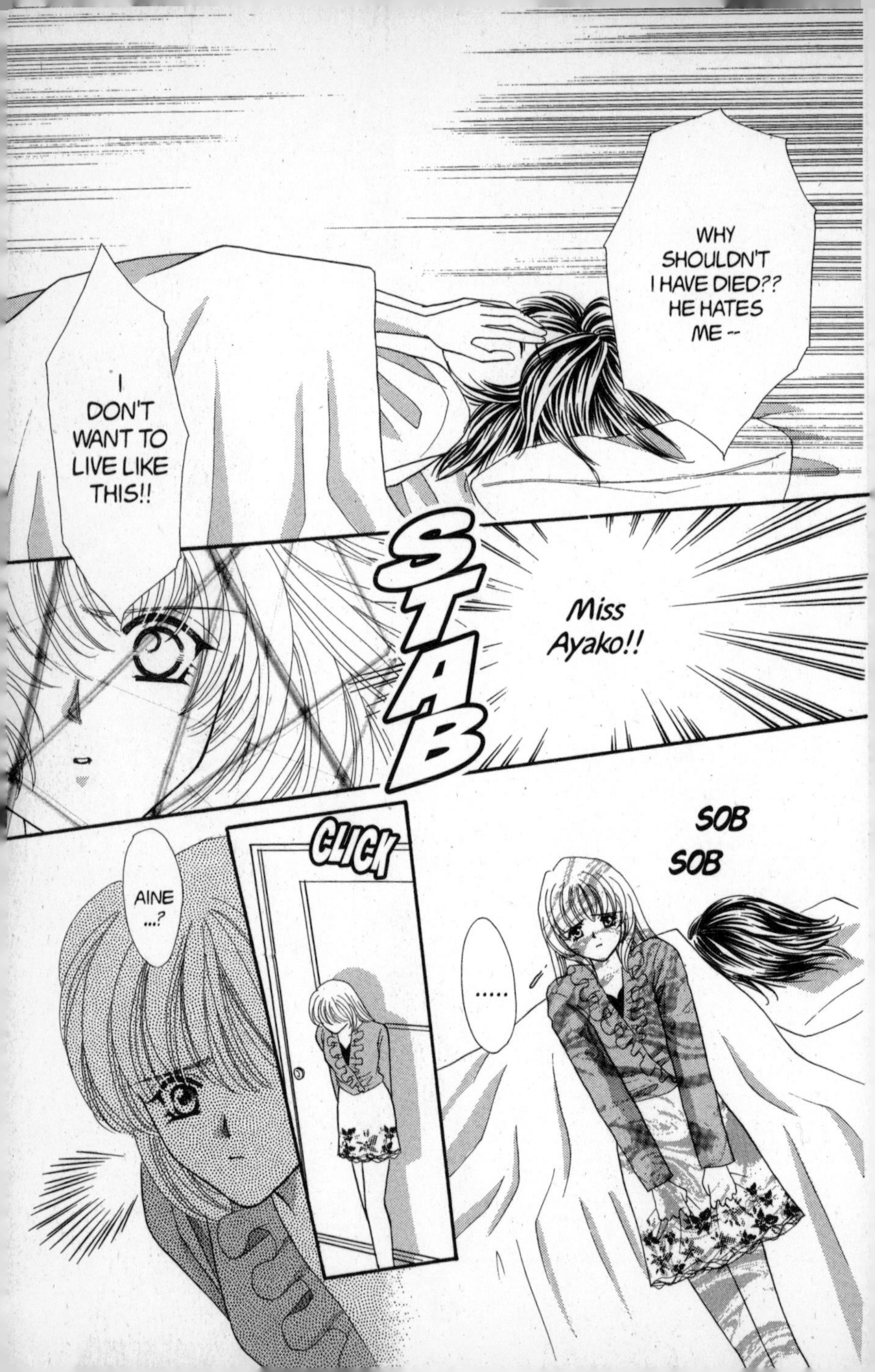
WHY SHOULDN'T I HAVE DIED?? HE HATES ME --
I DON'T WANT TO LIVE LIKE THIS!!
Miss Ayako!!
STAB
SOB SOB
.....
CLICK
AINE ...?

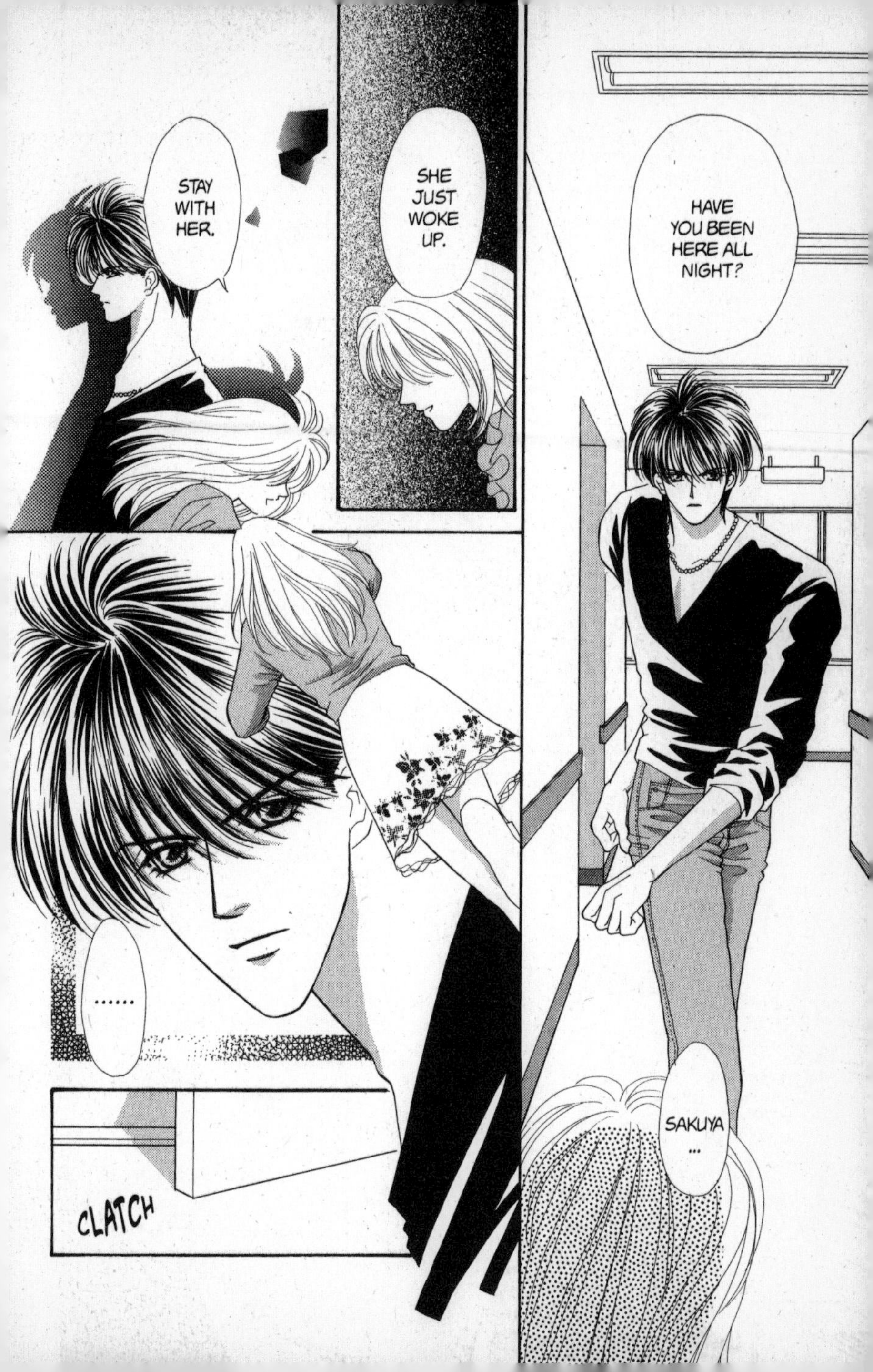
HAVE YOU BEEN HERE ALL NIGHT?
SAKUYA ...
SHE JUST WOKE UP.
STAY WITH HER.
......
CLATCH

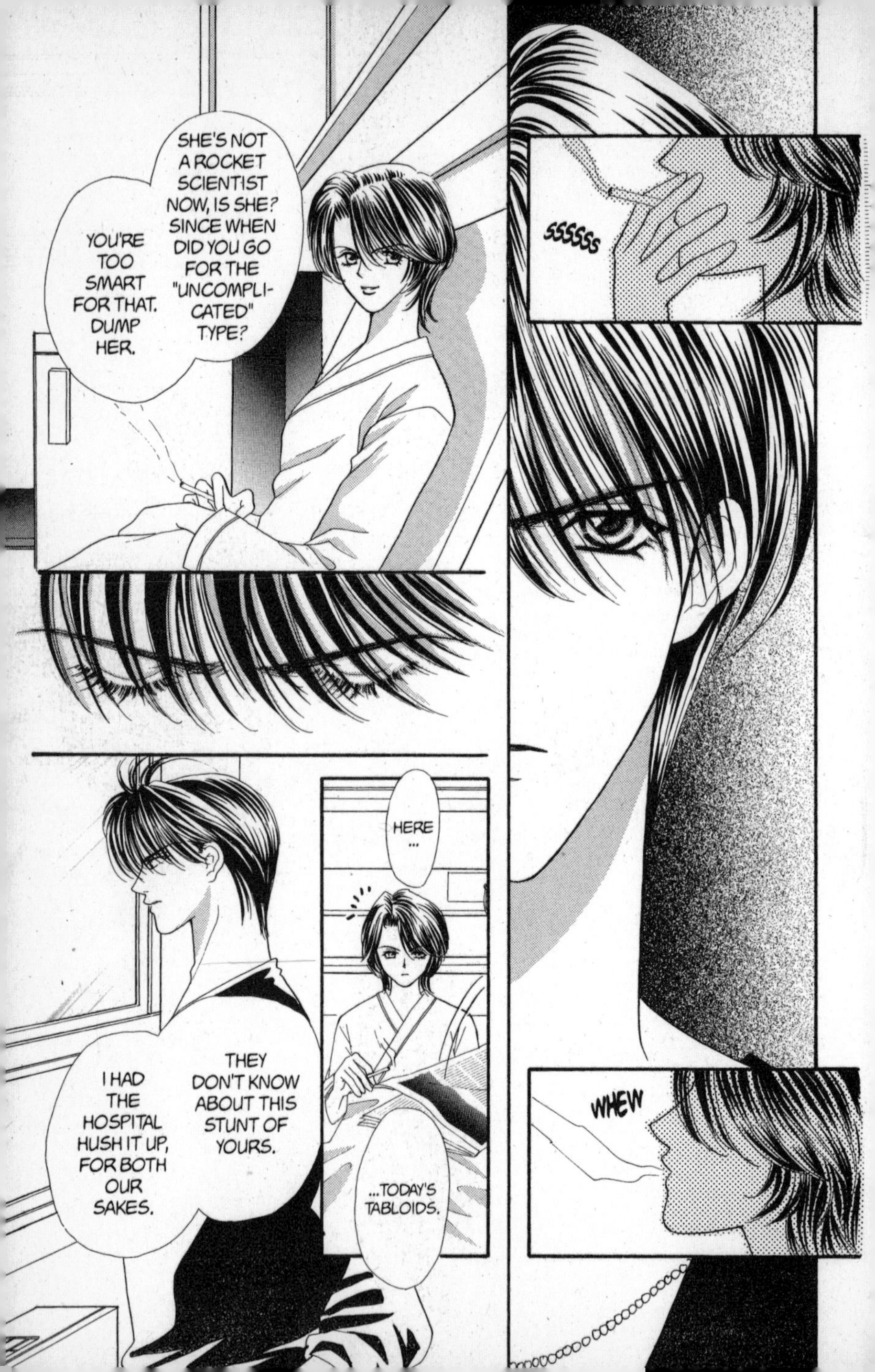
SSSSSS
WHEW
SHE'S NOT A ROCKET SCIENTIST NOW, IS SHE? SINCE WHEN DID YOU GO FOR THE "UNCOMPLICATED" TYPE?
YOU'RE TOO SMART FOR THAT. DUMP HER.
HERE ...
...TODAY'S TABLOIDS.
THEY DON'T KNOW ABOUT THIS STUNT OF YOURS.
I HAD THE HOSPITAL HUSH IT UP, FOR BOTH OUR SAKES.

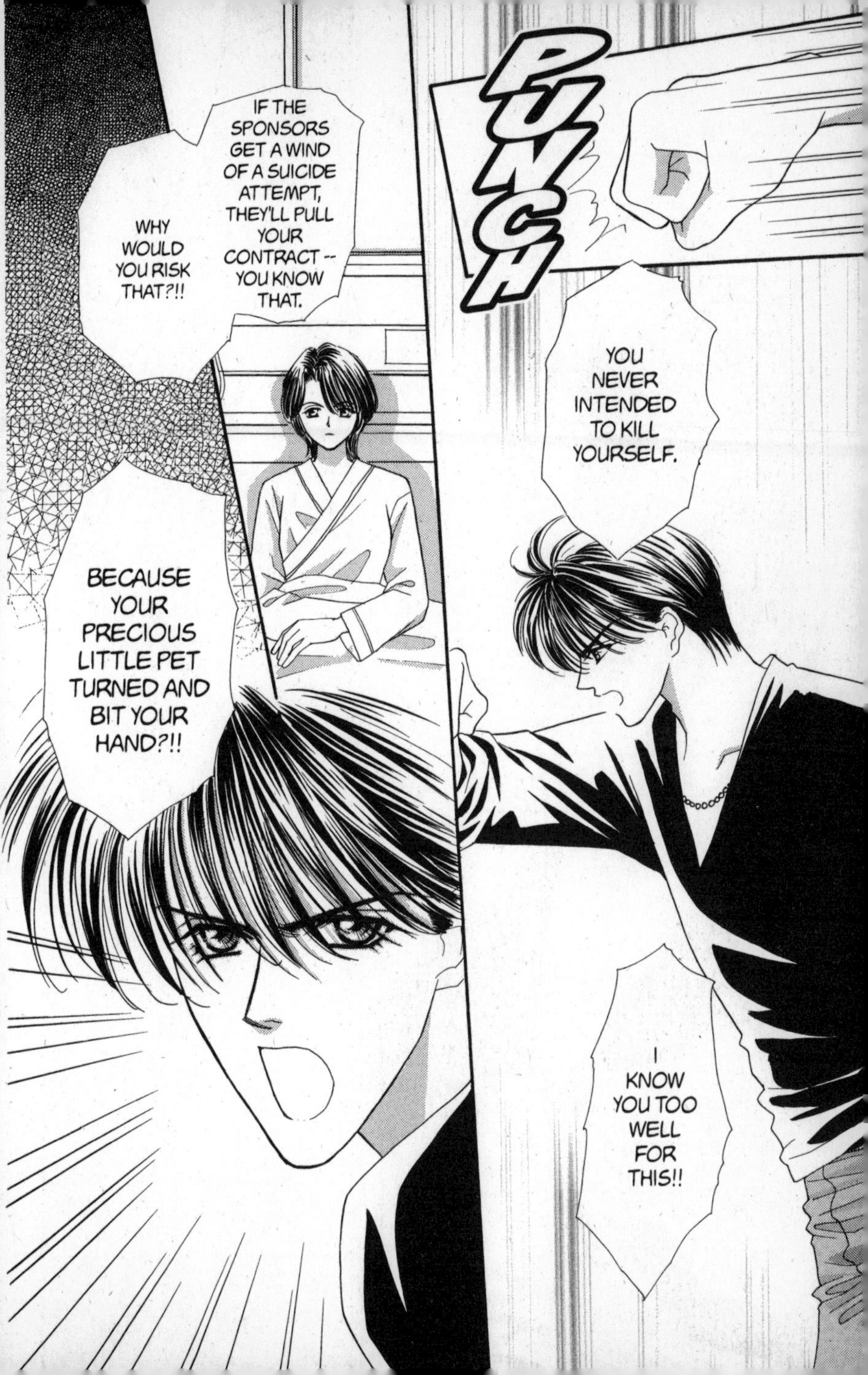
PUNCH
YOU NEVER INTENDED TO KILL YOURSELF.
I KNOW YOU TOO WELL FOR THIS!!
IF THE SPONSORS GET A WIND OF A SUICIDE ATTEMPT, THEY'LL PULL YOUR CONTRACT -- YOU KNOW THAT.
WHY WOULD YOU RISK THAT?!!
BECAUSE YOUR PRECIOUS LITTLE PET TURNED AND BIT YOUR HAND?!!

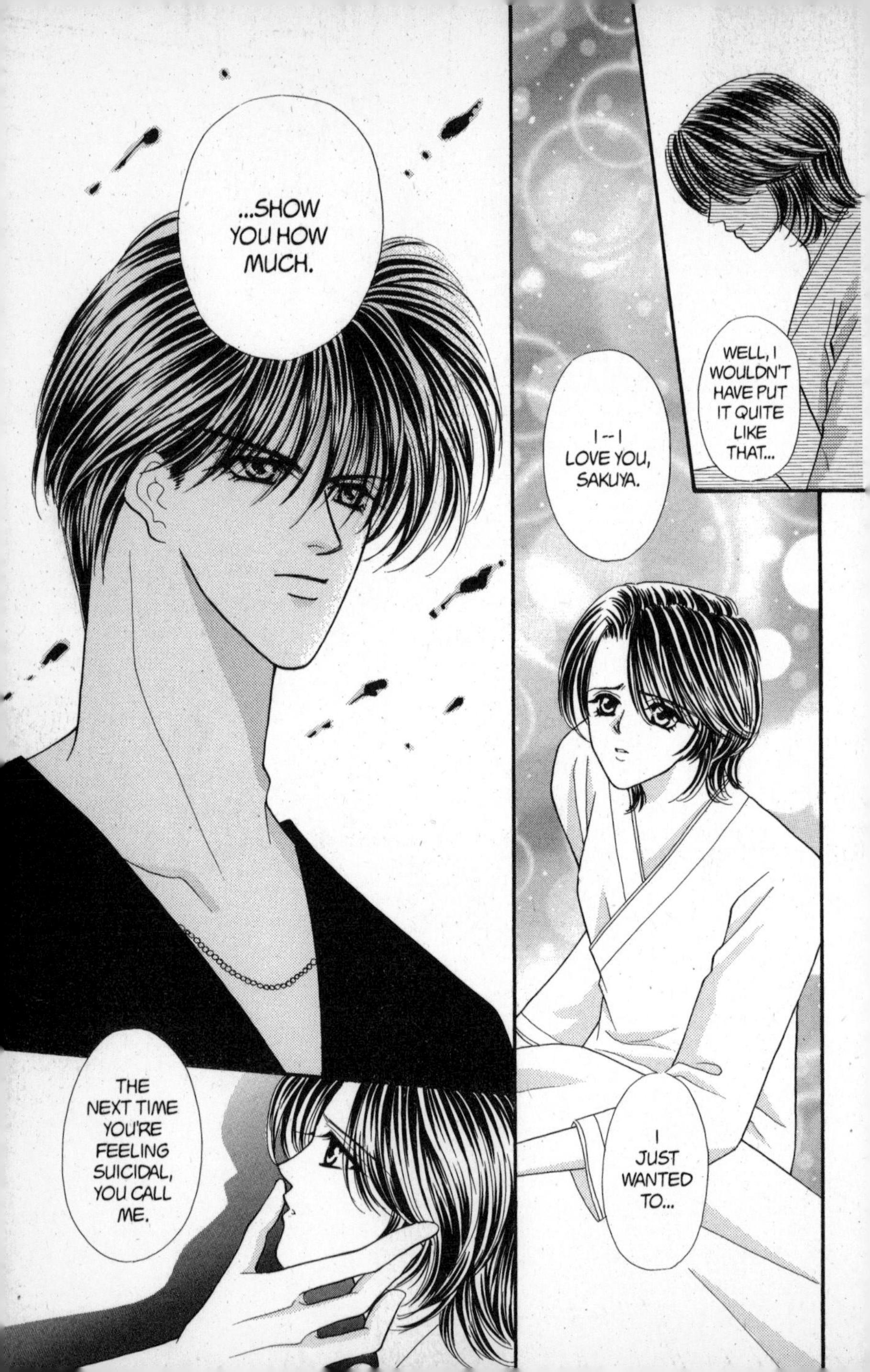
WELL, I WOULDN'T HAVE PUT IT QUITE LIKE THAT...
I -- I LOVE YOU, SAKUYA.
I JUST WANTED TO...
...SHOW YOU HOW MUCH.
THE NEXT TIME YOU'RE FEELING SUICIDAL, YOU CALL ME.

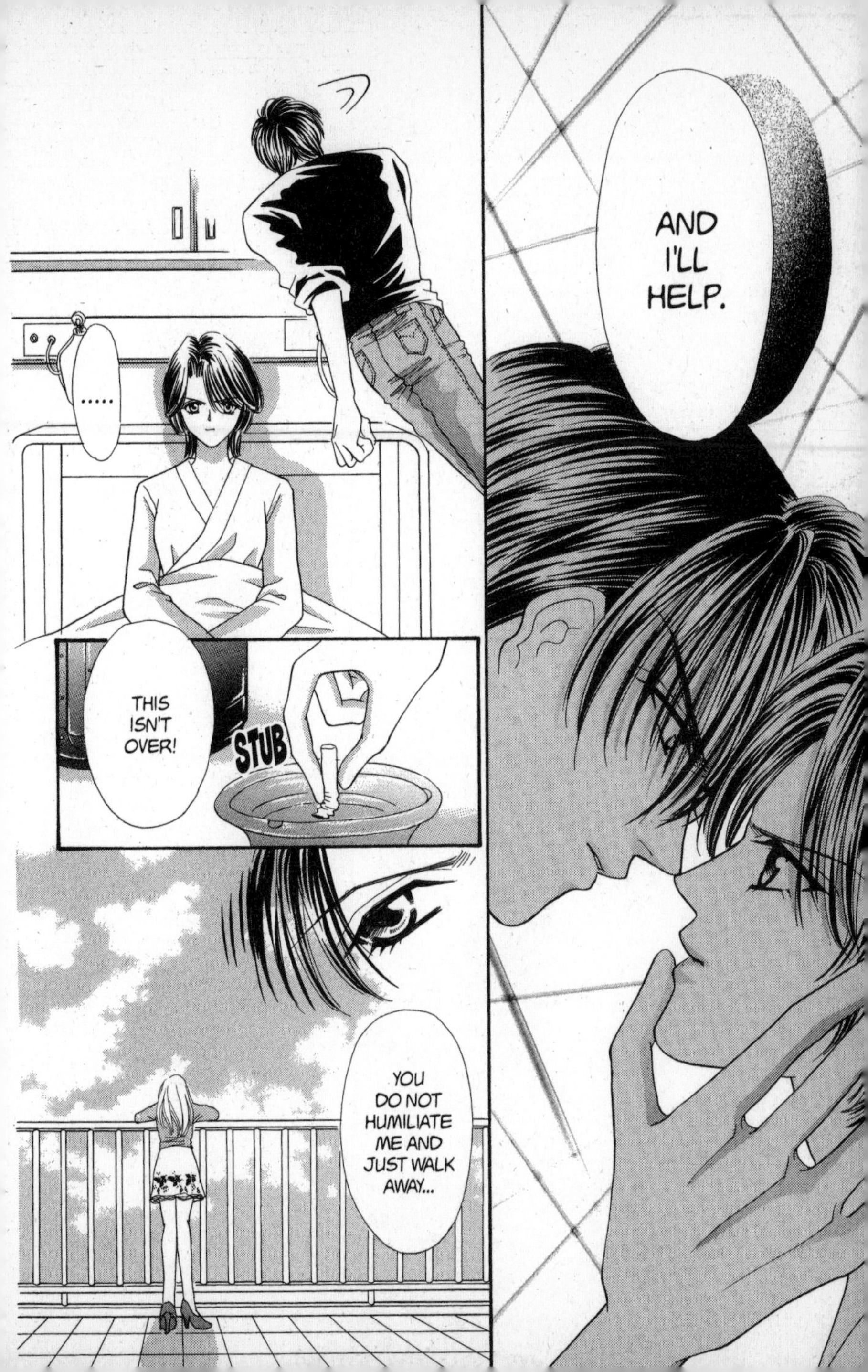
AND I'LL HELP.
......
THIS ISN'T OVER!
STUB
YOU DO NOT HUMILIATE ME AND JUST WALK AWAY...

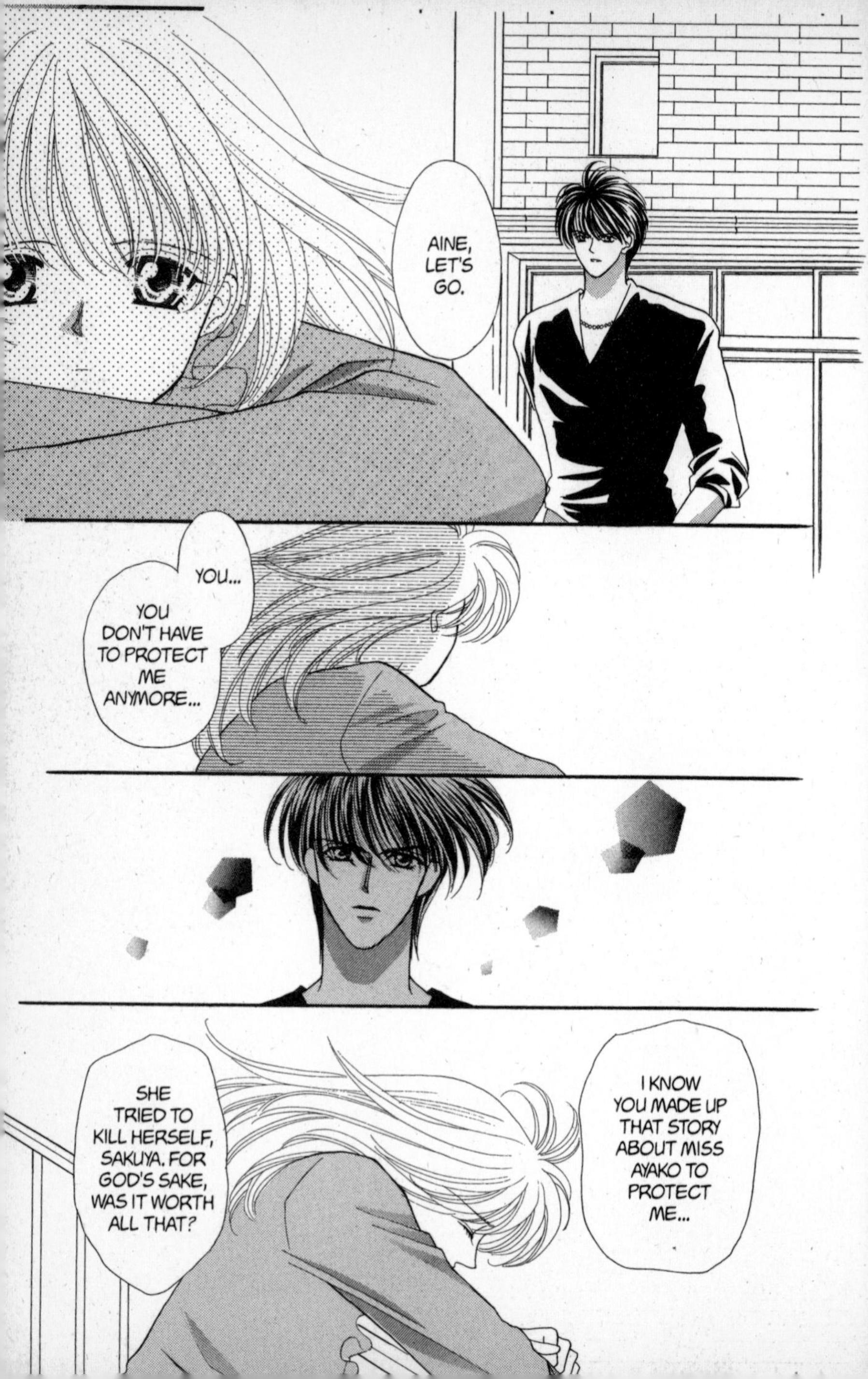
AINE, LET'S GO.
YOU...
YOU DON'T HAVE TO PROTECT ME ANYMORE...
I KNOW YOU MADE UP THAT STORY ABOUT MISS AYAKO TO PROTECT ME...
SHE TRIED TO KILL HERSELF, SAKUYA. FOR GOD'S SAKE, WAS IT WORTH ALL THAT?

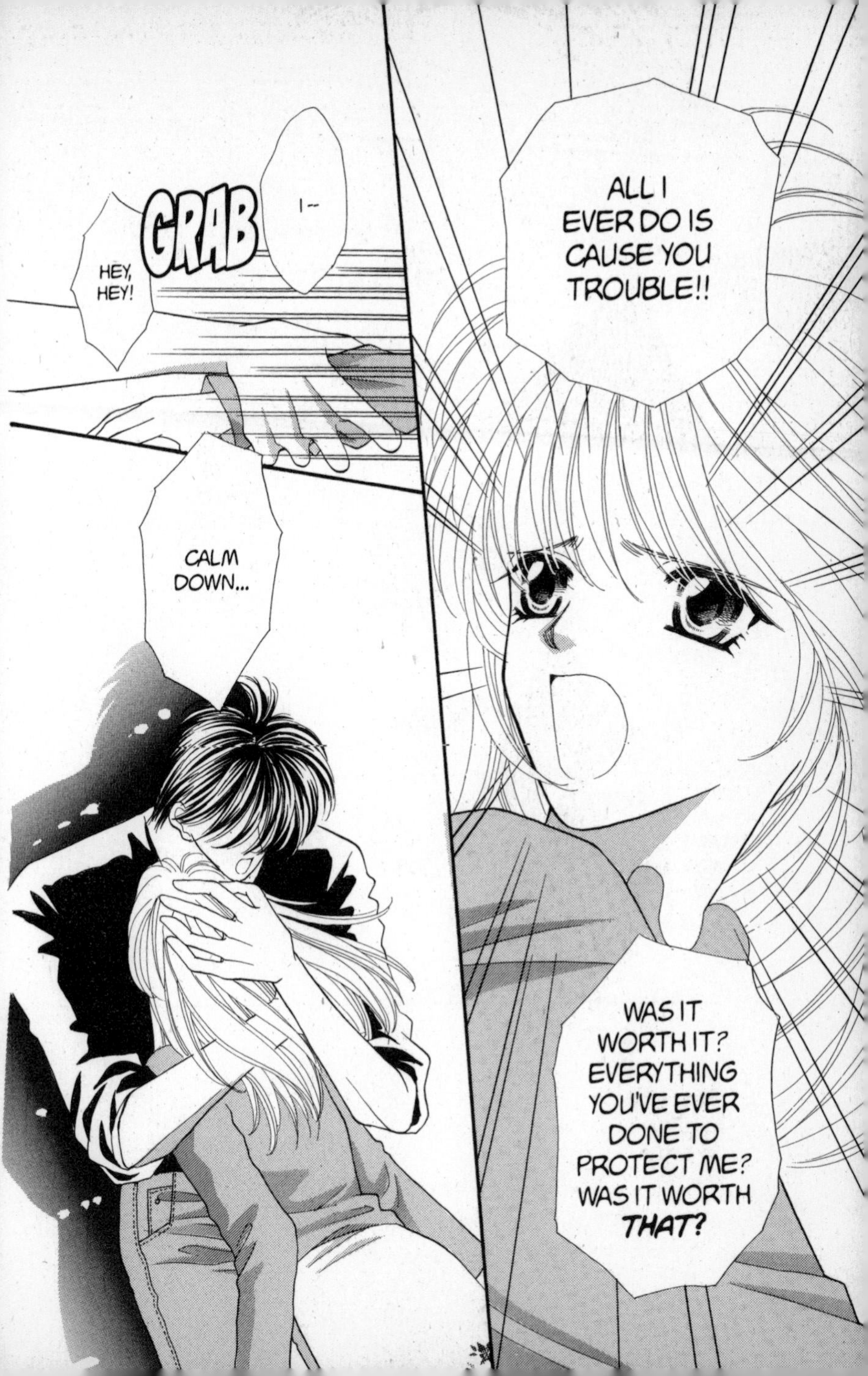

ALL I EVER DO IS CAUSE YOU TROUBLE!!
WAS IT WORTH IT? EVERYTHING YOU'VE EVER DONE TO PROTECT ME? WAS IT WORTH *THAT?*
I--
GRAB
HEY, HEY!
CALM DOWN...

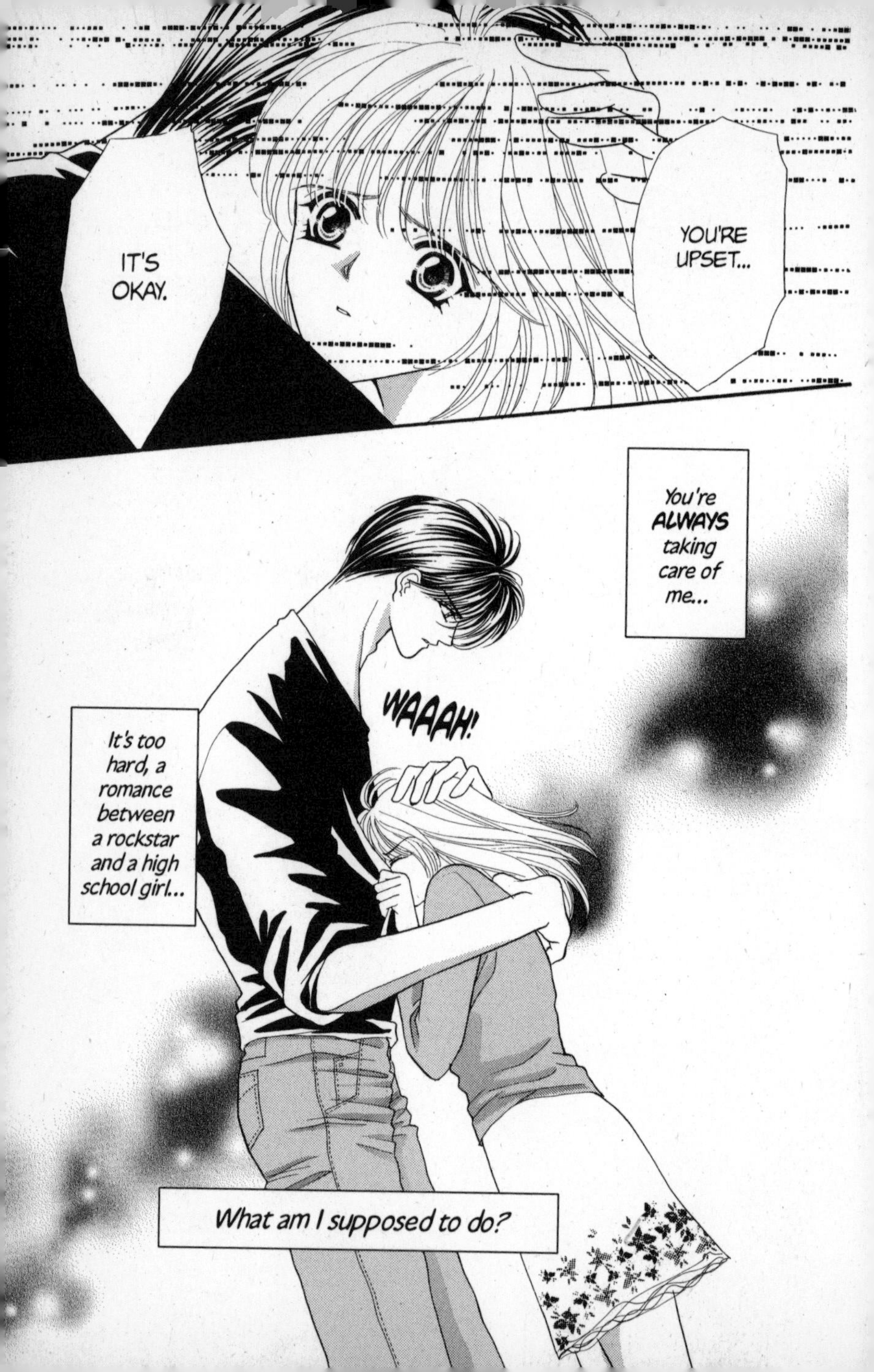
YOU'RE UPSET...
IT'S OKAY.
You're **ALWAYS** taking care of me...
WAAAH!
It's too hard, a romance between a rockstar and a high school girl...
What am I supposed to do?

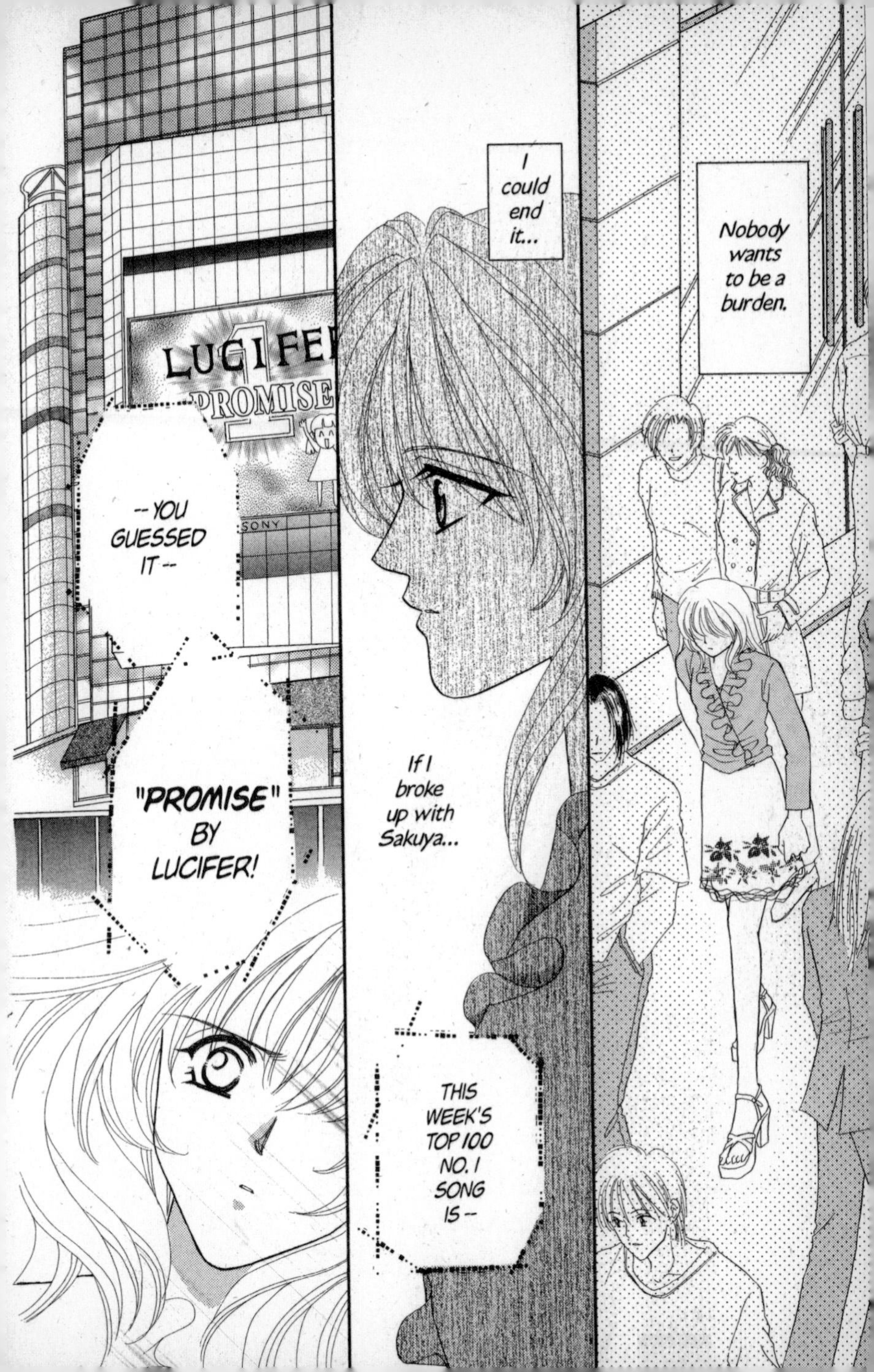
Nobody wants to be a burden.
I could end it...
If I broke up with Sakuya...
THIS WEEK'S TOP 100 NO. 1 SONG IS --
PROMISE
SONY
-- YOU GUESSED IT --
"PROMISE" BY LUCIFER!

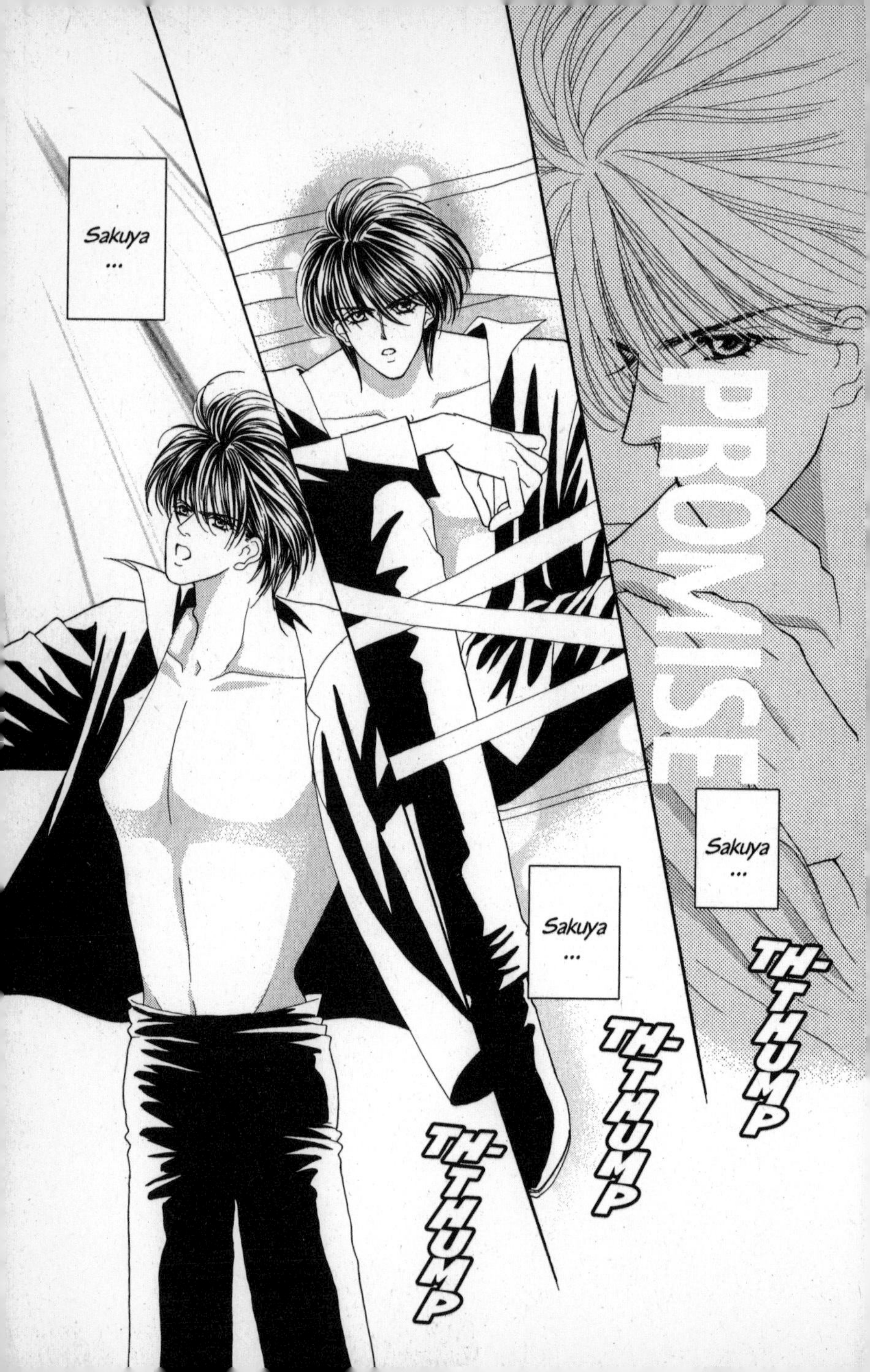
PROMISE
Sakuya ...
TH-THUMP
Sakuya ...
TH-THUMP
Sakuya ...
TH-THUMP

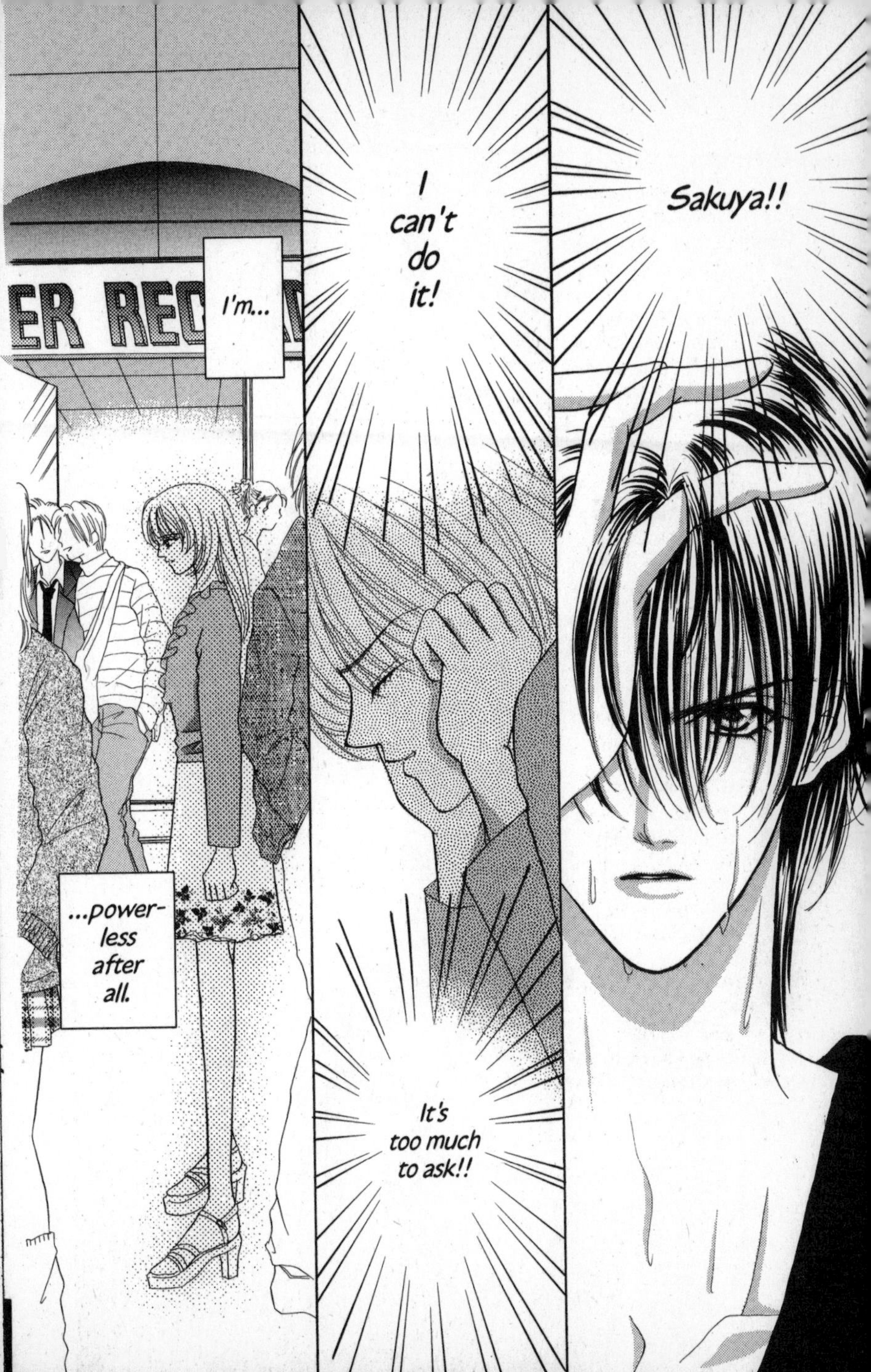
Sakuya!!
I can't do it!
It's too much to ask!!
I'm...
...power-less after all.

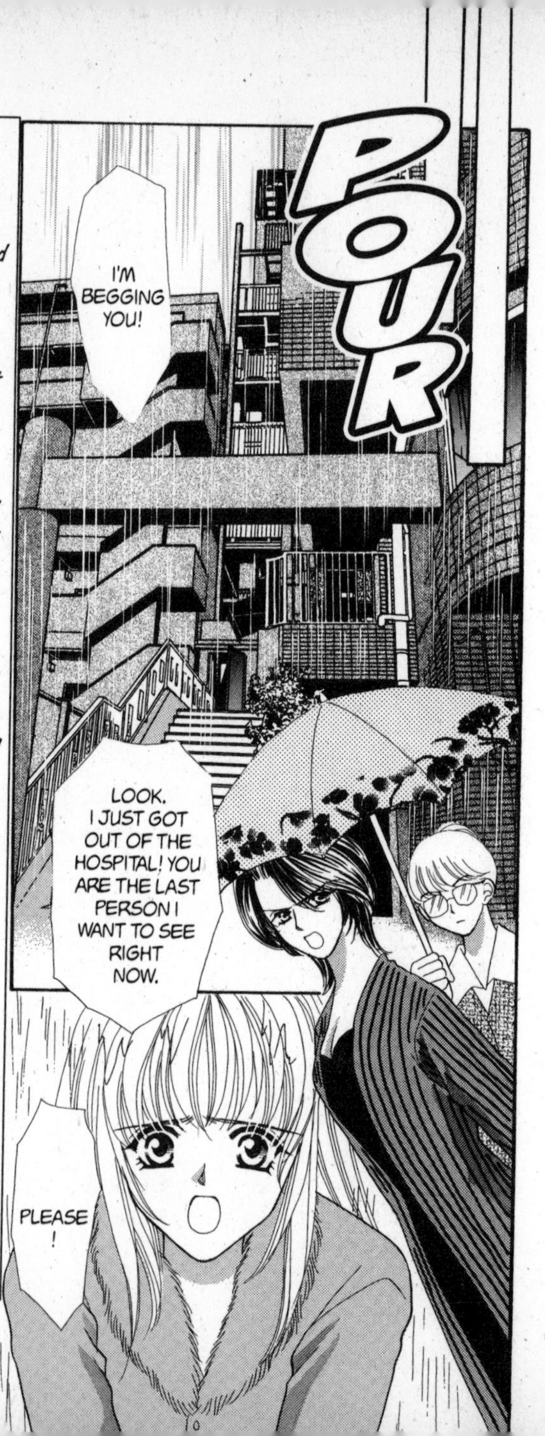
POUR
I'M BEGGING YOU!
LOOK. I JUST GOT OUT OF THE HOSPITAL! YOU ARE THE LAST PERSON I WANT TO SEE RIGHT NOW.
PLEASE!

It's about the rock bands these days. Actually when I first started working on this comic, everyone around me thought a comic about a band was a tired idea. Pre-fab boy bands were popular at the time...at one point I almost gave up. But then my old editor heard about my project and got behind the idea...and that's how it started. Shortly thereafter, Glay hit big and before I even knew it, rock bands were all the rage again.

The release of Vol. 1 was perfectly timed -- by accident! More than anything, I was lucky. I wish I could take credit for being "ahead of my time!"

This book has overcome a lot of obstacles, but I hope it can rouse the readers' interest in ROCK!

As always, I read all the letters saying I want a story like this, or I want to see this side of Sakuya. Quite a few of them are incorporated into the story so please keep those cards and letters coming!

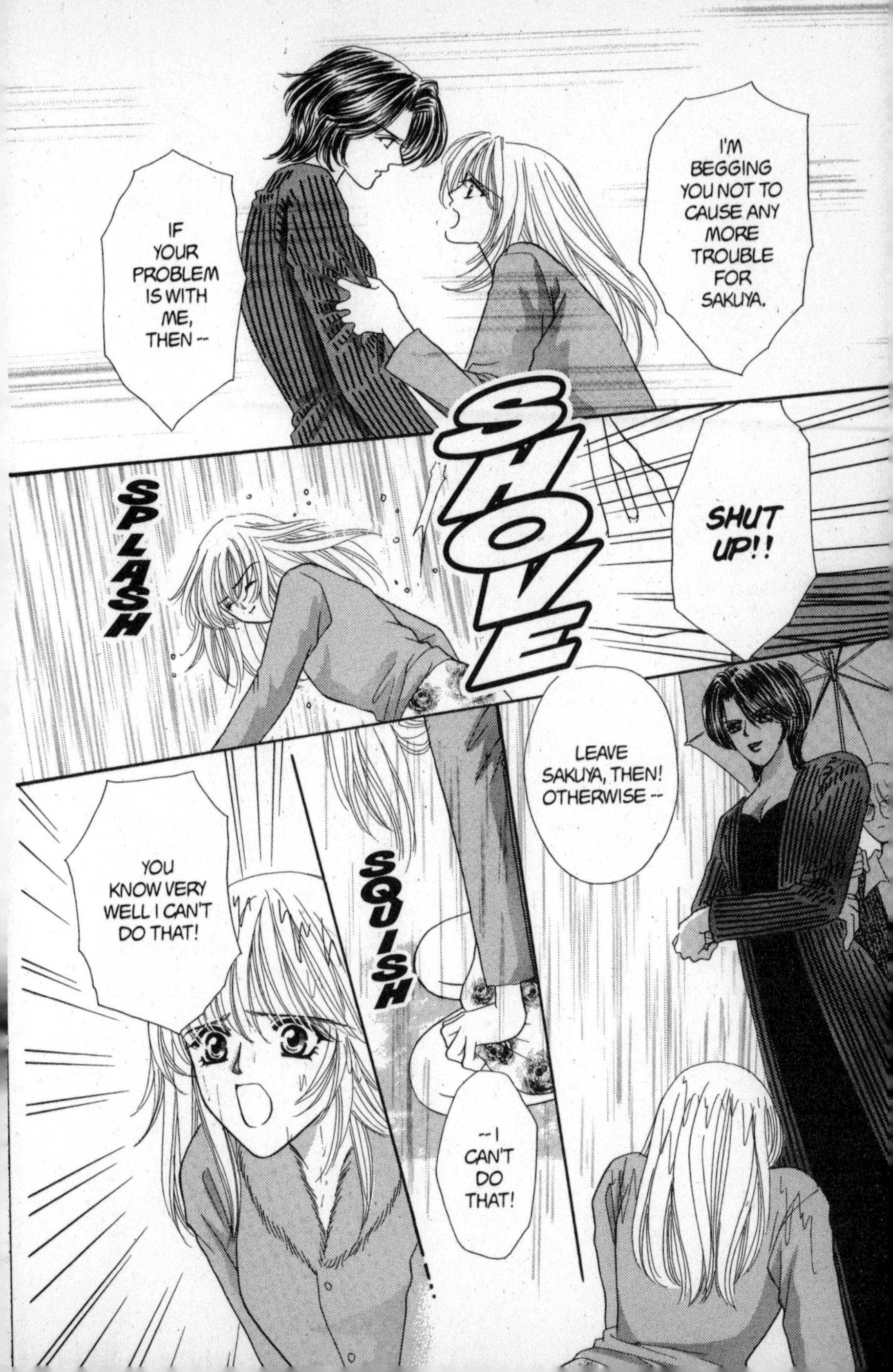
I'M BEGGING YOU NOT TO CAUSE ANY MORE TROUBLE FOR SAKUYA.
IF YOUR PROBLEM IS WITH ME, THEN --
SHUT UP!!
SHOVE
SPLASH
LEAVE SAKUYA, THEN! OTHERWISE --
SQUISH
YOU KNOW VERY WELL I CAN'T DO THAT!
-- I CAN'T DO THAT!

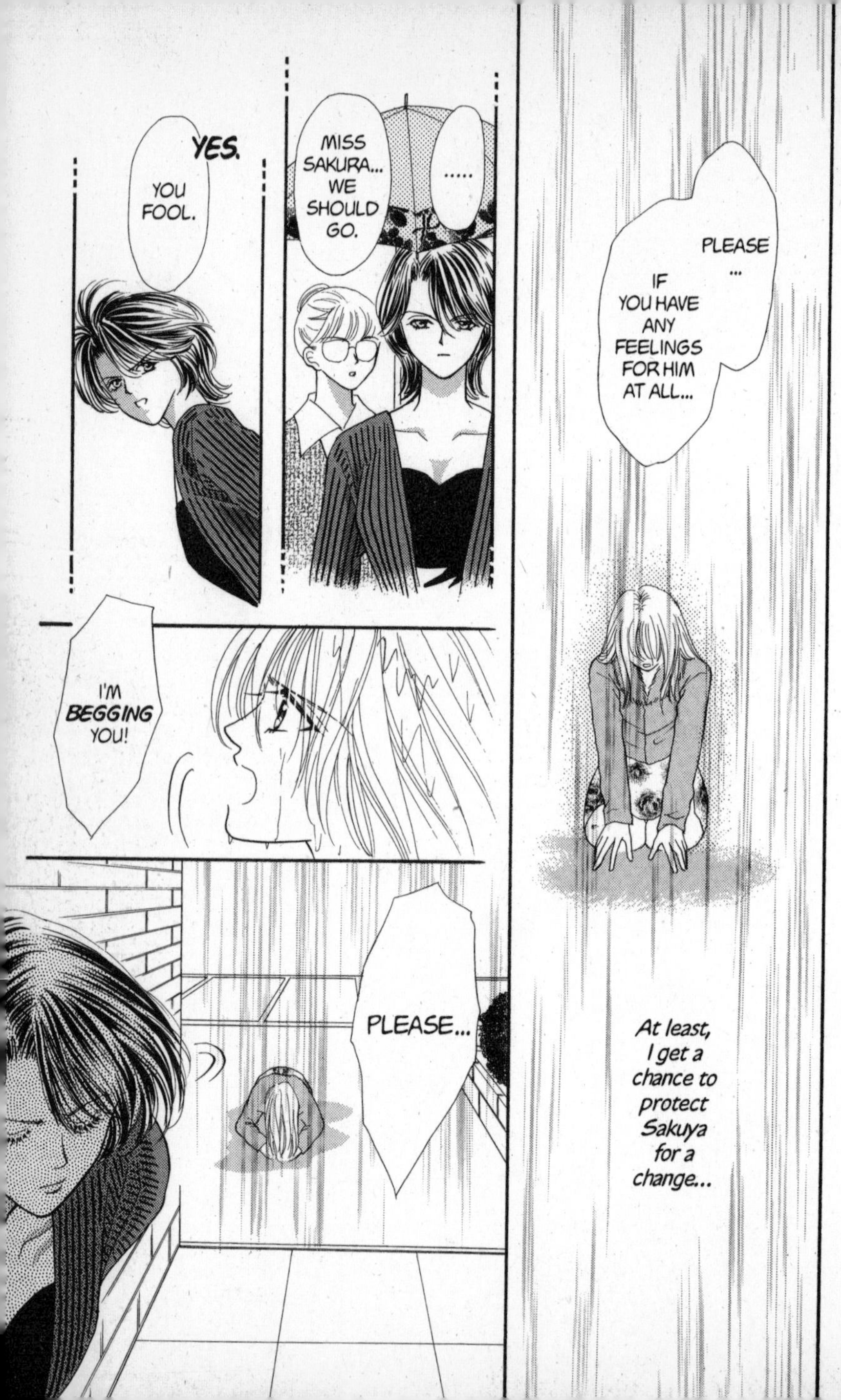
PLEASE ...
IF YOU HAVE ANY FEELINGS FOR HIM AT ALL...
At least, I get a chance to protect Sakuya for a change...
.....
MISS SAKURA... WE SHOULD GO.
YES.
YOU FOOL.
I'M **BEGGING** YOU!
PLEASE...

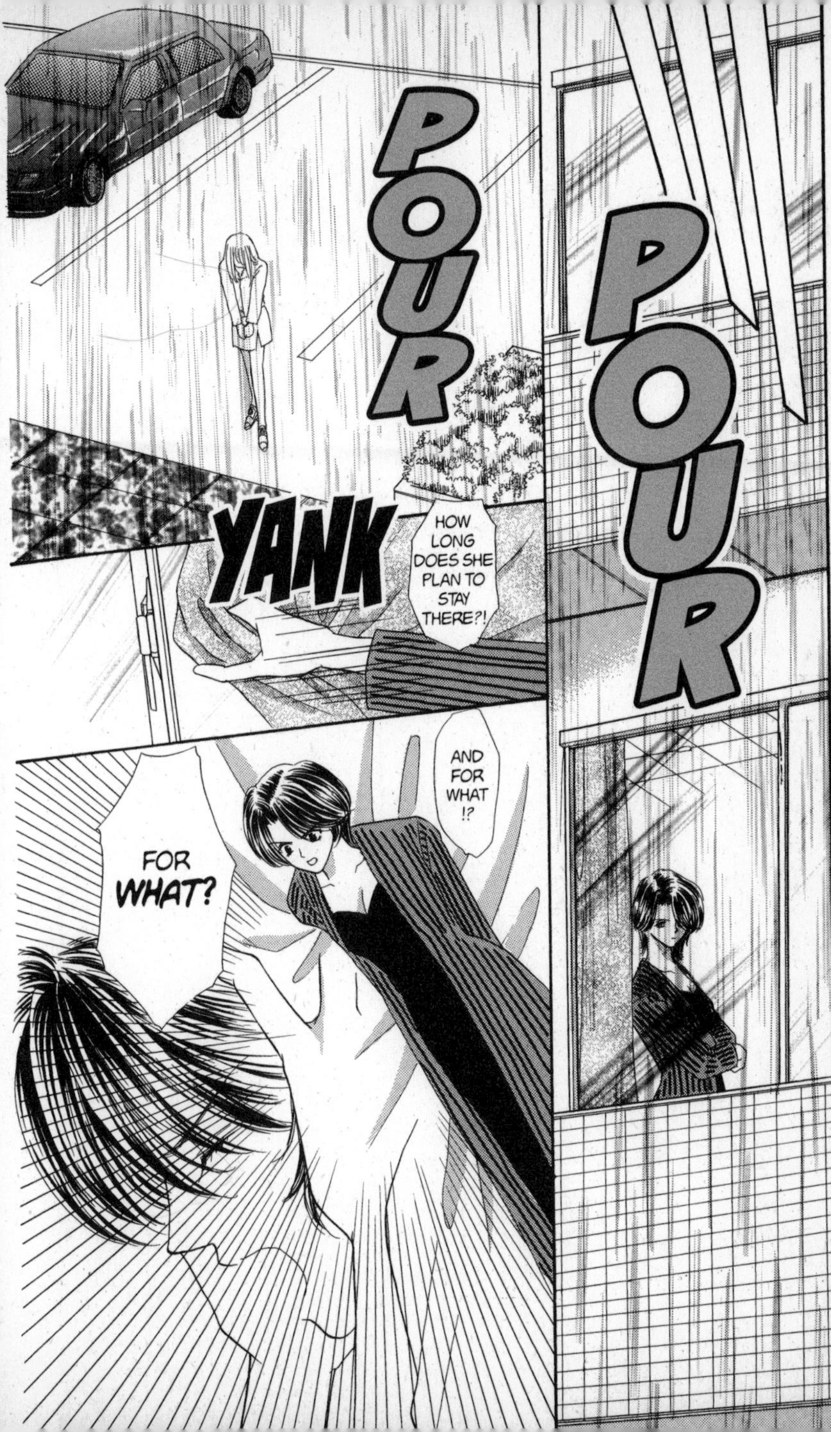
POUR
POUR
YANK
HOW LONG DOES SHE PLAN TO STAY THERE?!
AND FOR WHAT!?
FOR WHAT?

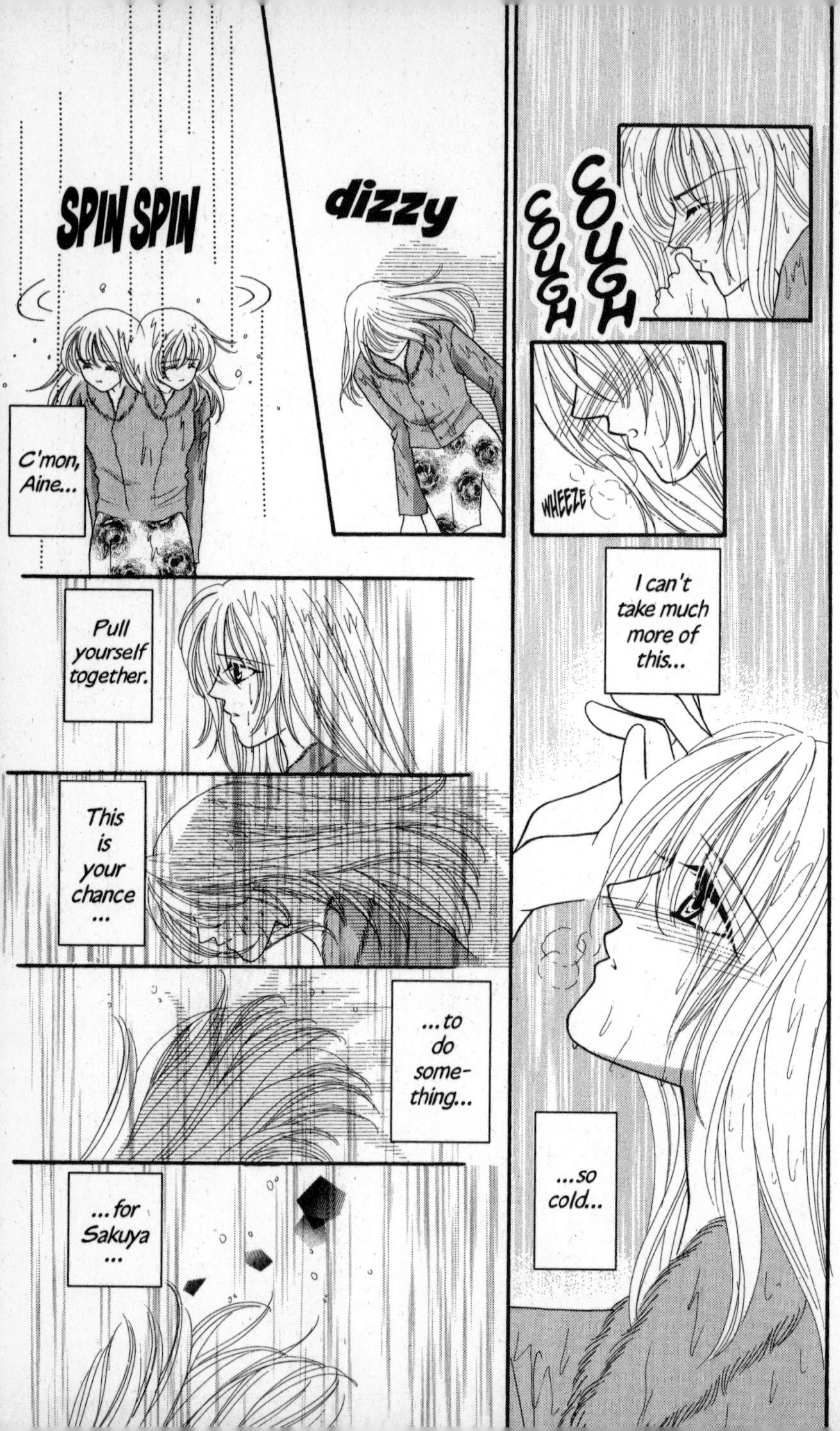
COUGH COUGH
WHEEZE
I can't take much more of this...
...so cold...
dizzy
SPIN SPIN
C'mon, Aine...
Pull yourself together.
This is your chance...
...to do some-thing...
...for Sakuya...

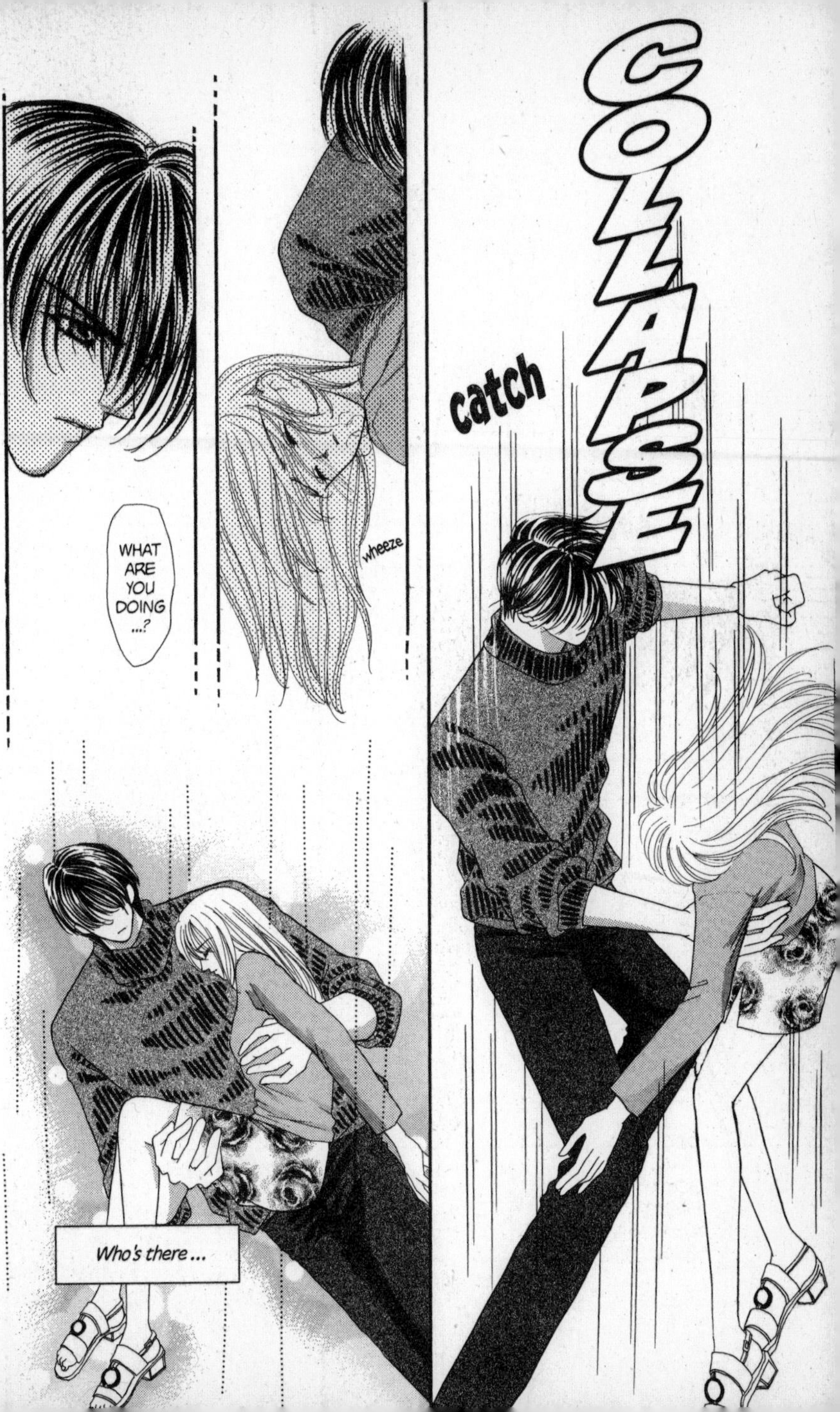
COLLAPSE
catch
wheeze
WHAT ARE YOU DOING ...?
Who's there ...

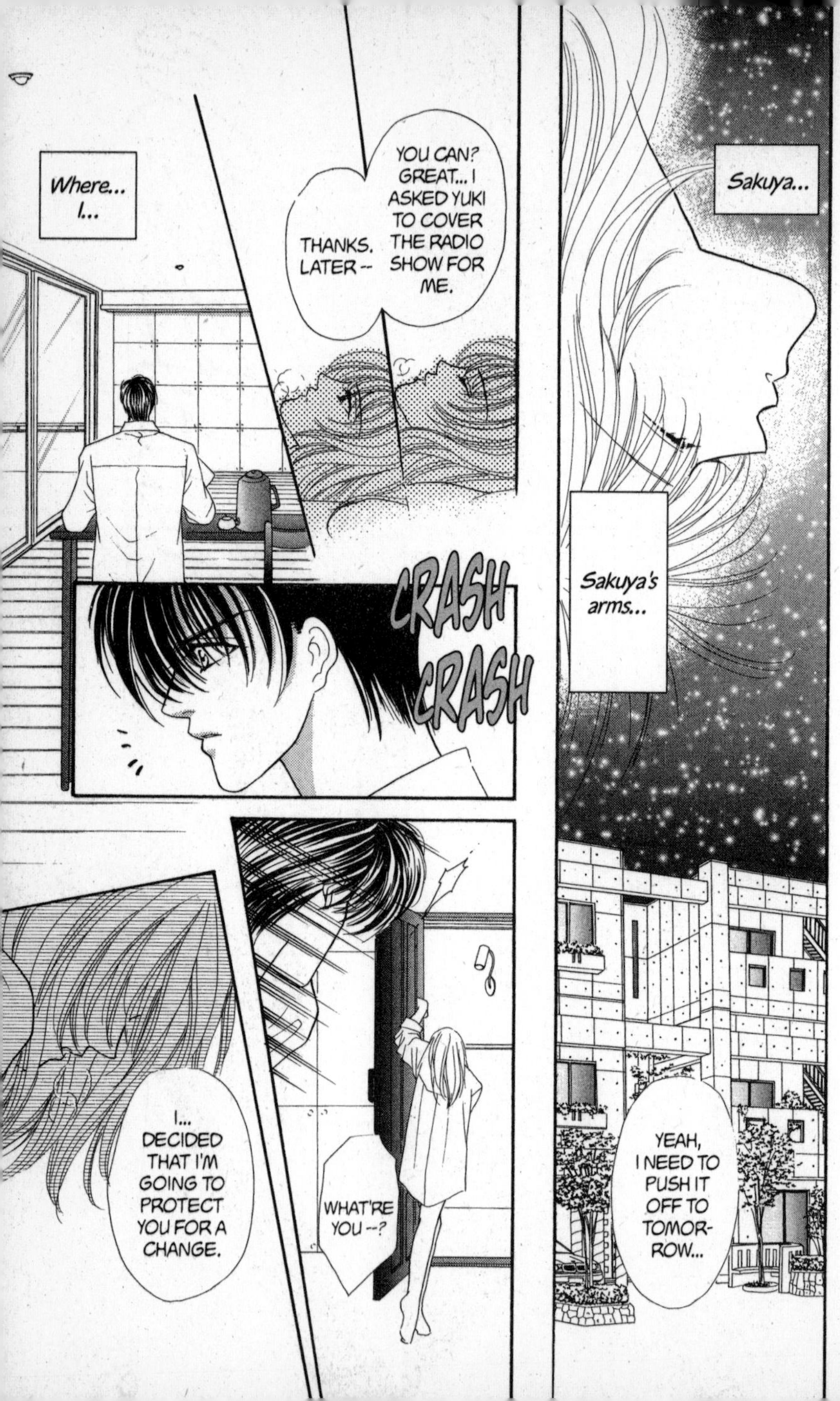
Sakuya...
Sakuya's arms...
YEAH, I NEED TO PUSH IT OFF TO TOMORROW...
YOU CAN? GREAT... I ASKED YUKI TO COVER THE RADIO SHOW FOR ME.
THANKS. LATER --
Where... I...
CRASH CRASH
WHAT'RE YOU --?
I... DECIDED THAT I'M GOING TO PROTECT YOU FOR A CHANGE.

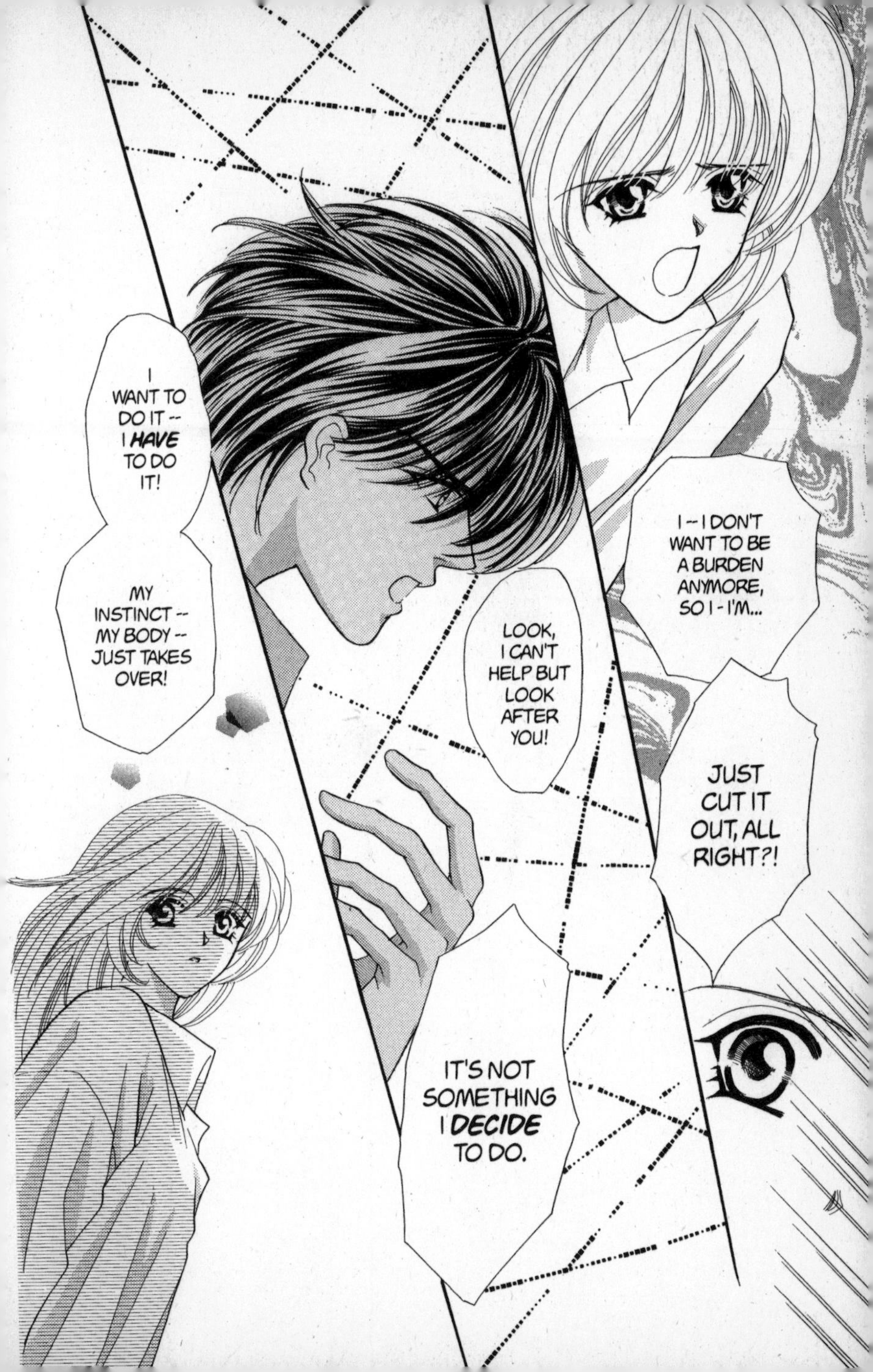
I -- I DON'T WANT TO BE A BURDEN ANYMORE, SO I - I'M...
JUST CUT IT OUT, ALL RIGHT?!
LOOK, I CAN'T HELP BUT LOOK AFTER YOU!
IT'S NOT SOMETHING I **DECIDE** TO DO.
I WANT TO DO IT -- I **HAVE** TO DO IT!
MY INSTINCT -- MY BODY -- JUST TAKES OVER!

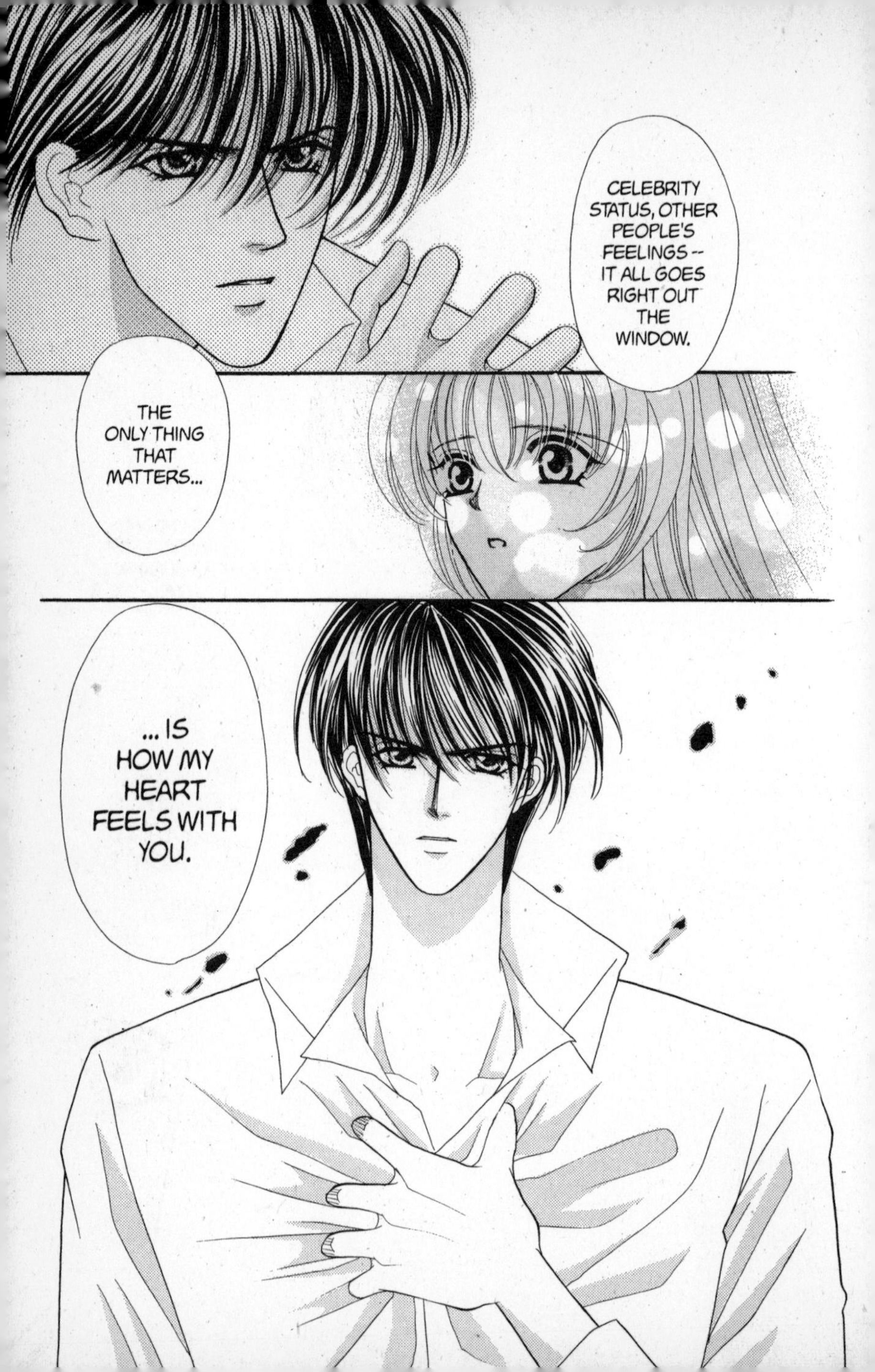
CELEBRITY STATUS, OTHER PEOPLE'S FEELINGS -- IT ALL GOES RIGHT OUT THE WINDOW.
THE ONLY THING THAT MATTERS...
... IS HOW MY HEART FEELS WITH YOU.

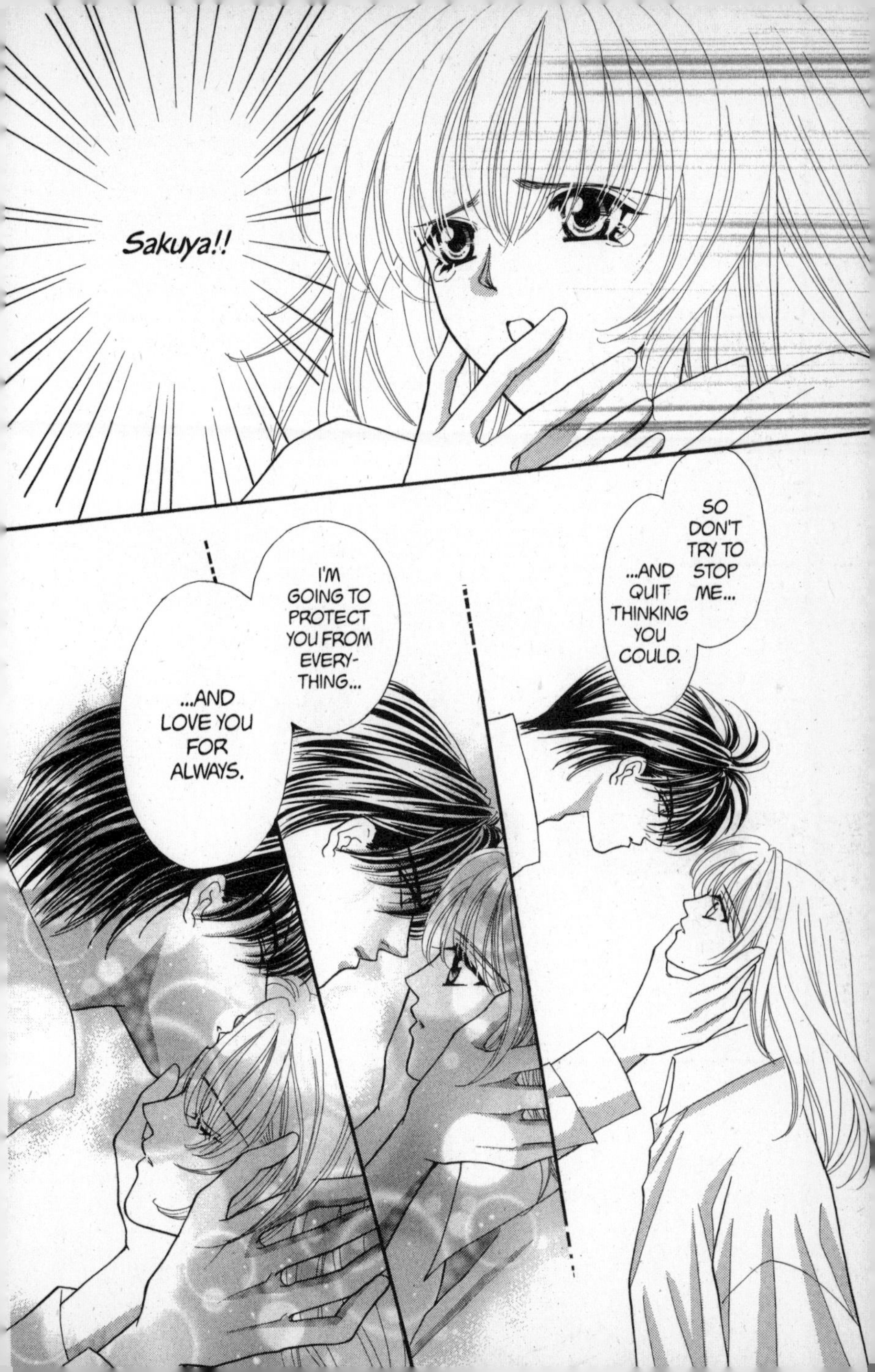
Sakuya!!
SO DON'T TRY TO STOP ME...
...AND QUIT THINKING YOU COULD.
I'M GOING TO PROTECT YOU FROM EVERY-THING...
...AND LOVE YOU FOR ALWAYS.

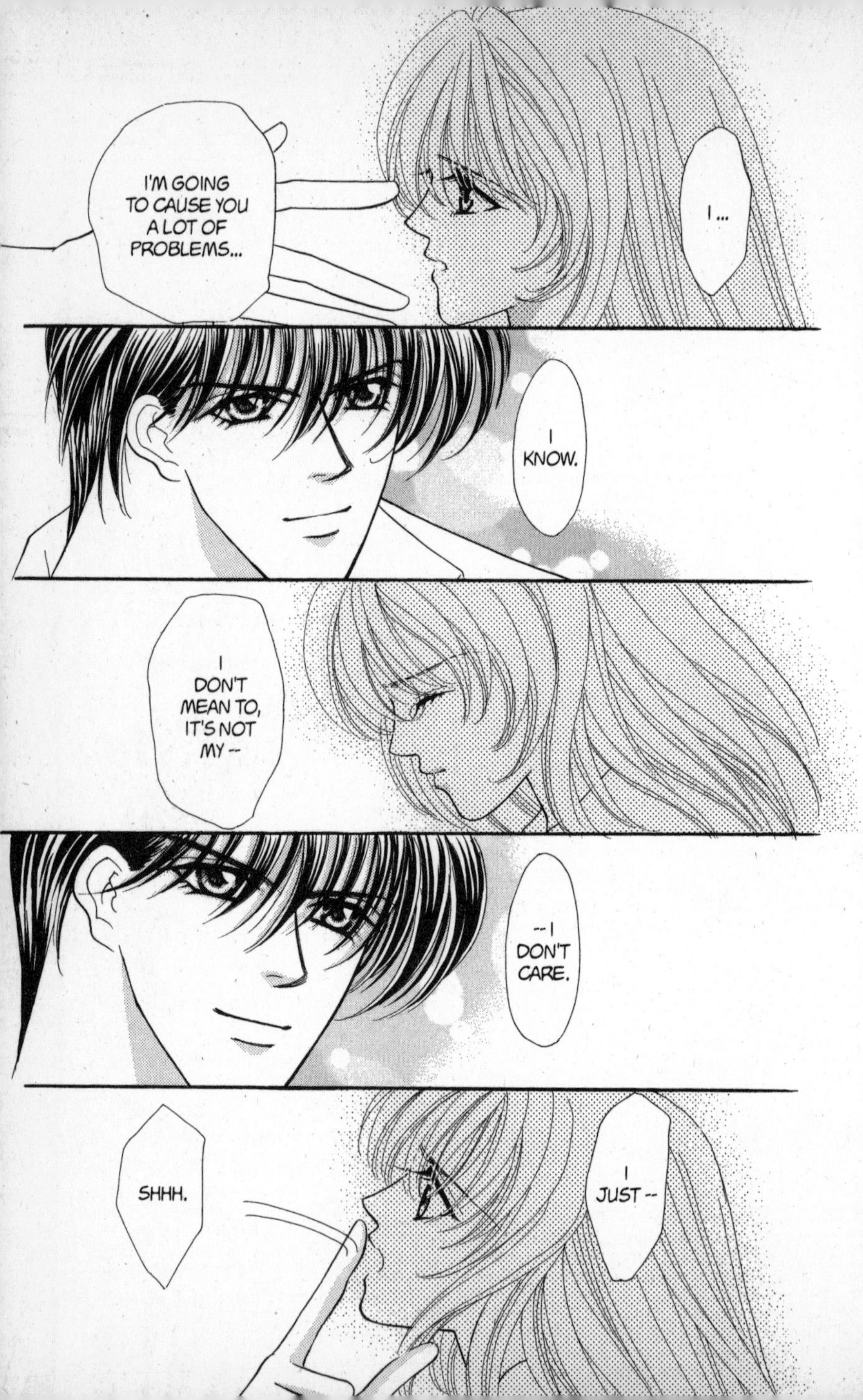
I...
I'M GOING TO CAUSE YOU A LOT OF PROBLEMS...
I KNOW.
I DON'T MEAN TO, IT'S NOT MY --
--I DON'T CARE.
I JUST --
SHHH.

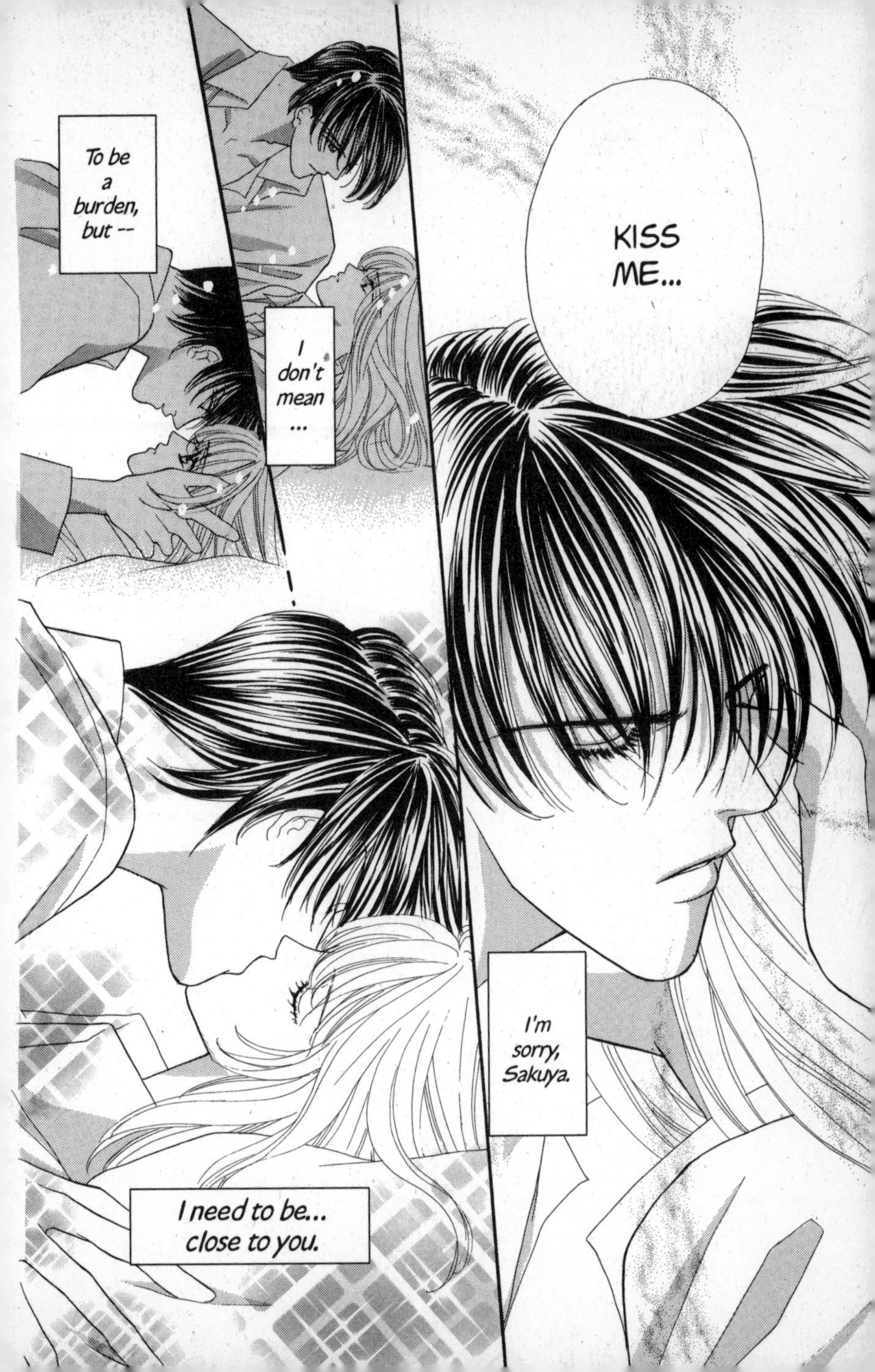
KISS ME...
I'm sorry, Sakuya.
I don't mean ...
To be a burden, but --
I need to be... close to you.

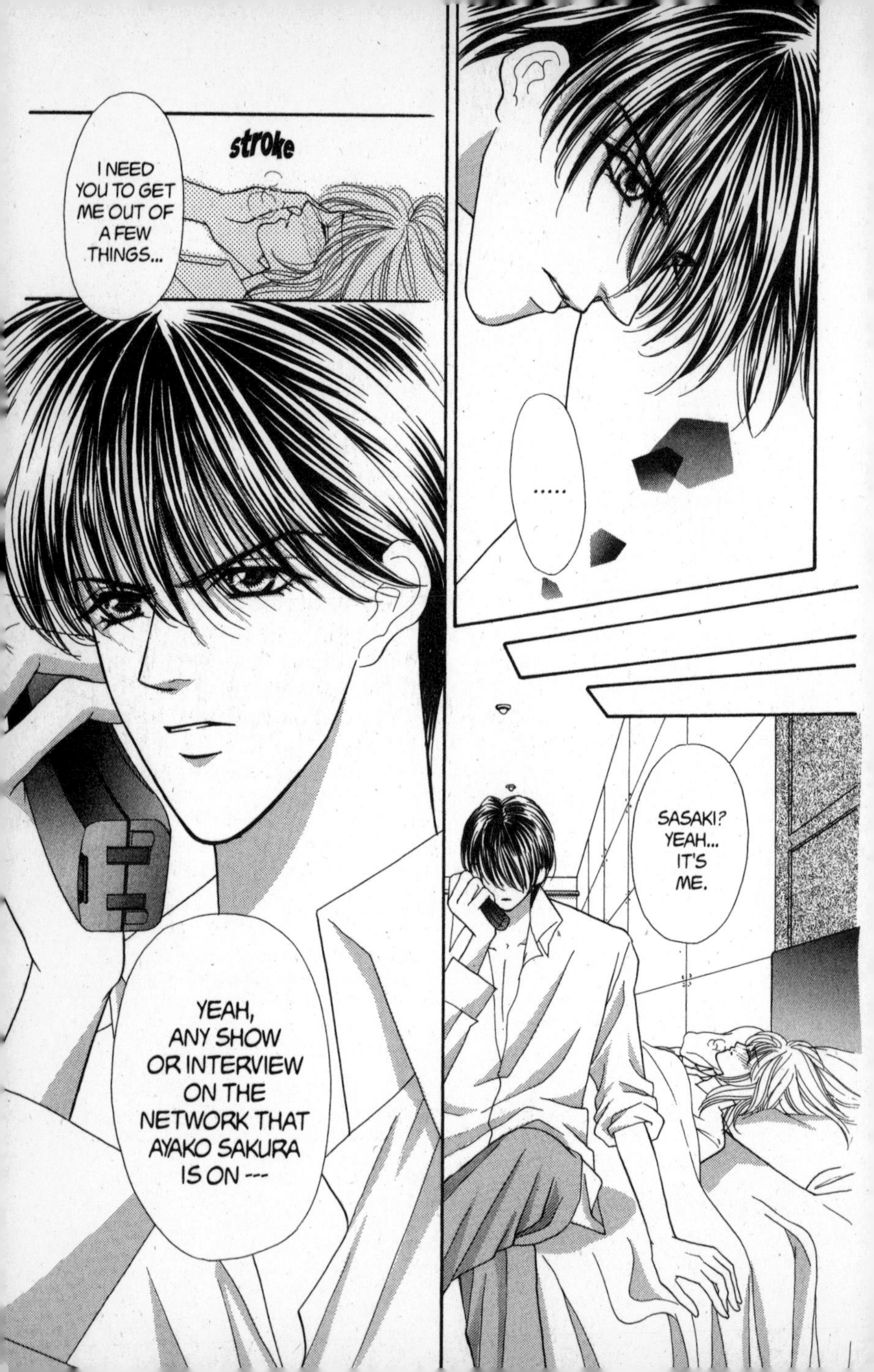
.....
SASAKI? YEAH... IT'S ME.
I NEED YOU TO GET ME OUT OF A FEW THINGS...
stroke
YEAH, ANY SHOW OR INTERVIEW ON THE NETWORK THAT AYAKO SAKURA IS ON ---

KAZUTO SAKUMA (19) - TOWA -

(Likes)
Color: Primary colors.
Season: Fall.
Cigarette: Parliament.
Food: Italian.
Drink: Wine.
Movie: English Patient.
Phrase: Dreams are to be realized.
Town: Akasaka, Ikejiri Ohashi.
Time: When I'm shopping.
Designer: Armani, Vivian Westwood.
Bands: Prodigy, Chemical Brothers.
Sports: Soccer.
Favorite Feature: My fingers.

(Dislikes)
Food: Blue Cheese.
People: Sneaky, Cheating.

(Personality)
Infatuated with foreign travel, pretty quiet, expensive taste. A bit of an outsider. Always daydreaming.

Hobby: Computers.
Weakness: Women.
Favorite Subject: Physics.
Least Favorite Subject: Classical literature.
Fave Place to Relax: My room.
How do you spend time off: Shopping.
What I want most: Time.
Gift you like receiving: Whatever I'm collecting at the time.
Habits: Frequent naps.
Need(s): Someone to look after.
Bathing Time: 30 minutes.
Girls you like: Opinionated girls.
Girls you hate: Loud, opinionated girls.
Thoughts on marriage: I'm looking forward to it.
Ideal family: One in which we need each other like air.
What are you like when you're drunk?: I'm a big baby.

(Thoughts on your band-mates)
Atsuro: We get along really well. He's got such a pure heart. His family really raised him right.
Sakuya: Can't argue with success, can you? He's easily got the best voice in rock music.
Yuki: He was brought up well, too. Classy and calm. And he's always right!
Santa: Hilarious! Big hearted, has a calming effect on the rest of us.

BORN: APRIL 10th
SIGN: ARIES
HEIGHT: 175 cm
WEIGHT: 60 kg
EYESIGHT: RIGHT 1.0, LEFT 0
SHOE SIZE: 26 cm
FROM: TOKYO
RESIDES IN: SETAGAYA

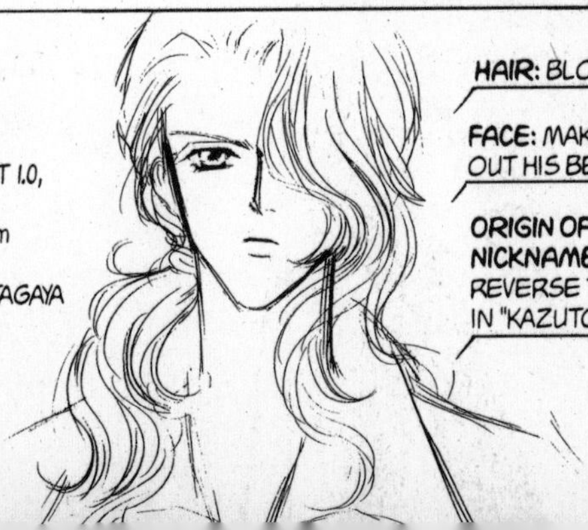

HAIR: BLONDE

FACE: MAKE UP BRINGS OUT HIS BEST FEATURES

ORIGIN OF NICKNAMETOWA: REVERSE THE KANJI IN "KAZUTO"

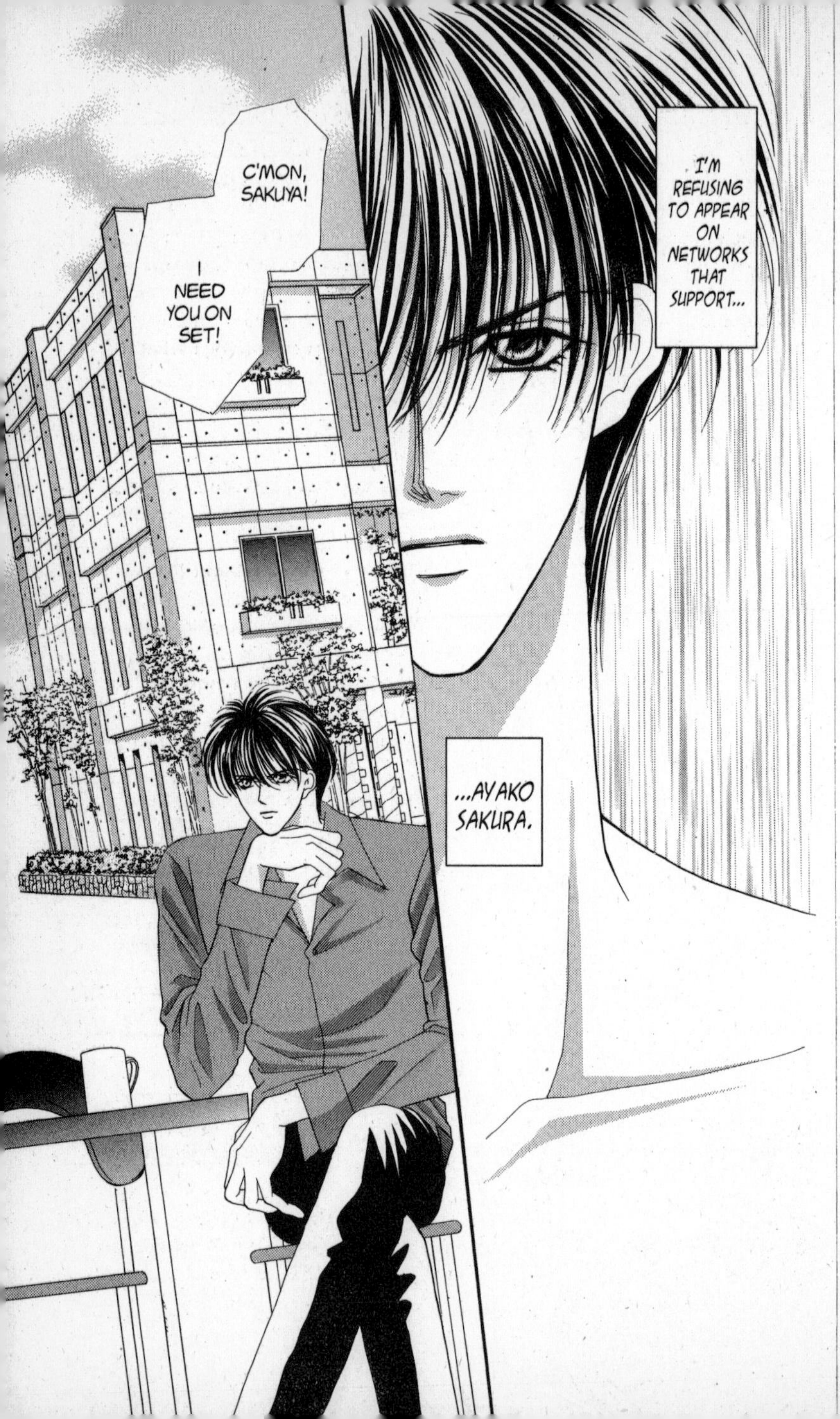
I'M REFUSING TO APPEAR ON NETWORKS THAT SUPPORT...
...AYAKO SAKURA.
C'MON, SAKUYA!
I NEED YOU ON SET!

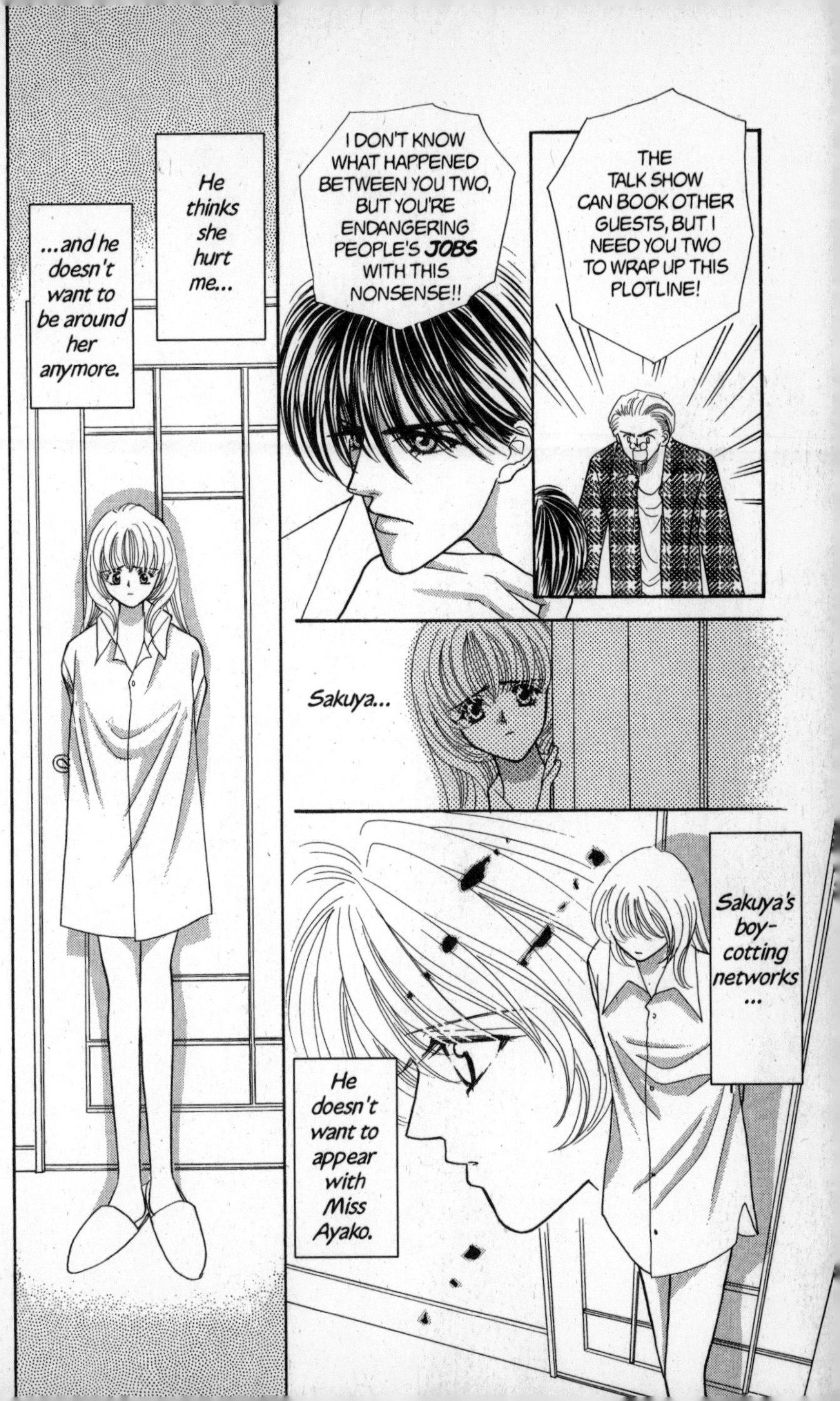
THE TALK SHOW CAN BOOK OTHER GUESTS, BUT I NEED YOU TWO TO WRAP UP THIS PLOTLINE!
I DON'T KNOW WHAT HAPPENED BETWEEN YOU TWO, BUT YOU'RE ENDANGERING PEOPLE'S JOBS WITH THIS NONSENSE!!
Sakuya...
Sakuya's boy-cotting networks ...
He doesn't want to appear with Miss Ayako.
He thinks she hurt me...
...and he doesn't want to be around her anymore.

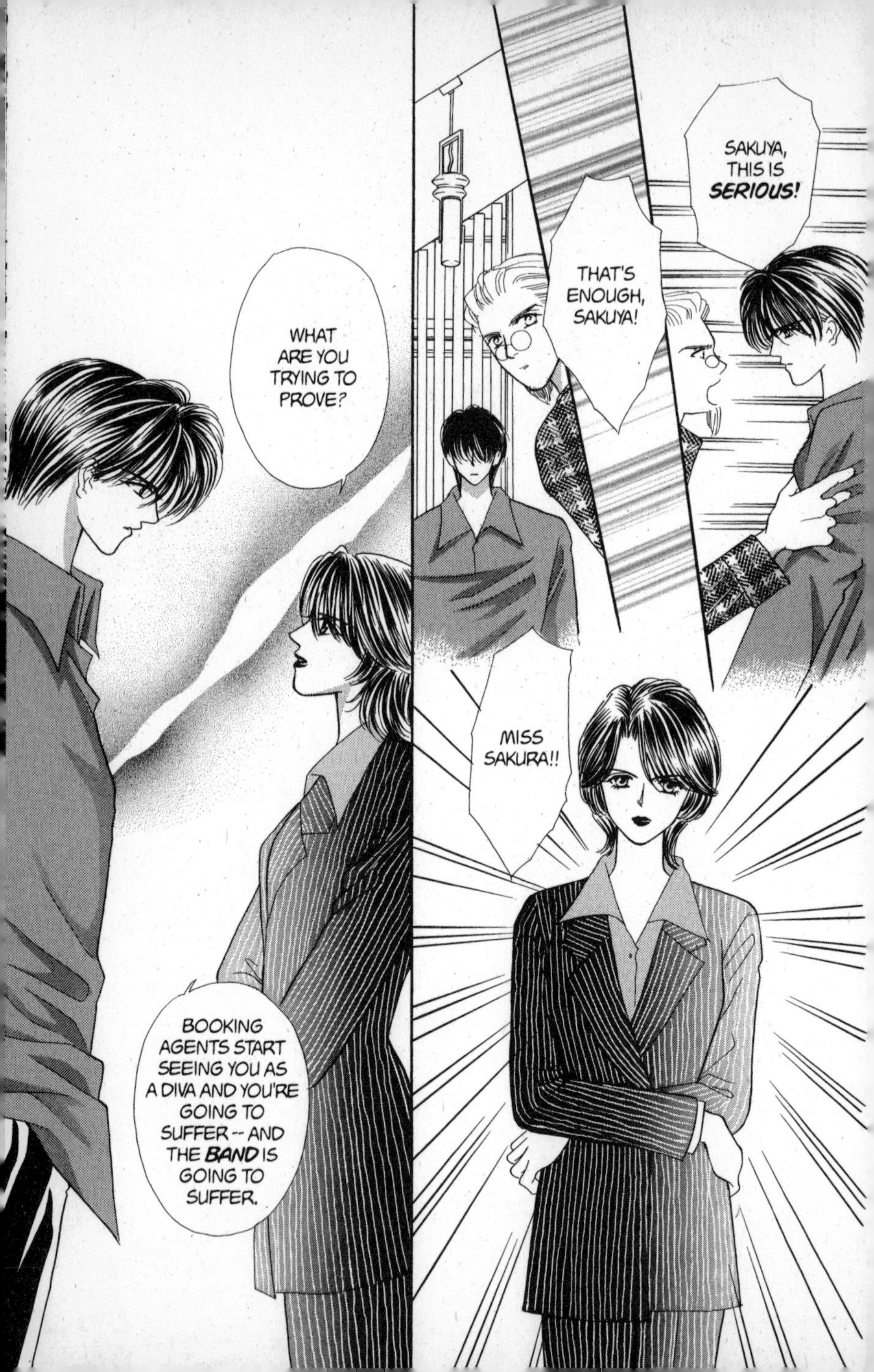
SAKUYA, THIS IS SERIOUS!
THAT'S ENOUGH, SAKUYA!
MISS SAKURA!!
WHAT ARE YOU TRYING TO PROVE?
BOOKING AGENTS START SEEING YOU AS A DIVA AND YOU'RE GOING TO SUFFER -- AND THE BAND IS GOING TO SUFFER.

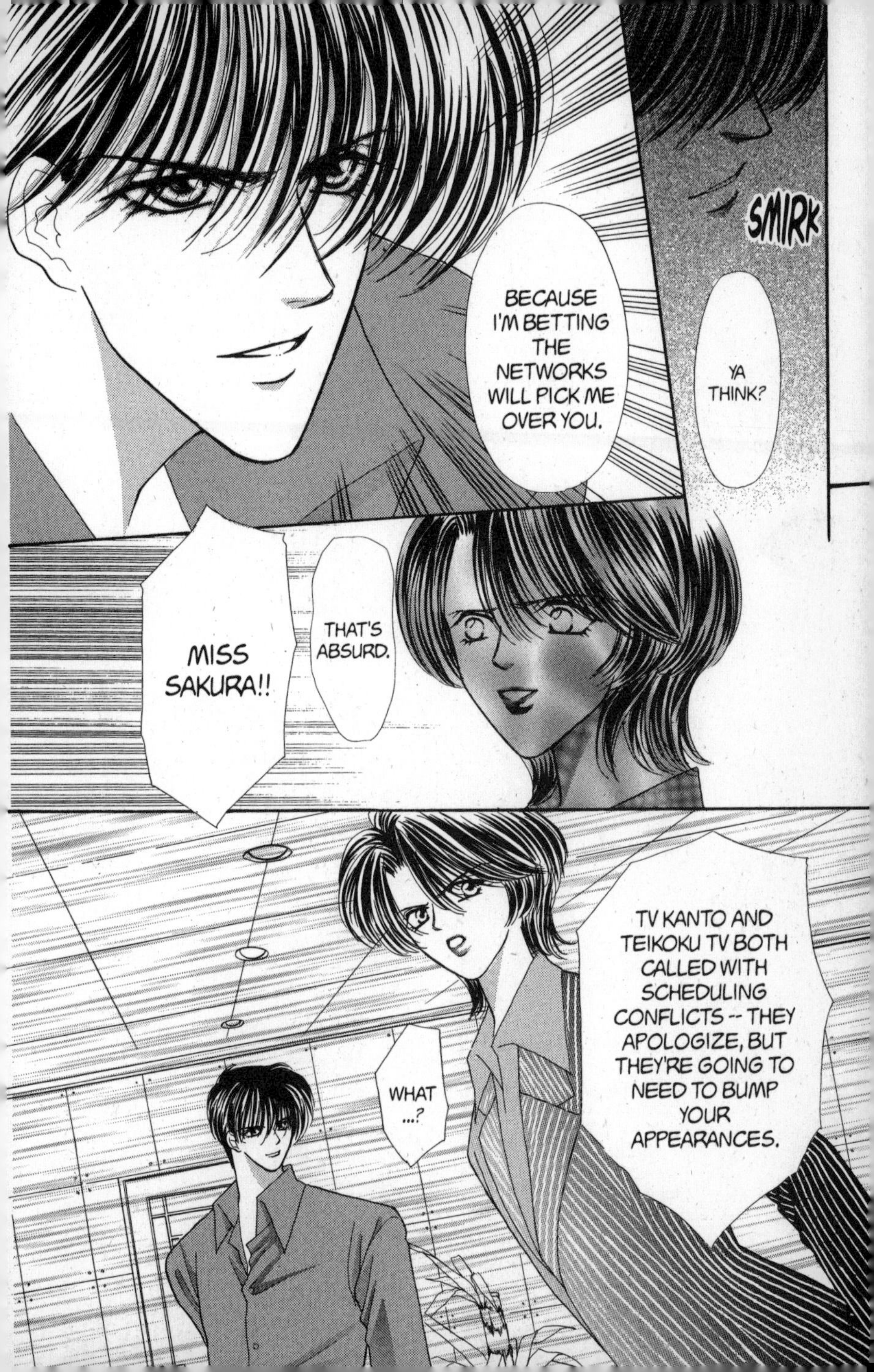
SMIRK
YA THINK?
BECAUSE I'M BETTING THE NETWORKS WILL PICK ME OVER YOU.
THAT'S ABSURD.
MISS SAKURA!!
TV KANTO AND TEIKOKU TV BOTH CALLED WITH SCHEDULING CONFLICTS -- THEY APOLOGIZE, BUT THEY'RE GOING TO NEED TO BUMP YOUR APPEARANCES.
WHAT ...?

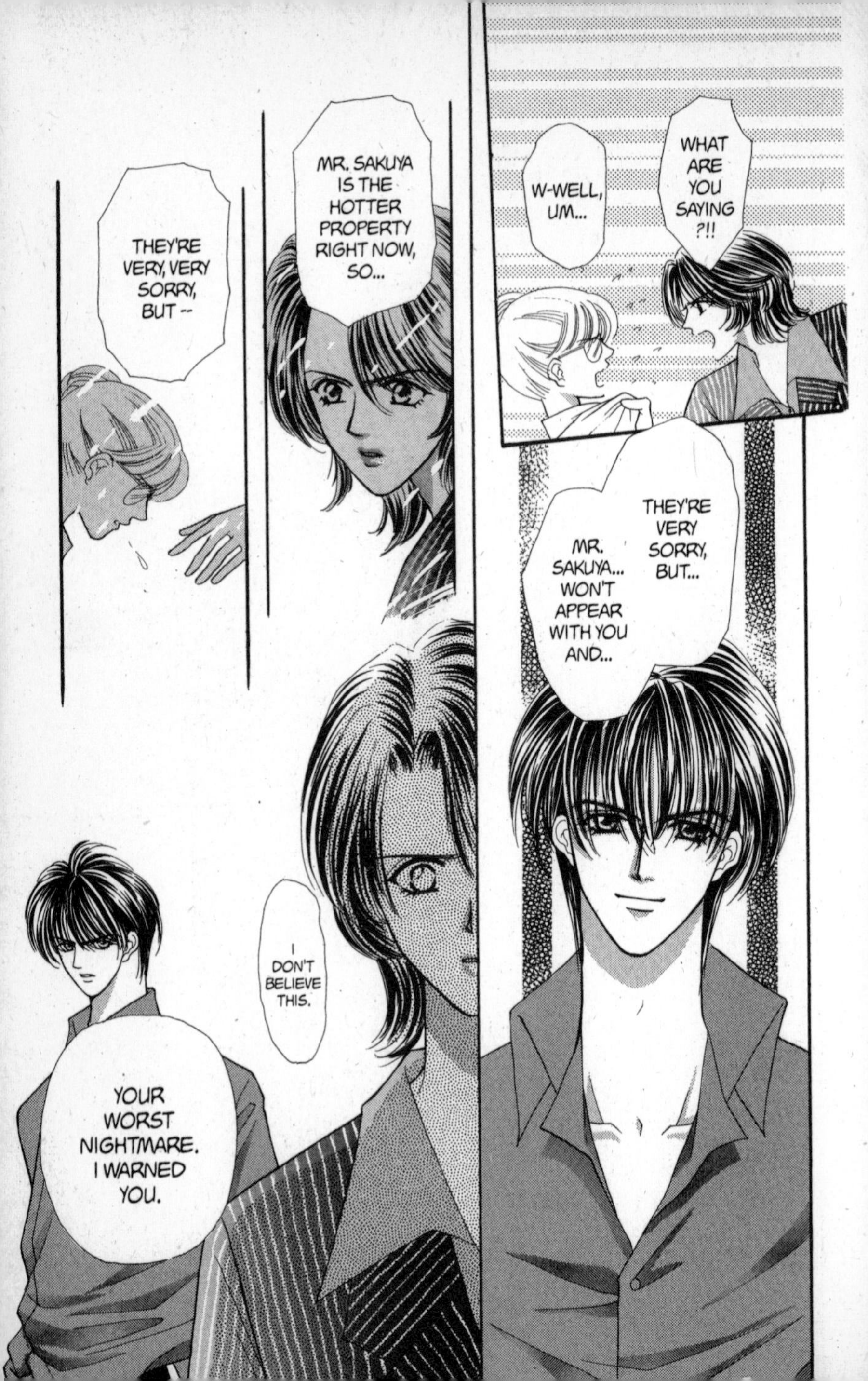
WHAT ARE YOU SAYING ?!!
W-WELL, UM...
THEY'RE VERY SORRY, BUT...
MR. SAKUYA... WON'T APPEAR WITH YOU AND...
MR. SAKUYA IS THE HOTTER PROPERTY RIGHT NOW, SO...
THEY'RE VERY, VERY SORRY, BUT --
I DON'T BELIEVE THIS.
YOUR WORST NIGHTMARE. I WARNED YOU.

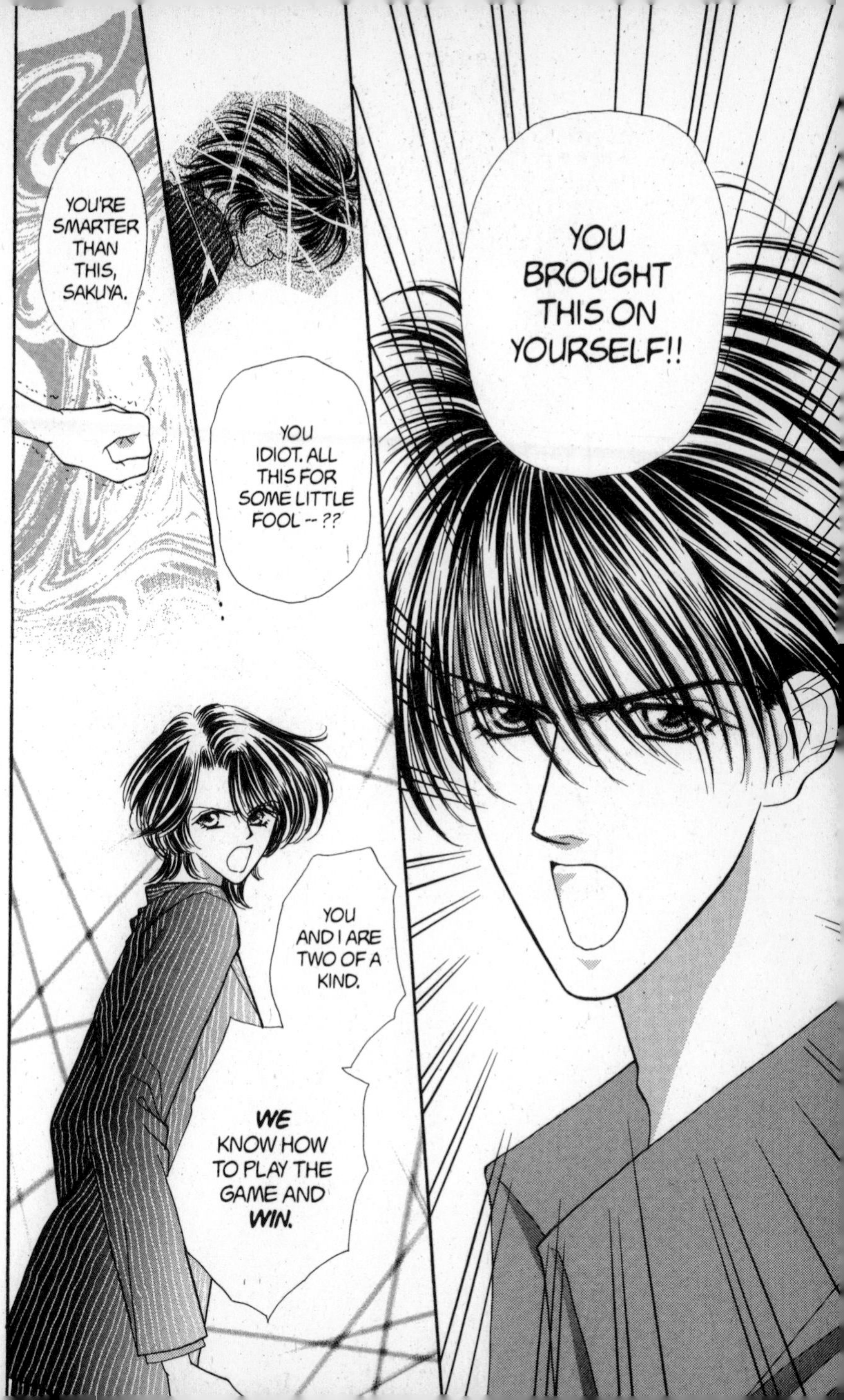
YOU BROUGHT THIS ON YOURSELF!!
YOU IDIOT. ALL THIS FOR SOME LITTLE FOOL--??
YOU'RE SMARTER THAN THIS, SAKUYA.
YOU AND I ARE TWO OF A KIND.
WE KNOW HOW TO PLAY THE GAME AND **WIN.**

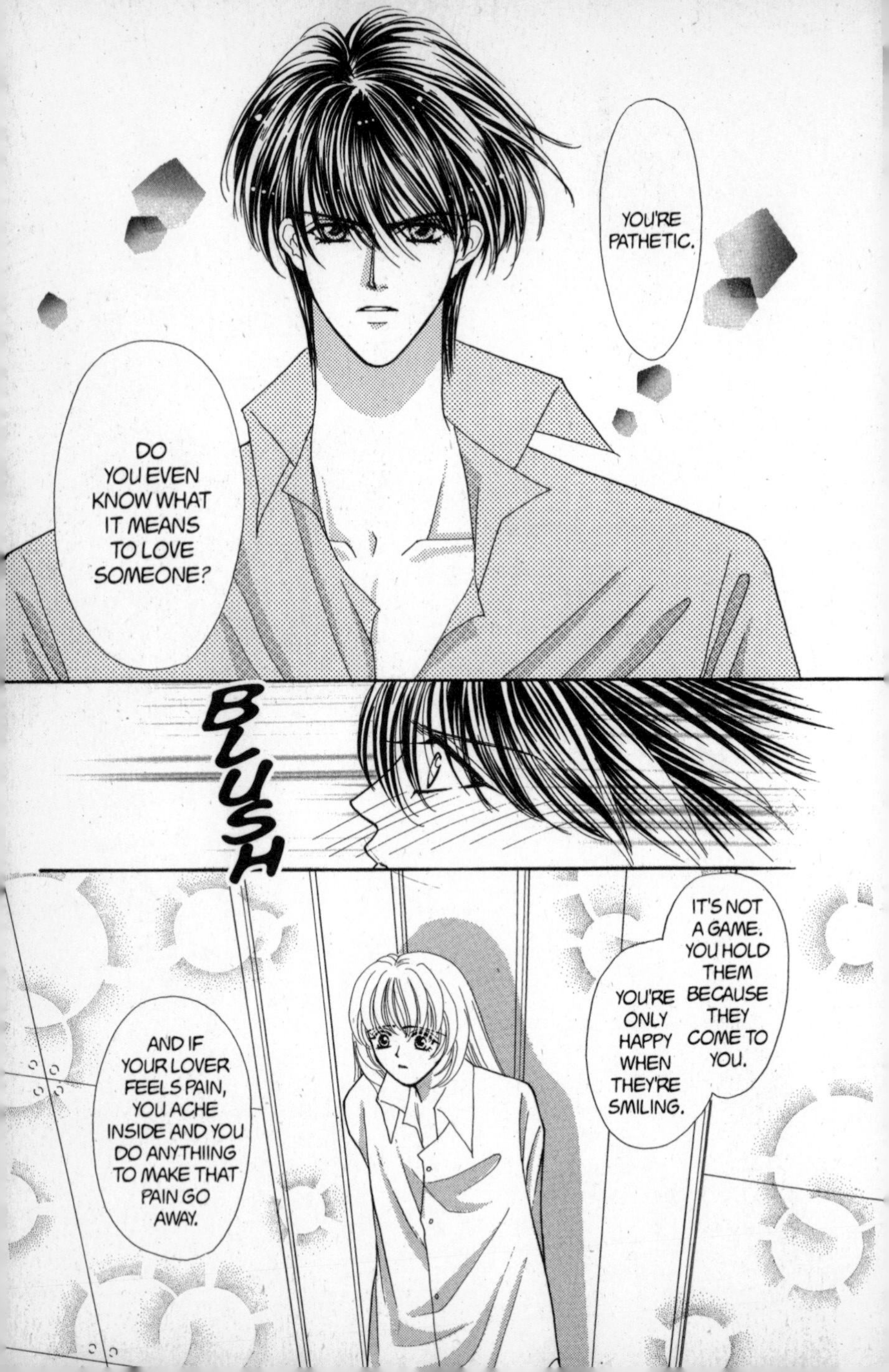
YOU'RE PATHETIC.
DO YOU EVEN KNOW WHAT IT MEANS TO LOVE SOMEONE?
BLUSH
IT'S NOT A GAME. YOU HOLD THEM BECAUSE THEY COME TO YOU.
YOU'RE ONLY HAPPY WHEN THEY'RE SMILING.
AND IF YOUR LOVER FEELS PAIN, YOU ACHE INSIDE AND YOU DO ANYTHIING TO MAKE THAT PAIN GO AWAY.

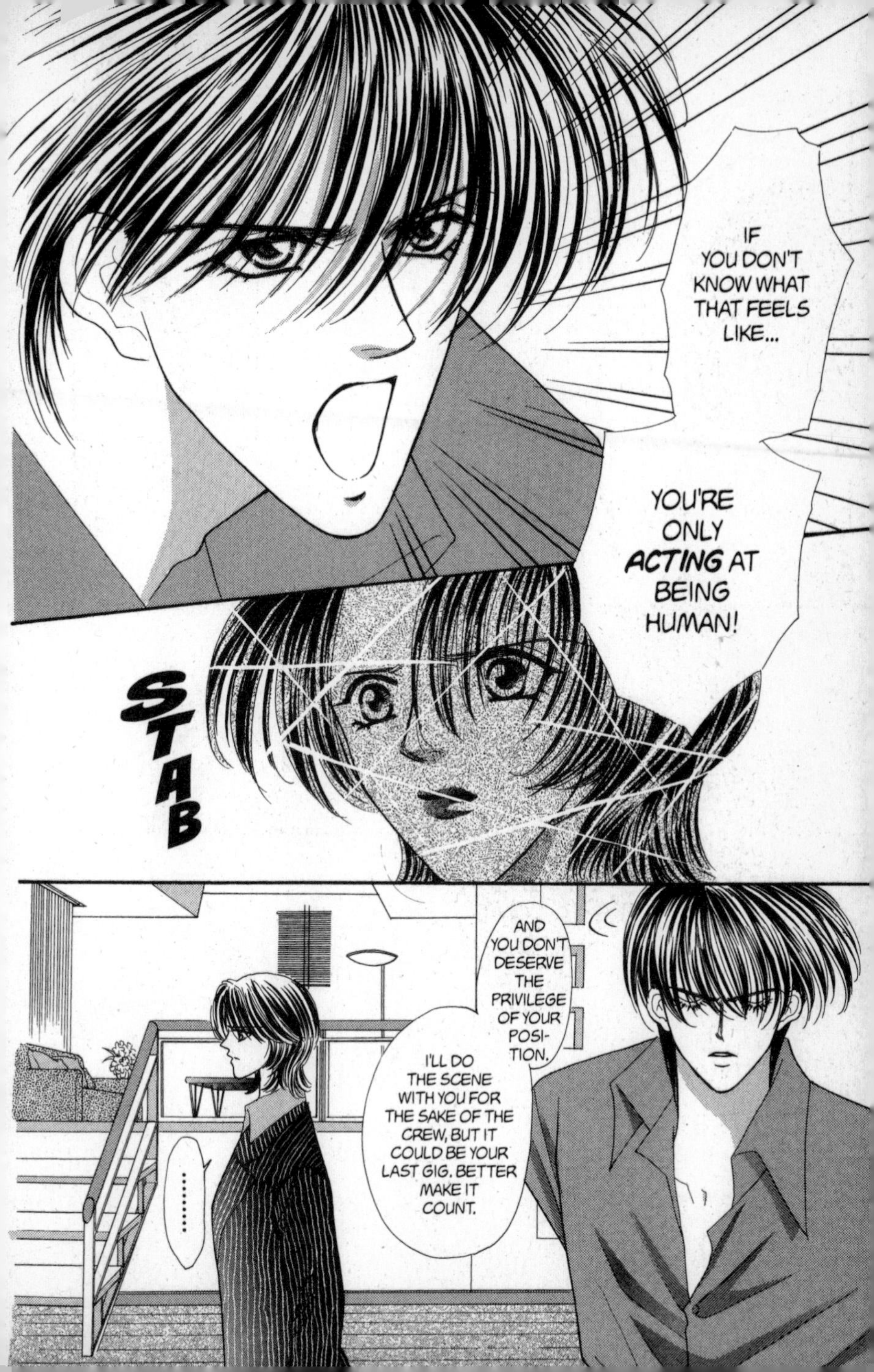
IF YOU DON'T KNOW WHAT THAT FEELS LIKE...
YOU'RE ONLY **ACTING** AT BEING HUMAN!
STAB
AND YOU DON'T DESERVE THE PRIVILEGE OF YOUR POSITION.
I'LL DO THE SCENE WITH YOU FOR THE SAKE OF THE CREW, BUT IT COULD BE YOUR LAST GIG. BETTER MAKE IT COUNT.
....

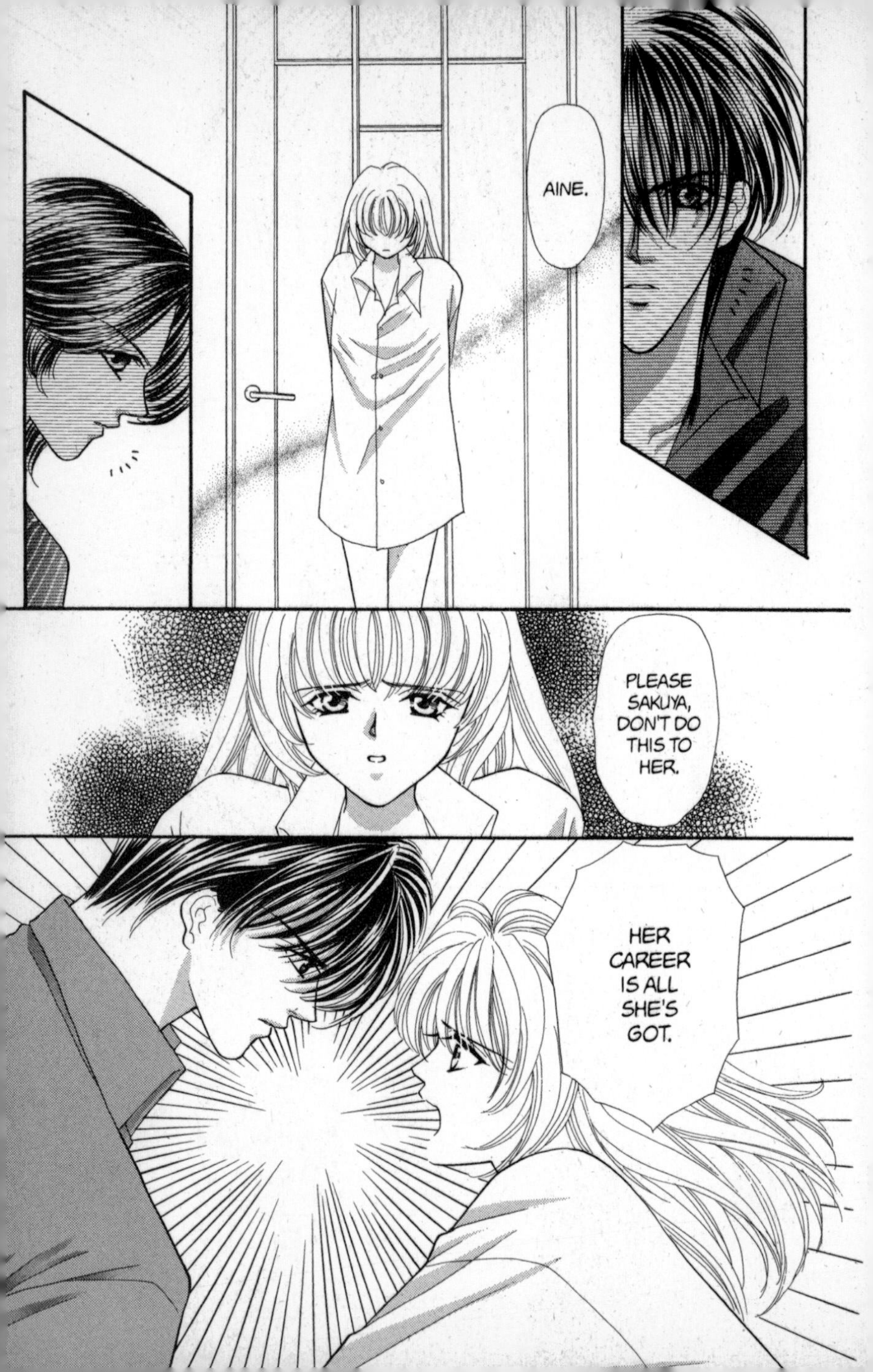
AINE.
PLEASE SAKUYA, DON'T DO THIS TO HER.
HER CAREER IS ALL SHE'S GOT.

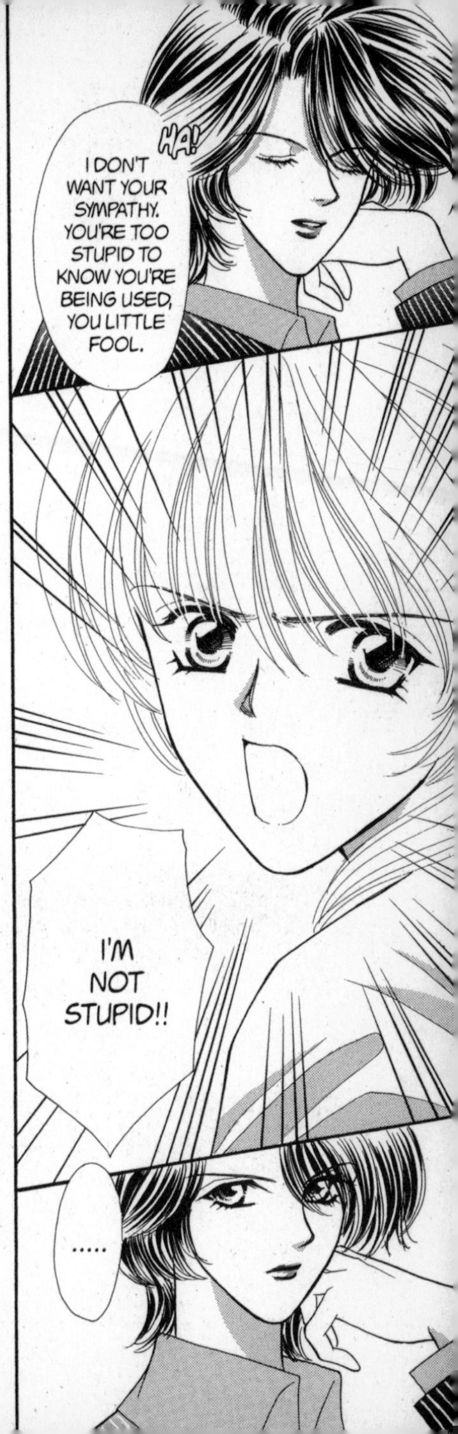
HA!
I DON'T WANT YOUR SYMPATHY. YOU'RE TOO STUPID TO KNOW YOU'RE BEING USED, YOU LITTLE FOOL.
I'M NOT STUPID!!
.....
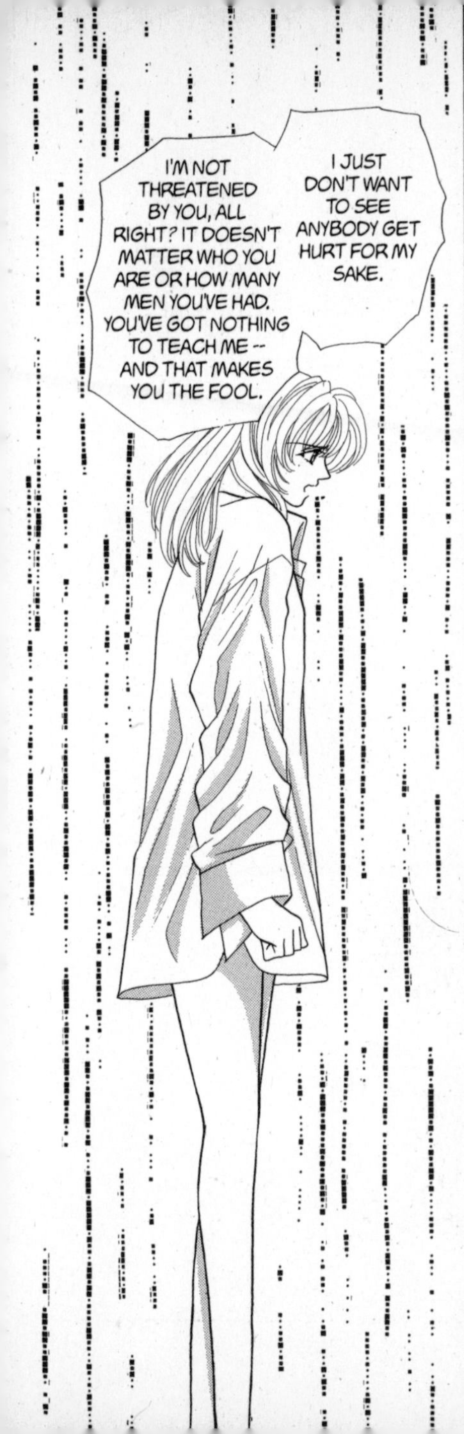
I JUST DON'T WANT TO SEE ANYBODY GET HURT FOR MY SAKE.
I'M NOT THREATENED BY YOU, ALL RIGHT? IT DOESN'T MATTER WHO YOU ARE OR HOW MANY MEN YOU'VE HAD. YOU'VE GOT NOTHING TO TEACH ME -- AND THAT MAKES YOU THE FOOL.

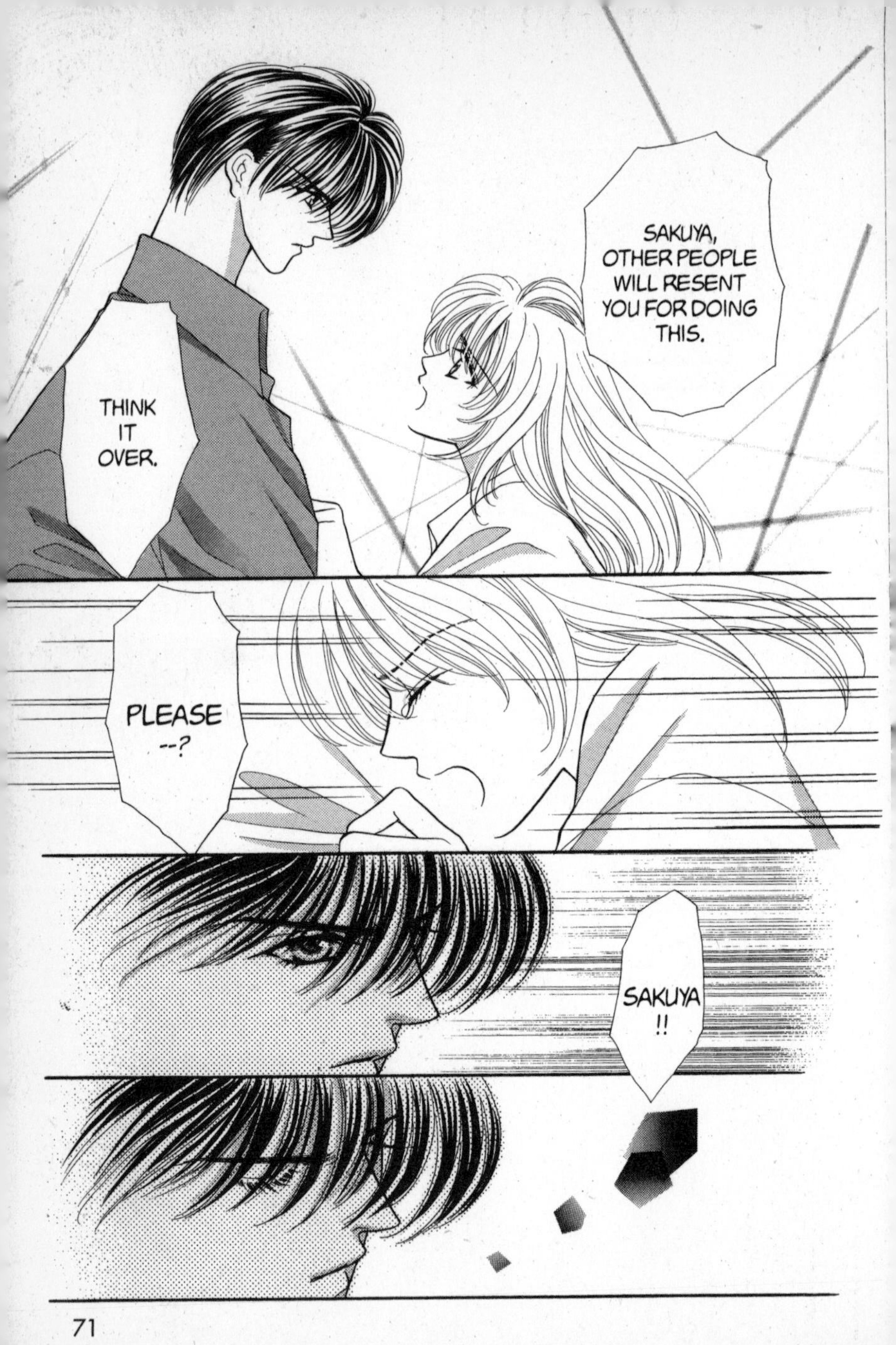
SAKUYA, OTHER PEOPLE WILL RESENT YOU FOR DOING THIS.
THINK IT OVER.
PLEASE --?
SAKUYA !!

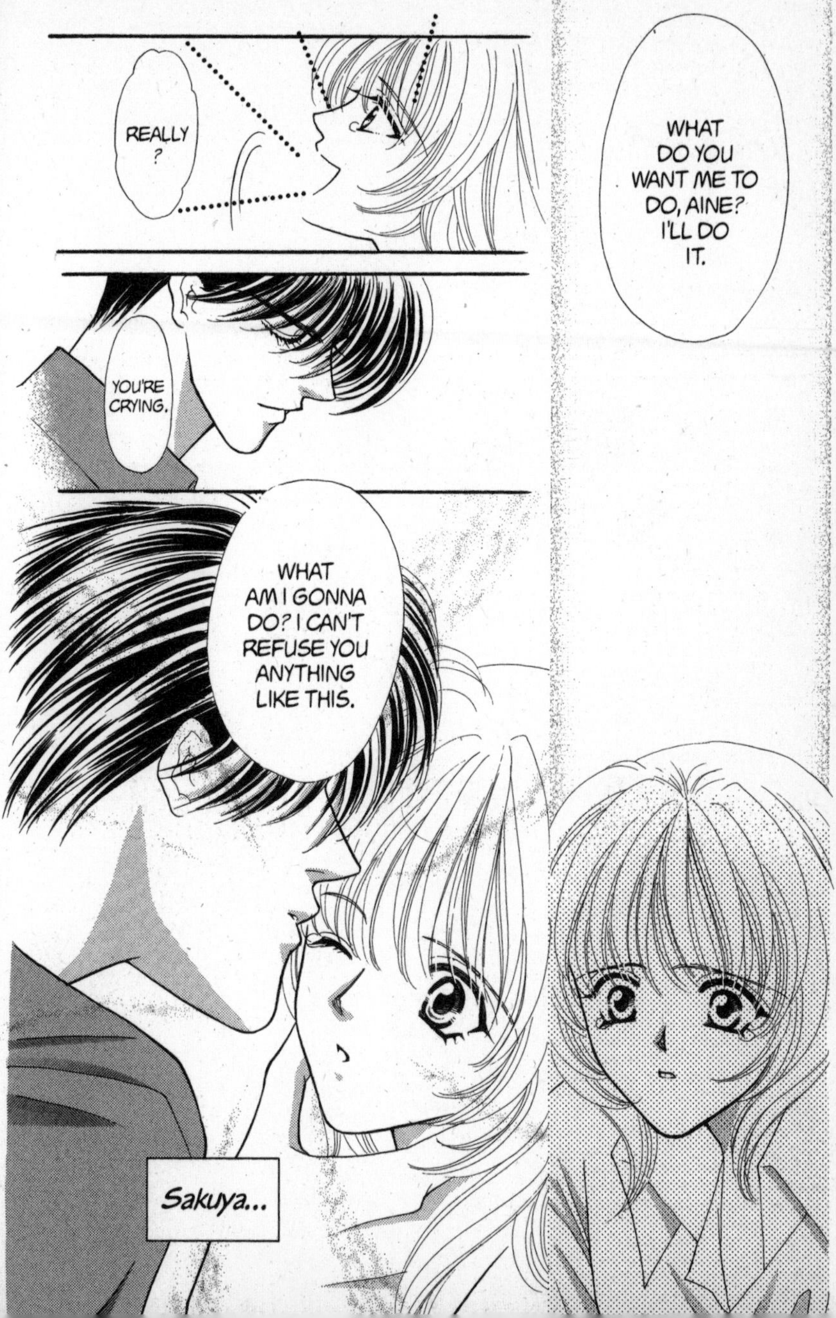
WHAT DO YOU WANT ME TO DO, AINE? I'LL DO IT.
REALLY ?
YOU'RE CRYING.
WHAT AM I GONNA DO? I CAN'T REFUSE YOU ANYTHING LIKE THIS.
Sakuya...

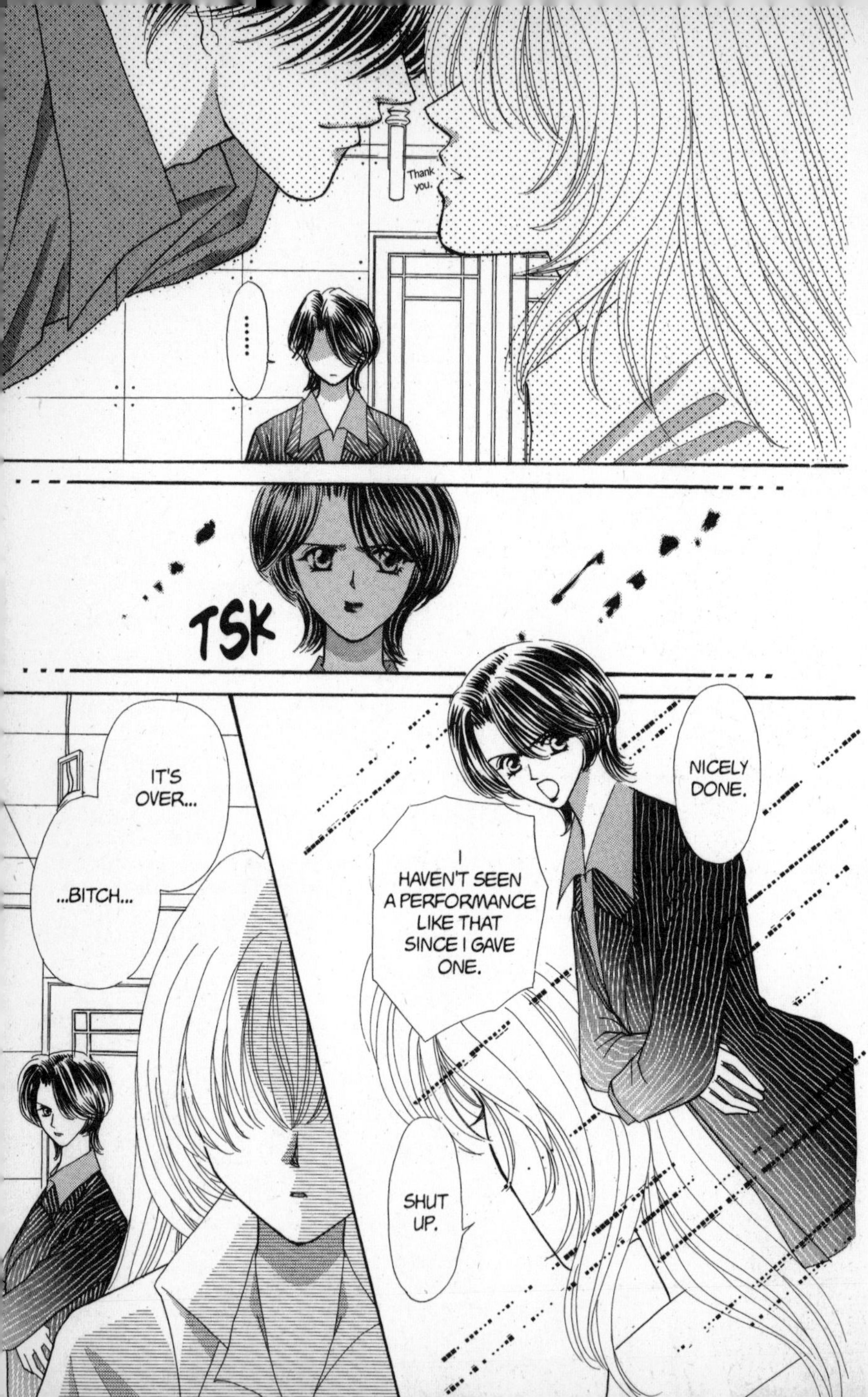
Thank you.
......
TSK
NICELY DONE.
I HAVEN'T SEEN A PERFORMANCE LIKE THAT SINCE I GAVE ONE.
SHUT UP.
IT'S OVER...
...BITCH...

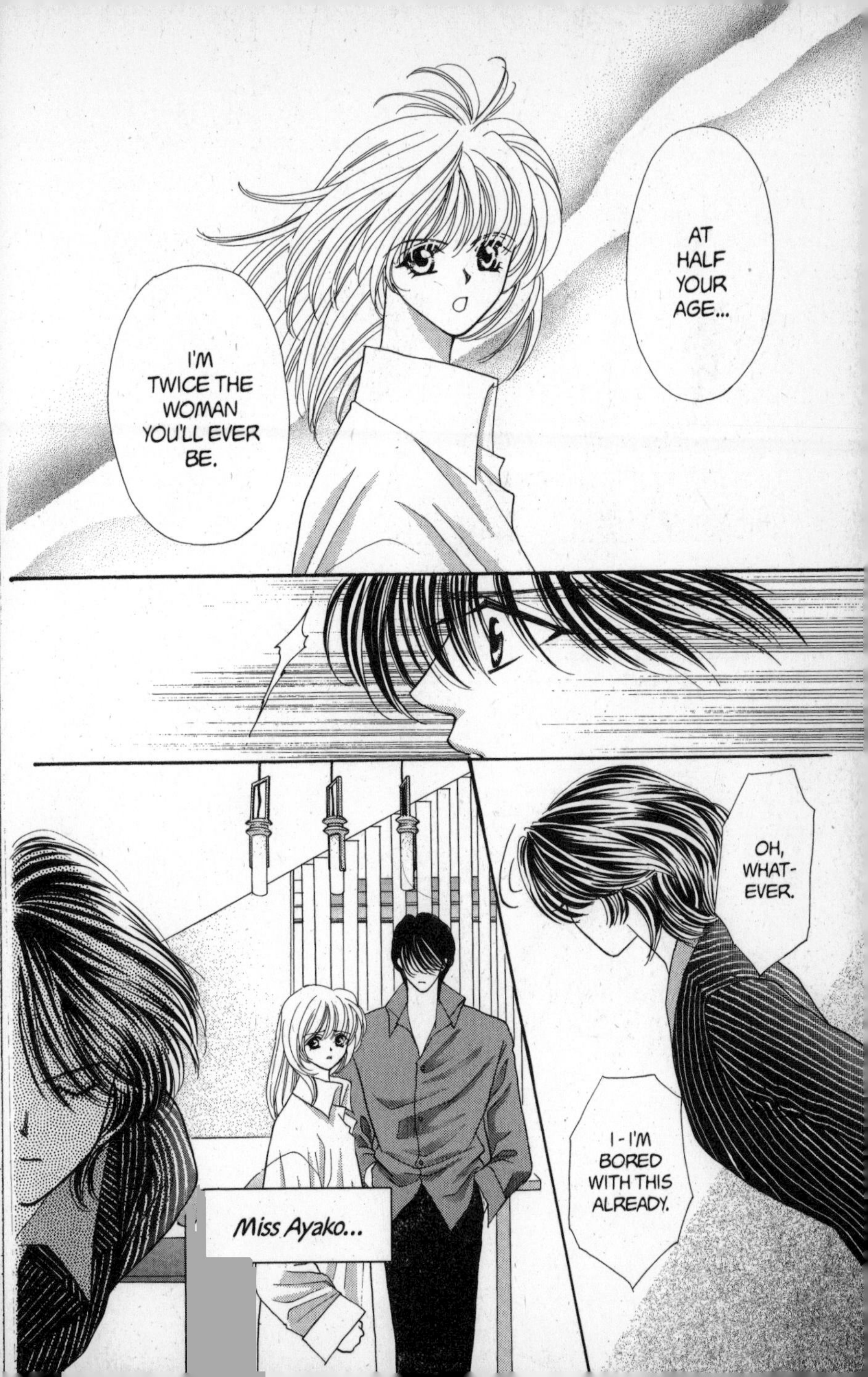
AT HALF YOUR AGE...
I'M TWICE THE WOMAN YOU'LL EVER BE.
OH, WHAT-EVER.
I-I'M BORED WITH THIS ALREADY.
Miss Ayako...

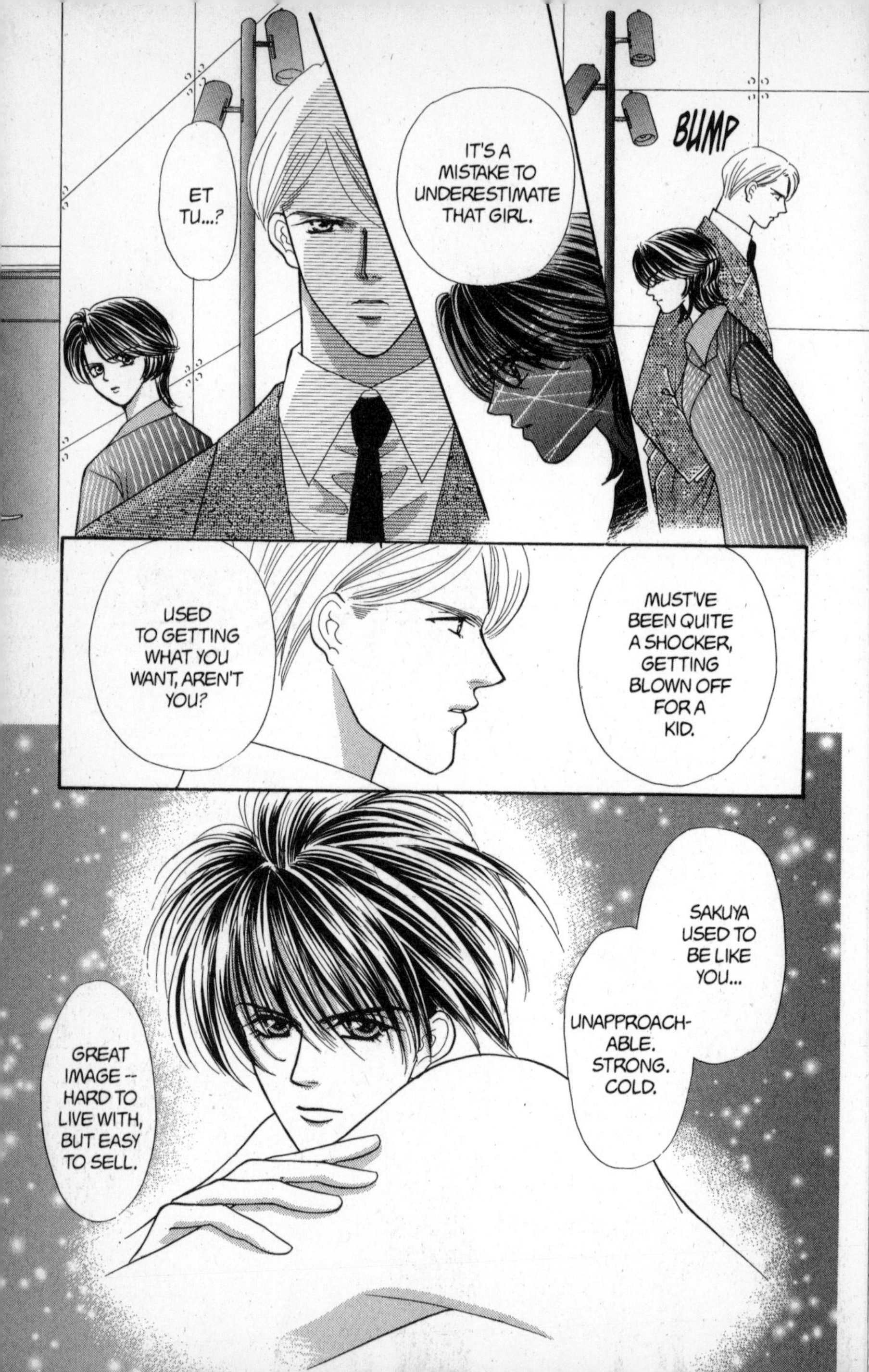
BUMP
IT'S A MISTAKE TO UNDERESTIMATE THAT GIRL.
ET TU...?
MUST'VE BEEN QUITE A SHOCKER, GETTING BLOWN OFF FOR A KID.
USED TO GETTING WHAT YOU WANT, AREN'T YOU?
SAKUYA USED TO BE LIKE YOU...
UNAPPROACH-ABLE. STRONG. COLD.
GREAT IMAGE -- HARD TO LIVE WITH, BUT EASY TO SELL.

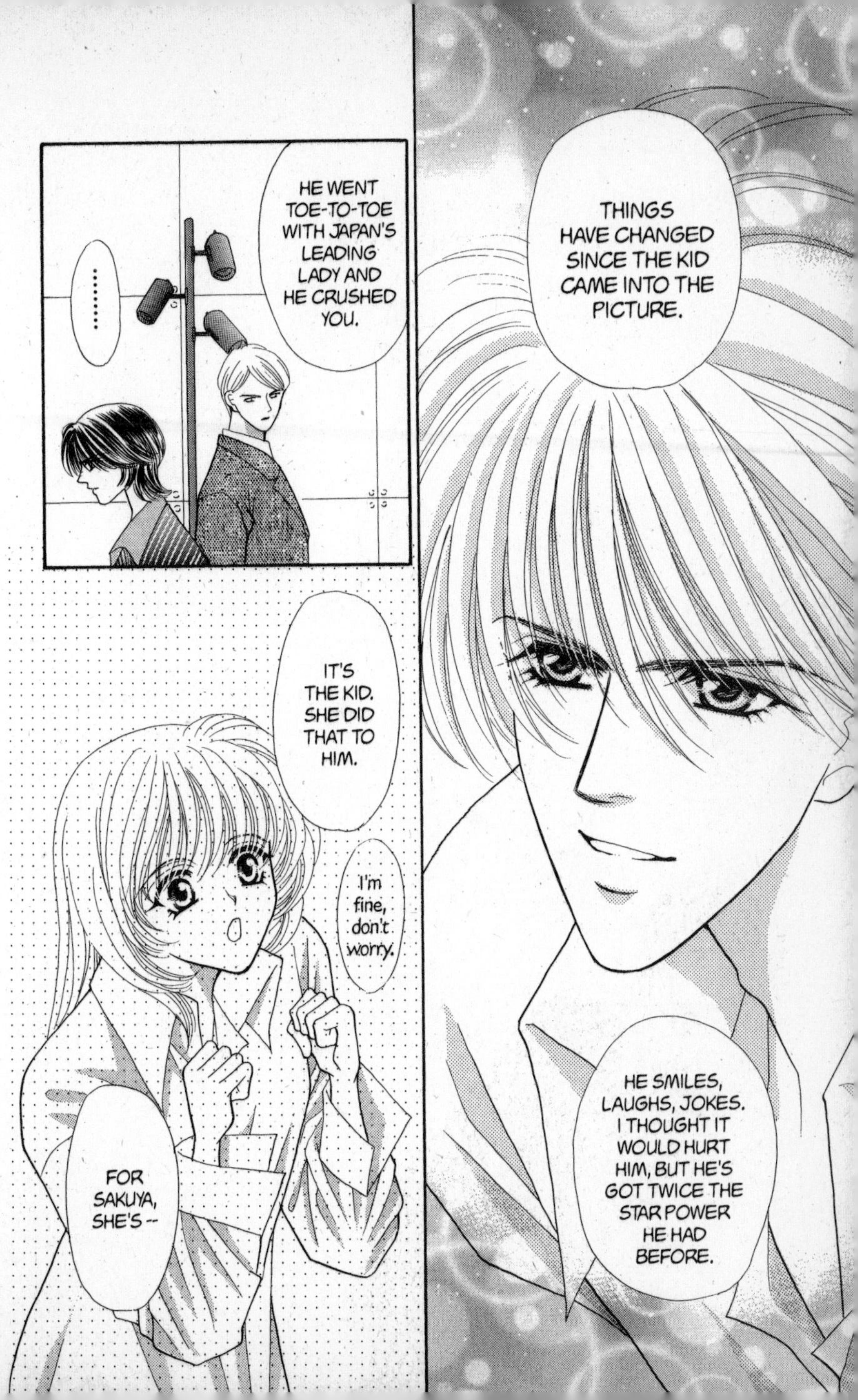
THINGS HAVE CHANGED SINCE THE KID CAME INTO THE PICTURE.
HE SMILES, LAUGHS, JOKES. I THOUGHT IT WOULD HURT HIM, BUT HE'S GOT TWICE THE STAR POWER HE HAD BEFORE.
HE WENT TOE-TO-TOE WITH JAPAN'S LEADING LADY AND HE CRUSHED YOU.
....
IT'S THE KID. SHE DID THAT TO HIM.
I'm fine, don't worry.
FOR SAKUYA, SHE'S --

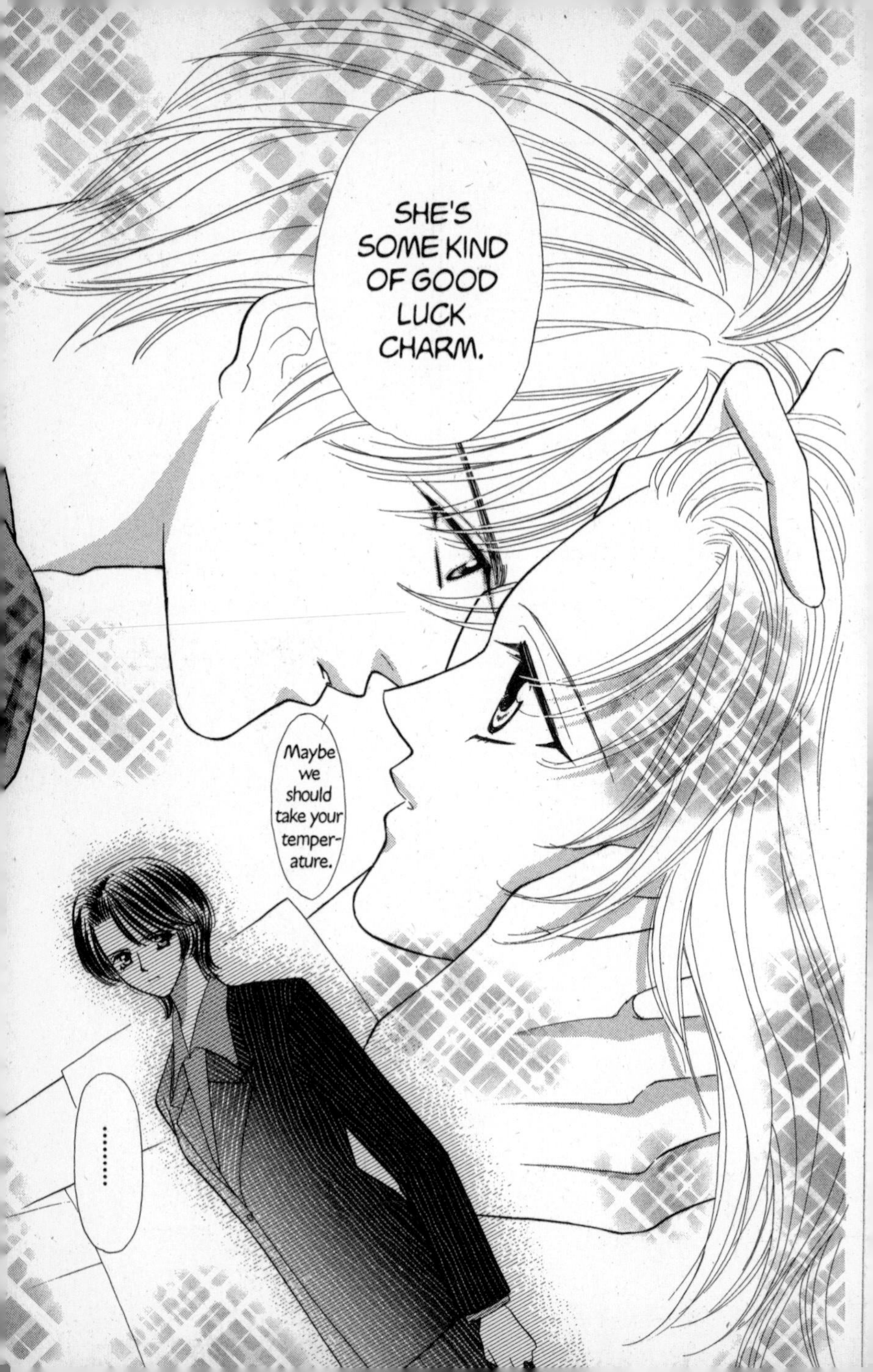
SHE'S SOME KIND OF GOOD LUCK CHARM.
Maybe we should take your temper-ature.
....

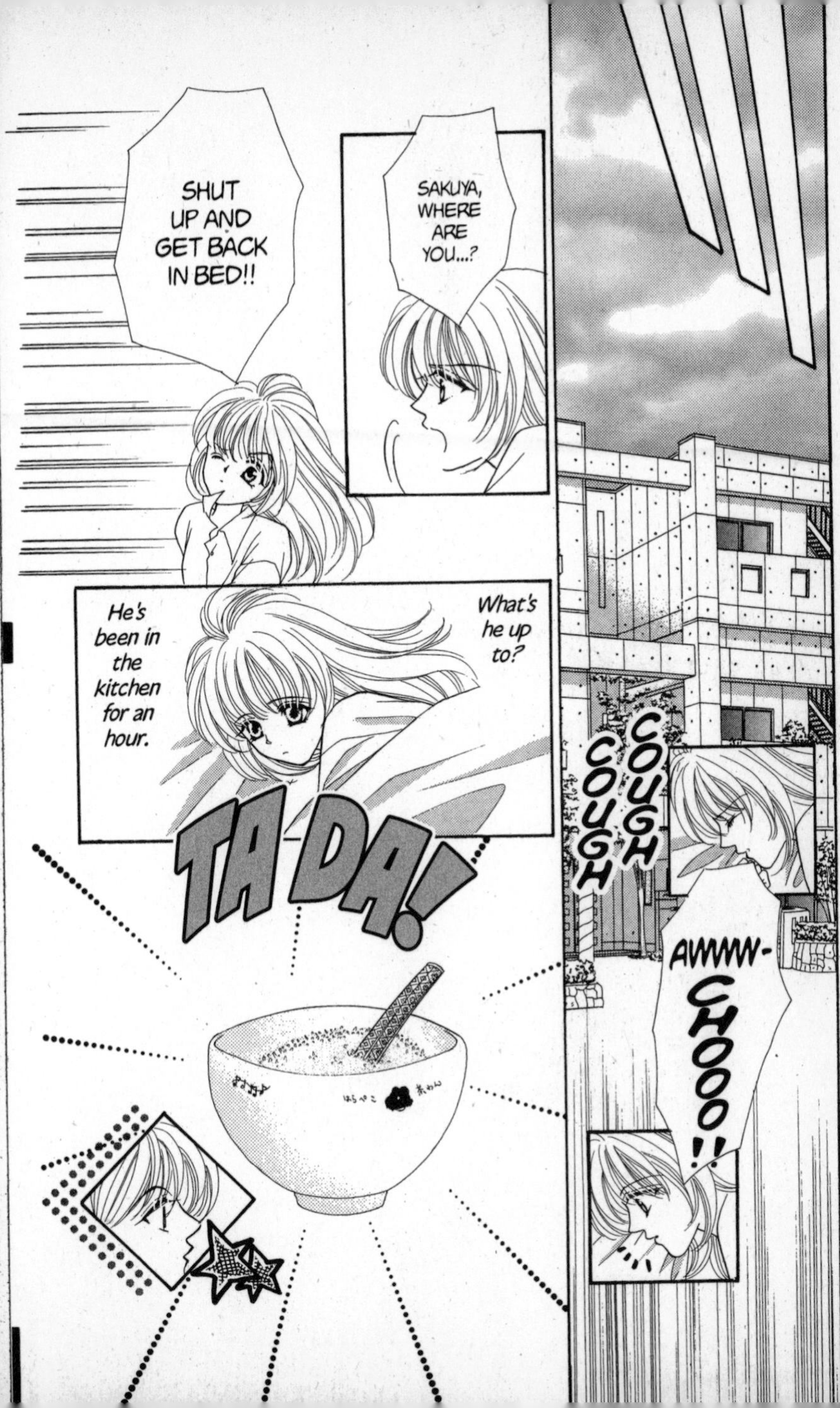
COUGH
COUGH
AWWW-CHOOOO!!
SAKUYA, WHERE ARE YOU...?
SHUT UP AND GET BACK IN BED!!
What's he up to?
He's been in the kitchen for an hour.
TA DA!

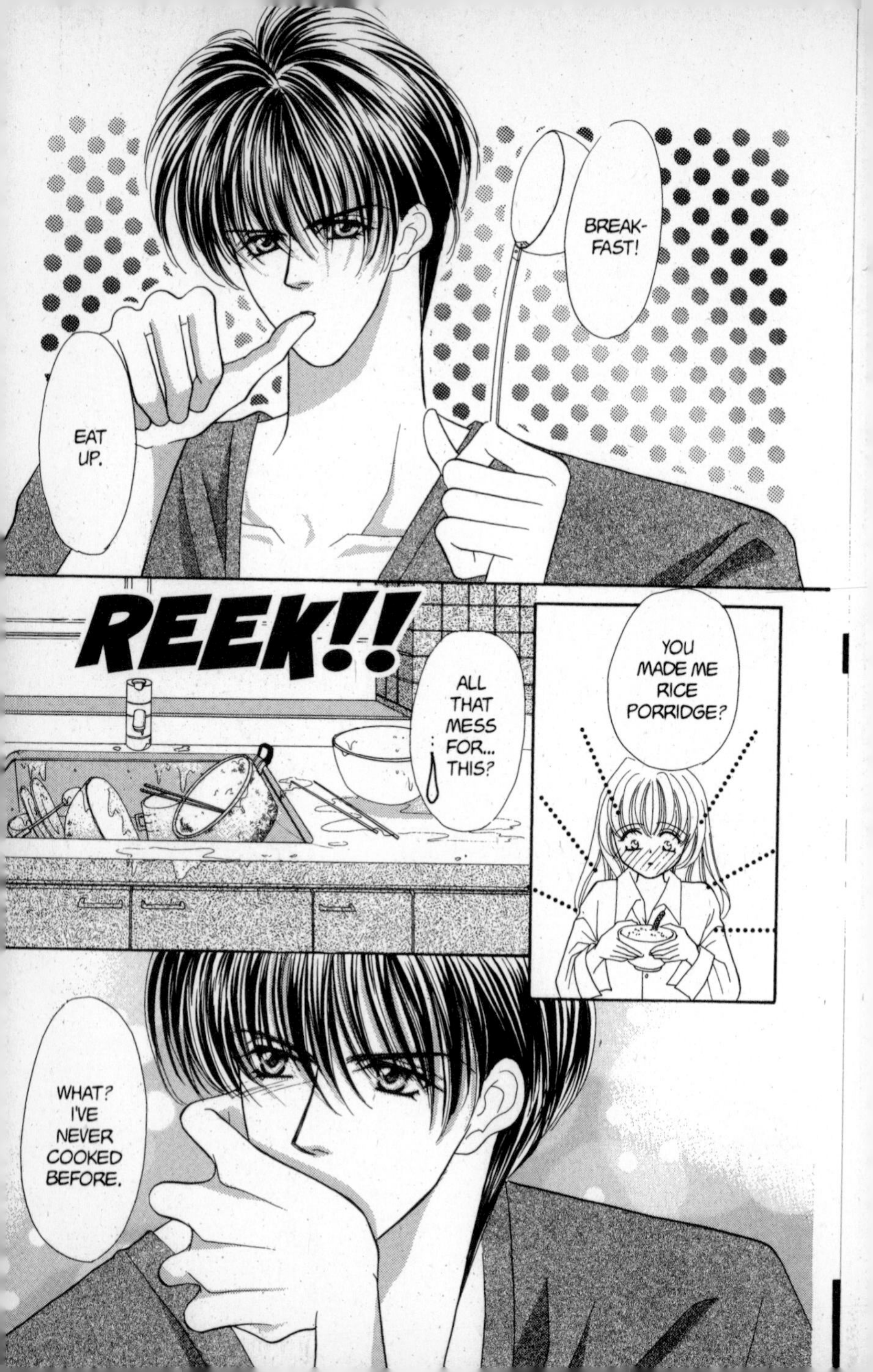
BREAK-FAST!
EAT UP.
YOU MADE ME RICE PORRIDGE?
REEK!!
ALL THAT MESS FOR... THIS?
WHAT? I'VE NEVER COOKED BEFORE.

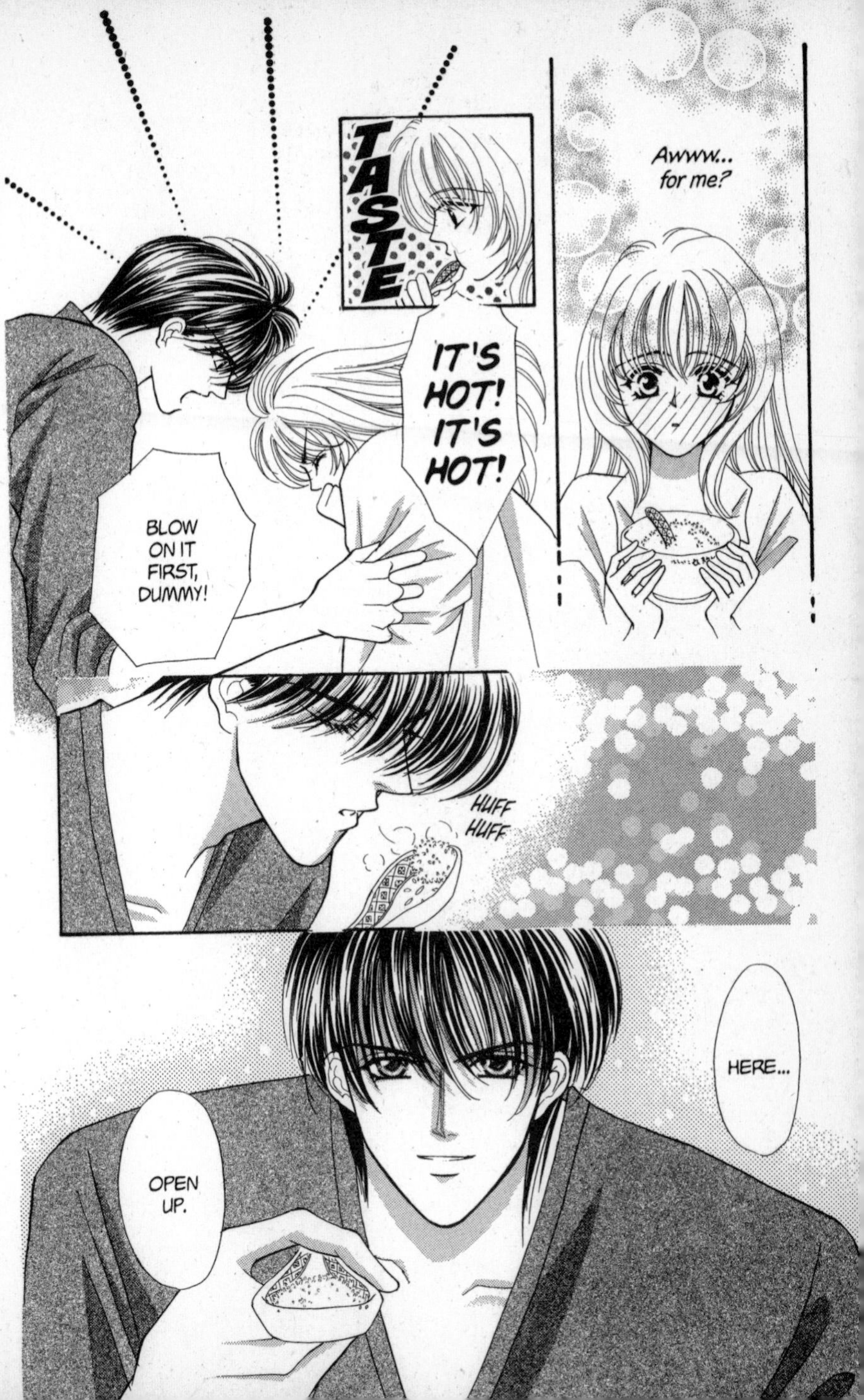
Awww... for me?
TASTE
IT'S HOT! IT'S HOT!
BLOW ON IT FIRST, DUMMY!
HUFF HUFF
HERE...
OPEN UP.

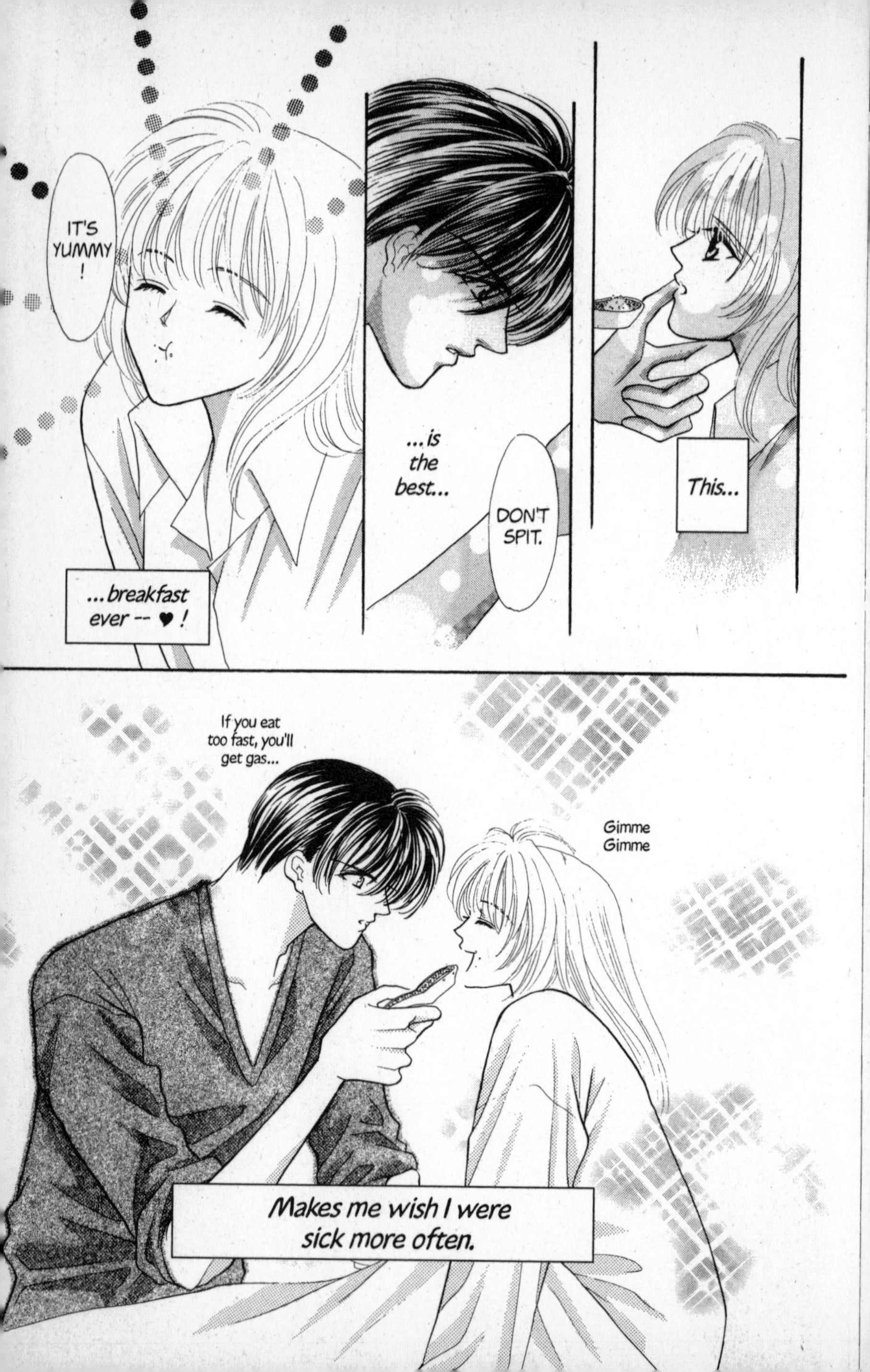
This...
...is the best...
DON'T SPIT.
IT'S YUMMY!
...breakfast ever -- ♥ !
Gimme Gimme
If you eat too fast, you'll get gas...
Makes me wish I were sick more often.

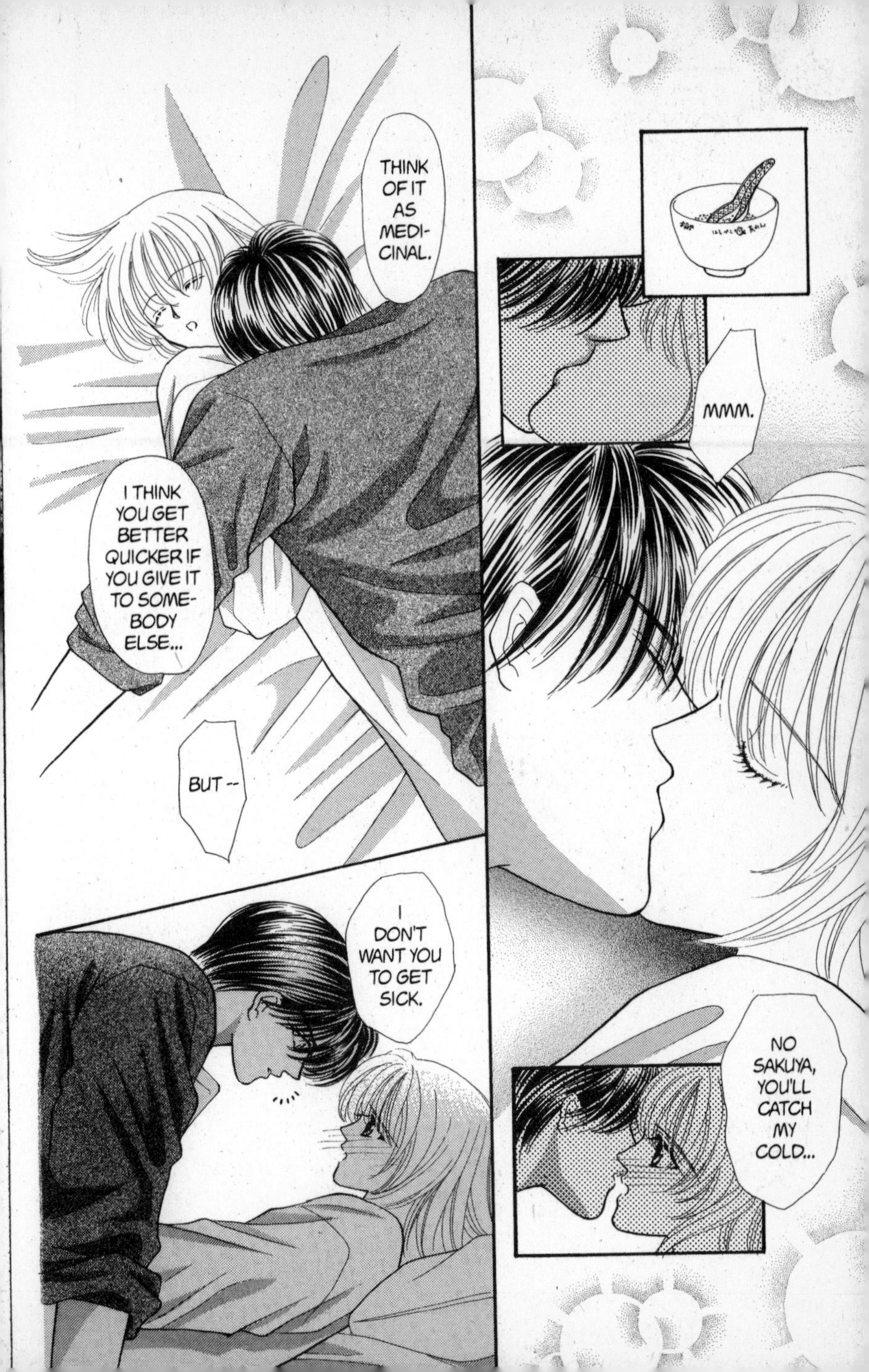
MMM.
NO SAKUYA, YOU'LL CATCH MY COLD...
THINK OF IT AS MEDI-CINAL.
I THINK YOU GET BETTER QUICKER IF YOU GIVE IT TO SOME-BODY ELSE...
BUT --
I DON'T WANT YOU TO GET SICK.

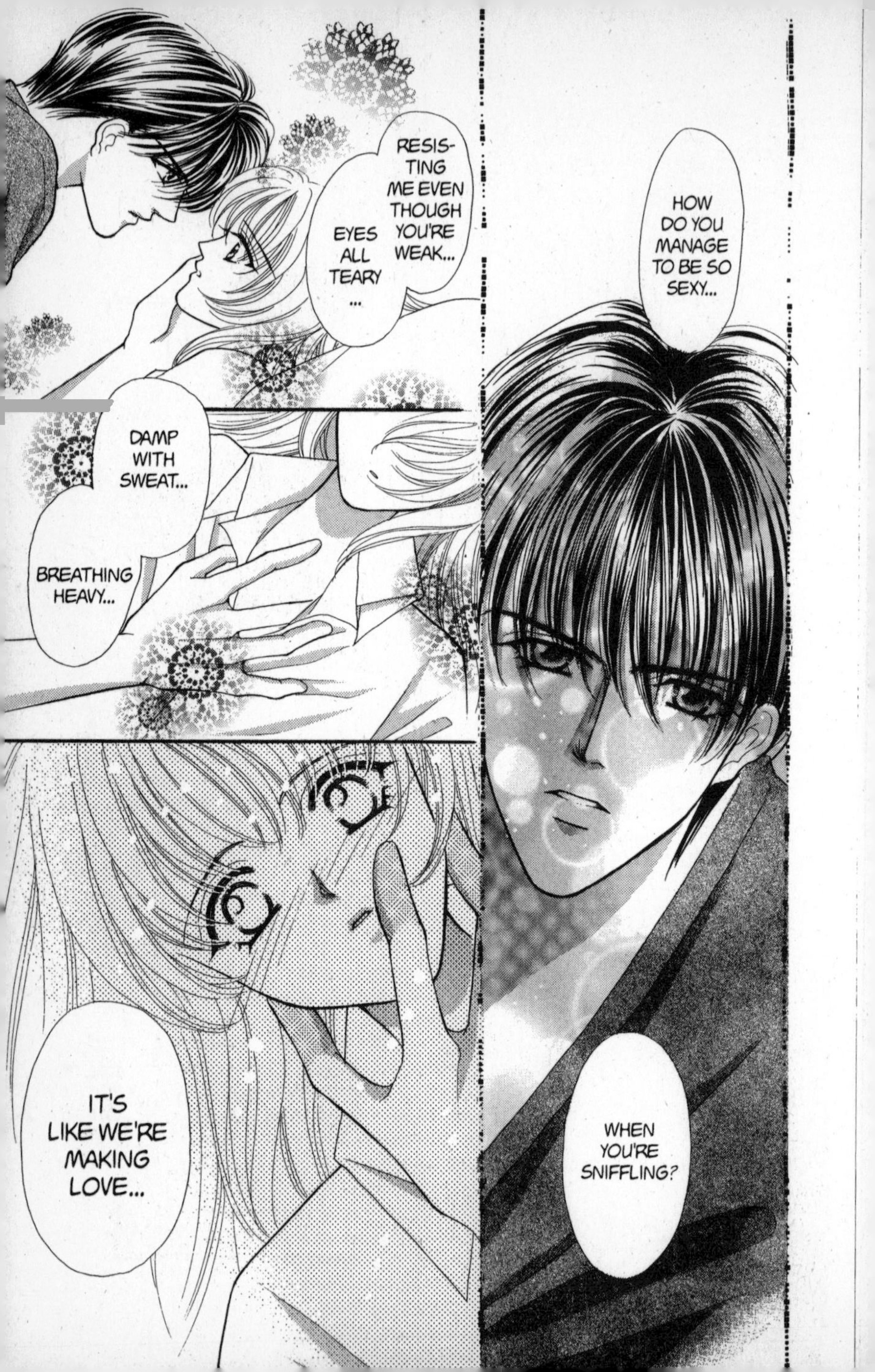
HOW DO YOU MANAGE TO BE SO SEXY...
WHEN YOU'RE SNIFFLING?
RESIS-TING ME EVEN THOUGH YOU'RE WEAK...
EYES ALL TEARY ...
DAMP WITH SWEAT...
BREATHING HEAVY...
IT'S LIKE WE'RE MAKING LOVE...

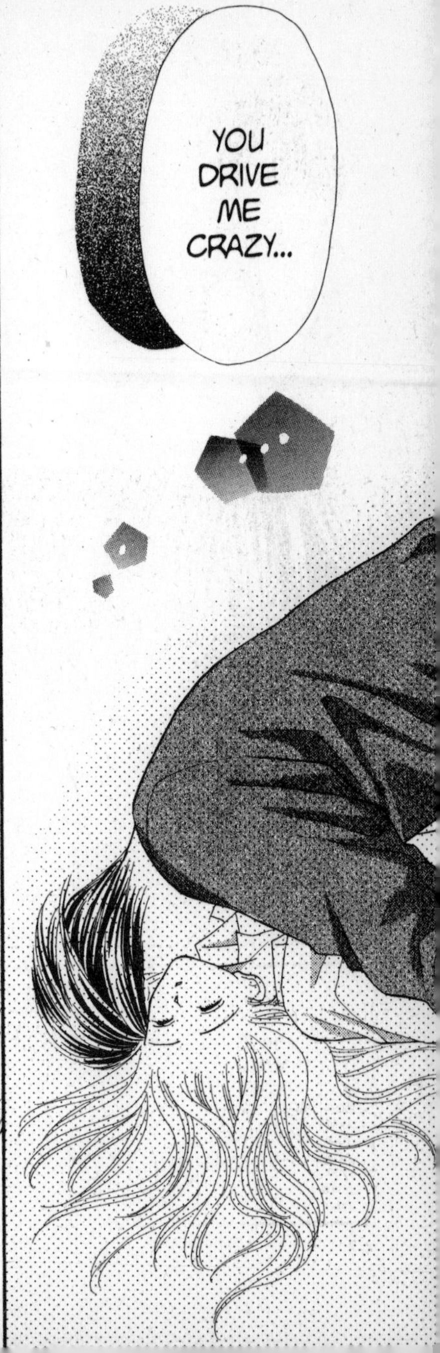
YOU DRIVE ME CRAZY...

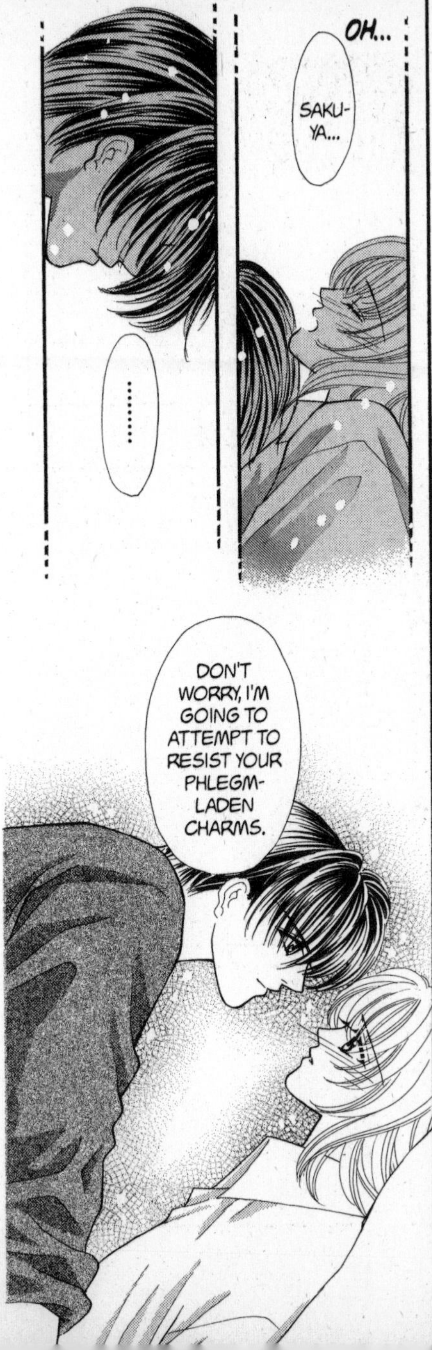
OH...
SAKU-YA...
......
DON'T WORRY, I'M GOING TO ATTEMPT TO RESIST YOUR PHLEGM-LADEN CHARMS.

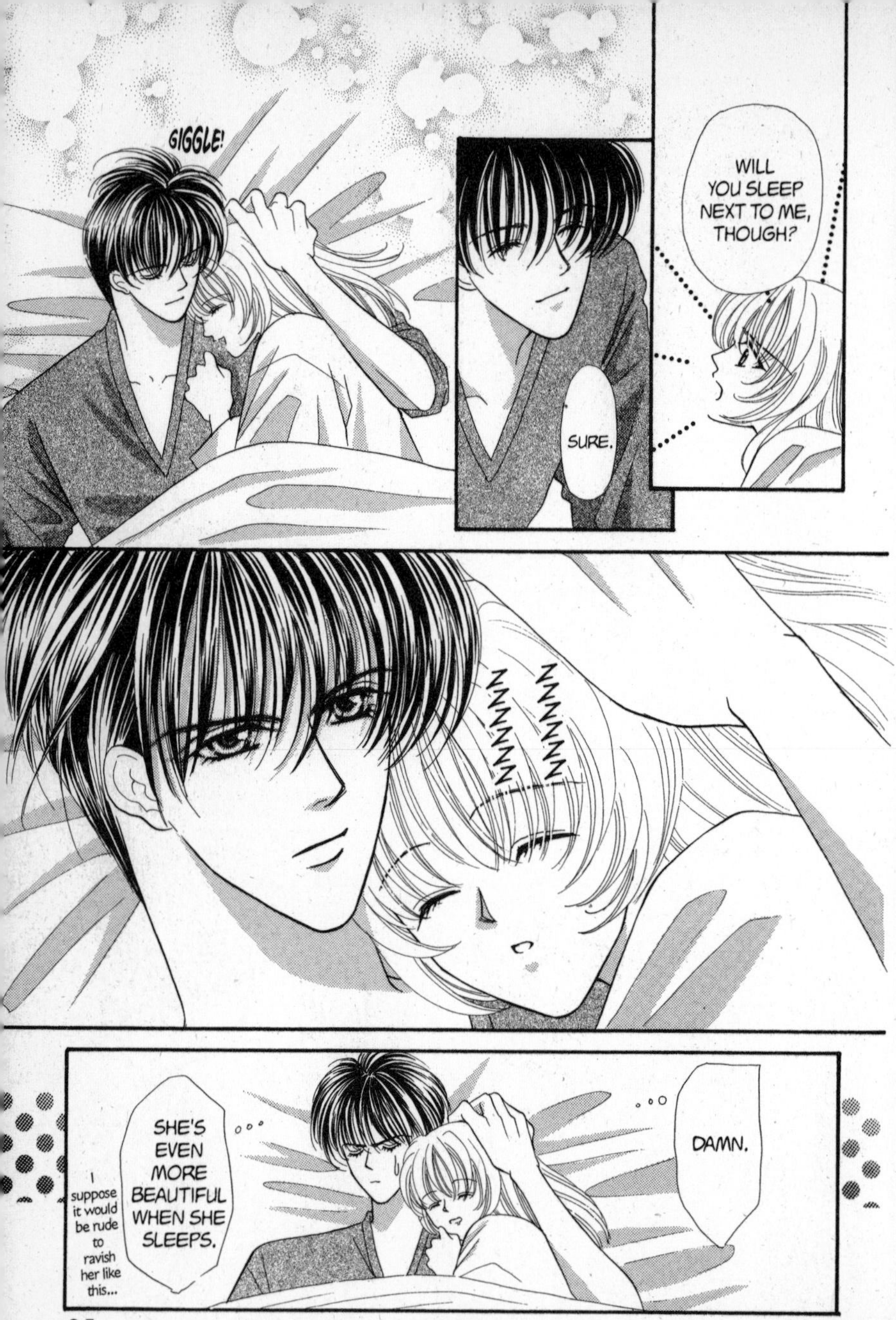
WILL YOU SLEEP NEXT TO ME, THOUGH?
SURE.
GIGGLE!
ZZZZZZ
ZZZZZZ
DAMN.
SHE'S EVEN MORE BEAUTIFUL WHEN SHE SLEEPS.
I suppose it would be rude to ravish her like this...

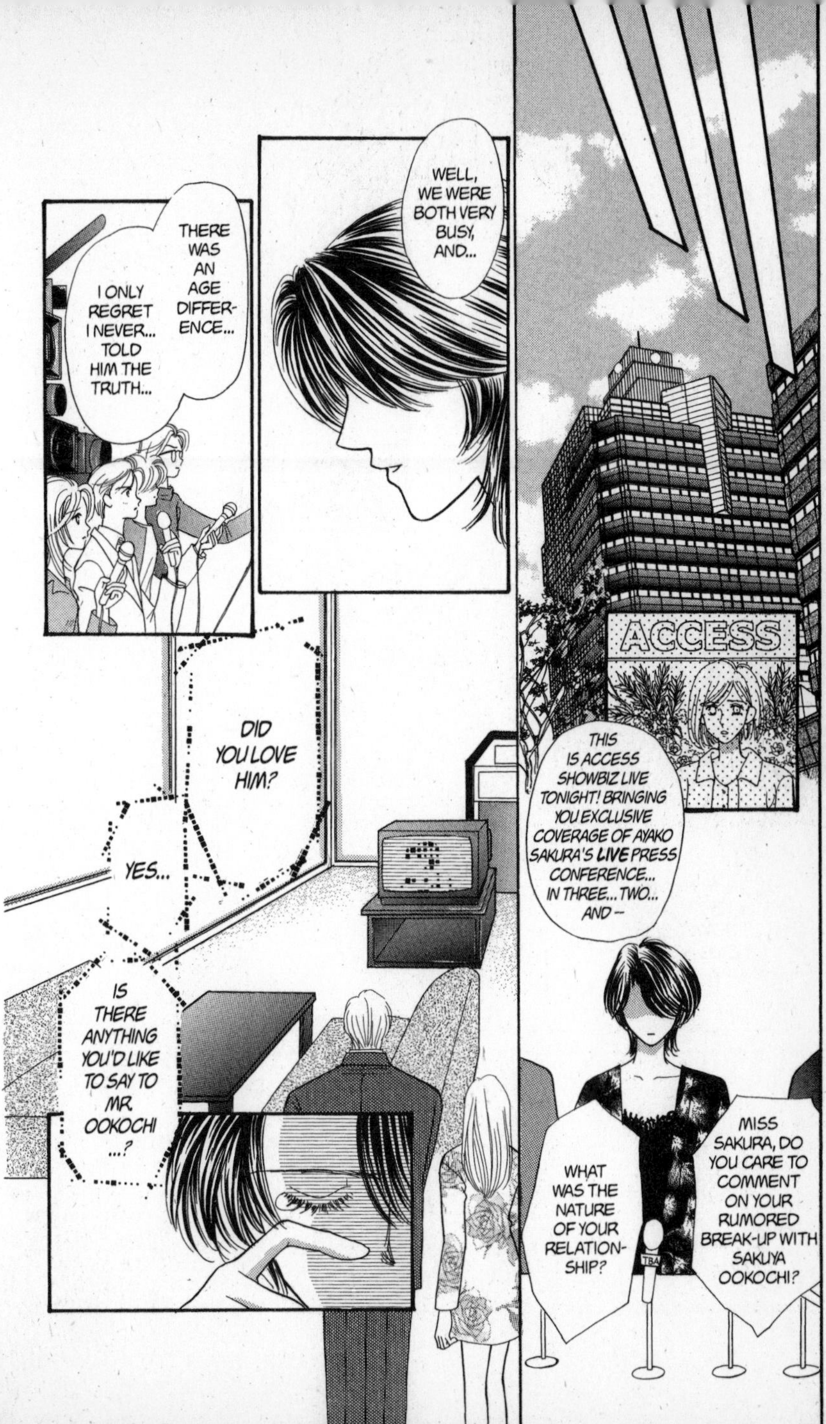
ACCESS
THIS IS ACCESS SHOWBIZ LIVE TONIGHT! BRINGING YOU EXCLUSIVE COVERAGE OF AYAKO SAKURA'S **LIVE** PRESS CONFERENCE... IN THREE... TWO... AND --
MISS SAKURA, DO YOU CARE TO COMMENT ON YOUR RUMORED BREAK-UP WITH SAKUYA OOKOCHI?
WHAT WAS THE NATURE OF YOUR RELATIONSHIP?
TBA
WELL, WE WERE BOTH VERY BUSY, AND...
THERE WAS AN AGE DIFFERENCE...
I ONLY REGRET I NEVER... TOLD HIM THE TRUTH...
DID YOU LOVE HIM?
YES...
IS THERE ANYTHING YOU'D LIKE TO SAY TO MR. OOKOCHI ...?

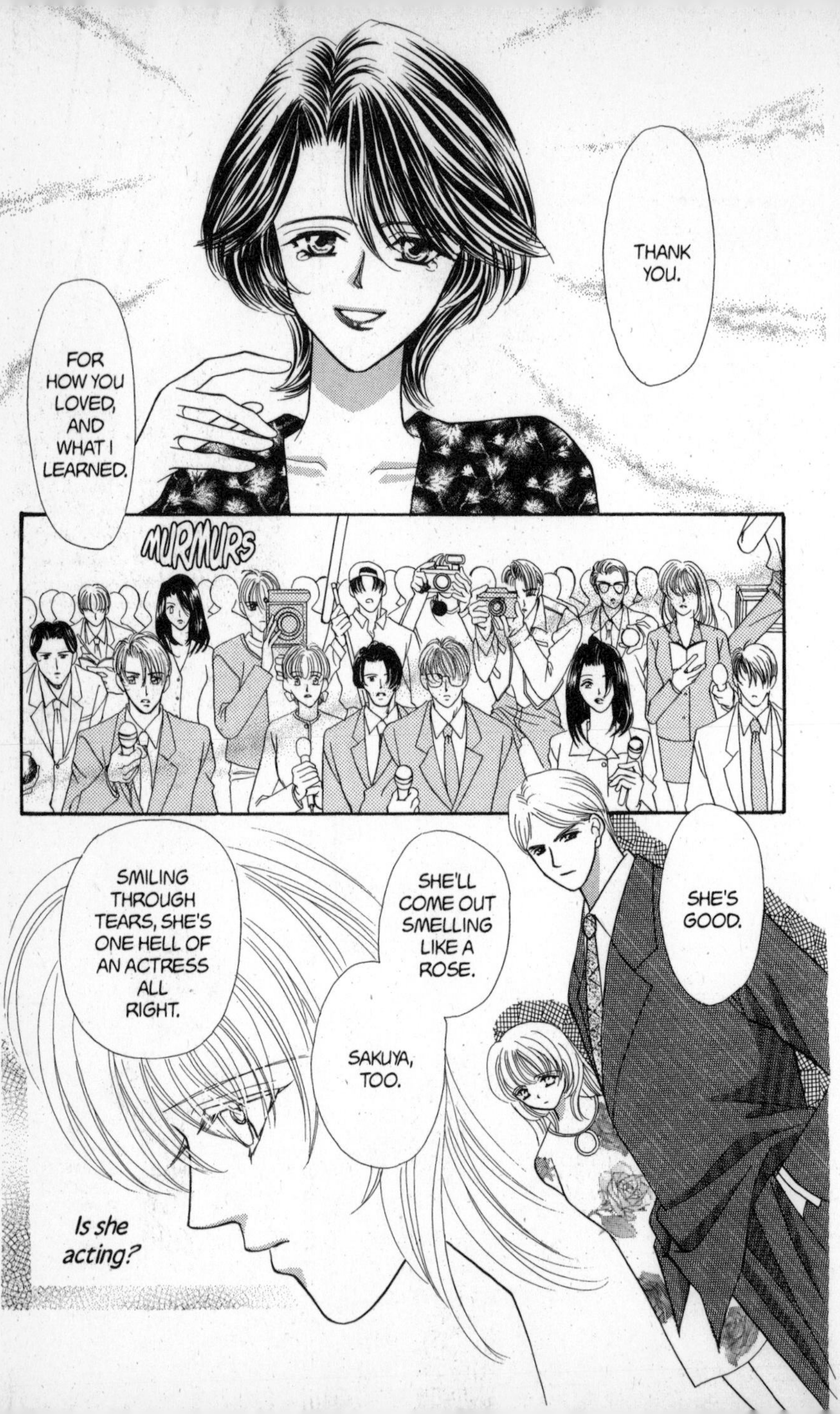
THANK YOU.
FOR HOW YOU LOVED, AND WHAT I LEARNED.
MURMURS
SHE'S GOOD.
SHE'LL COME OUT SMELLING LIKE A ROSE.
SAKUYA, TOO.
SMILING THROUGH TEARS, SHE'S ONE HELL OF AN ACTRESS ALL RIGHT.
Is she acting?

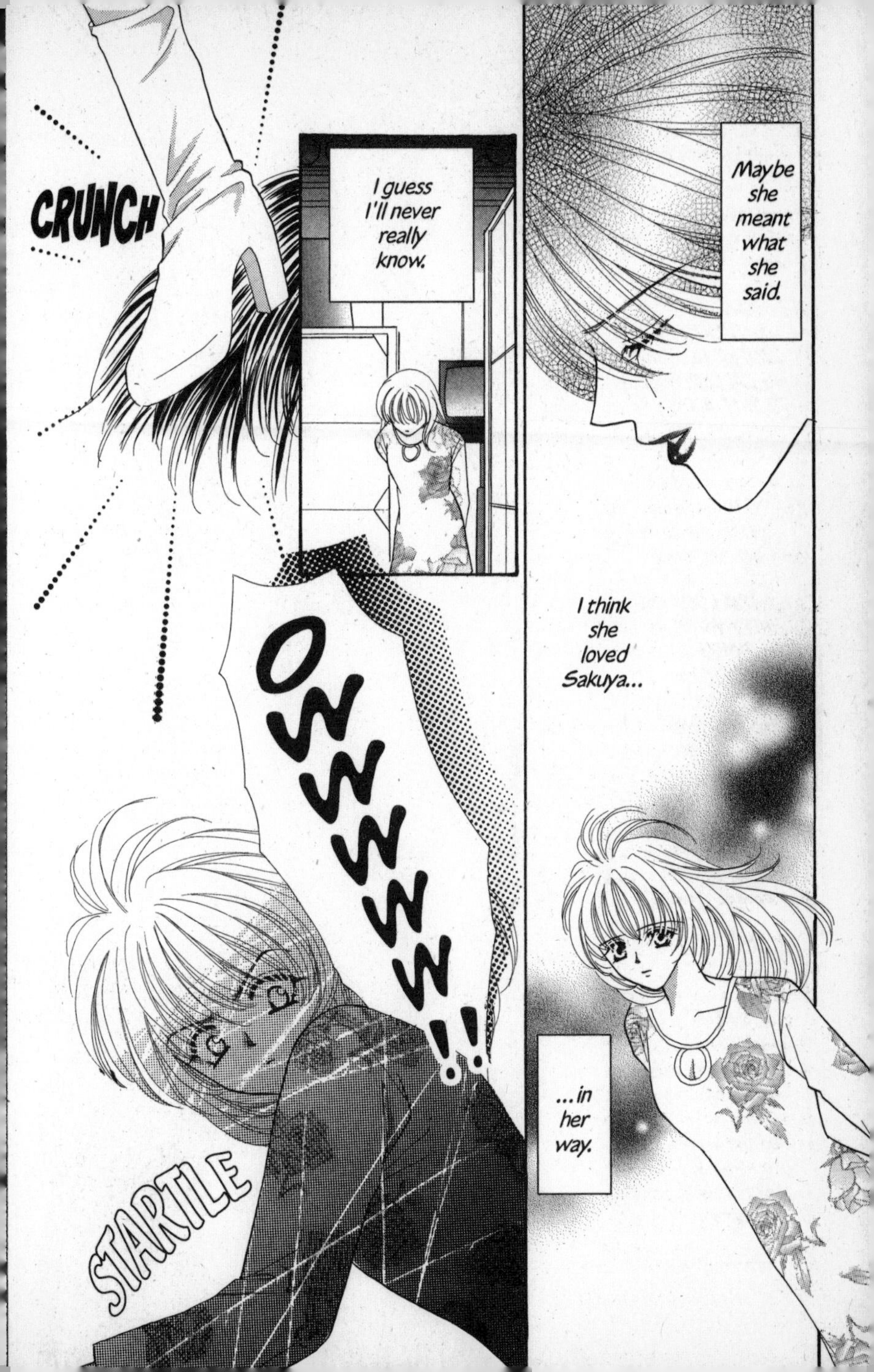

Maybe she meant what she said.
I think she loved Sakuya...
...in her way.
I guess I'll never really know.
CRUNCH
OWWWW!!
STARTLE

QUESTION SEGMENT!!

Yes...as usual, I'll be answering some of the questions sent in from the readers.

Q: IN SENSUAL PHRASE VOL. 1, THERE'S A GLIMPSE OF LUCIFER HOLDING SOMETHING CALLED PARADISE LOST. IS IT A REFERENCE TO THE CONTROVERSIAL FILM BY THE SAME TITLE?
A: Lucifer's first album is titled "Paradise Lost," but it's a reference to Milton's poem, not the movie.

Q: SAKUYA LOST HIS VIRGINITY WHEN HE WAS IN SIXTH GRADE TO A WOMAN IN HER TWENTIES...? HOW'D HE DO?
A: Completely fine!! Ha! In her defense, Sakuya looked more like a ninth grader than a sixth grader...He was, uh, big for his age, so Ayako was very satisfied!! (I can't believe I'm having this conversation...)

Q: IS ATSURO IN LOVE WITH SAKUYA?
A: No. I was surprised I got a lot of letters like this. I responded to a request to see Atsuro and Sakuya having a good time, and I guess that scene apparently created the impression that Atsuro might have a thing for Sakuya. He doesn't. Atsuro has a girlfriend, anyway.

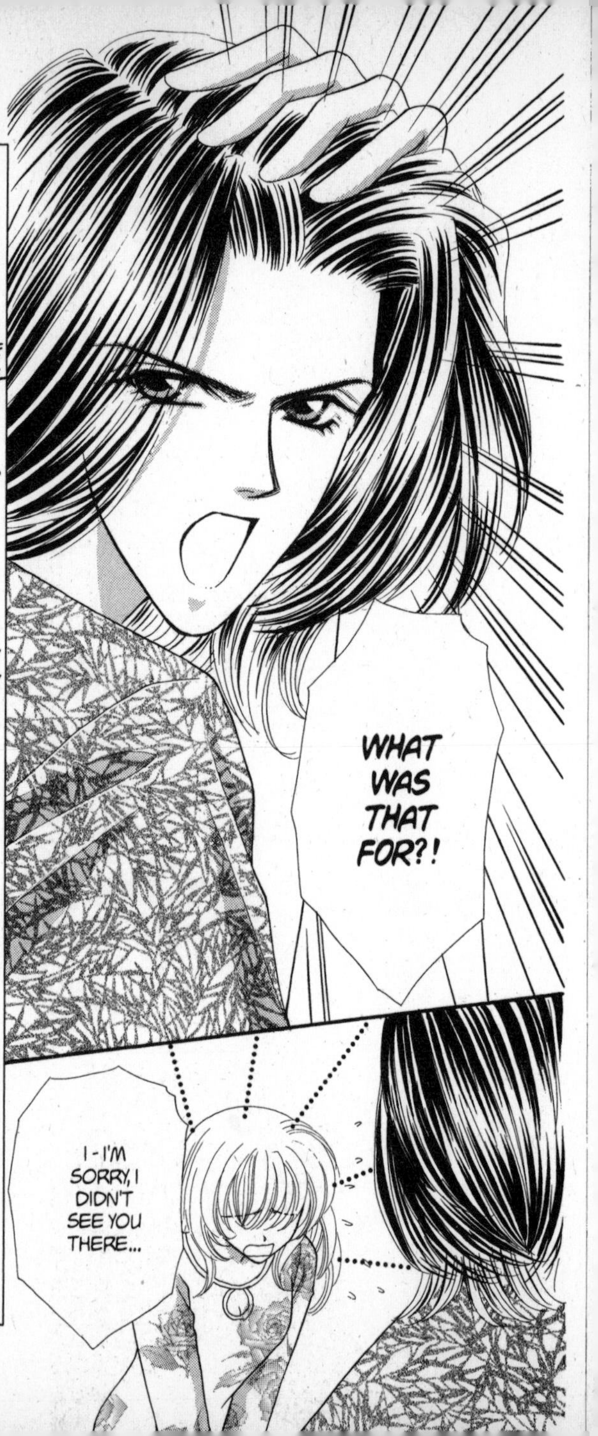
WHAT WAS THAT FOR?!
I-I'M SORRY, I DIDN'T SEE YOU THERE...

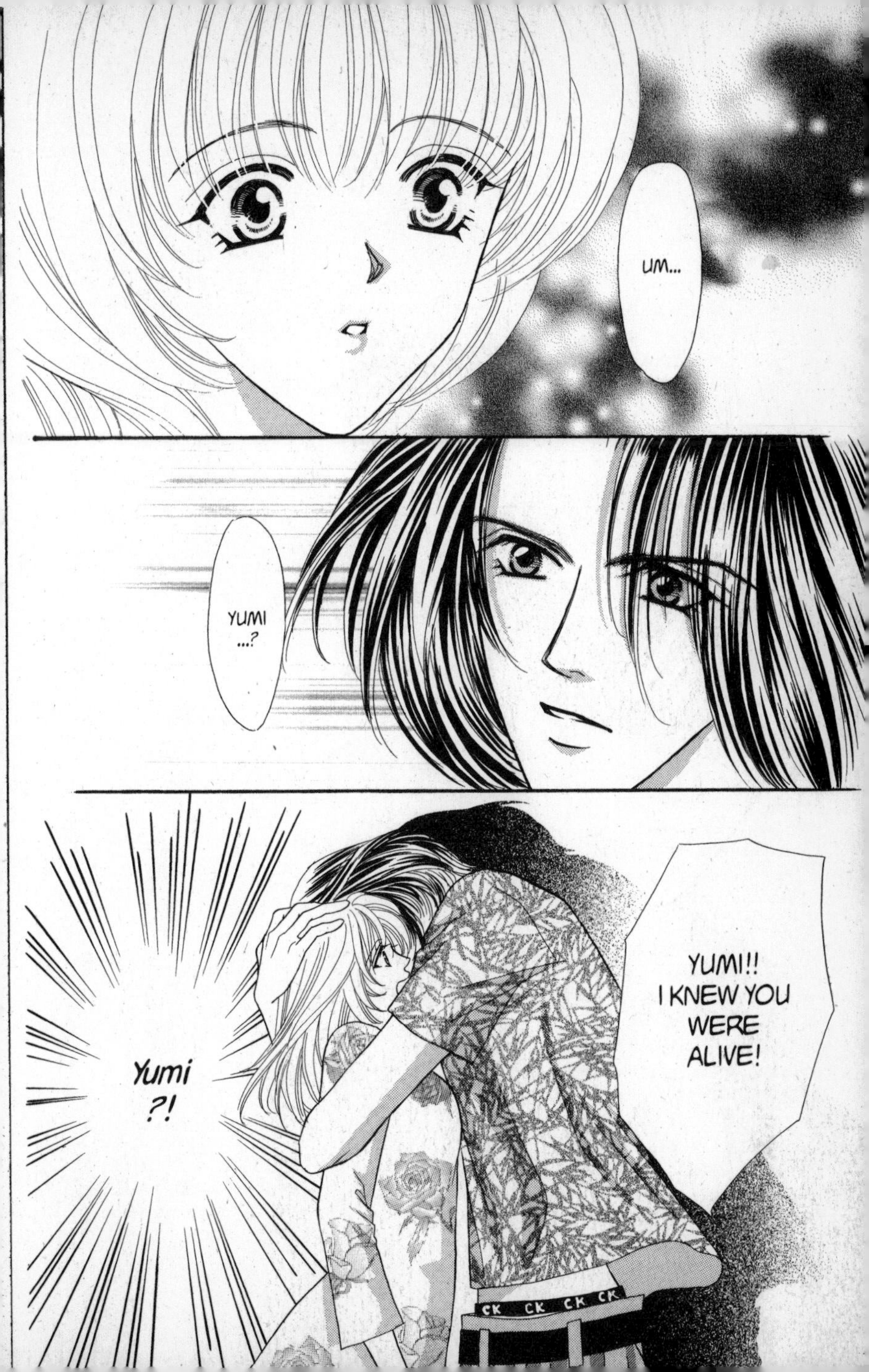
UM...
YUMI ...?
YUMI!! I KNEW YOU WERE ALIVE!
Yumi ?!

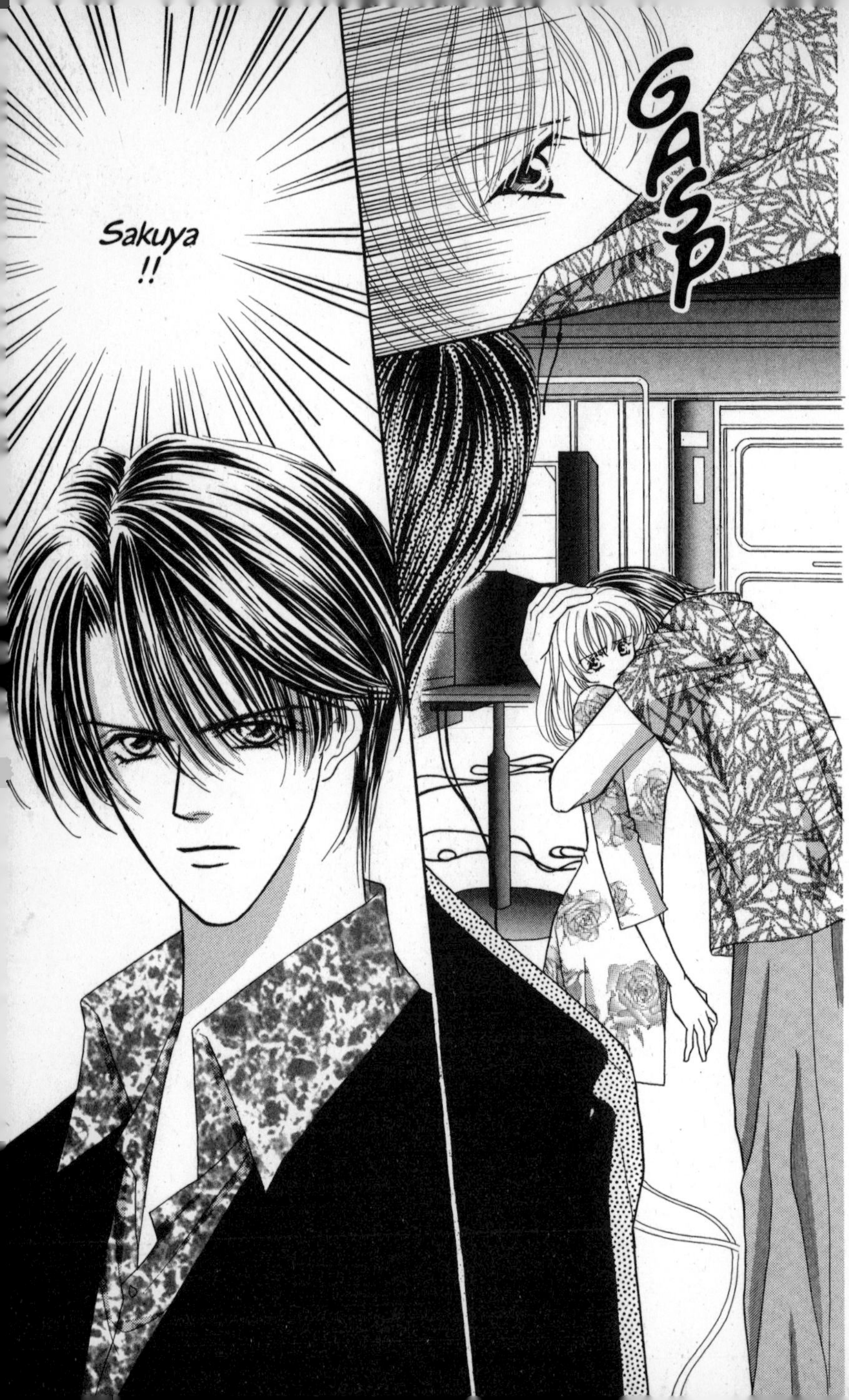
GASP
Sakuya !!

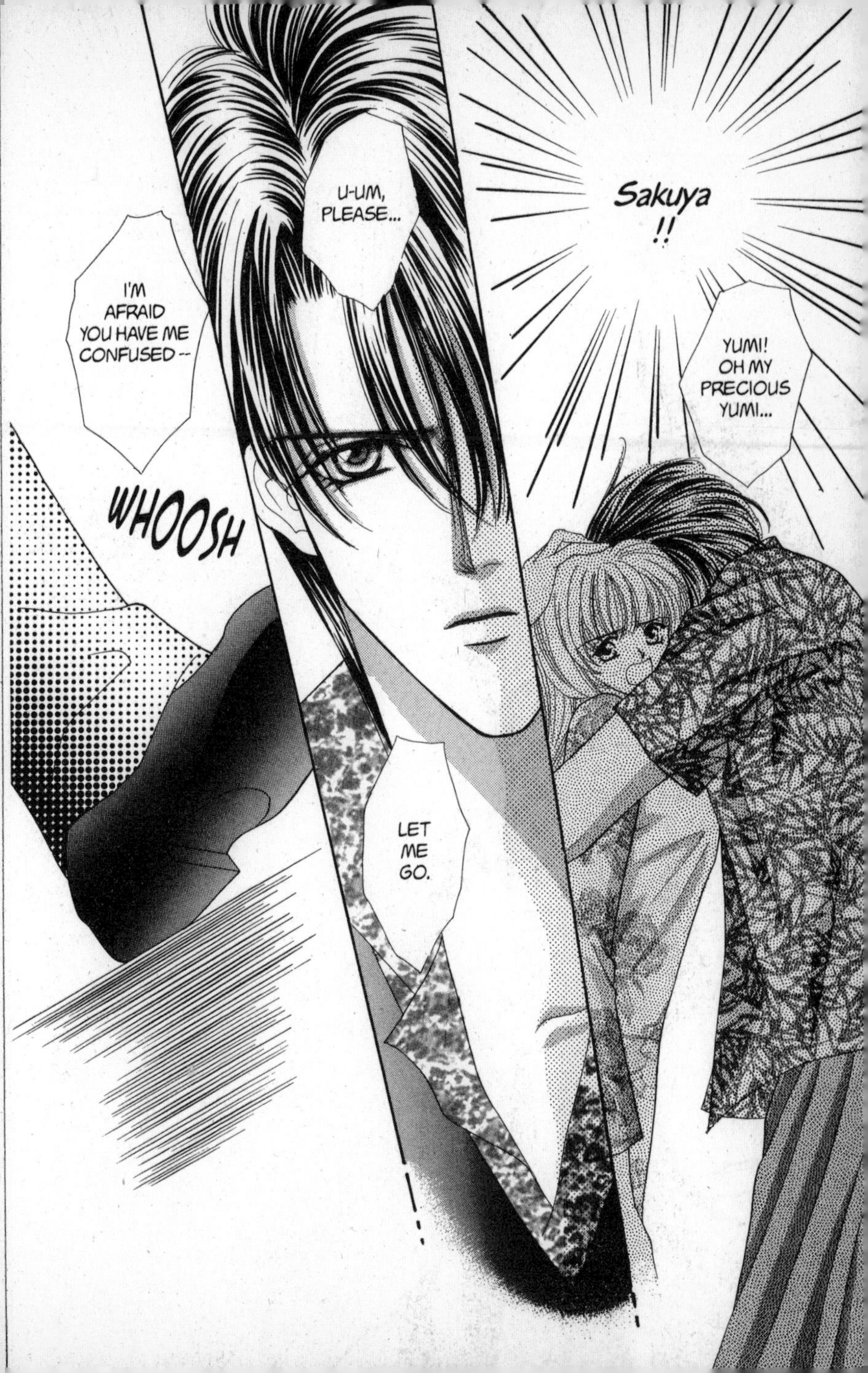
Sakuya !!
YUMI! OH MY PRECIOUS YUMI...
U-UM, PLEASE...
LET ME GO.
I'M AFRAID YOU HAVE ME CONFUSED --
WHOOSH

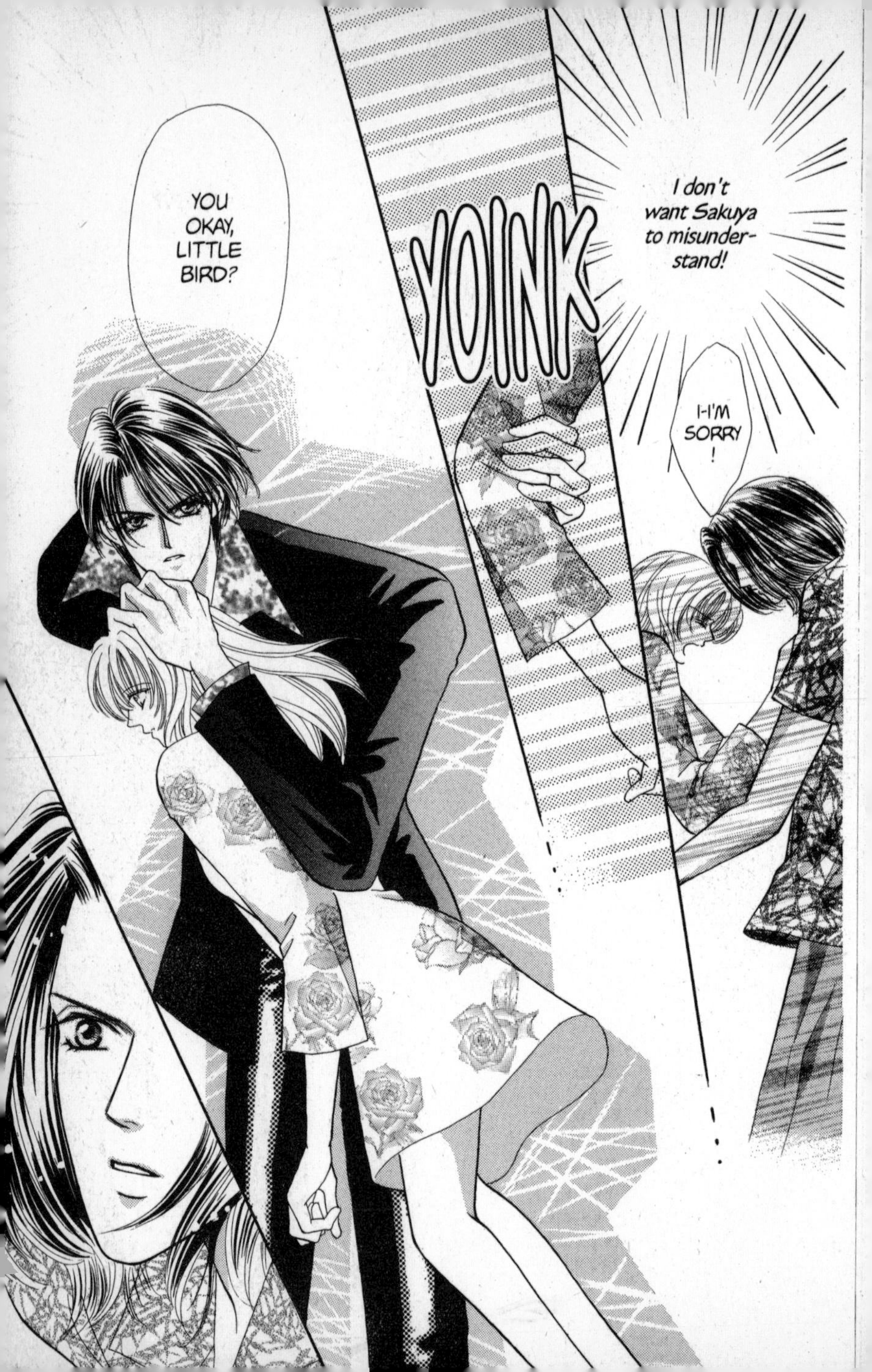
I don't want Sakuya to misunder-stand!
I-I'M SORRY!
YOINK
YOU OKAY, LITTLE BIRD?

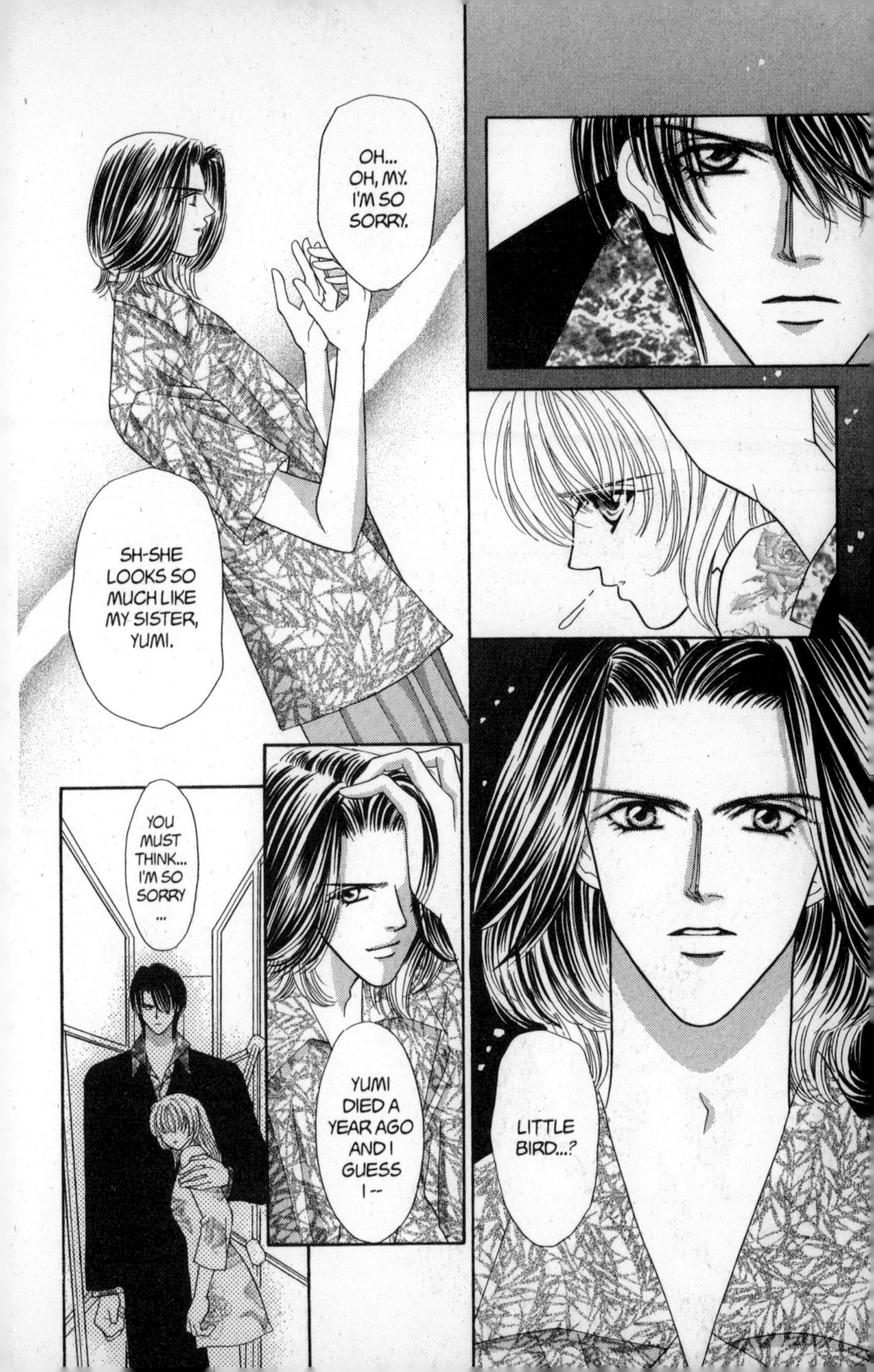
LITTLE BIRD...?
OH... OH, MY. I'M SO SORRY.
SH-SHE LOOKS SO MUCH LIKE MY SISTER, YUMI.
YUMI DIED A YEAR AGO AND I GUESS I --
YOU MUST THINK... I'M SO SORRY ...

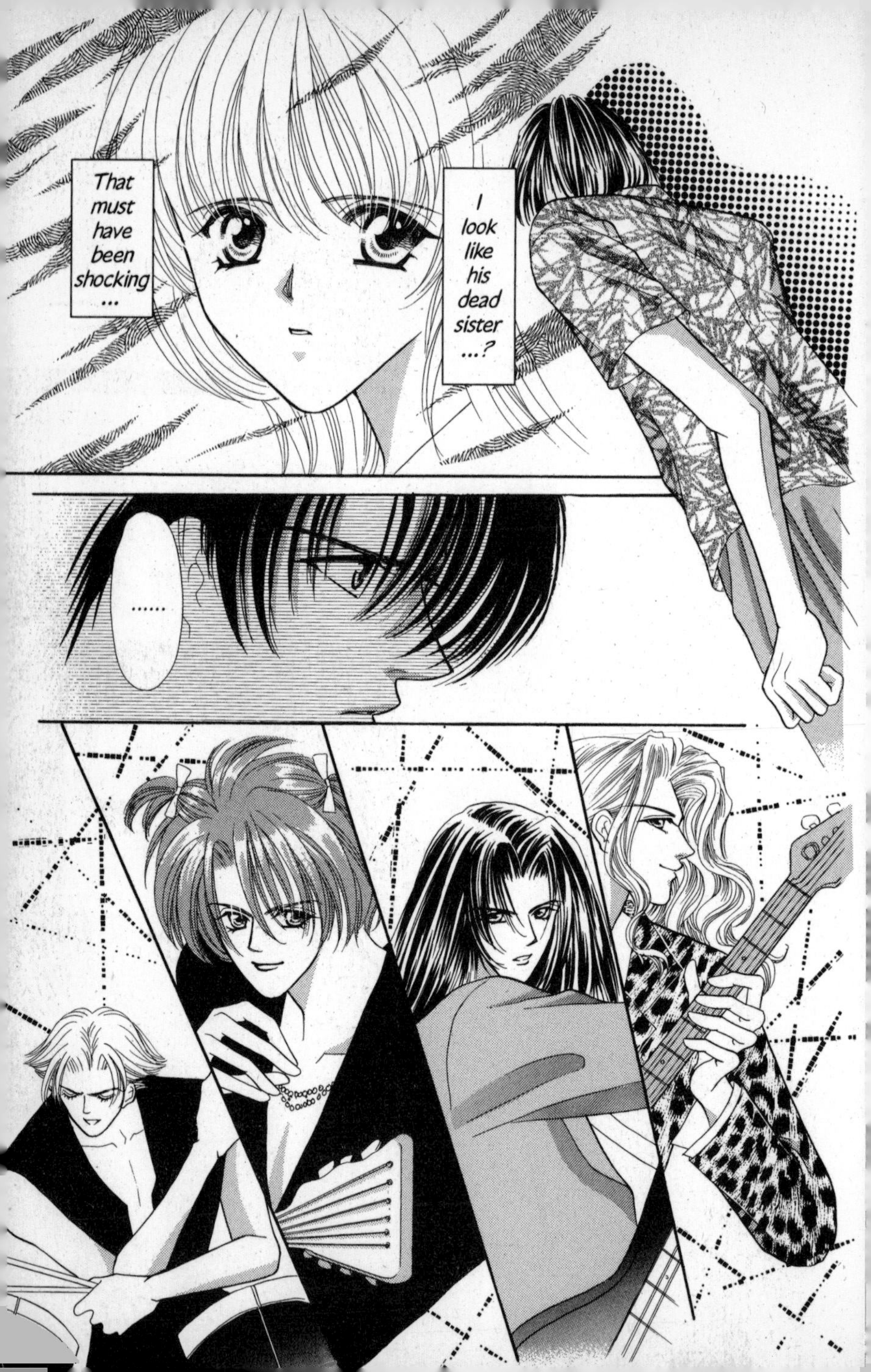
I look like his dead sister ...?
That must have been shocking ...
......

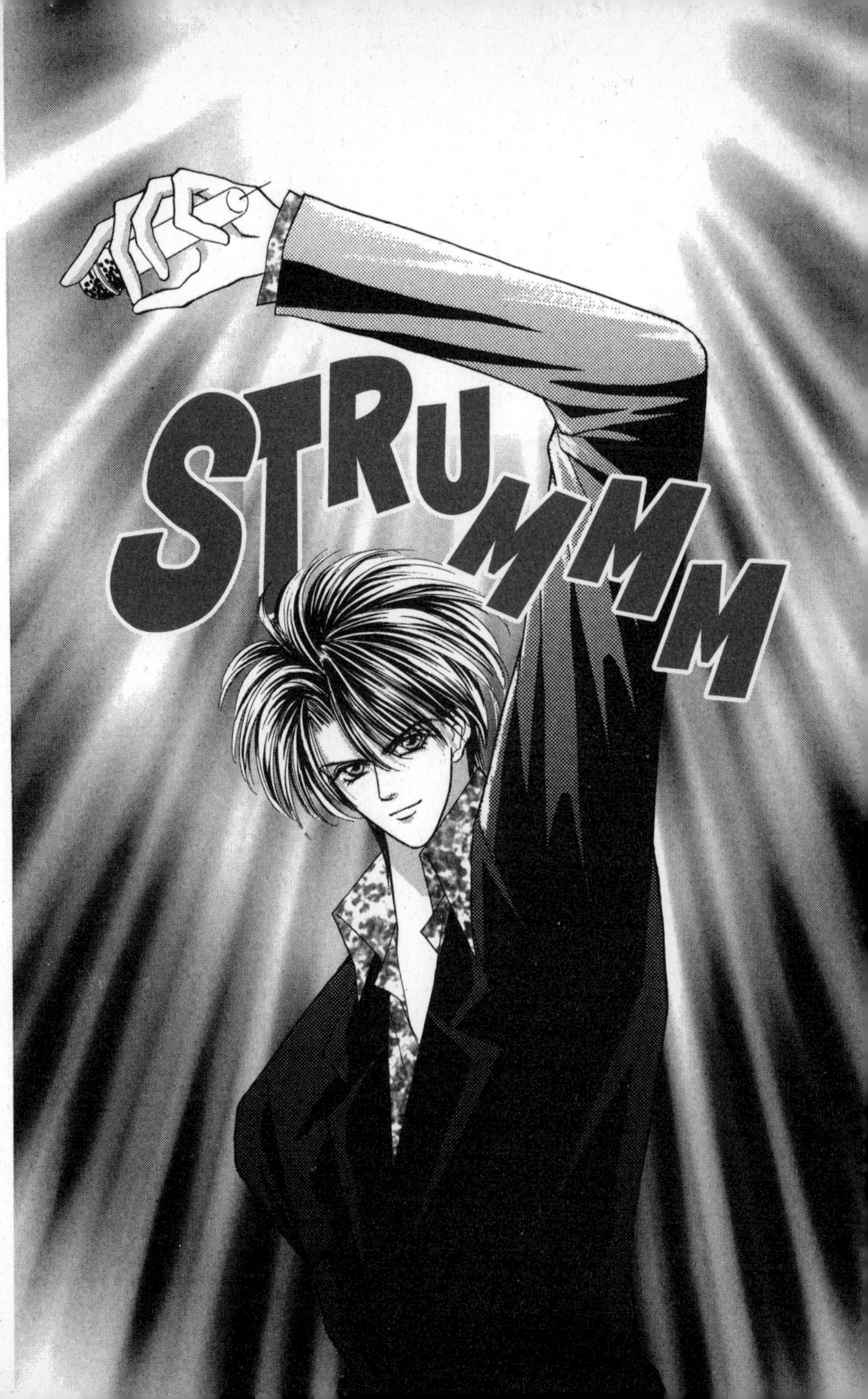
STRUMMM

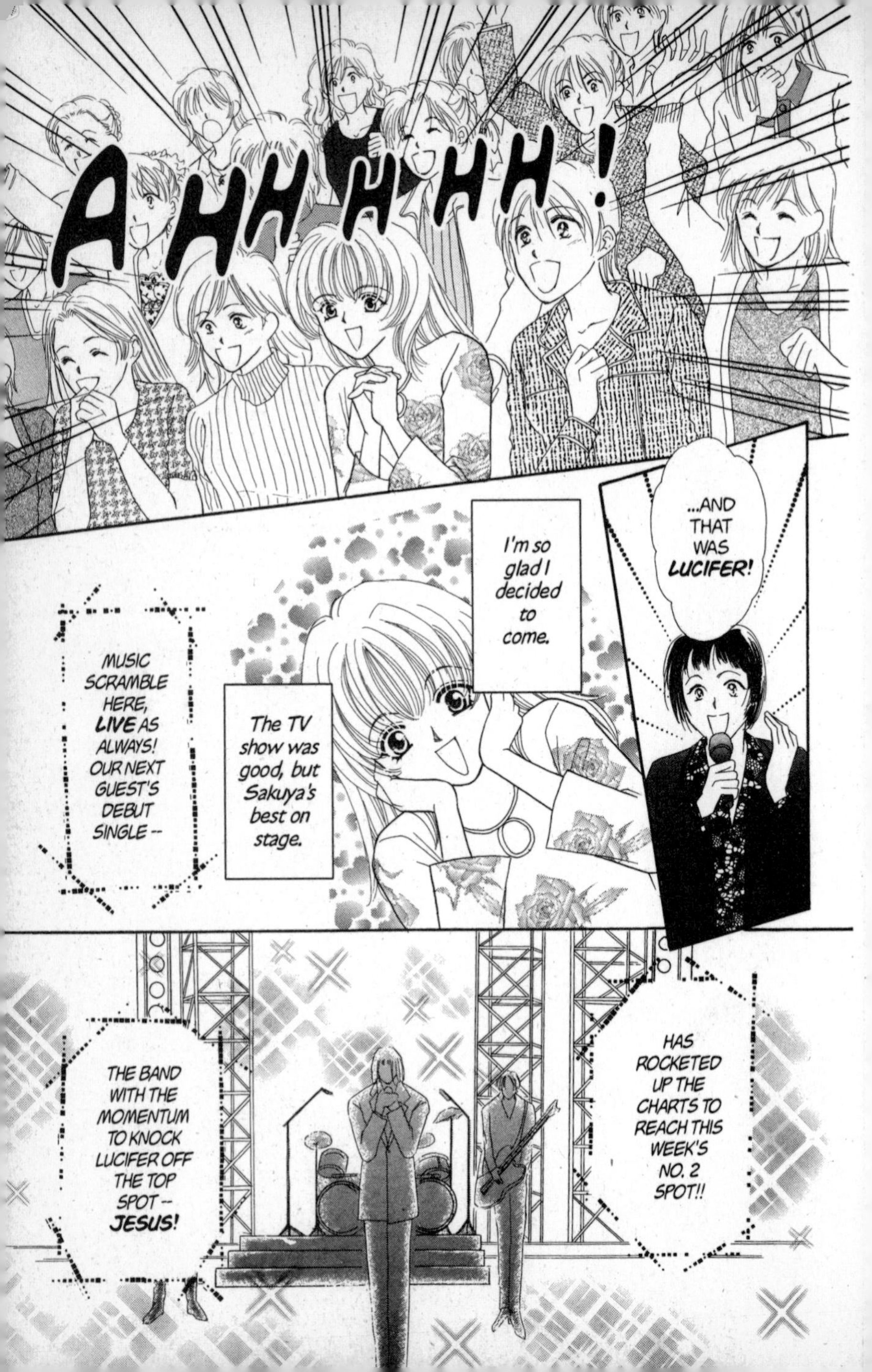
AHHHHHH!
...AND THAT WAS LUCIFER!
I'm so glad I decided to come.
The TV show was good, but Sakuya's best on stage.
MUSIC SCRAMBLE HERE, LIVE AS ALWAYS! OUR NEXT GUEST'S DEBUT SINGLE --
HAS ROCKETED UP THE CHARTS TO REACH THIS WEEK'S NO. 2 SPOT!!
THE BAND WITH THE MOMENTUM TO KNOCK LUCIFER OFF THE TOP SPOT -- JESUS!

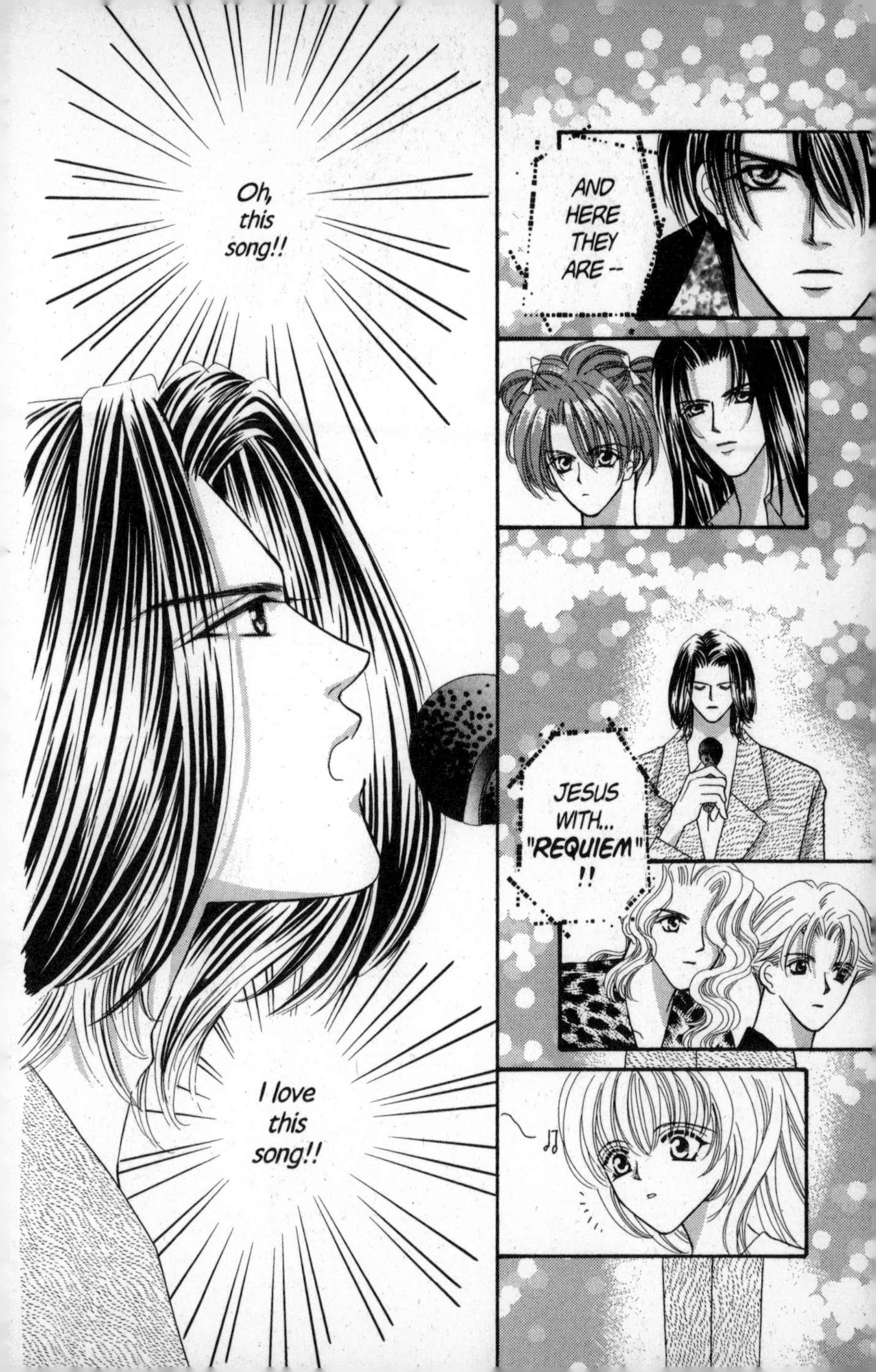
AND HERE THEY ARE --
JESUS WITH... "REQUIEM" !!
Oh, this song!!
I love this song!!

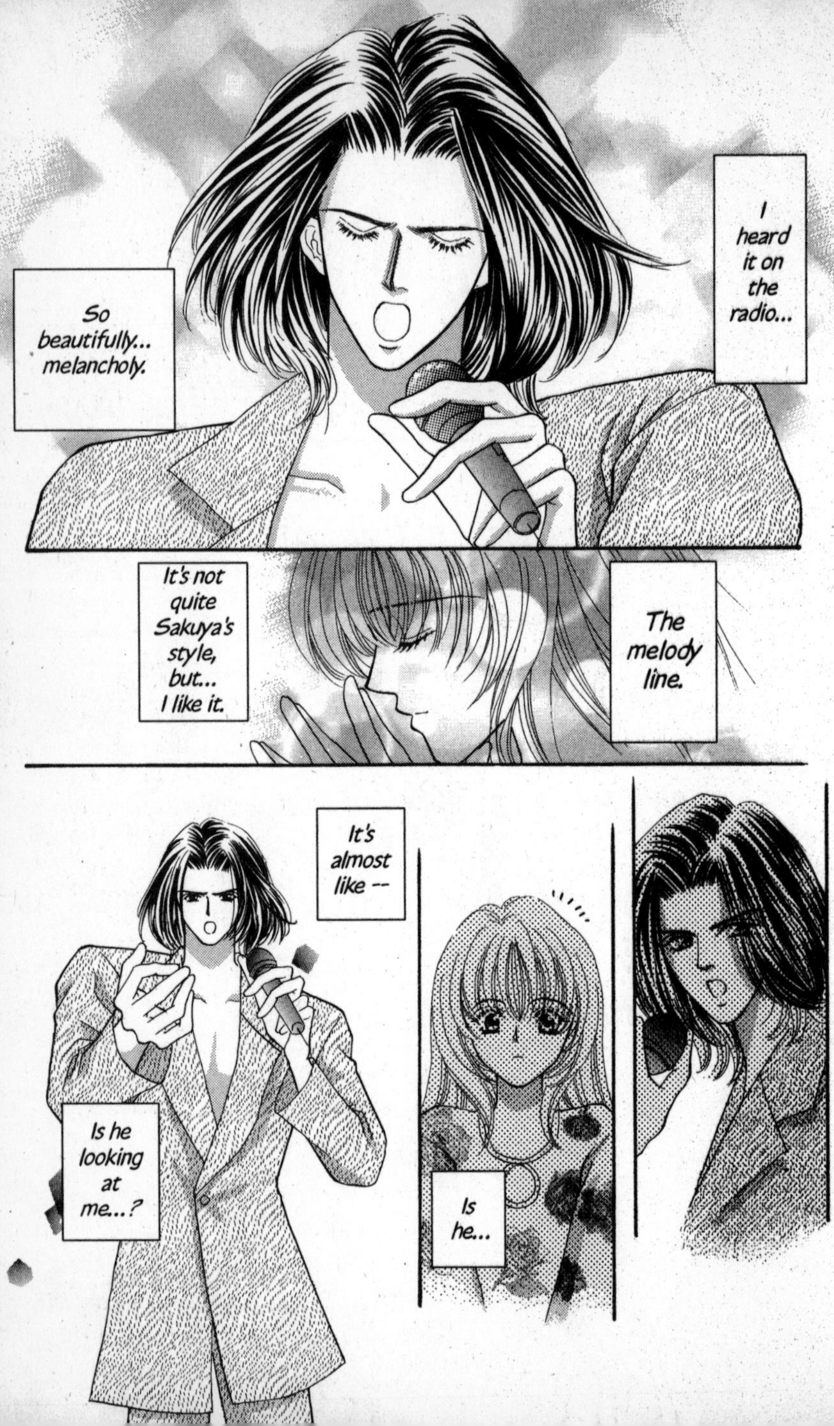
I heard it on the radio...
So beautifully... melancholy.
The melody line.
It's not quite Sakuya's style, but... I like it.
Is he...
It's almost like --
Is he looking at me...?

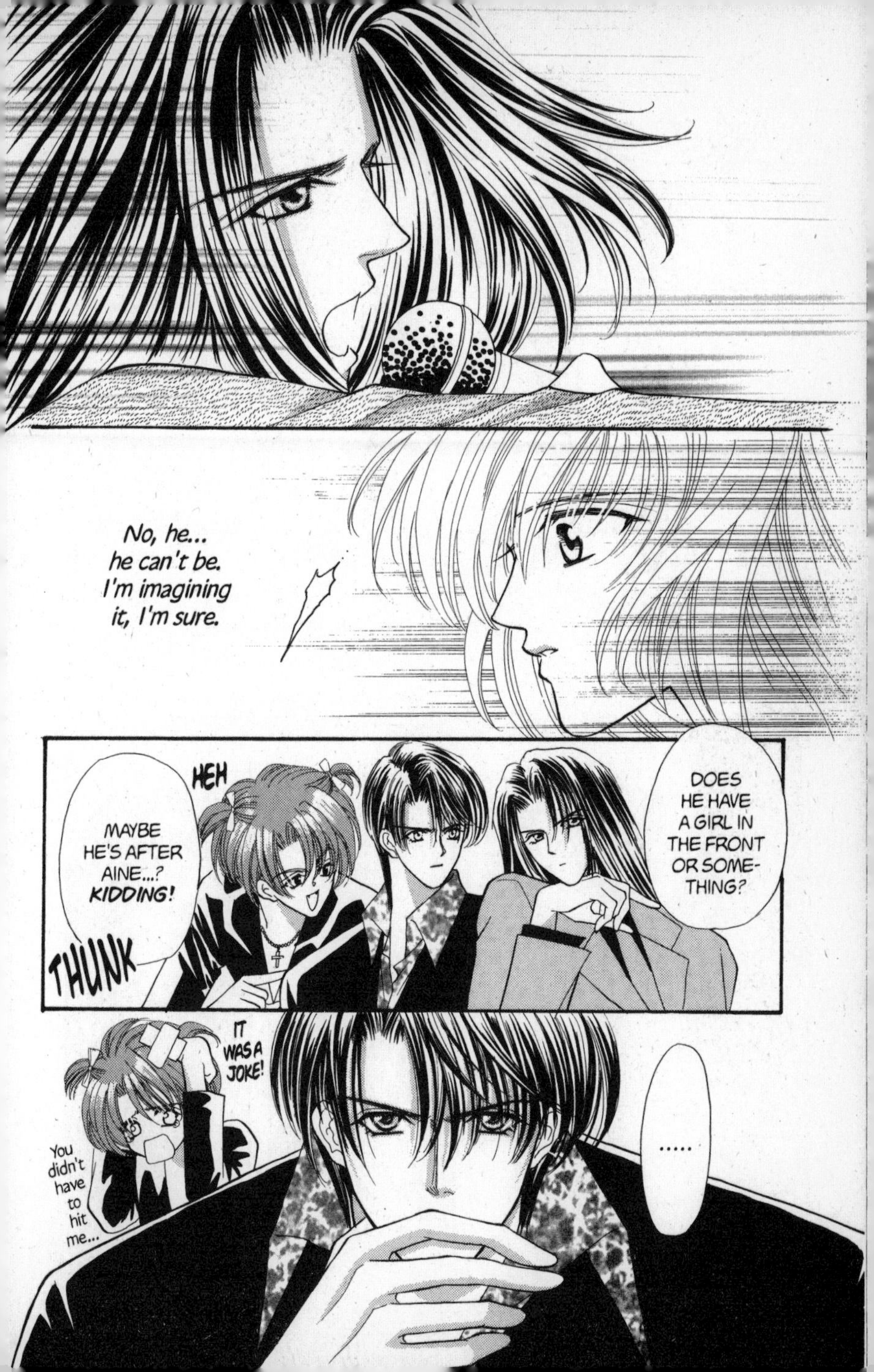
No, he... he can't be. I'm imagining it, I'm sure.
DOES HE HAVE A GIRL IN THE FRONT OR SOME-THING?
HEH
MAYBE HE'S AFTER AINE...? KIDDING!
THUNK
.....
IT WAS A JOKE!
You didn't have to hit me...

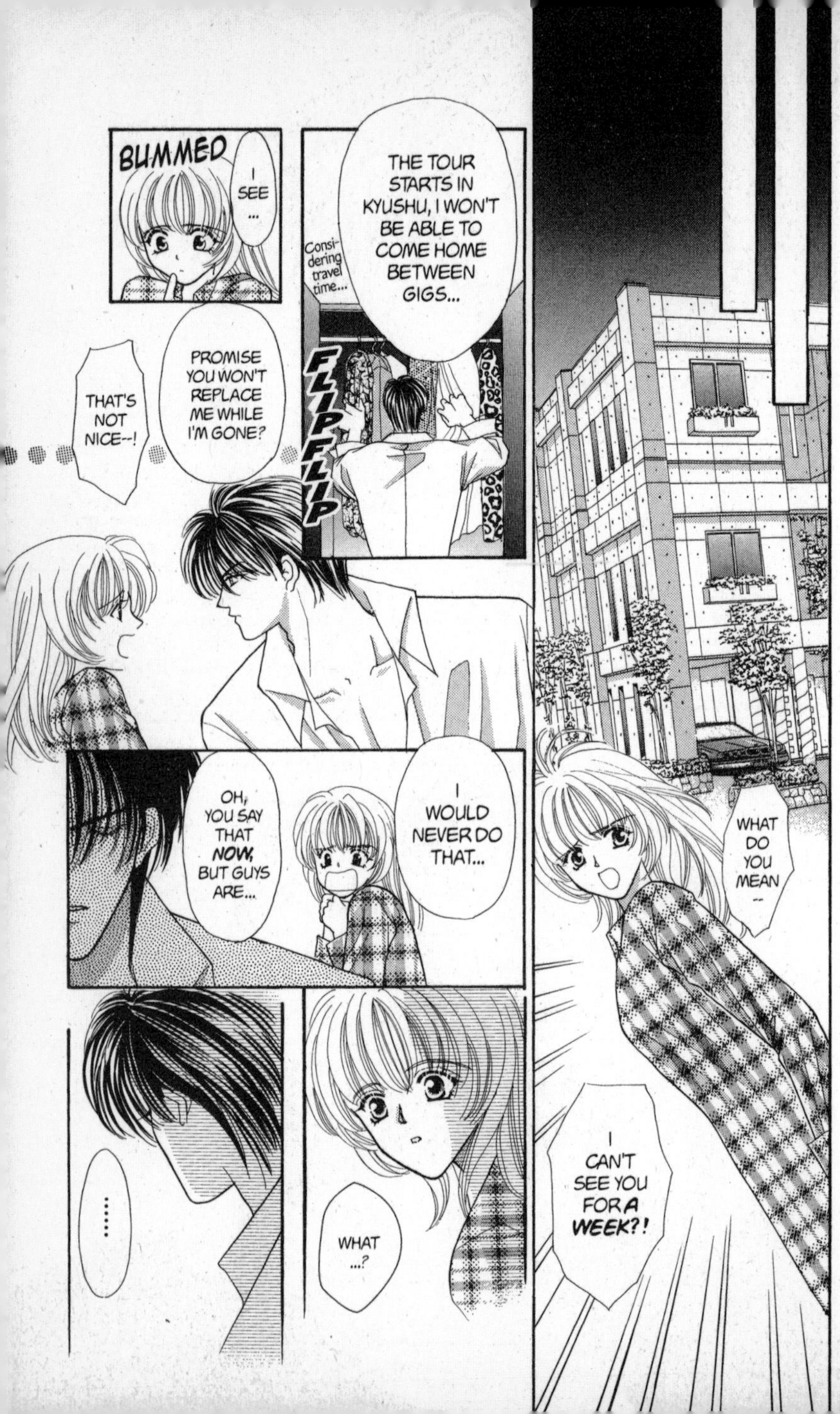
WHAT DO YOU MEAN --
I CAN'T SEE YOU FOR A WEEK?!
THE TOUR STARTS IN KYUSHU, I WON'T BE ABLE TO COME HOME BETWEEN GIGS...
Considering travel time...
FLIPFLIP
BUMMED
I SEE ...
PROMISE YOU WON'T REPLACE ME WHILE I'M GONE?
THAT'S NOT NICE--!
I WOULD NEVER DO THAT...
OH, YOU SAY THAT NOW, BUT GUYS ARE...
WHAT ...?
......

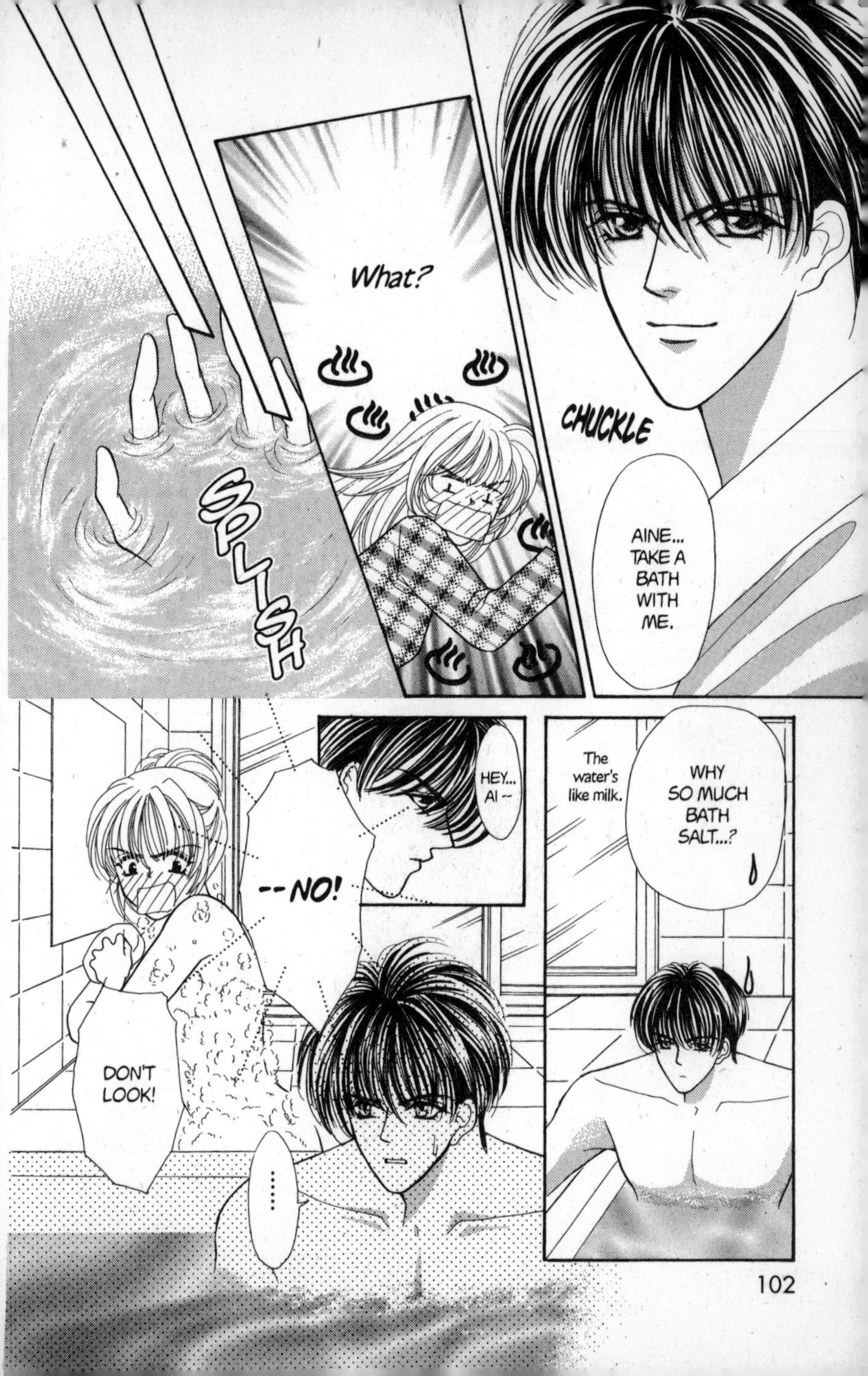
CHUCKLE
AINE... TAKE A BATH WITH ME.
What?
SPLISH
WHY SO MUCH BATH SALT...?
The water's like milk.
HEY... AI --
--NO!
DON'T LOOK!
......

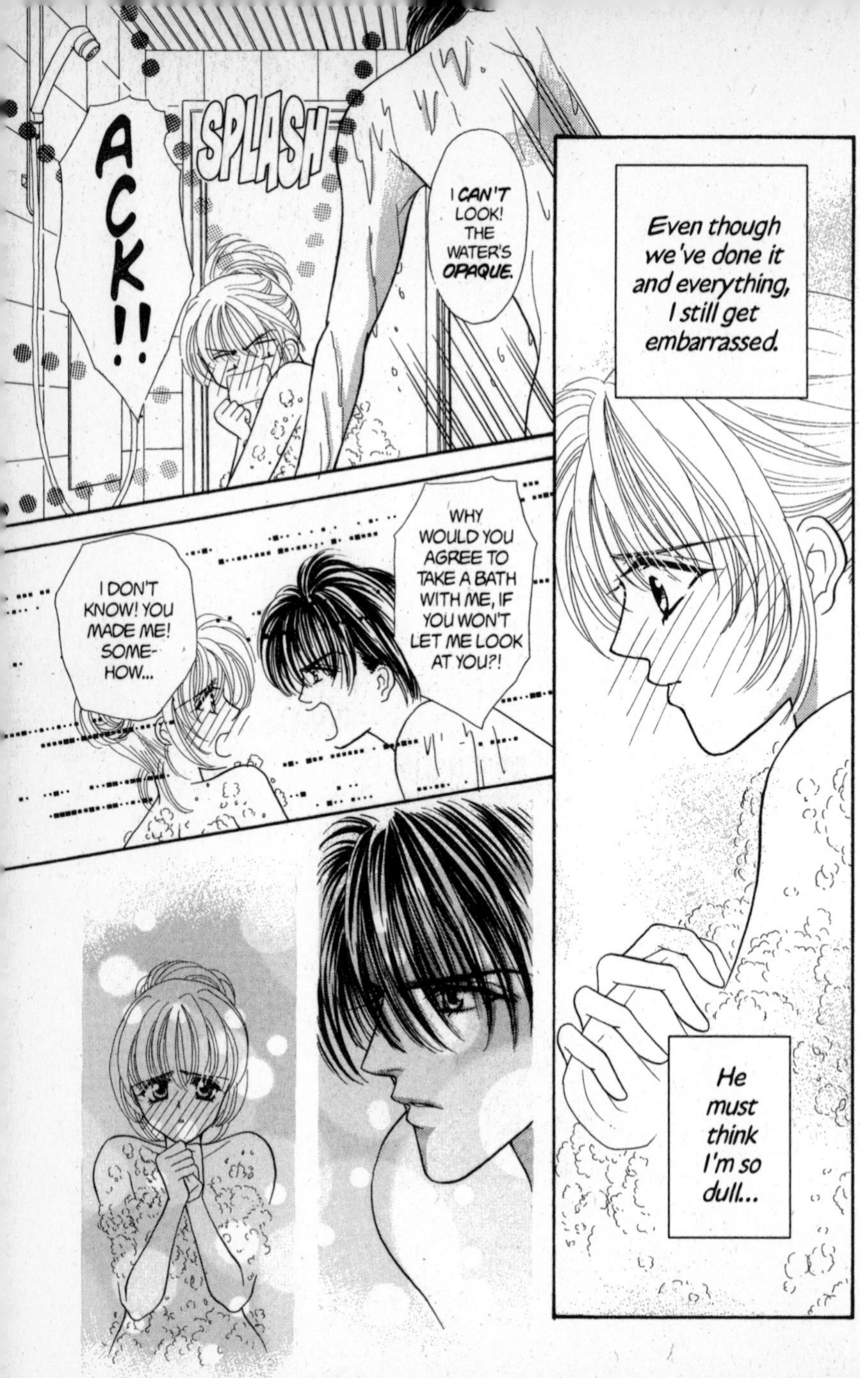
SPLASH
ACK!!
I CAN'T LOOK! THE WATER'S OPAQUE.
WHY WOULD YOU AGREE TO TAKE A BATH WITH ME, IF YOU WON'T LET ME LOOK AT YOU?!
I DON'T KNOW! YOU MADE ME! SOME-HOW...
Even though we've done it and everything, I still get embarrassed.
He must think I'm so dull...

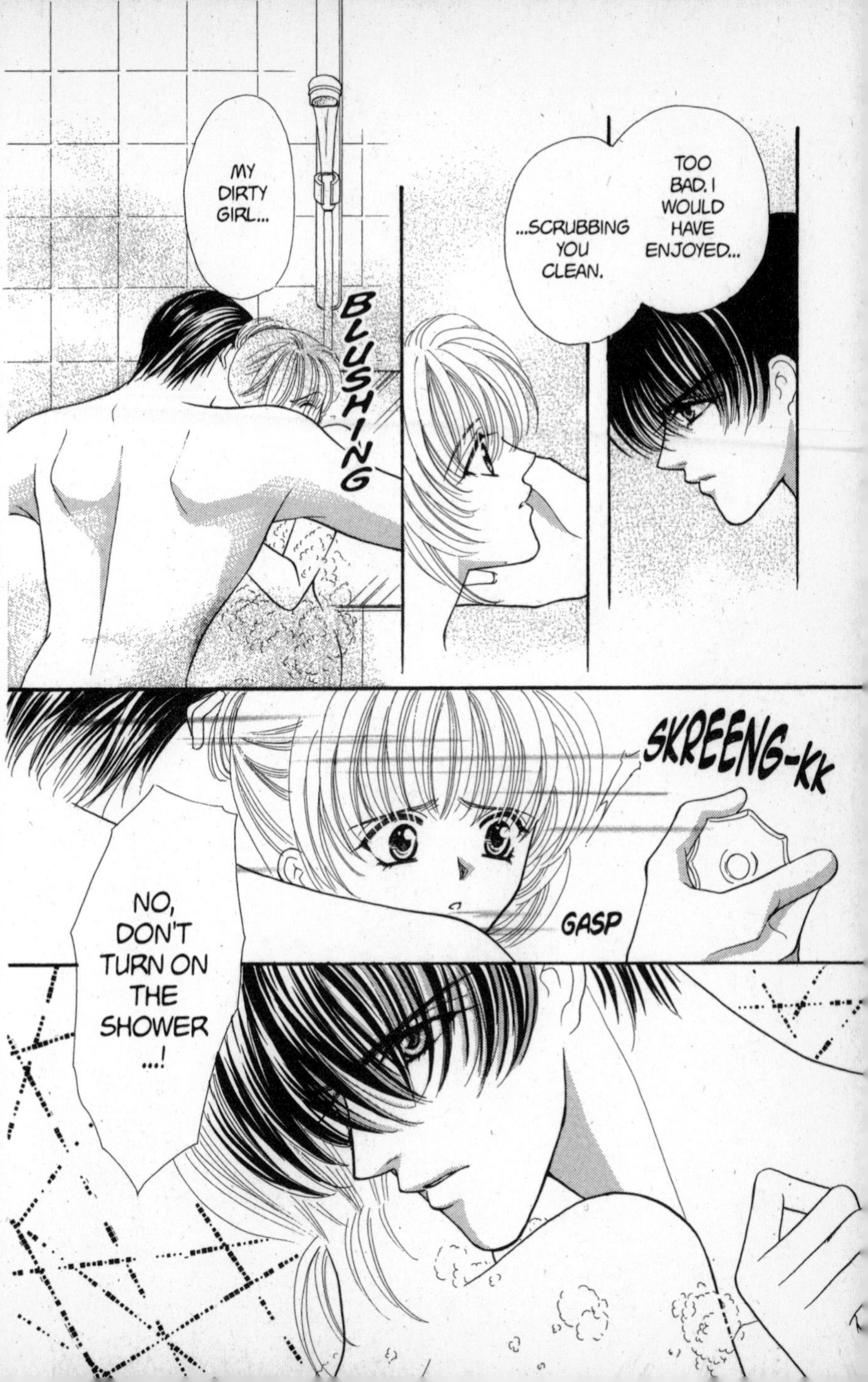
TOO BAD. I WOULD HAVE ENJOYED... ...SCRUBBING YOU CLEAN.
MY DIRTY GIRL...
BLUSHING
SKREENG-KK
GASP
NO, DON'T TURN ON THE SHOWER ...!

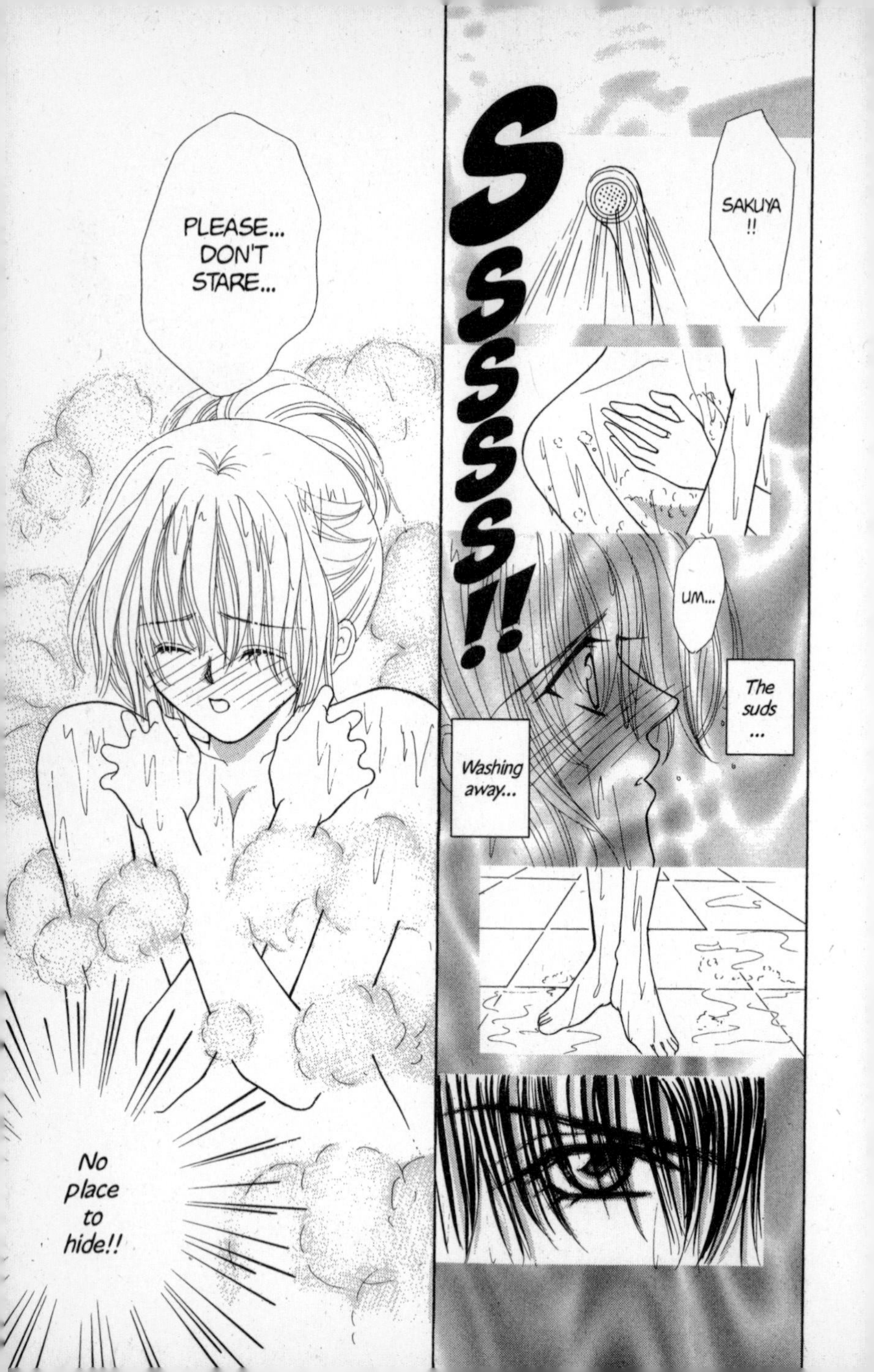
SAKUYA !!
SSSSSS!!
UM...
The suds ...
Washing away...
PLEASE... DON'T STARE...
No place to hide!!

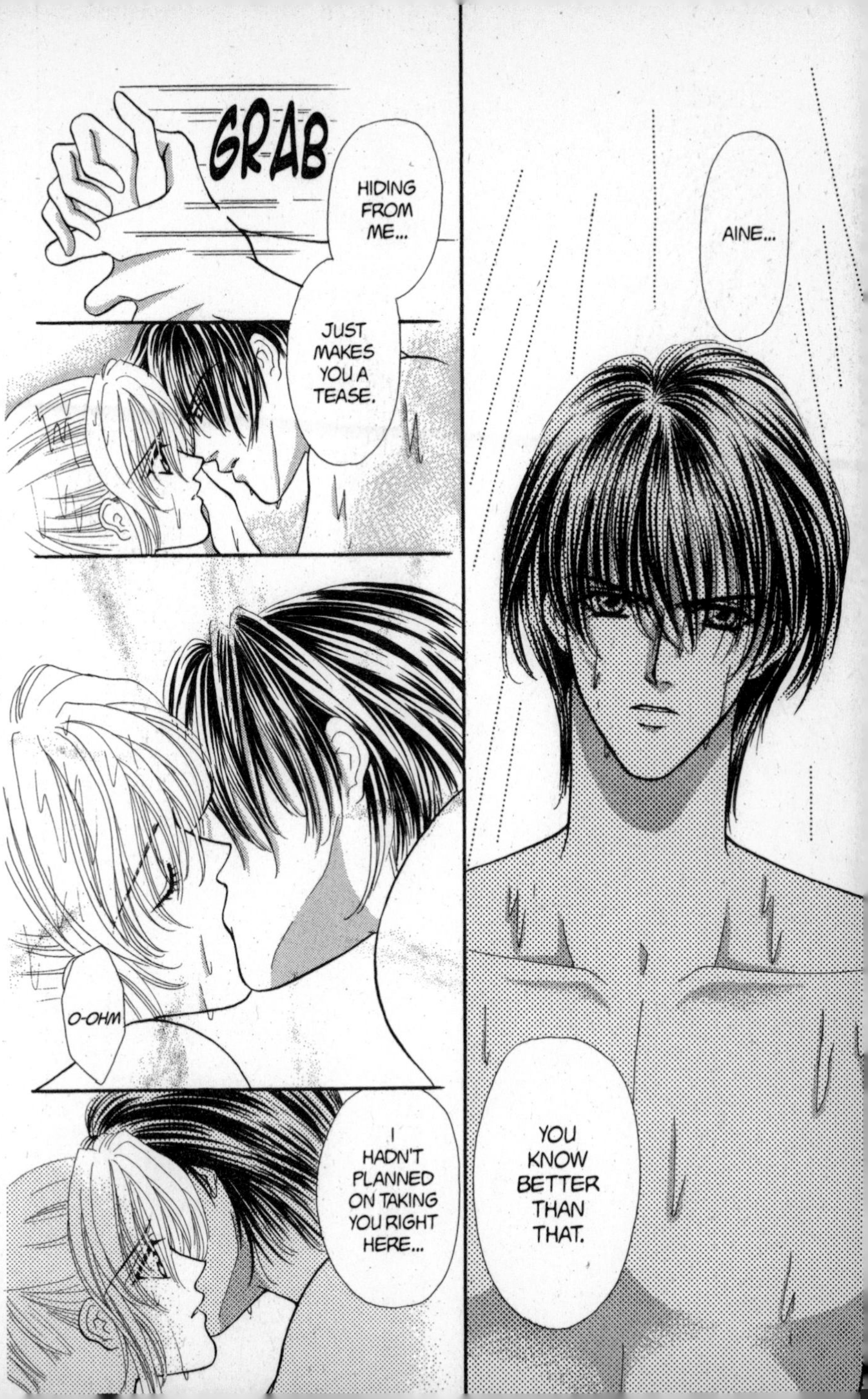
AINE...
YOU KNOW BETTER THAN THAT.
GRAB
HIDING FROM ME...
JUST MAKES YOU A TEASE.
O-OHM
I HADN'T PLANNED ON TAKING YOU RIGHT HERE...

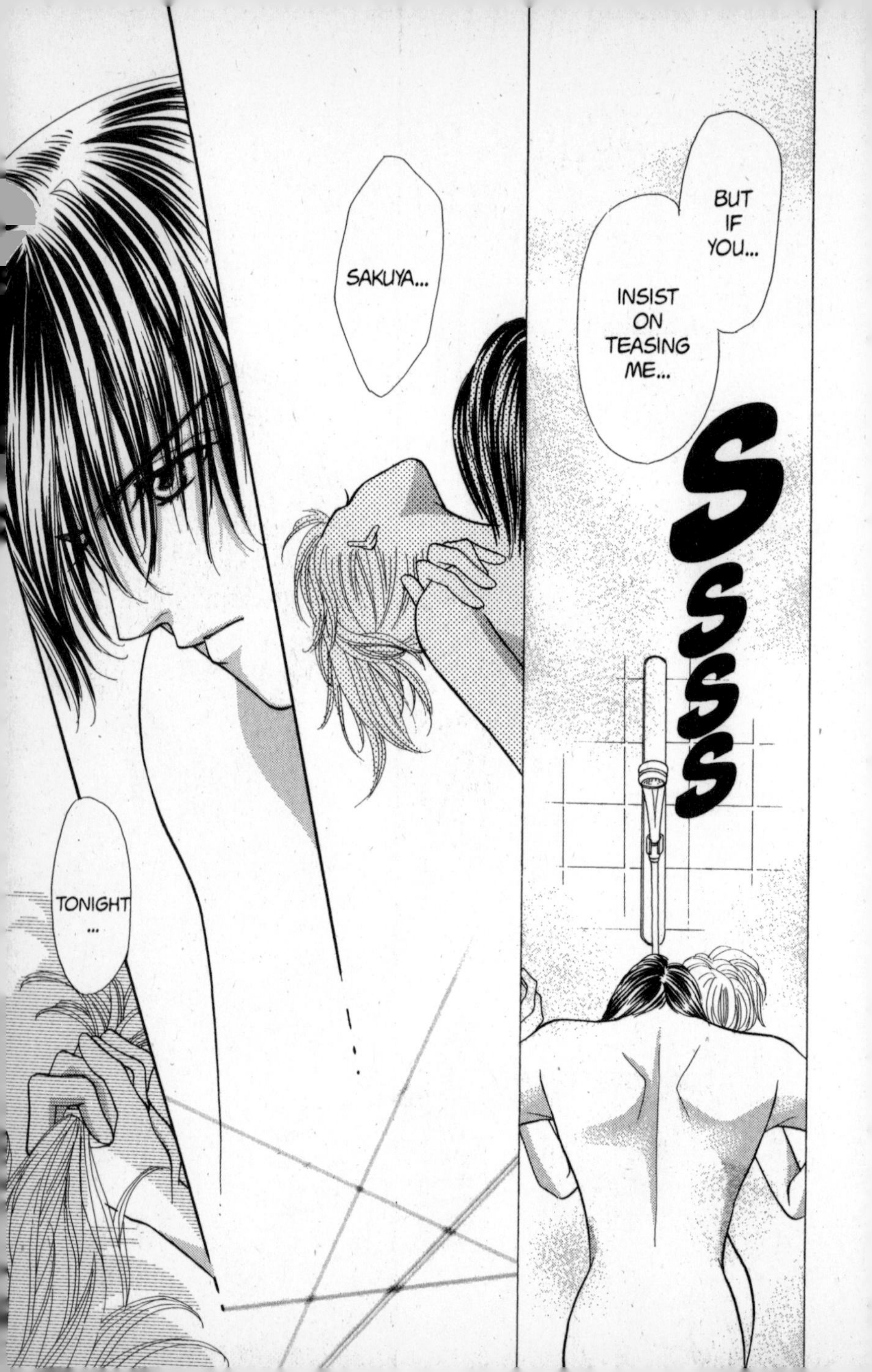
BUT IF YOU...
INSIST ON TEASING ME...
SSSSS
SAKUYA...
TONIGHT ...

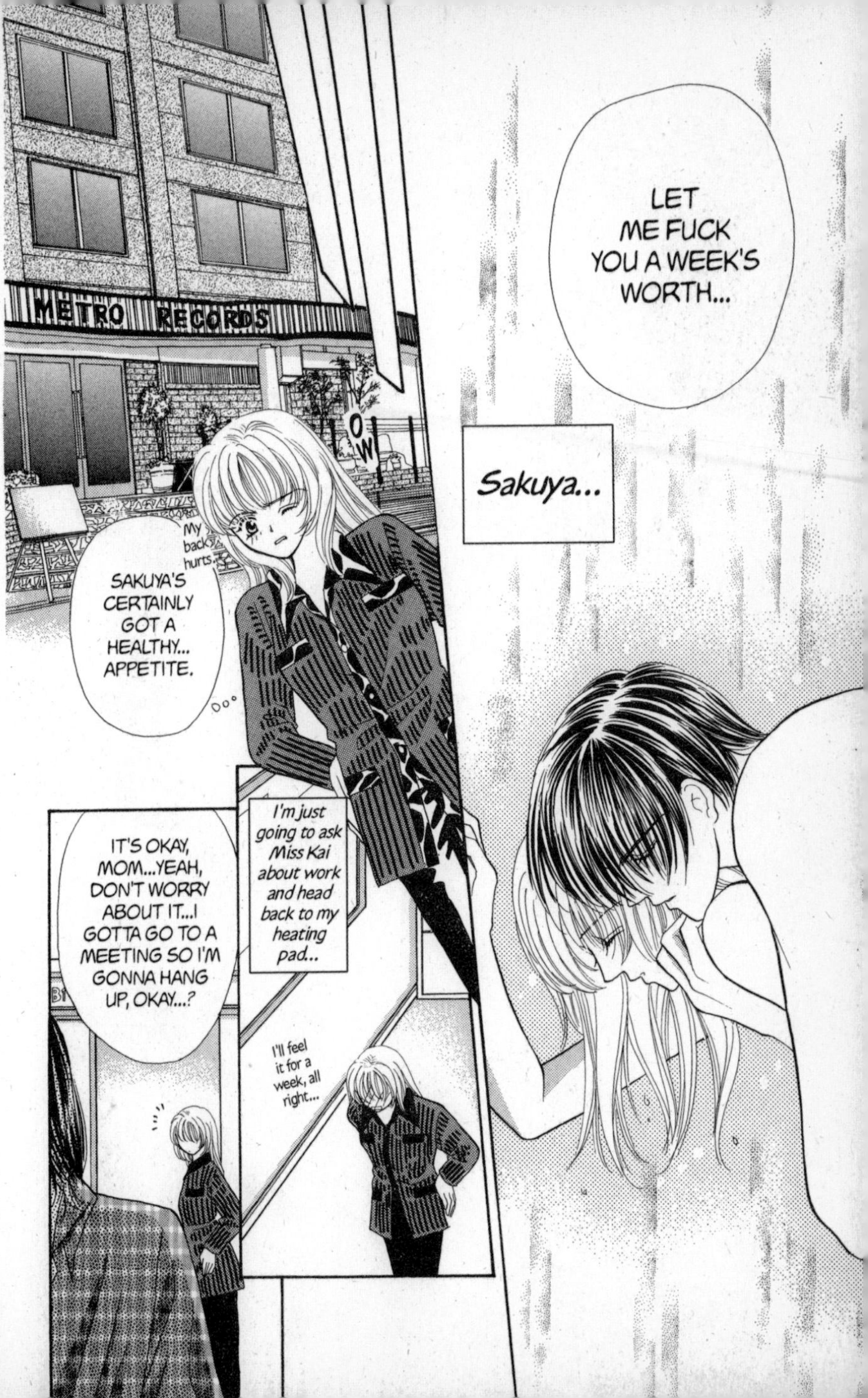
LET ME FUCK YOU A WEEK'S WORTH...
Sakuya...
METRO RECORDS
OW
My back hurts.
SAKUYA'S CERTAINLY GOT A HEALTHY... APPETITE.
Doo
I'm just going to ask Miss Kai about work and head back to my heating pad...
I'll feel it for a week, all right...
IT'S OKAY, MOM...YEAH, DON'T WORRY ABOUT IT...I GOTTA GO TO A MEETING SO I'M GONNA HANG UP, OKAY...?

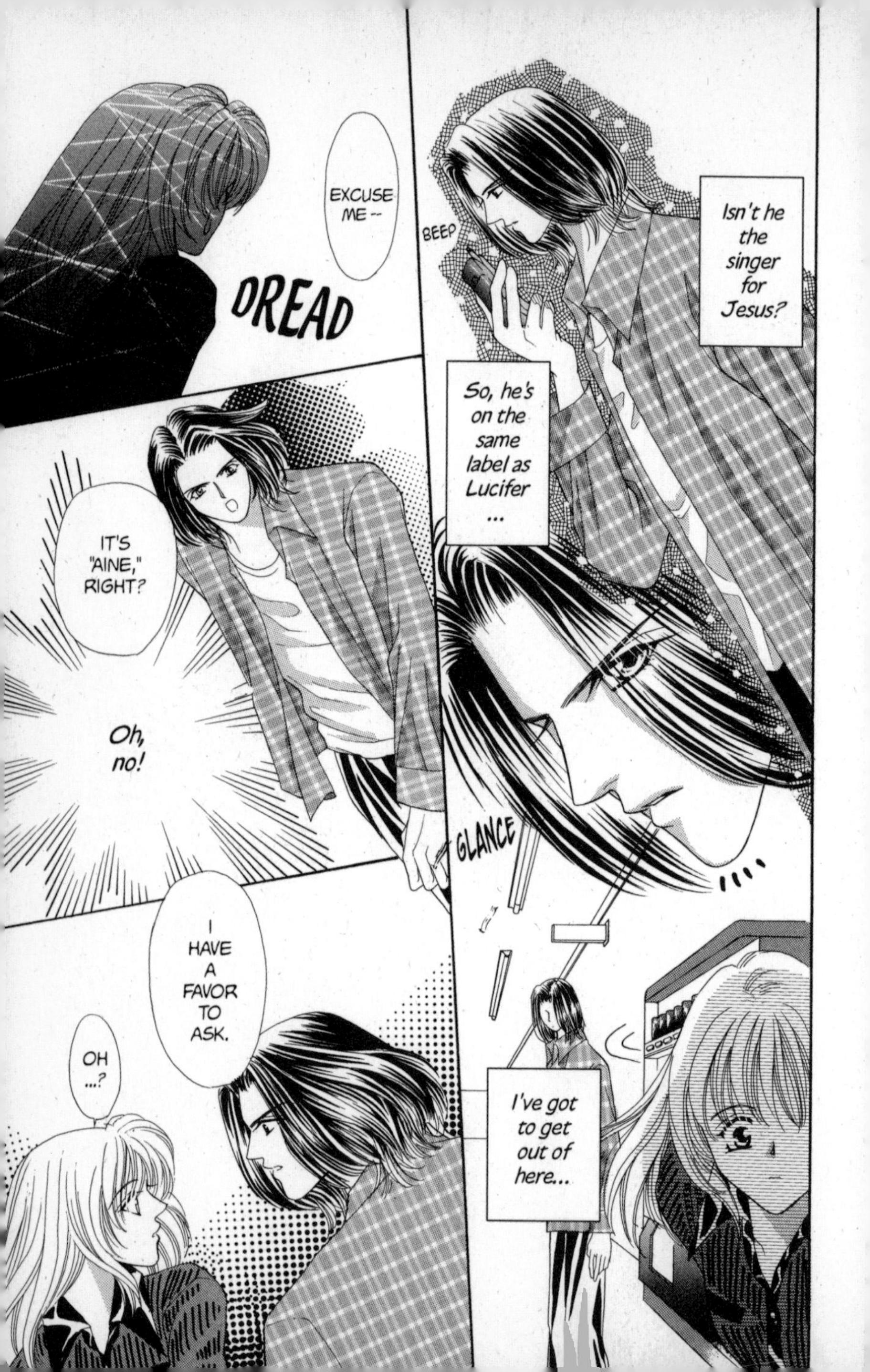
Isn't he the singer for Jesus?
BEEP
So, he's on the same label as Lucifer ...
GLANCE
I've got to get out of here...
EXCUSE ME --
DREAD
IT'S "AINE," RIGHT?
Oh, no!
I HAVE A FAVOR TO ASK.
OH ...?

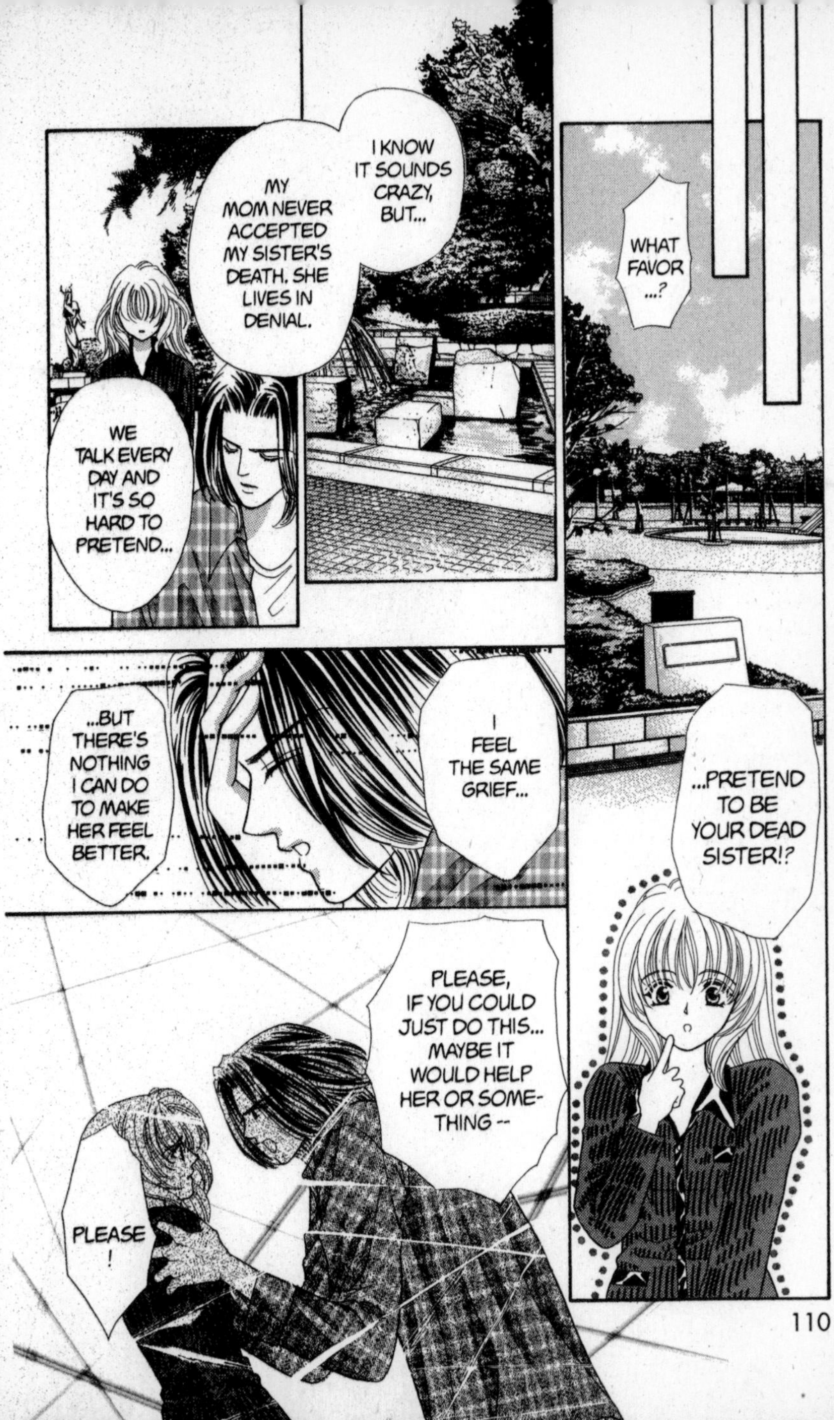
WHAT FAVOR ...?
...PRETEND TO BE YOUR DEAD SISTER!?
I KNOW IT SOUNDS CRAZY, BUT...
MY MOM NEVER ACCEPTED MY SISTER'S DEATH. SHE LIVES IN DENIAL.
WE TALK EVERY DAY AND IT'S SO HARD TO PRETEND...
I FEEL THE SAME GRIEF...
...BUT THERE'S NOTHING I CAN DO TO MAKE HER FEEL BETTER.
PLEASE, IF YOU COULD JUST DO THIS... MAYBE IT WOULD HELP HER OR SOME-THING --
PLEASE !

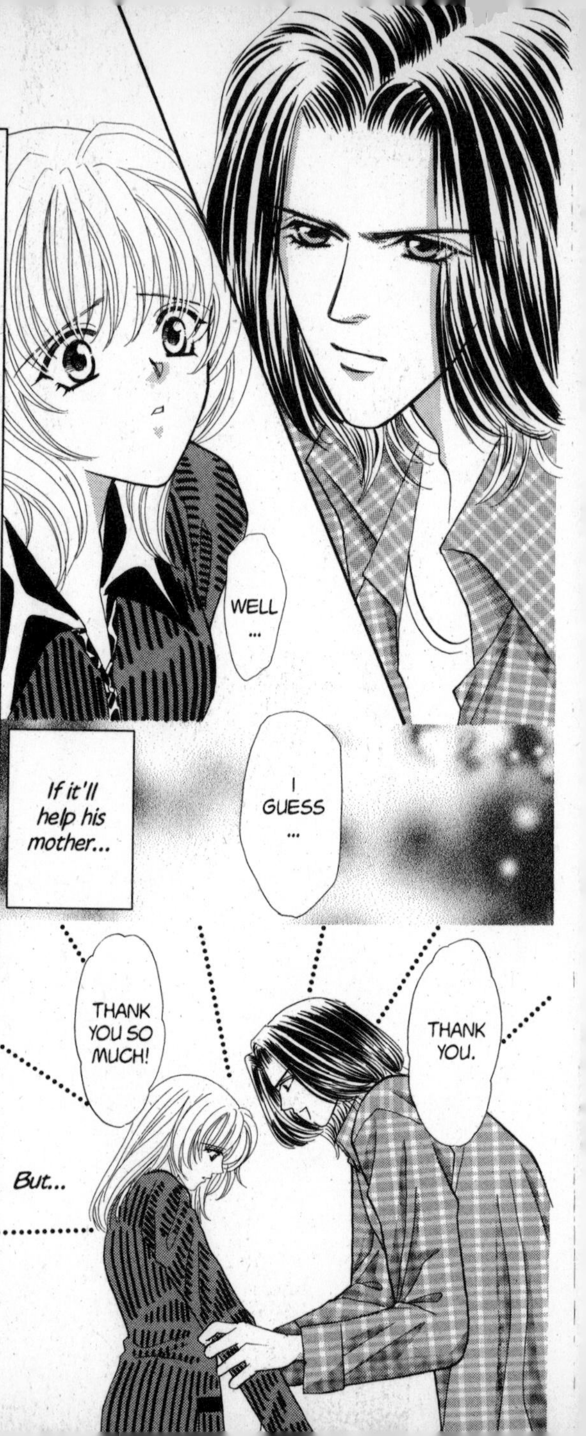
WELL...
I GUESS...
If it'll help his mother...
THANK YOU.
THANK YOU SO MUCH!
But...

Q: WHAT DO YOU LISTEN TO WHILE YOU WORK?
A: Right now I'm into Glay, Luna Sea, T.M.R., Shikao Suga, Siam Shade, and B'z. And some Top 40 stuff, too.

Q: IF YOU WEREN'T A COMIC ARTIST, WHAT WOULD YOU BE?
A: Hmm. I don't know. I imagine I'd work in the entertainment industry in some capacity. Or do night work (hee hee).

Q: IS SAKUYA YOUR TYPE?
A: Hm...Yes and no, I guess? It's kind of like this: more than wanting to DATE Sakuya, I want to BE Sakuya. Does that sound weird? Wealth, power, fame, talent, adoration...I fantasize about that stuff. When I see footage of live shows, I envy the performers. It looks like it feels great, doesn't it? Oh, and I totally want to spin the mic stand!

We play a game at the studio called 'ultimate choice.' It works like this: if you could either be Tetsuya Komuro or Teru of Glay, who would you be? The answer is Teru, three to one.

Q: WHERE'S AINE'S PROFILE?
A: I'm thinking about putting it in Volume 5.

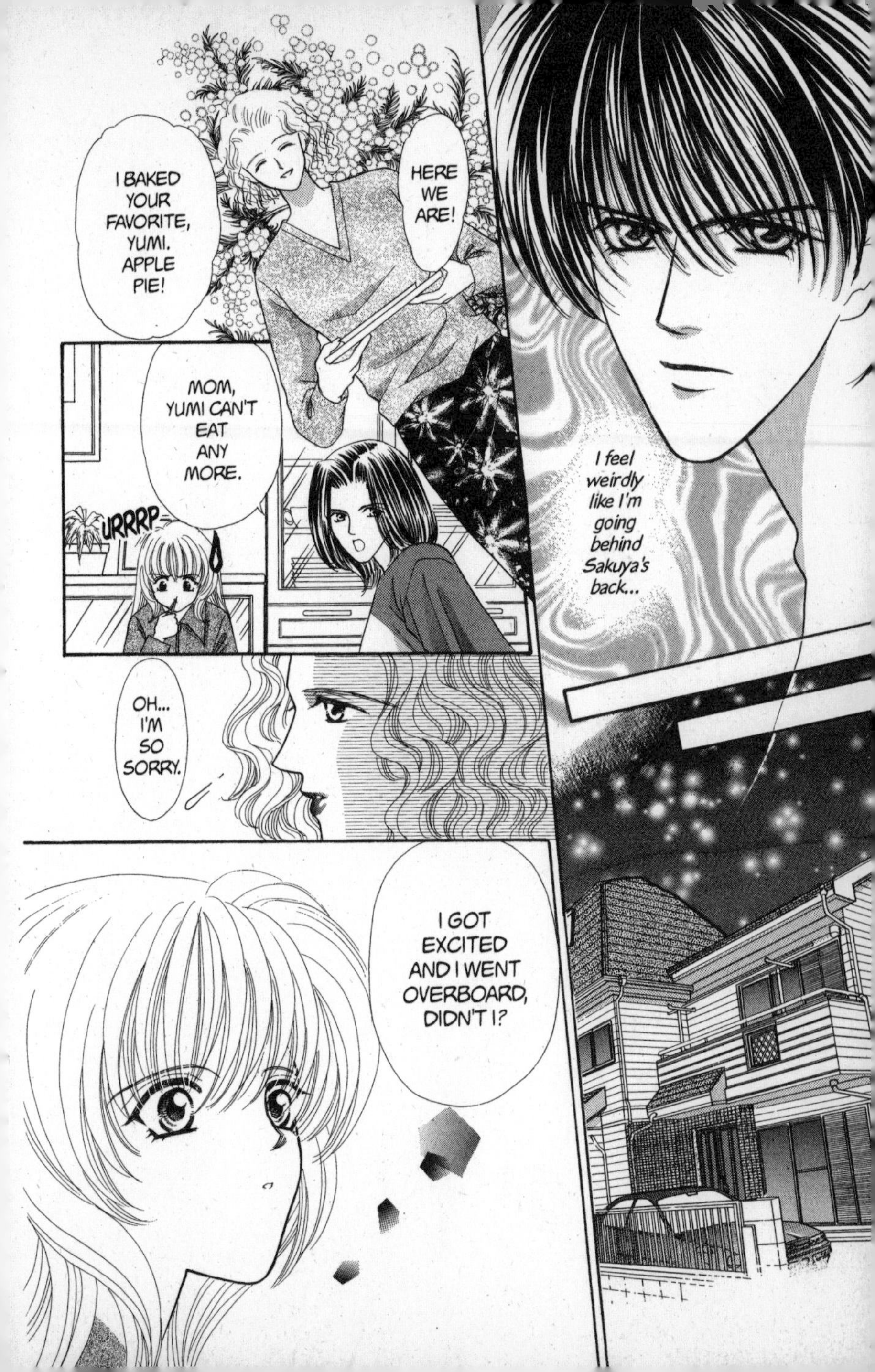
I feel weirdly like I'm going behind Sakuya's back...
HERE WE ARE!
I BAKED YOUR FAVORITE, YUMI. APPLE PIE!
MOM, YUMI CAN'T EAT ANY MORE.
URRRP
OH... I'M SO SORRY.
I GOT EXCITED AND I WENT OVERBOARD, DIDN'T I?

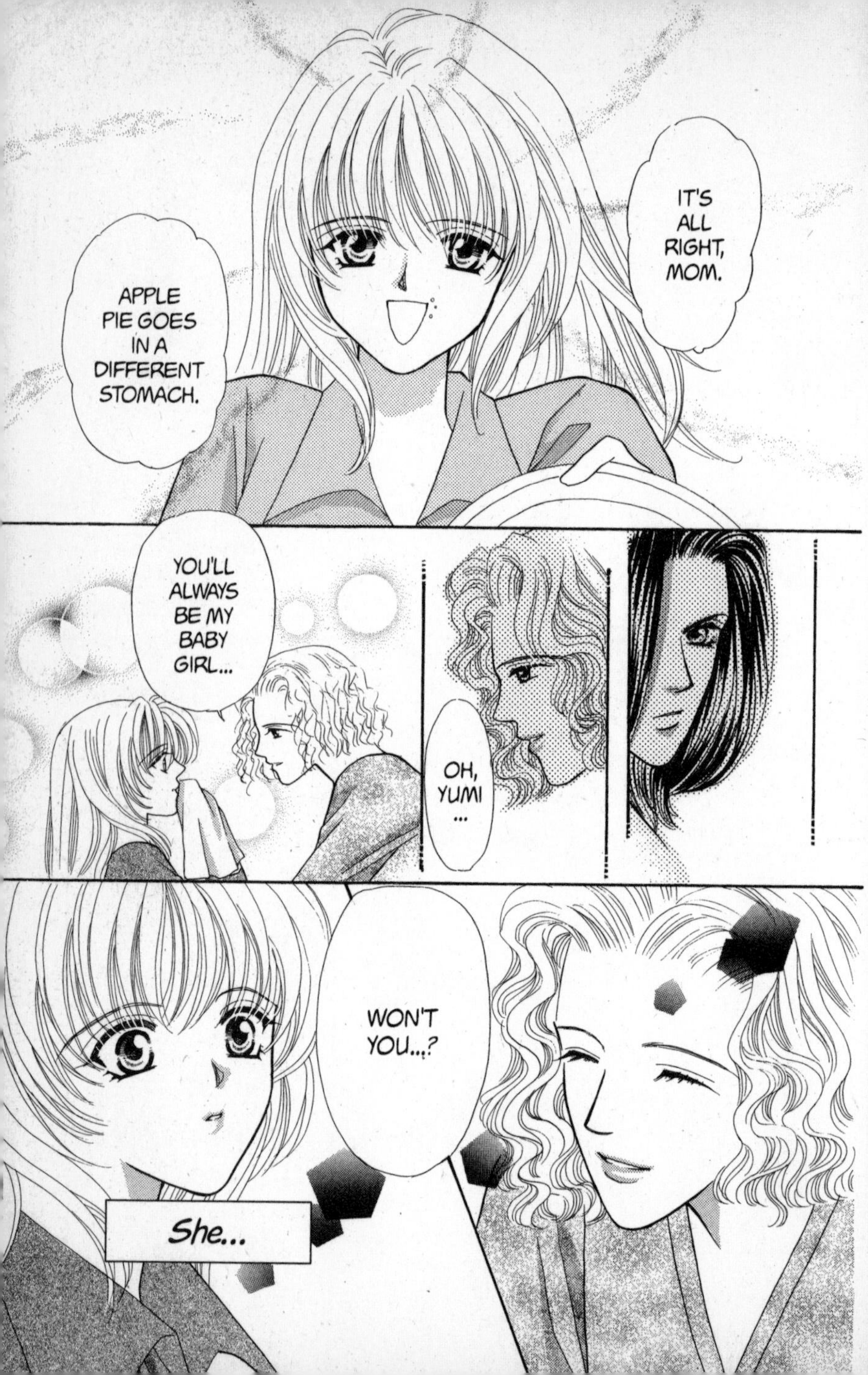
IT'S ALL RIGHT, MOM.
APPLE PIE GOES IN A DIFFERENT STOMACH.
OH, YUMI...
YOU'LL ALWAYS BE MY BABY GIRL...
WON'T YOU...?
She...

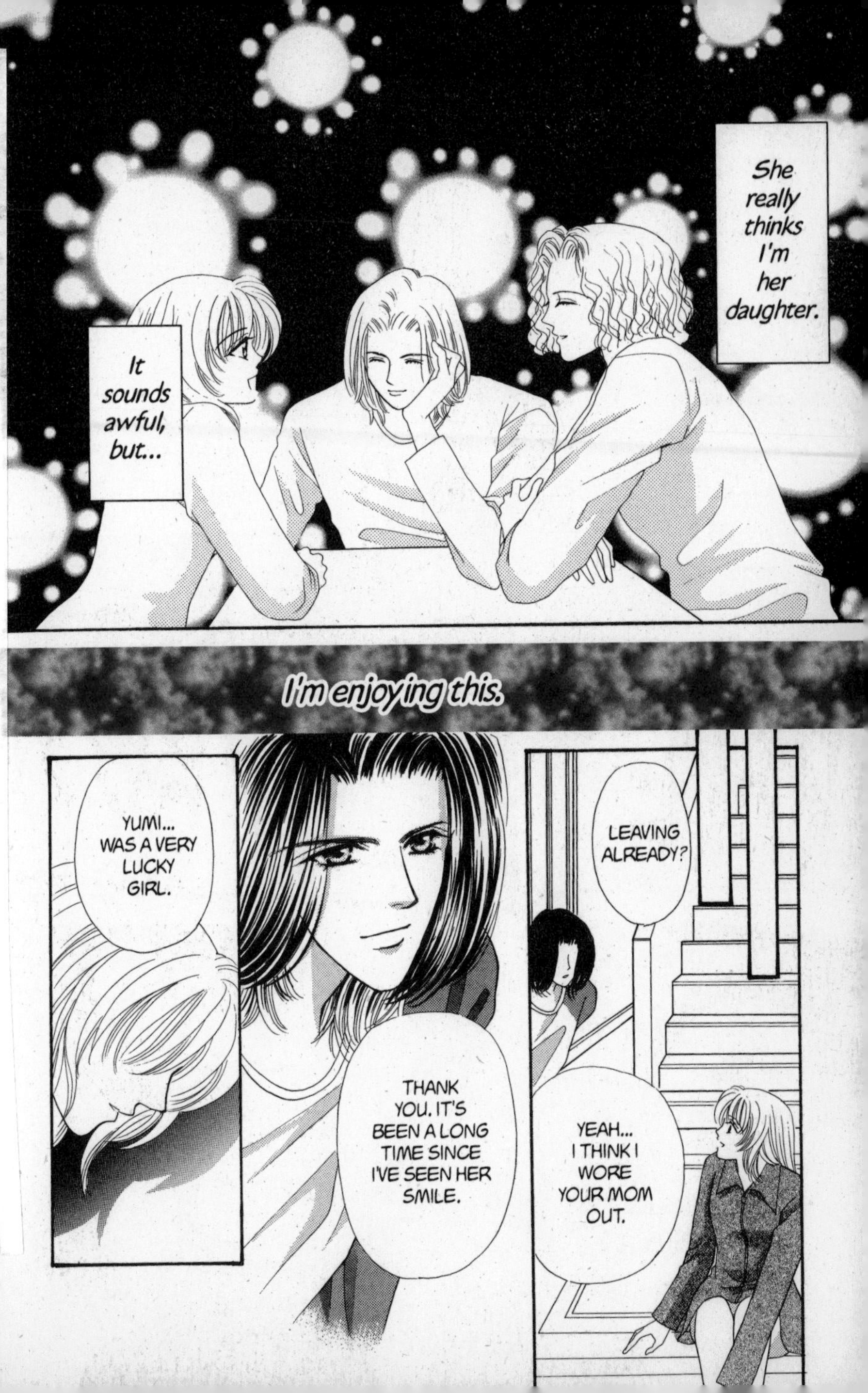
She really thinks I'm her daughter.
It sounds awful, but...
I'm enjoying this.
LEAVING ALREADY?
YEAH... I THINK I WORE YOUR MOM OUT.
YUMI... WAS A VERY LUCKY GIRL.
THANK YOU. IT'S BEEN A LONG TIME SINCE I'VE SEEN HER SMILE.

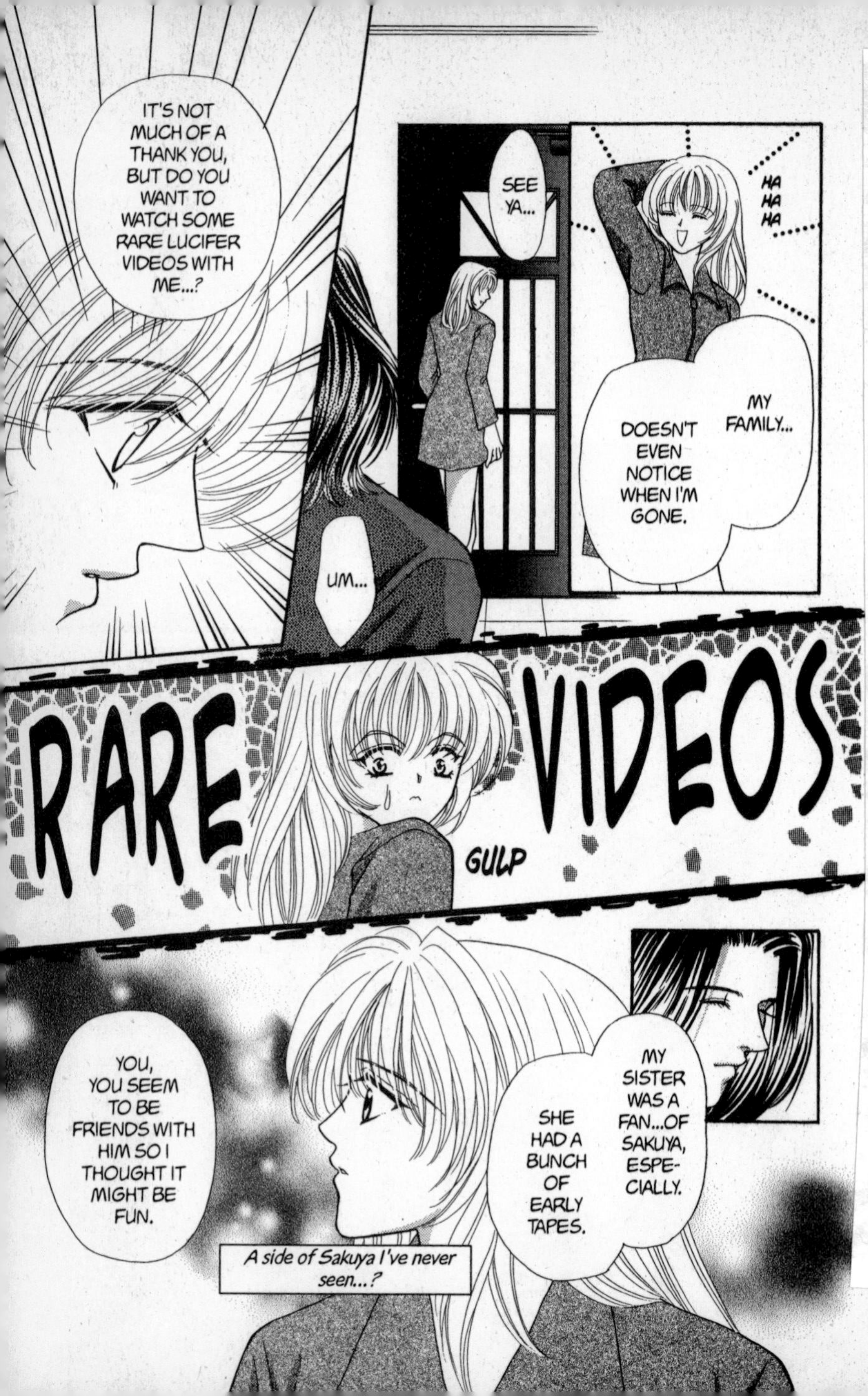
HA HA HA
MY FAMILY... DOESN'T EVEN NOTICE WHEN I'M GONE.
SEE YA...
UM...
IT'S NOT MUCH OF A THANK YOU, BUT DO YOU WANT TO WATCH SOME RARE LUCIFER VIDEOS WITH ME...?
RARE VIDEOS
GULP
MY SISTER WAS A FAN...OF SAKUYA, ESPECIALLY.
SHE HAD A BUNCH OF EARLY TAPES.
YOU, YOU SEEM TO BE FRIENDS WITH HIM SO I THOUGHT IT MIGHT BE FUN.
A side of Sakuya I've never seen...?

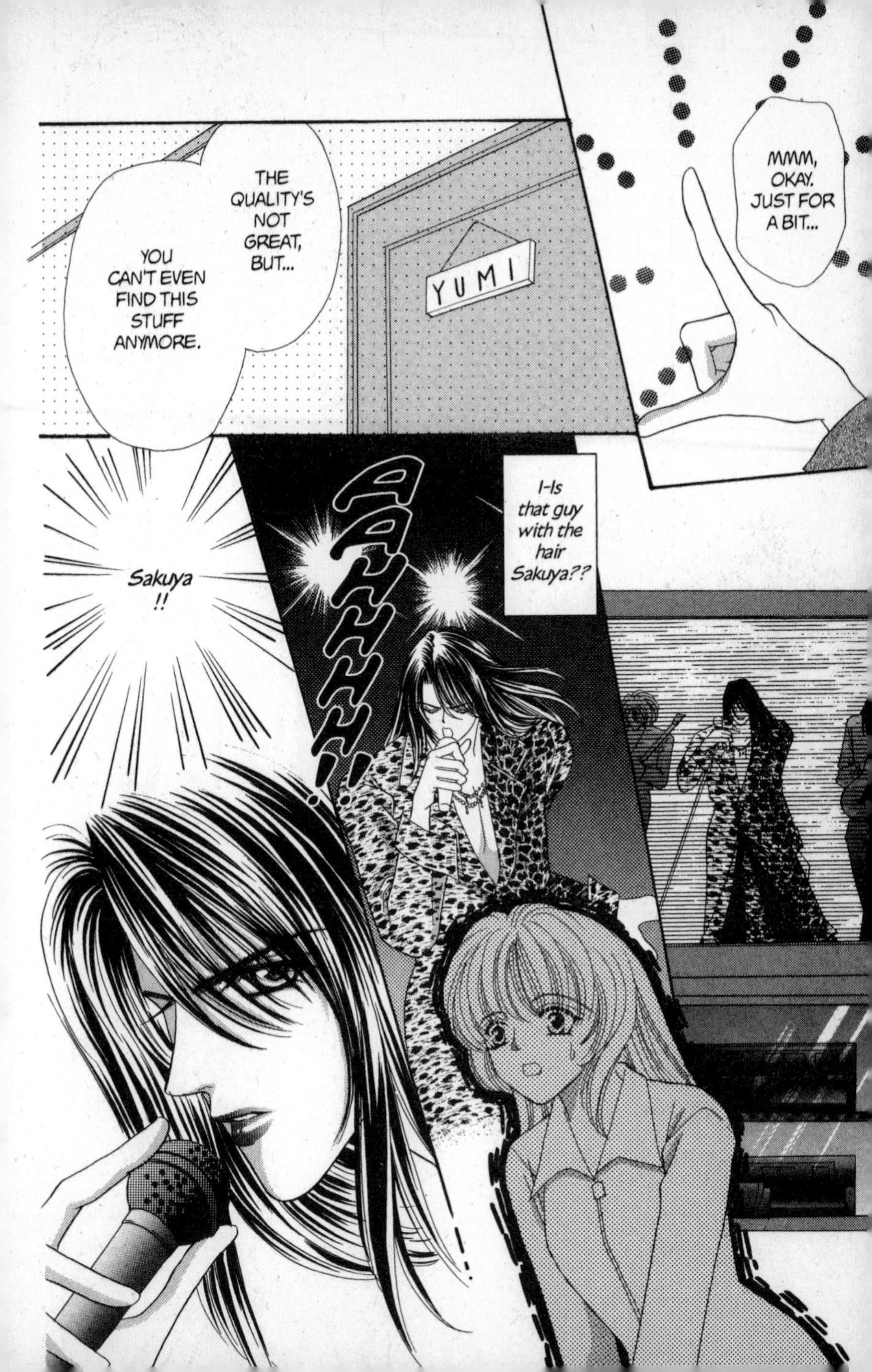
MMM, OKAY. JUST FOR A BIT...
THE QUALITY'S NOT GREAT, BUT...
YOU CAN'T EVEN FIND THIS STUFF ANYMORE.
YUMI
I-Is that guy with the hair Sakuya??
AAHHHHH!!
Sakuya !!

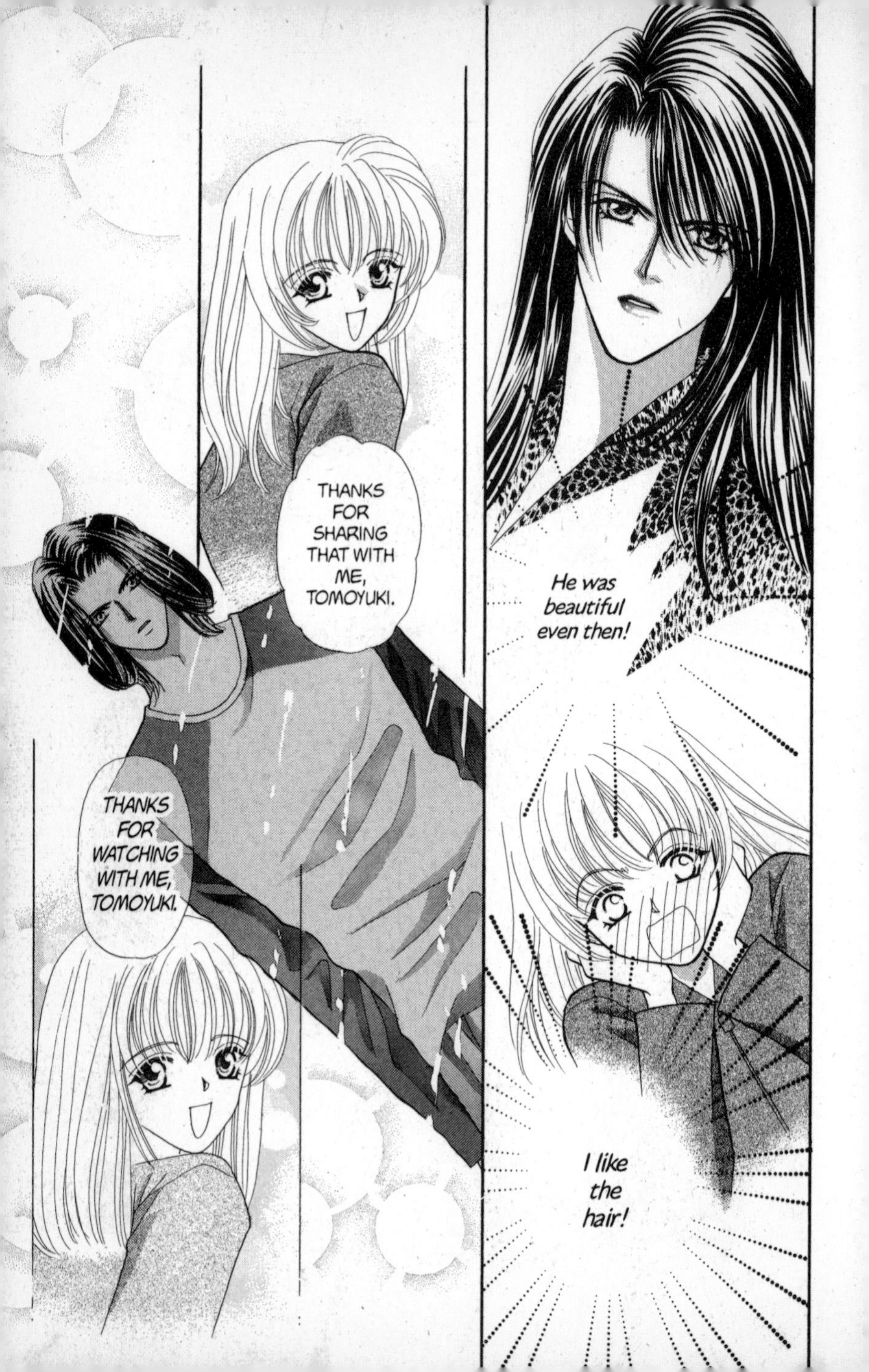
He was beautiful even then!
I like the hair!
THANKS FOR SHARING THAT WITH ME, TOMOYUKI.
THANKS FOR WATCHING WITH ME, TOMOYUKI.

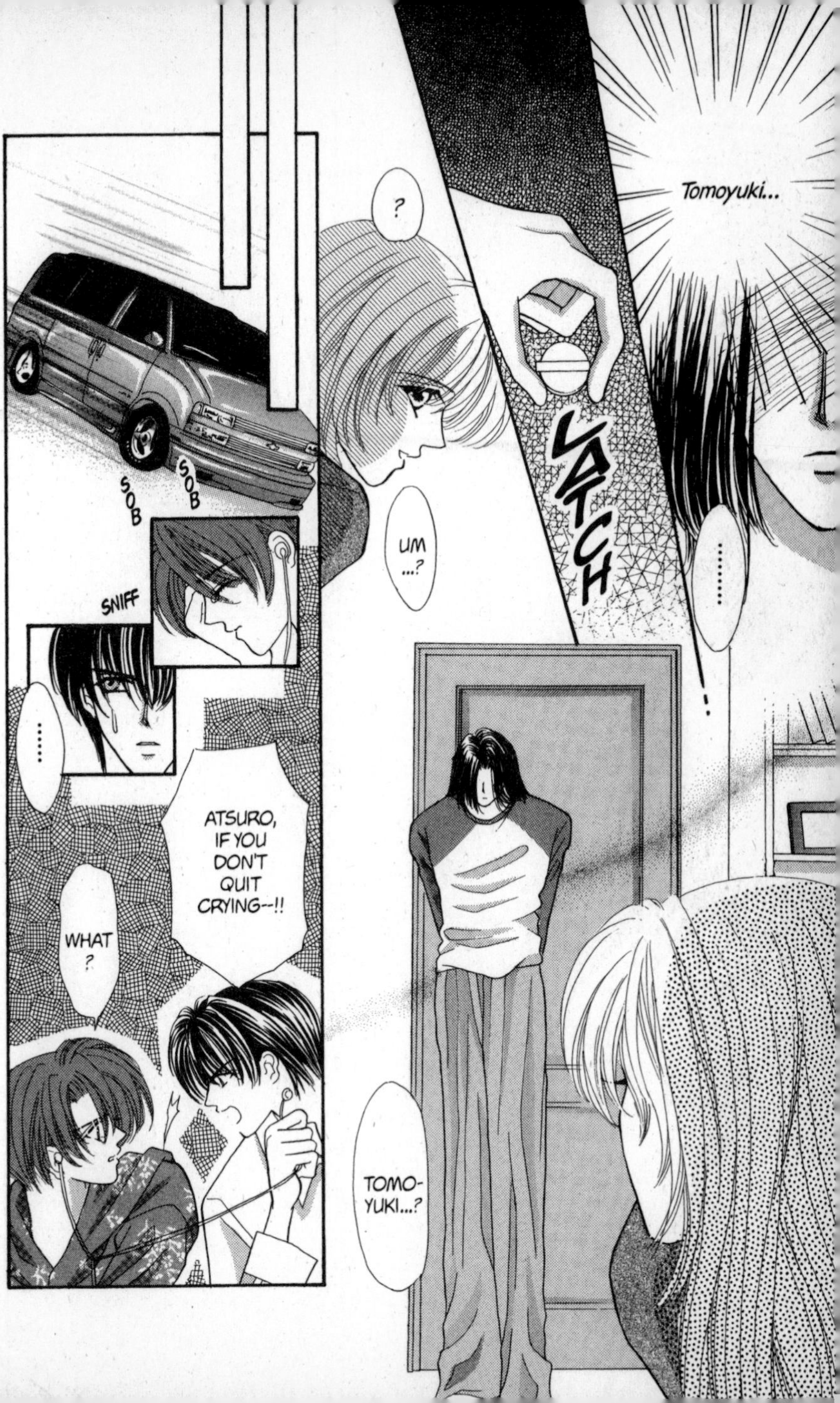
Tomoyuki...
......
LATCH
?
UM ...?
TOMO-YUKI...?
SOB SOB
SNIFF
......
ATSURO, IF YOU DON'T QUIT CRYING--!!
WHAT?

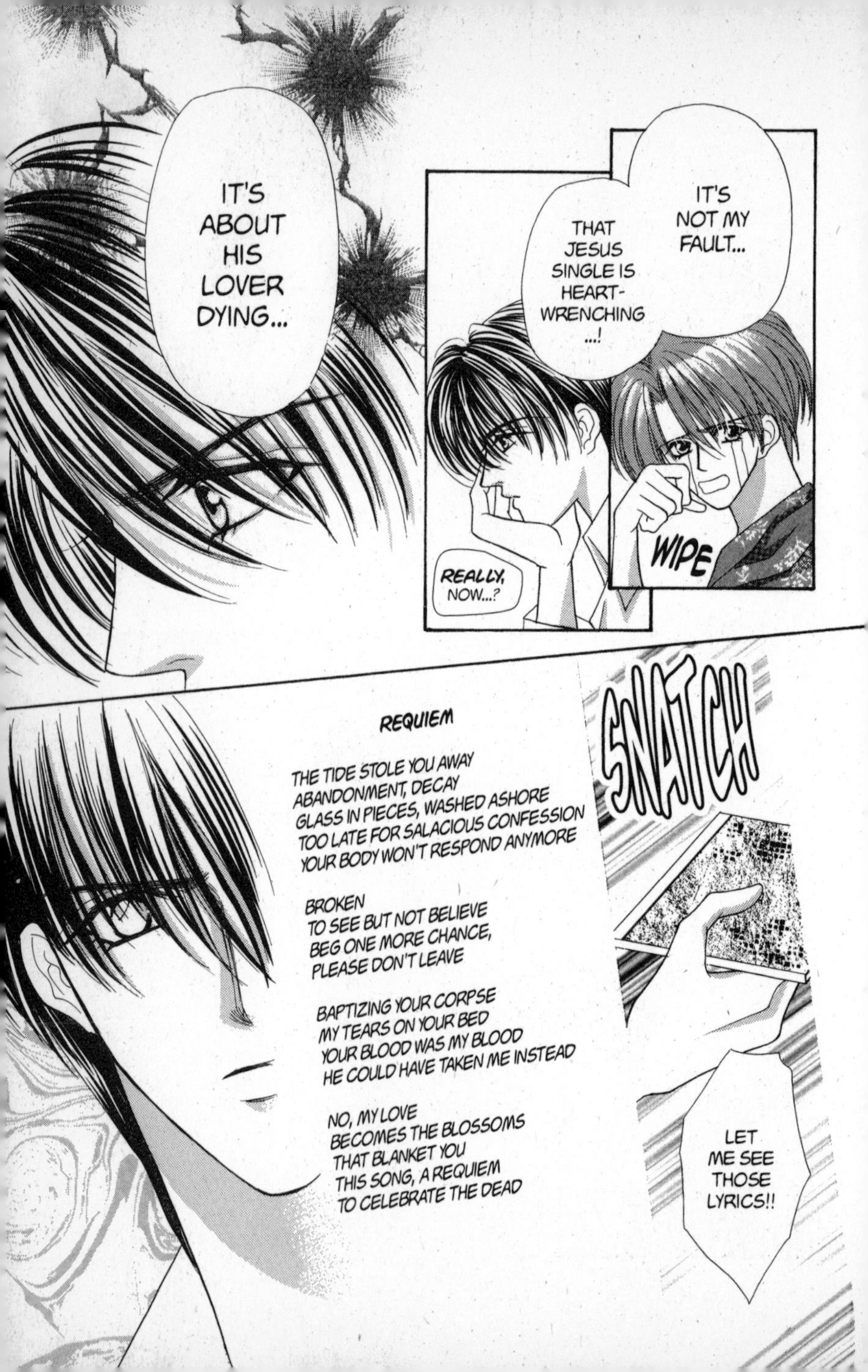
IT'S NOT MY FAULT...
THAT JESUS SINGLE IS HEART-WRENCHING ...!
WIPE
REALLY, NOW...?
IT'S ABOUT HIS LOVER DYING...
SNATCH
LET ME SEE THOSE LYRICS!!
REQUIEM
THE TIDE STOLE YOU AWAY
ABANDONMENT, DECAY
GLASS IN PIECES, WASHED ASHORE
TOO LATE FOR SALACIOUS CONFESSION
YOUR BODY WON'T RESPOND ANYMORE
BROKEN
TO SEE BUT NOT BELIEVE
BEG ONE MORE CHANCE,
PLEASE DON'T LEAVE
BAPTIZING YOUR CORPSE
MY TEARS ON YOUR BED
YOUR BLOOD WAS MY BLOOD
HE COULD HAVE TAKEN ME INSTEAD
NO, MY LOVE
BECOMES THE BLOSSOMS
THAT BLANKET YOU
THIS SONG, A REQUIEM
TO CELEBRATE THE DEAD

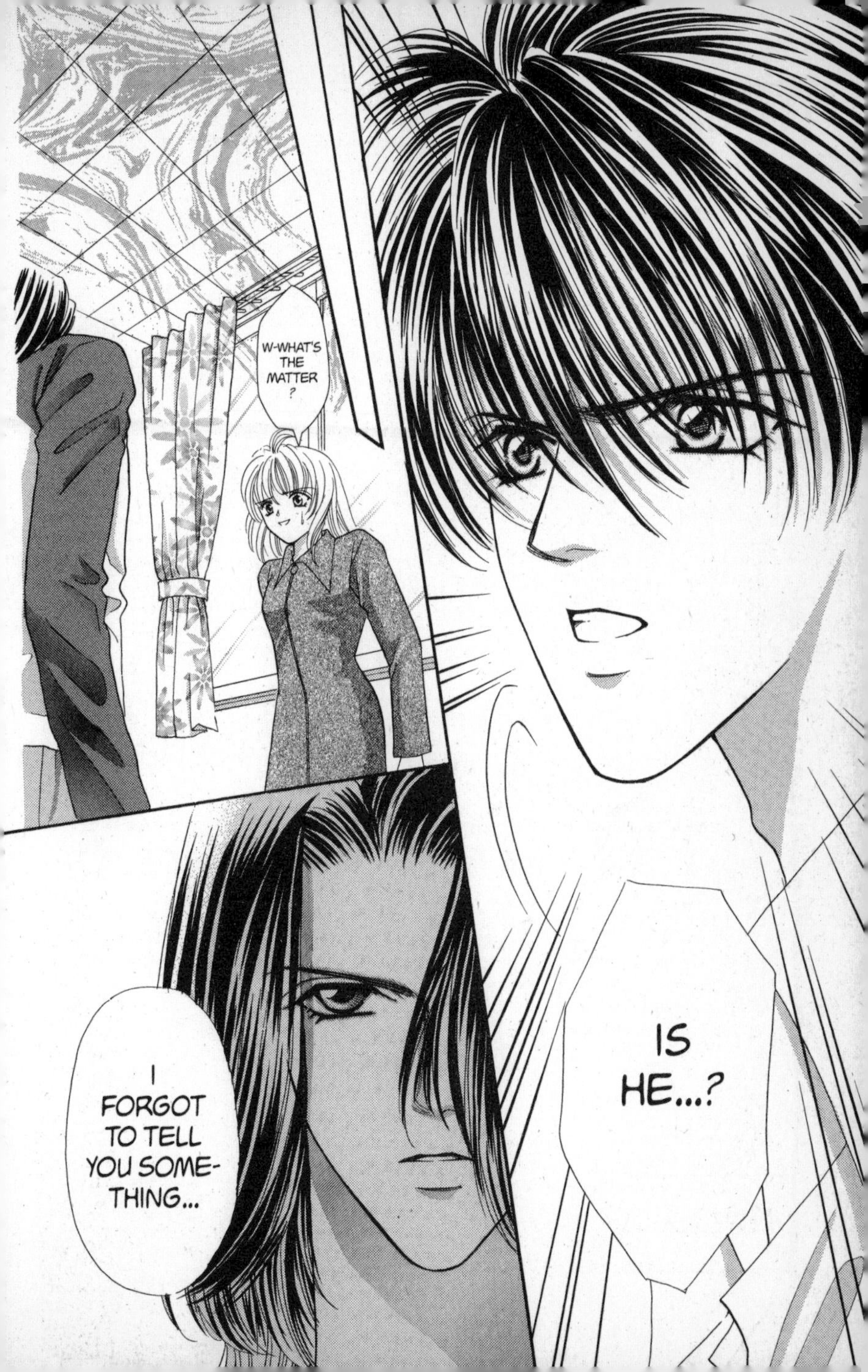
IS HE...?
W-WHAT'S THE MATTER?
I FORGOT TO TELL YOU SOMETHING...

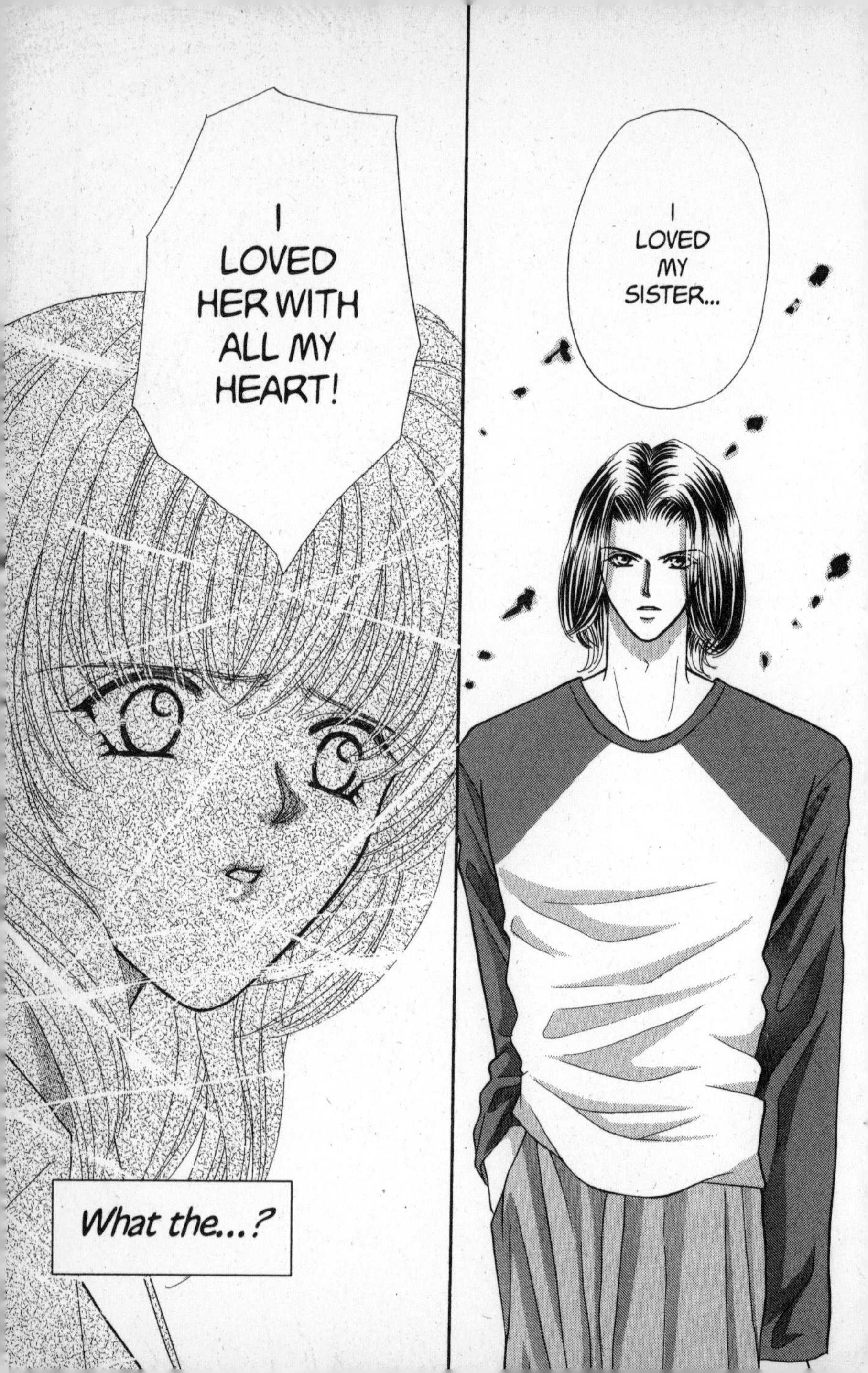
I LOVED MY SISTER...
I LOVED HER WITH ALL MY HEART!
What the...?

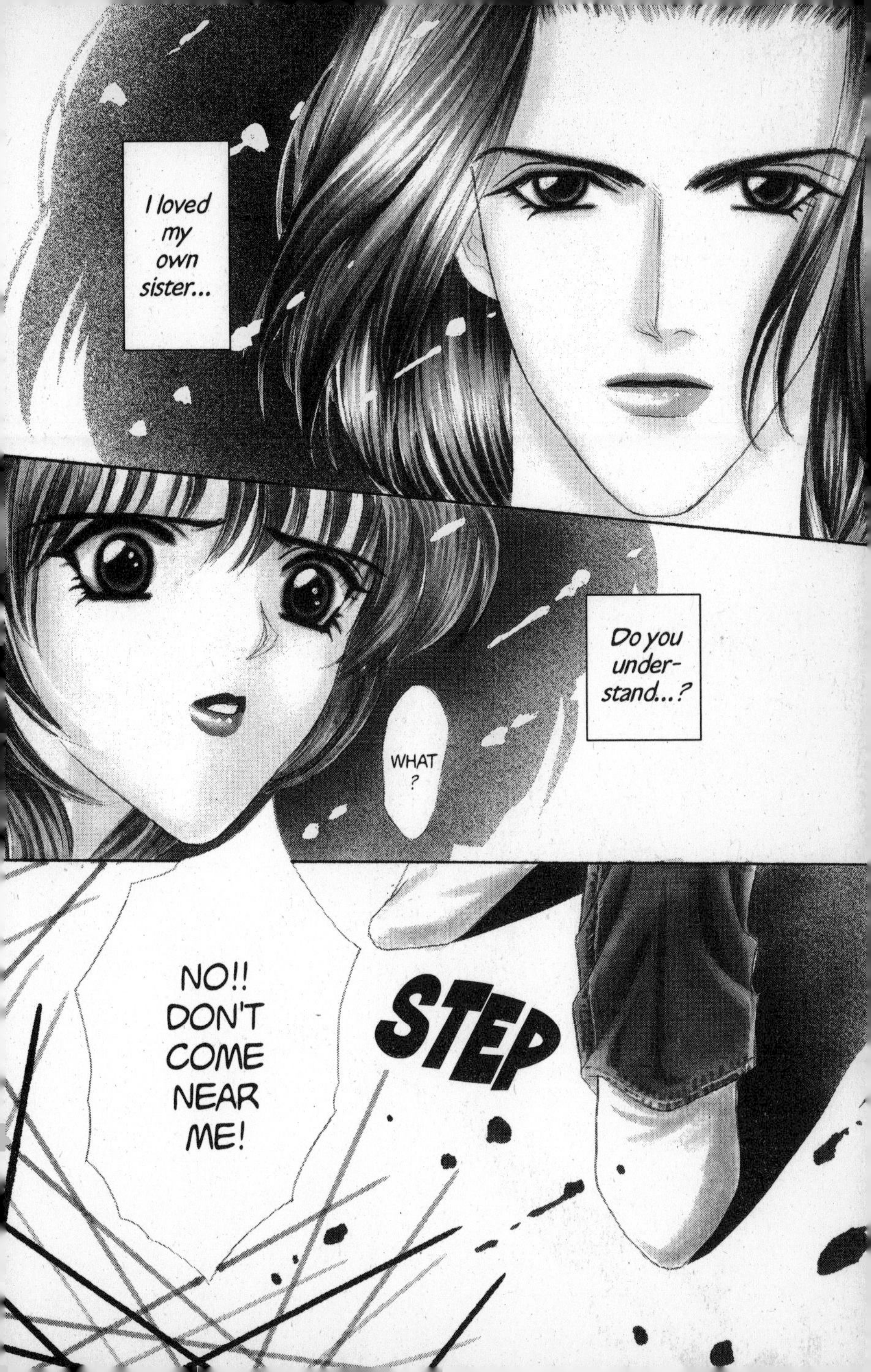
I loved my own sister...
Do you under-stand...?
WHAT ?
STEP
NO!! DON'T COME NEAR ME!

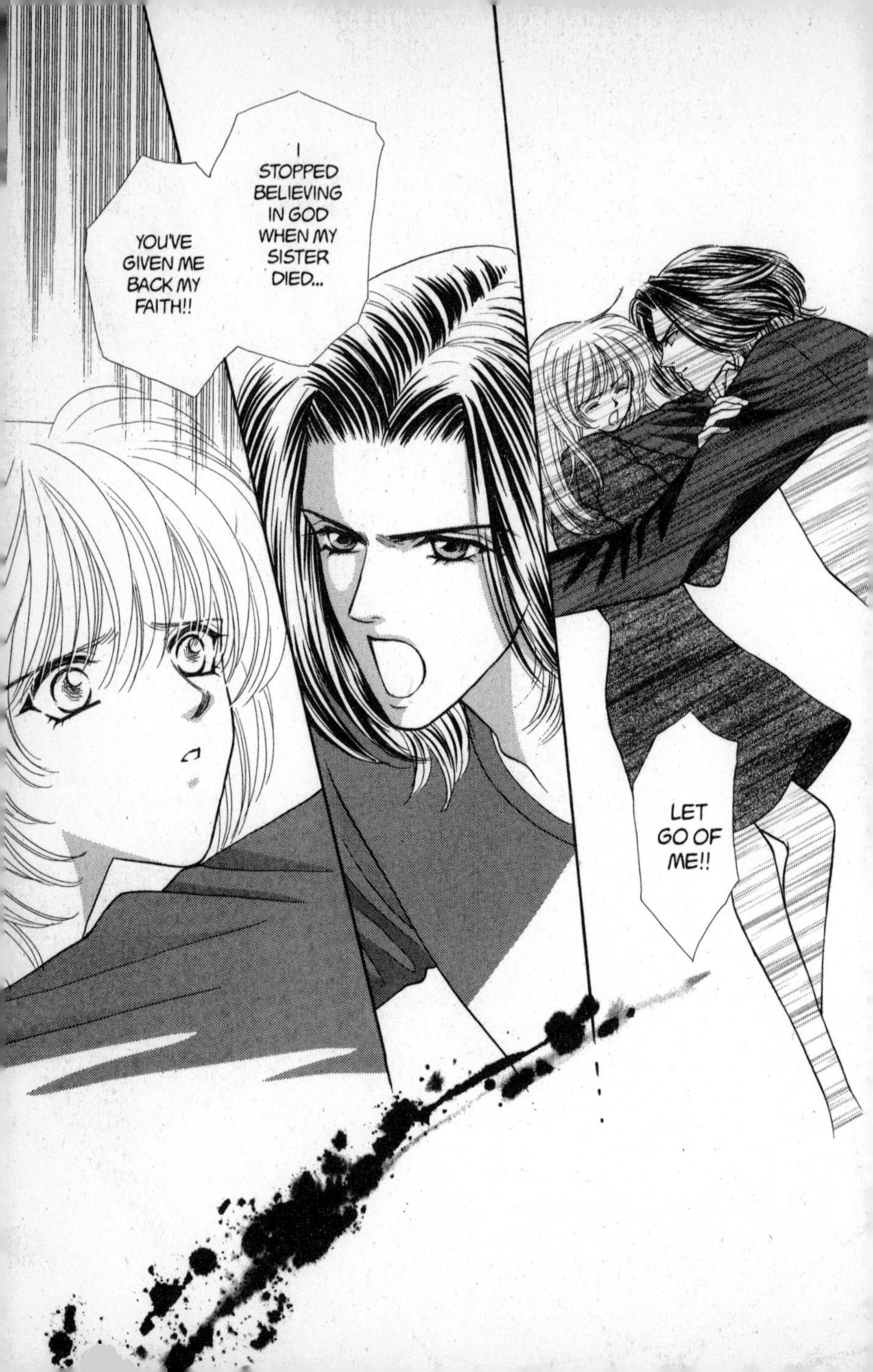
LET GO OF ME!!
I STOPPED BELIEVING IN GOD WHEN MY SISTER DIED...
YOU'VE GIVEN ME BACK MY FAITH!!

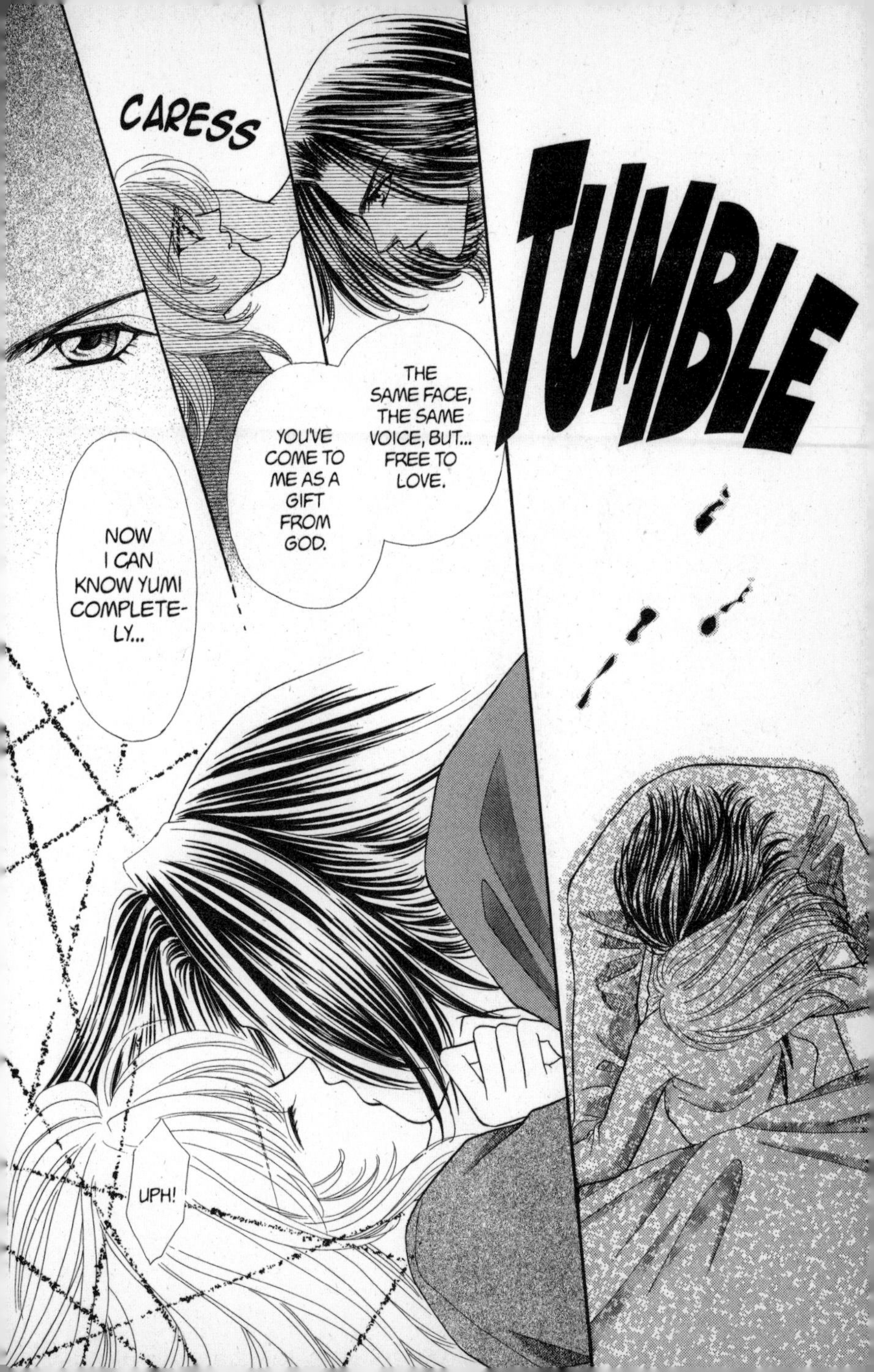
TUMBLE
THE SAME FACE, THE SAME VOICE, BUT... FREE TO LOVE.
YOU'VE COME TO ME AS A GIFT FROM GOD.
CARESS
NOW I CAN KNOW YUMI COMPLETE-LY...
UPH!

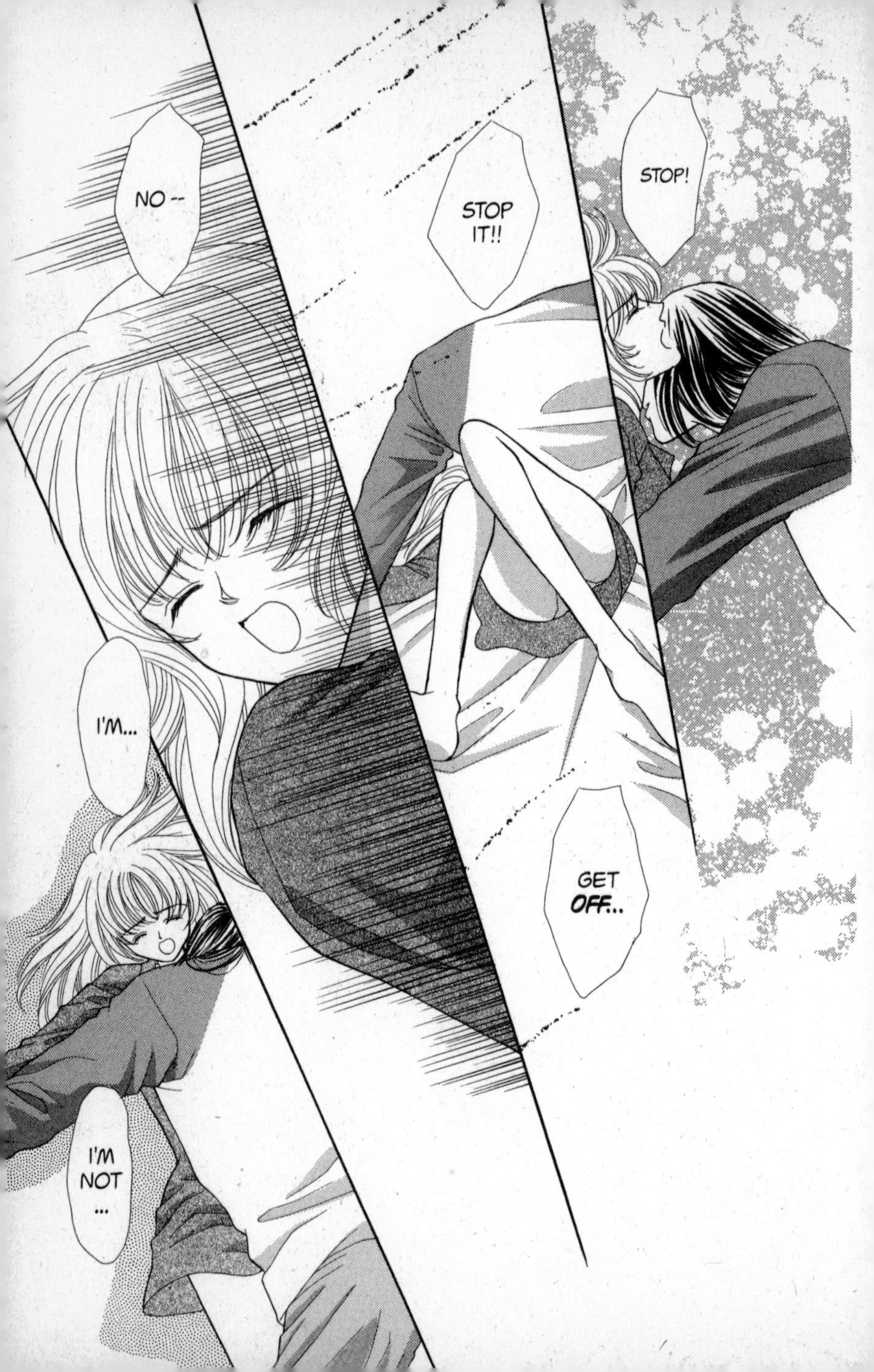
STOP!
STOP IT!!
GET OFF...
NO --
I'M...
I'M NOT ...

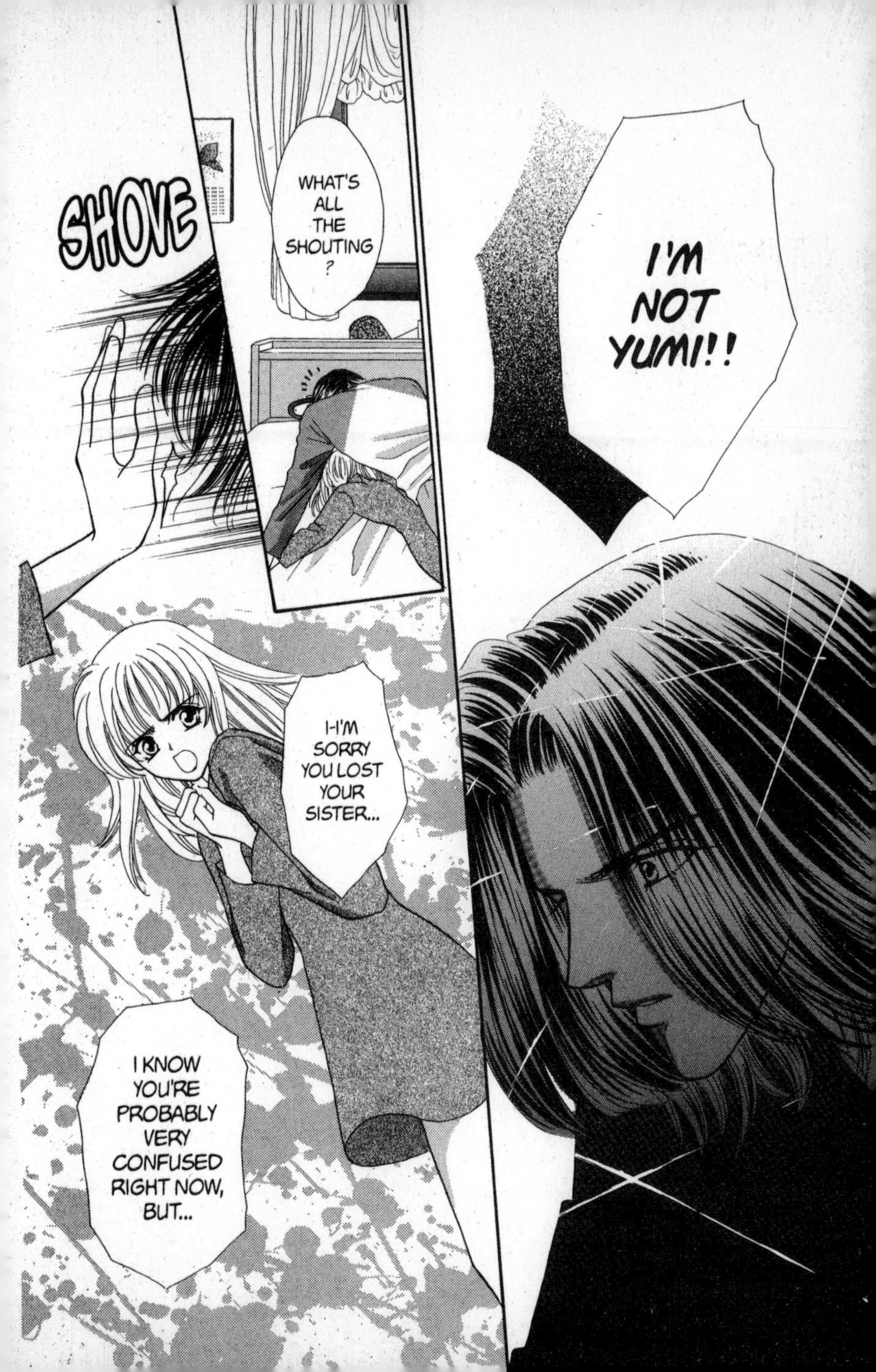
I'M NOT YUMI!!
WHAT'S ALL THE SHOUTING?
SHOVE
I-I'M SORRY YOU LOST YOUR SISTER...
I KNOW YOU'RE PROBABLY VERY CONFUSED RIGHT NOW, BUT...

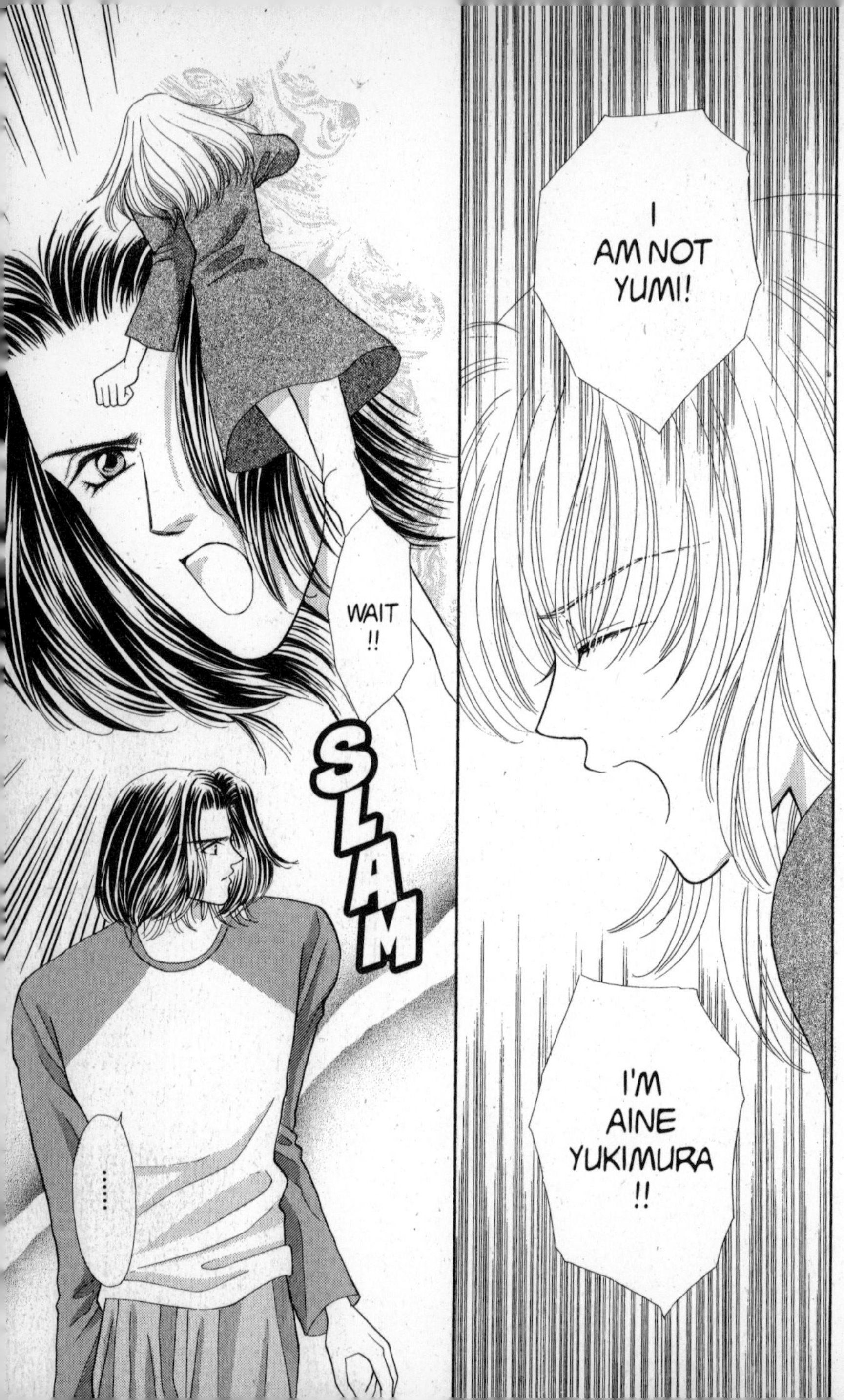
I AM NOT YUMI!
I'M AINE YUKIMURA !!
WAIT !!
SLAM
……

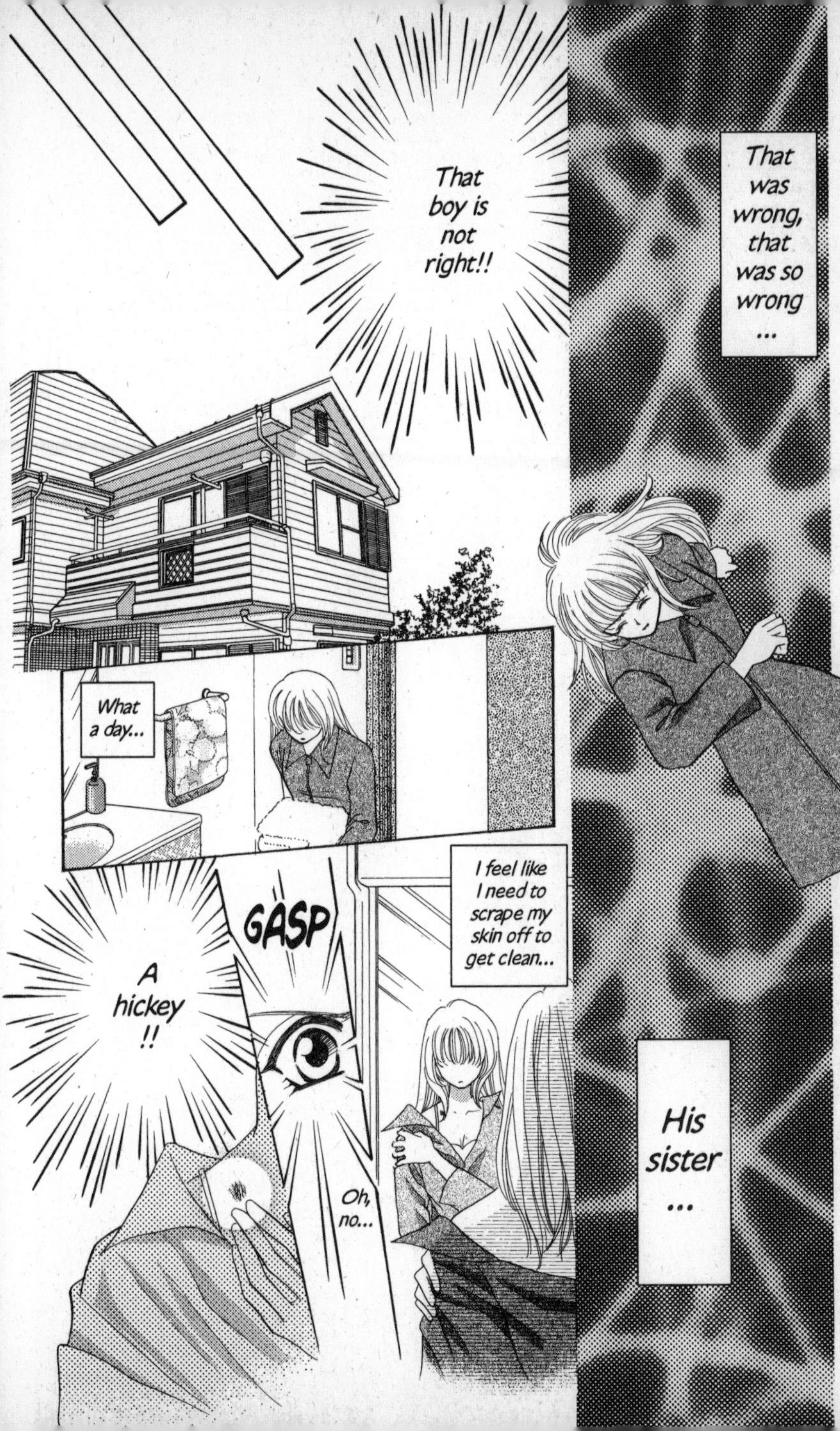
That was wrong, that was so wrong...
His sister...
That boy is not right!!
What a day...
I feel like I need to scrape my skin off to get clean...
Oh, no...
GASP
A hickey!!

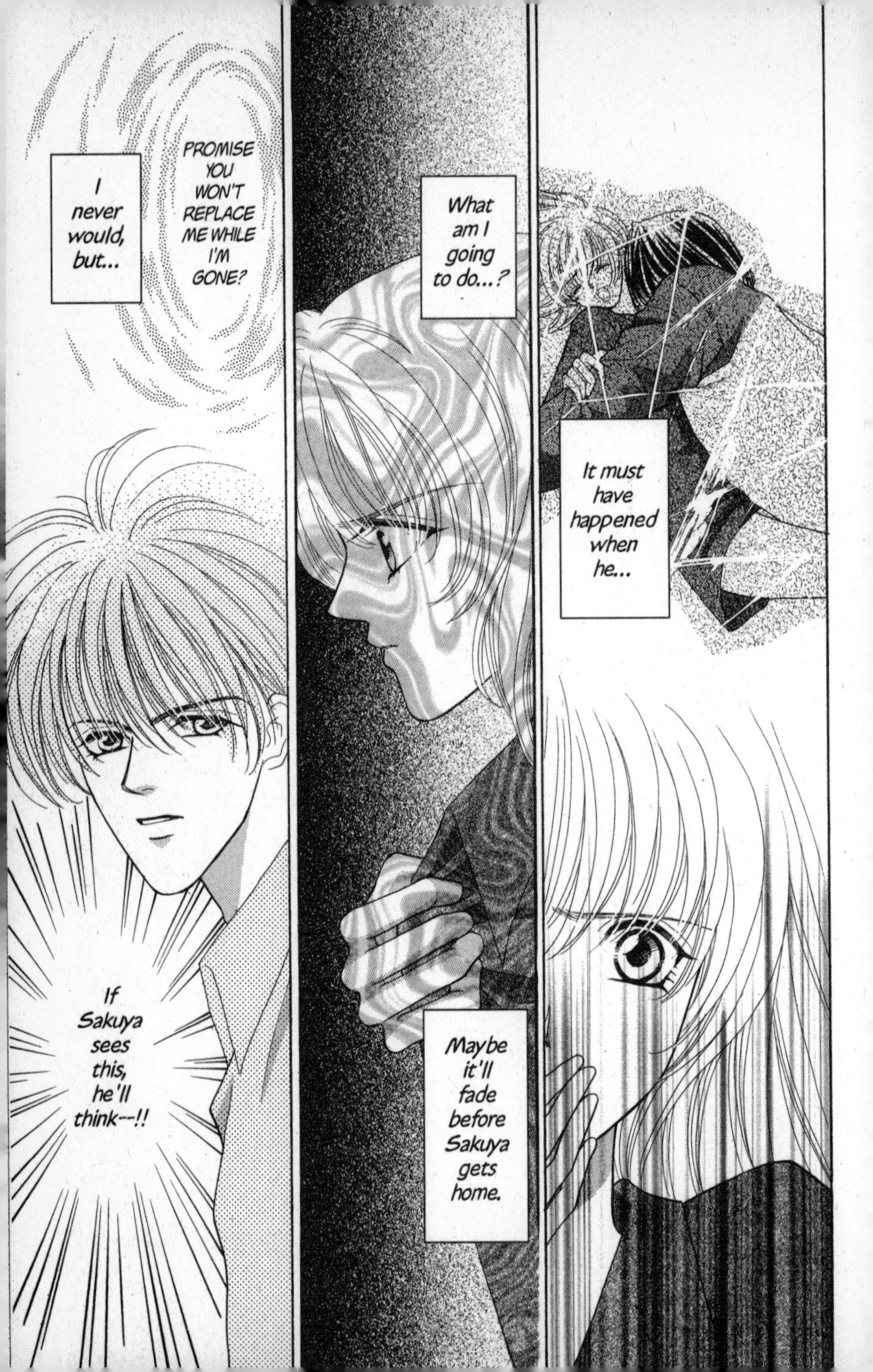
It must have happened when he...
What am I going to do...?
Maybe it'll fade before Sakuya gets home.
PROMISE YOU WON'T REPLACE ME WHILE I'M GONE?
I never would, but...
If Sakuya sees this, he'll think--!!

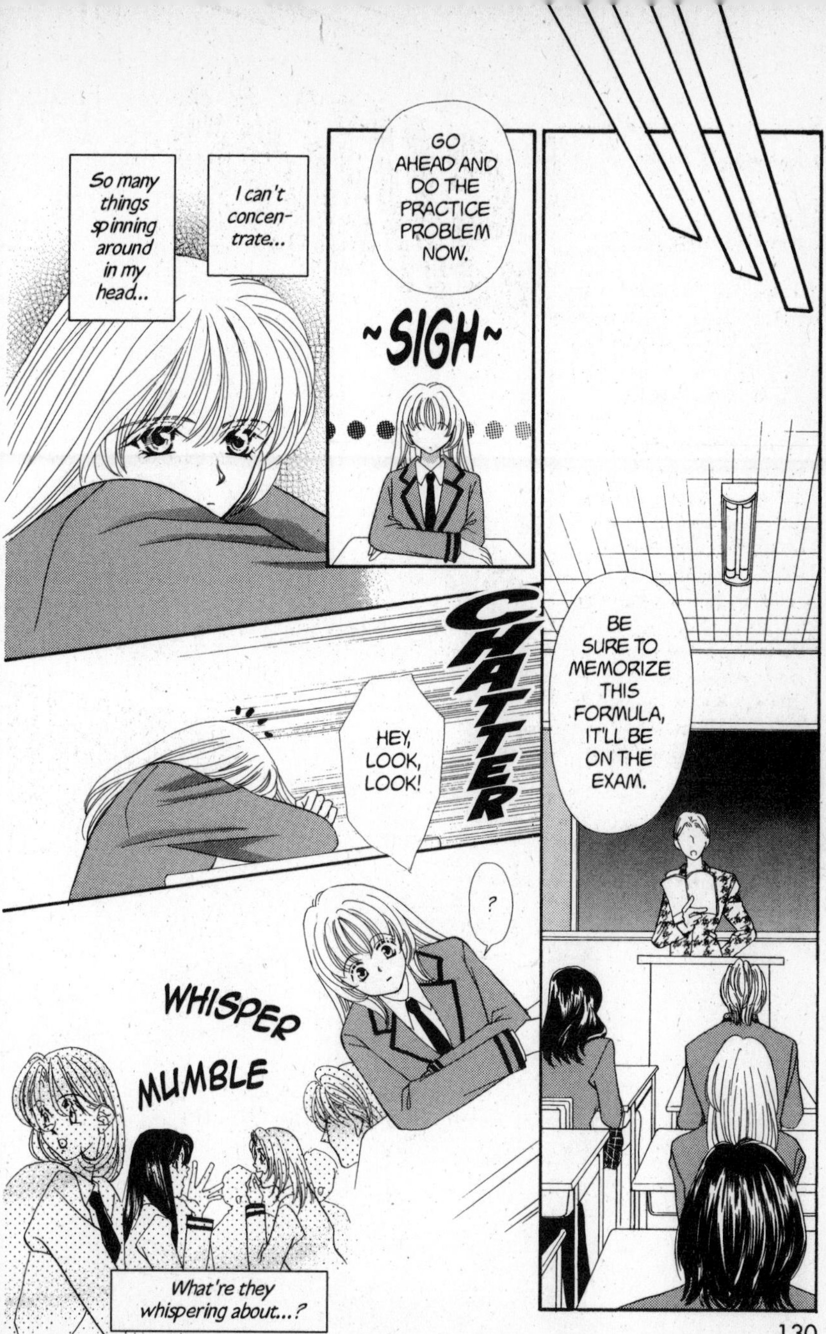

BE SURE TO MEMORIZE THIS FORMULA, IT'LL BE ON THE EXAM.
GO AHEAD AND DO THE PRACTICE PROBLEM NOW.
~SIGH~
I can't concen-trate...
So many things spinning around in my head...
CHATTER
HEY, LOOK, LOOK!
?
WHISPER
MUMBLE
What're they whispering about...?

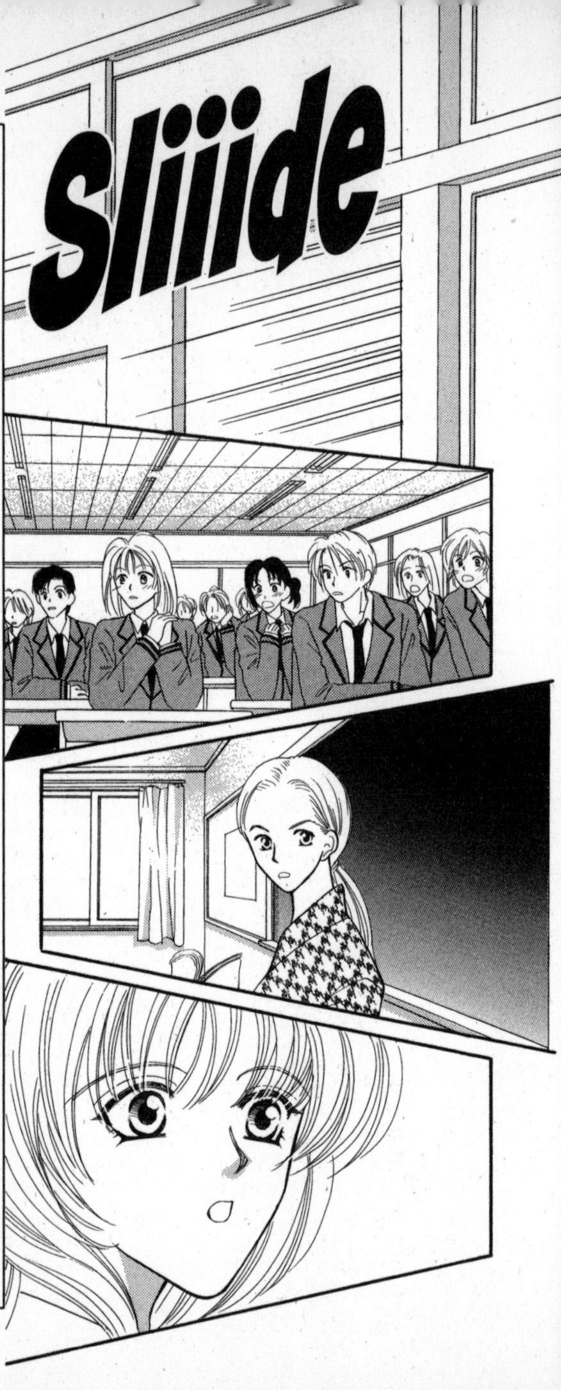
Sliiide

BIG NEWS!!

Finally!!
Sensual Phrase on CD!!

Songs like "Birdsong" and "Cruel Jones" finally set to music! There'll be other fun features, too, so look for details in Sho-comics!

When I started this project, I hoped that something like this might happen one day, but it's turning out even better than I had hoped. Start saving your allowance! I'm really excited.

The only cast member confirmed so far is Takehito Koyasu as Sakuya, but by the time this volume comes out, I should know a lot more.

So, those of you who requested it, your interest made it happen! Thank you!

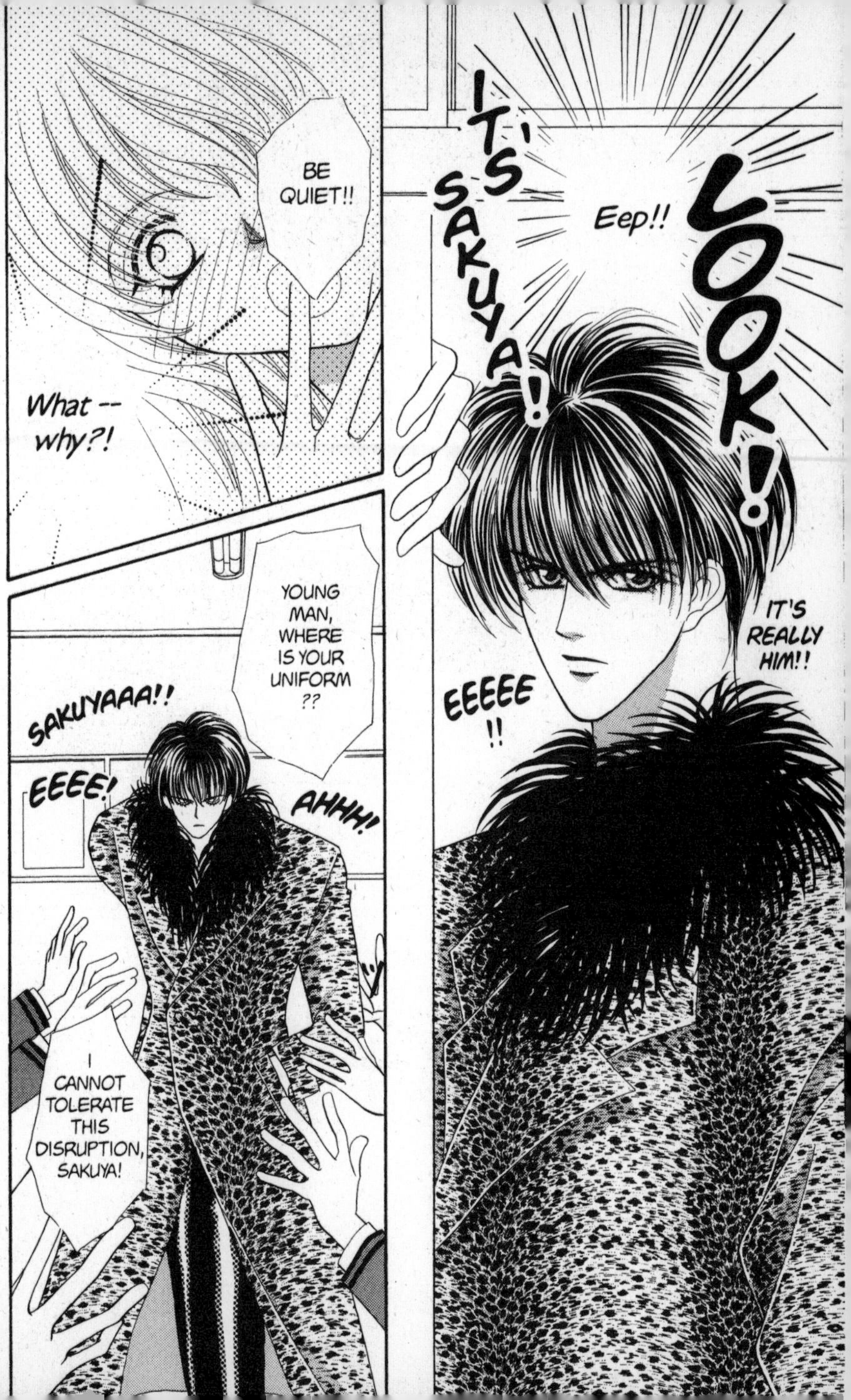
LOOK!
Eep!!
IT'S SAKUYA!
IT'S REALLY HIM!!
EEEEE !!
BE QUIET!!
What -- why?!
YOUNG MAN, WHERE IS YOUR UNIFORM ??
SAKUYAAA!!
AHHH!
EEEE!
I CANNOT TOLERATE THIS DISRUPTION, SAKUYA!

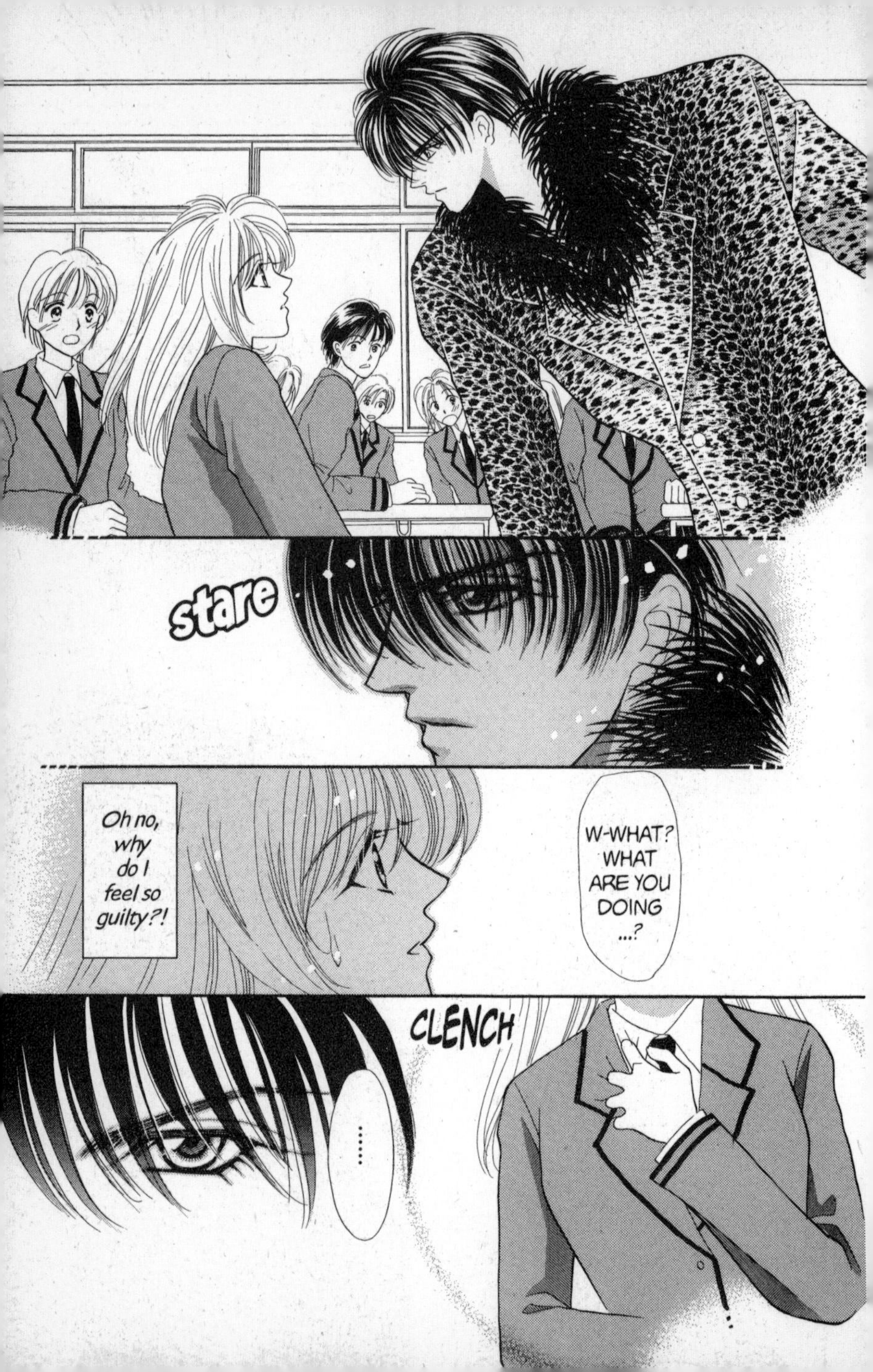
stare
W-WHAT? WHAT ARE YOU DOING ...?
Oh no, why do I feel so guilty?!
CLENCH
......

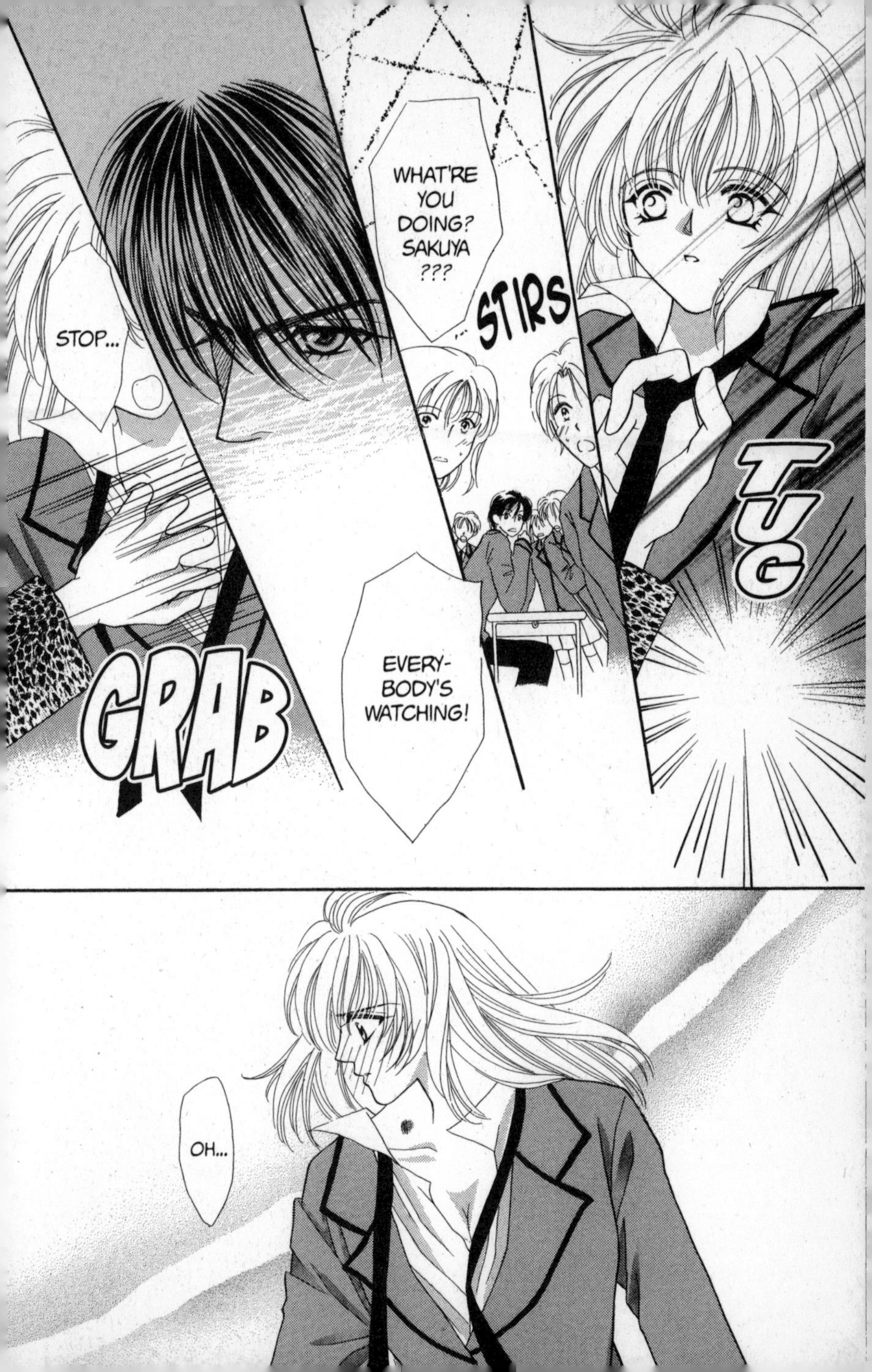
TUG
WHAT'RE YOU DOING? SAKUYA ???
STIRS
EVERY-BODY'S WATCHING!
STOP...
GRAB
OH...

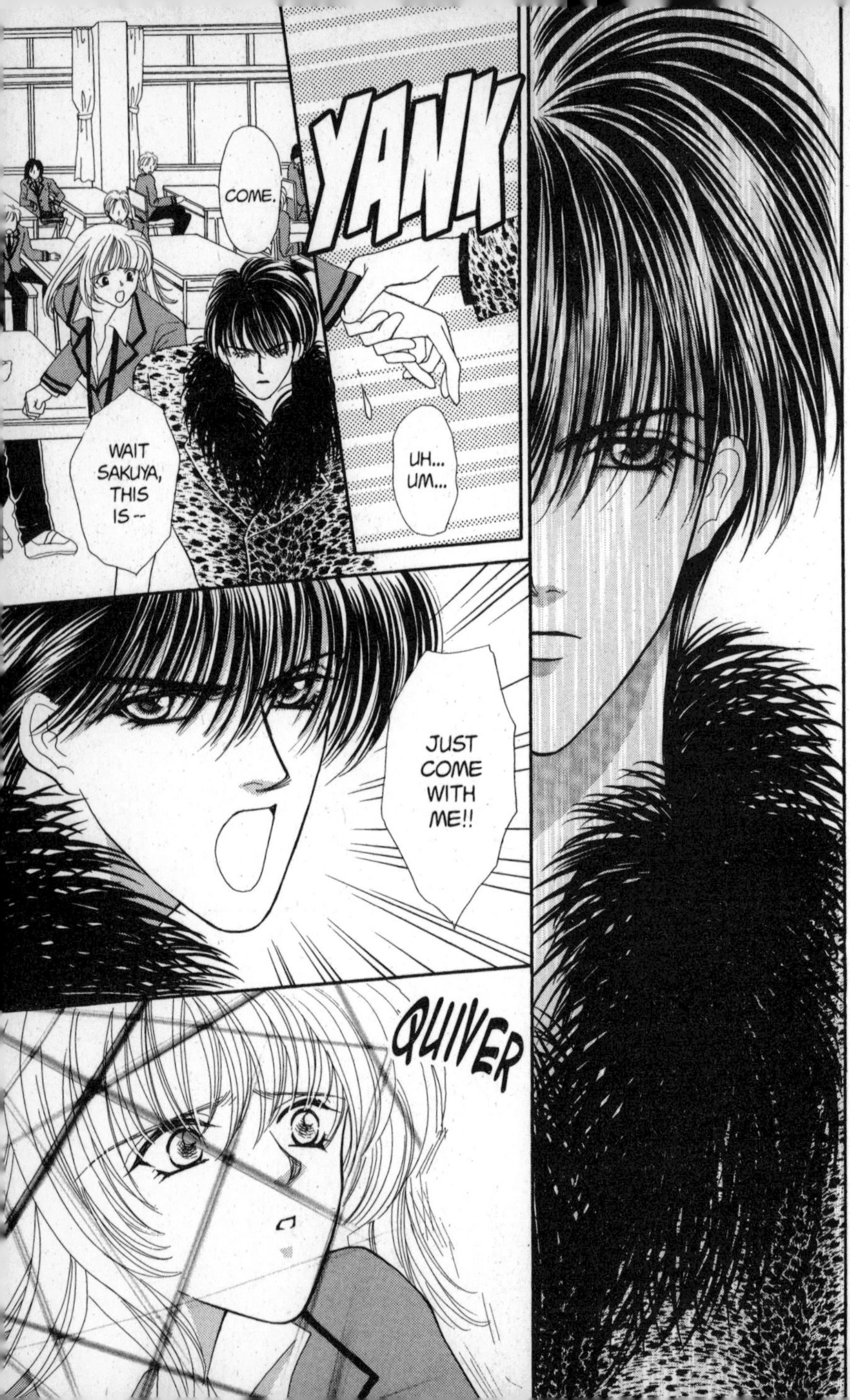
YANK
UH... UM...
COME.
WAIT SAKUYA, THIS IS --
JUST COME WITH ME!!
QUIVER

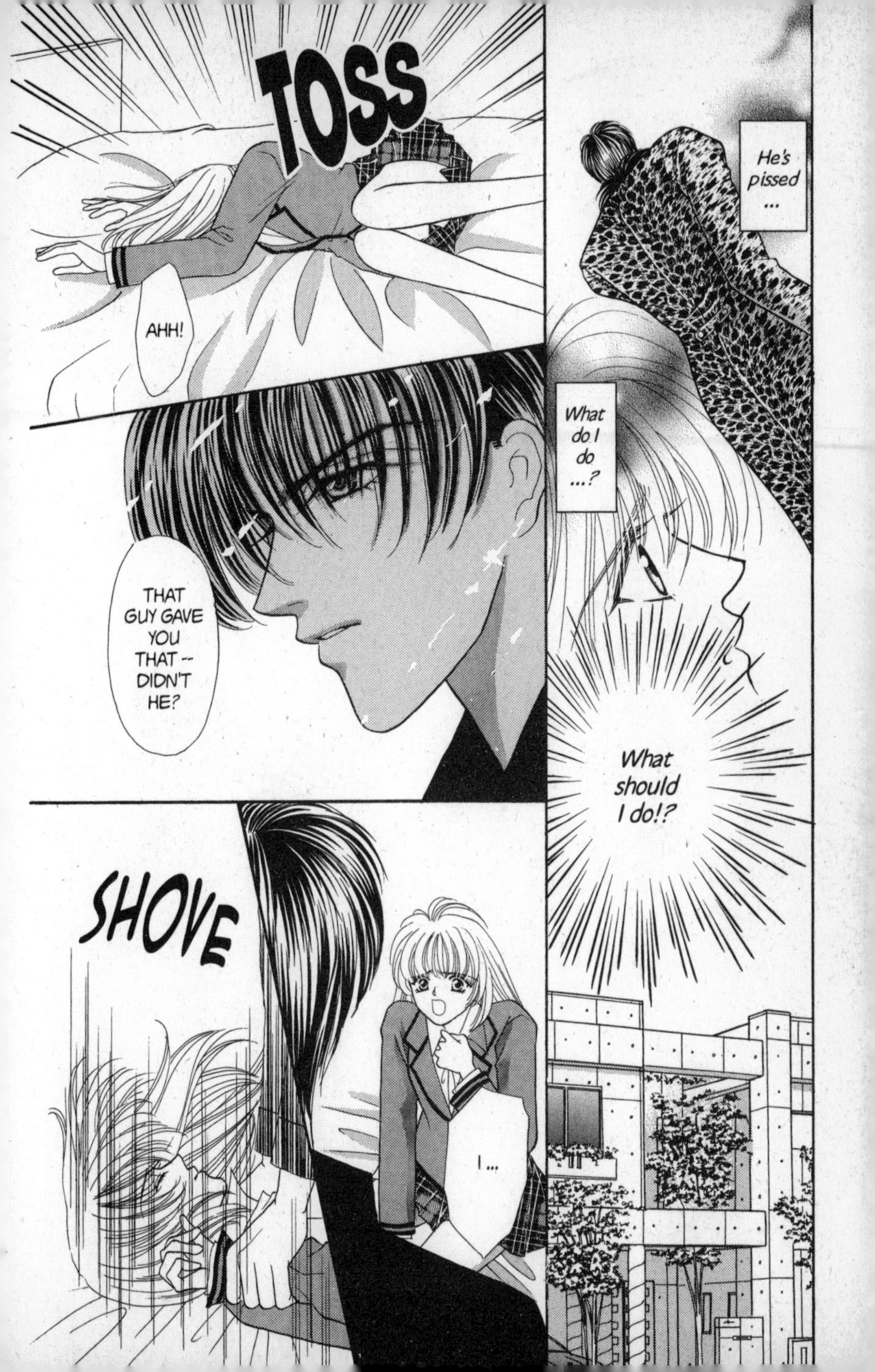
He's pissed ...
What do I do ...?
What should I do!?
TOSS
AHH!
THAT GUY GAVE YOU THAT -- DIDN'T HE?
SHOVE
I ...

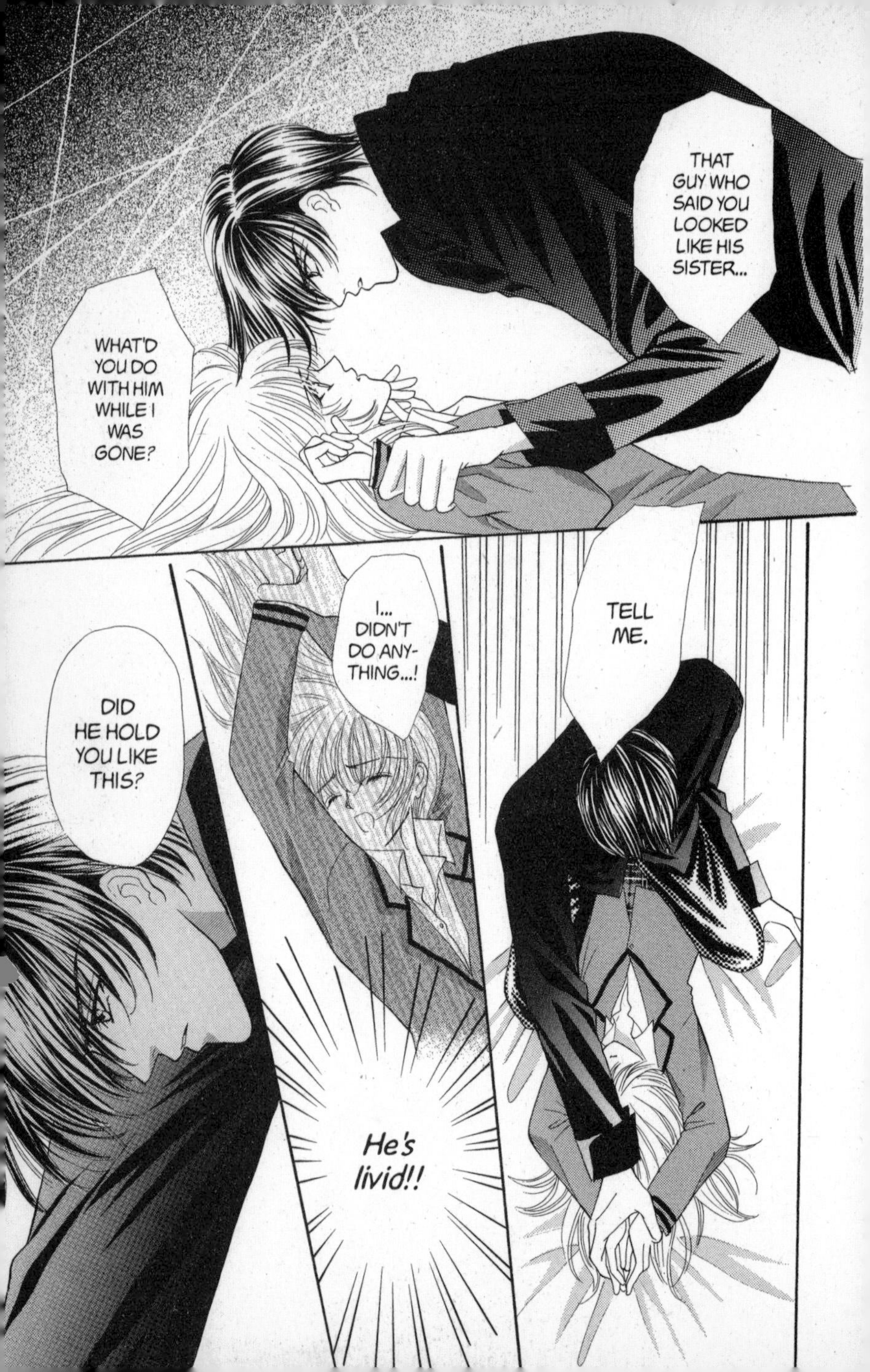
THAT GUY WHO SAID YOU LOOKED LIKE HIS SISTER...
WHAT'D YOU DO WITH HIM WHILE I WAS GONE?
TELL ME.
I... DIDN'T DO ANY-THING...!
He's livid!!
DID HE HOLD YOU LIKE THIS?

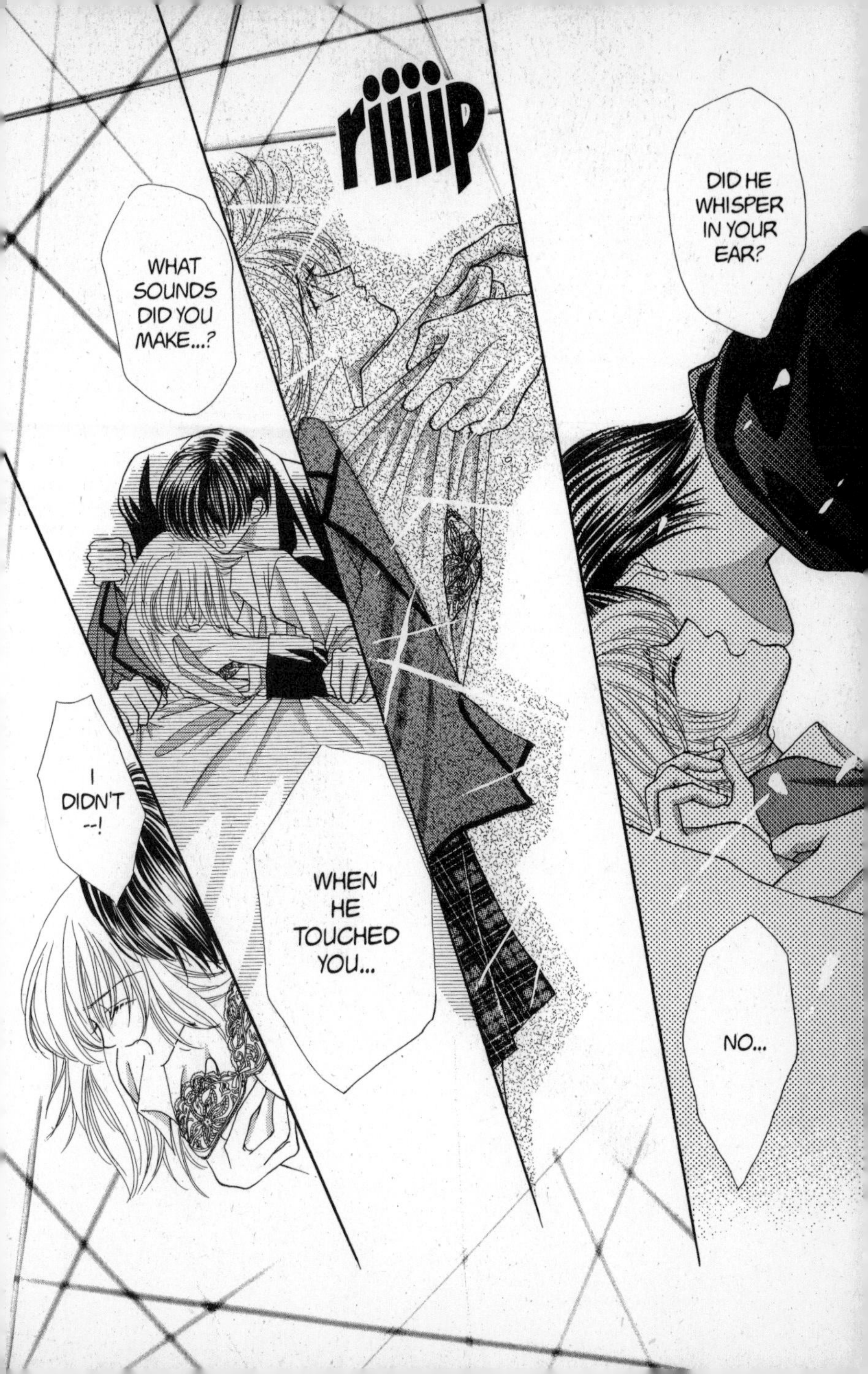
DID HE WHISPER IN YOUR EAR?
NO...
riiiip
WHAT SOUNDS DID YOU MAKE...?
WHEN HE TOUCHED YOU...
I DIDN'T --!

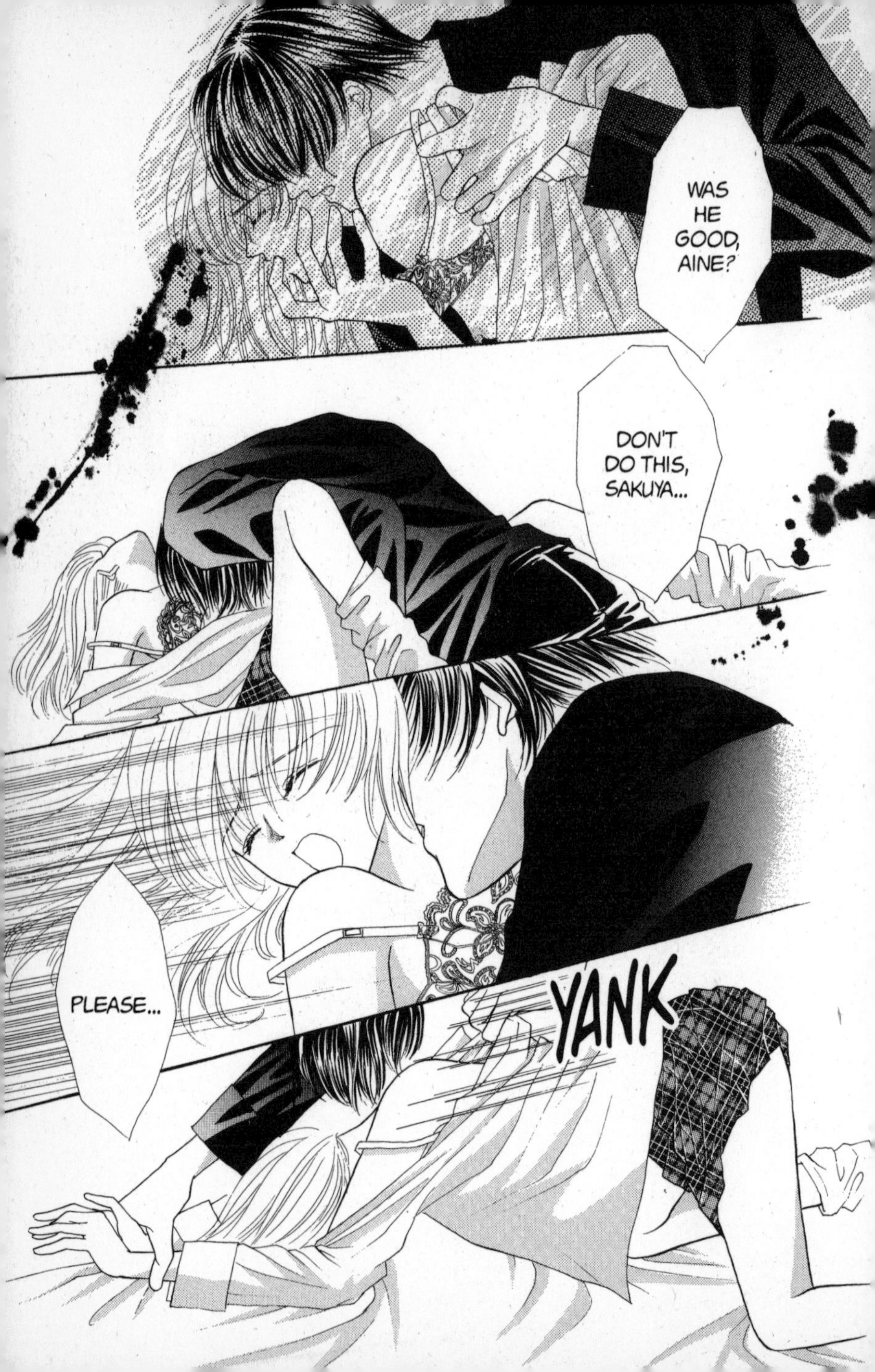
WAS HE GOOD, AINE?
DON'T DO THIS, SAKUYA...
YANK
PLEASE...

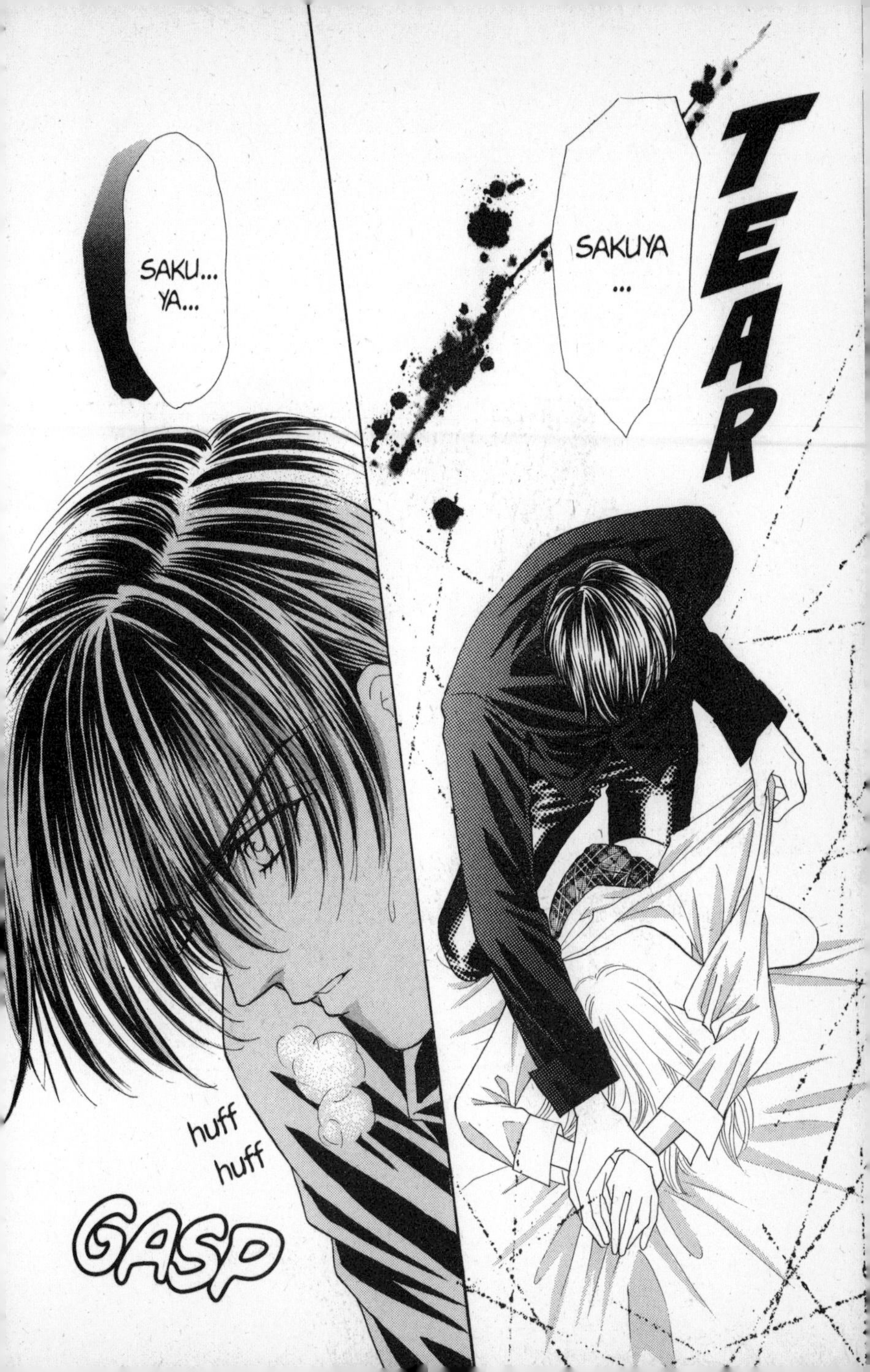
SAKUYA ...
TEAR
SAKU... YA...
huff huff
GASP

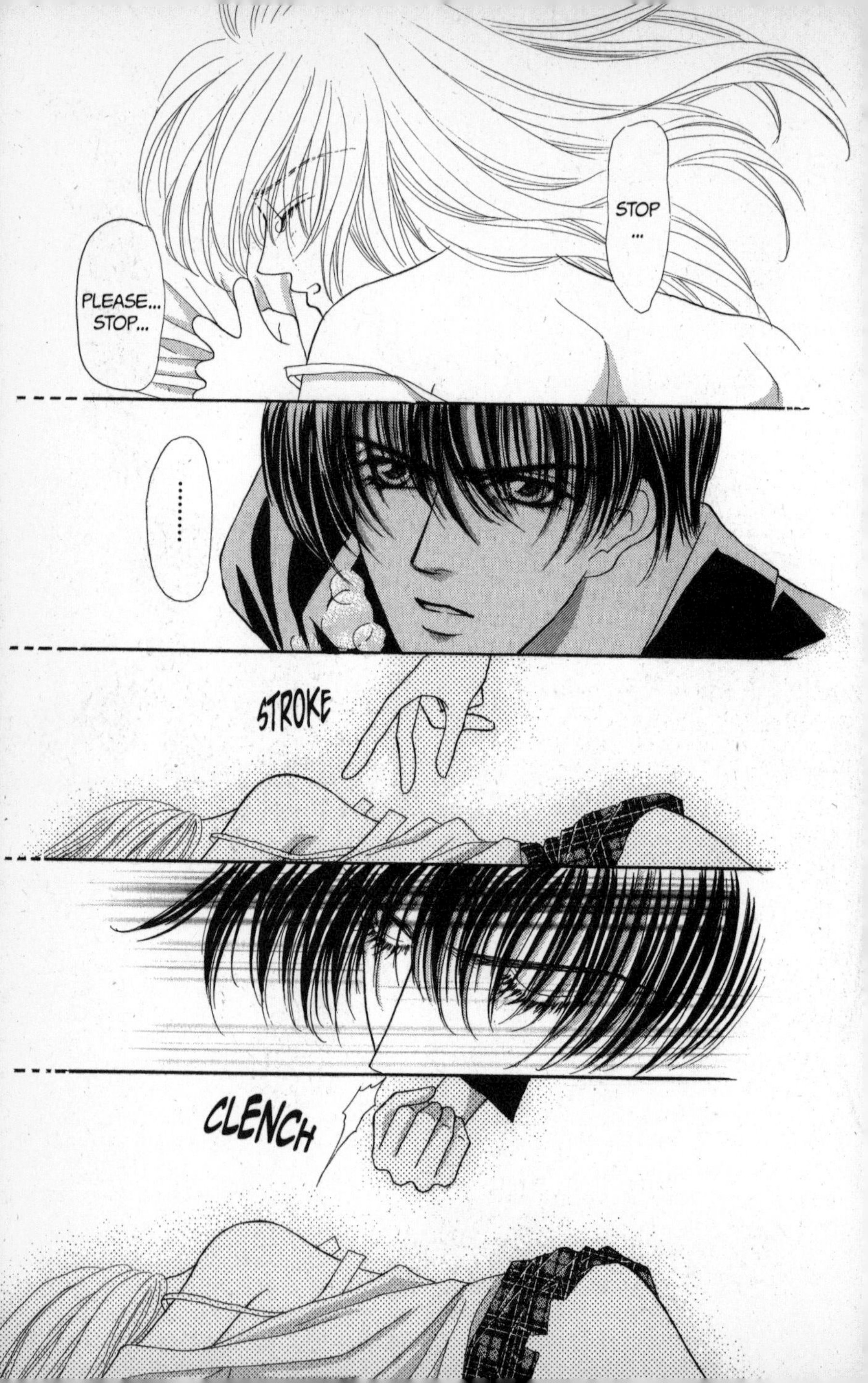
STOP ...
PLEASE... STOP...
......
STROKE
CLENCH

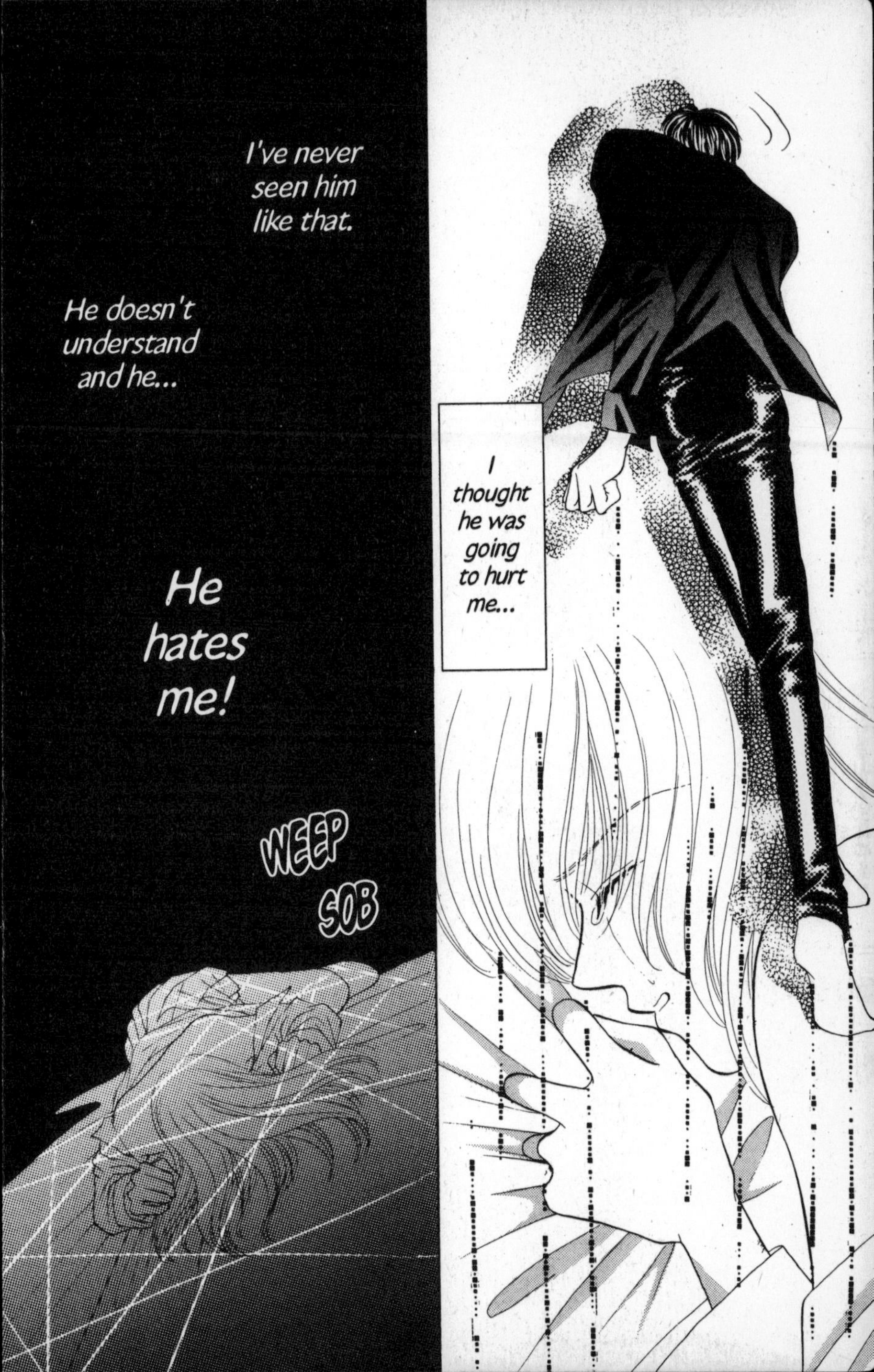
I thought he was going to hurt me...
I've never seen him like that.
He doesn't understand and he...
He hates me!
WEEP
SOB

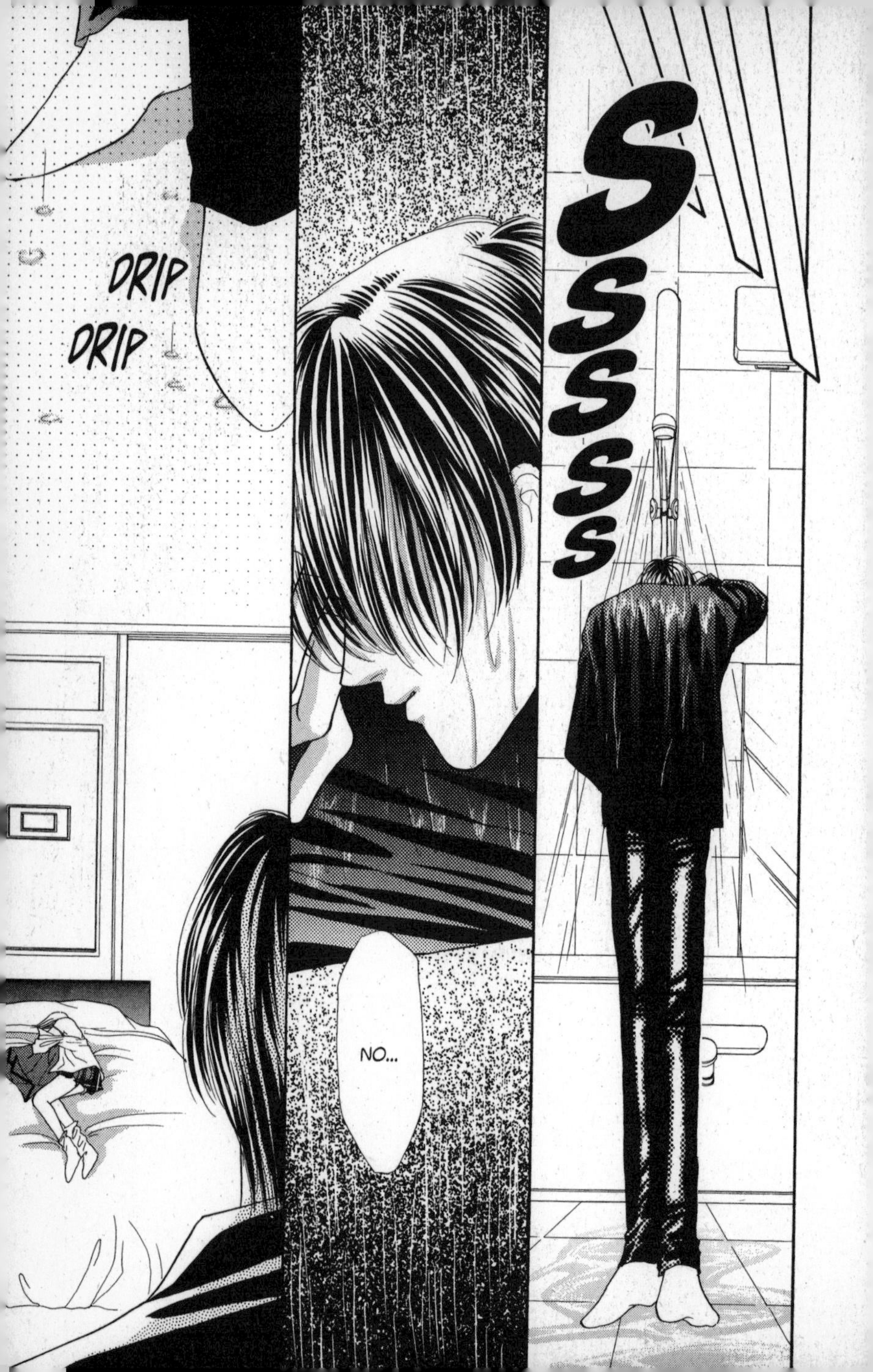
SSSSSS
NO...
DRIP
DRIP

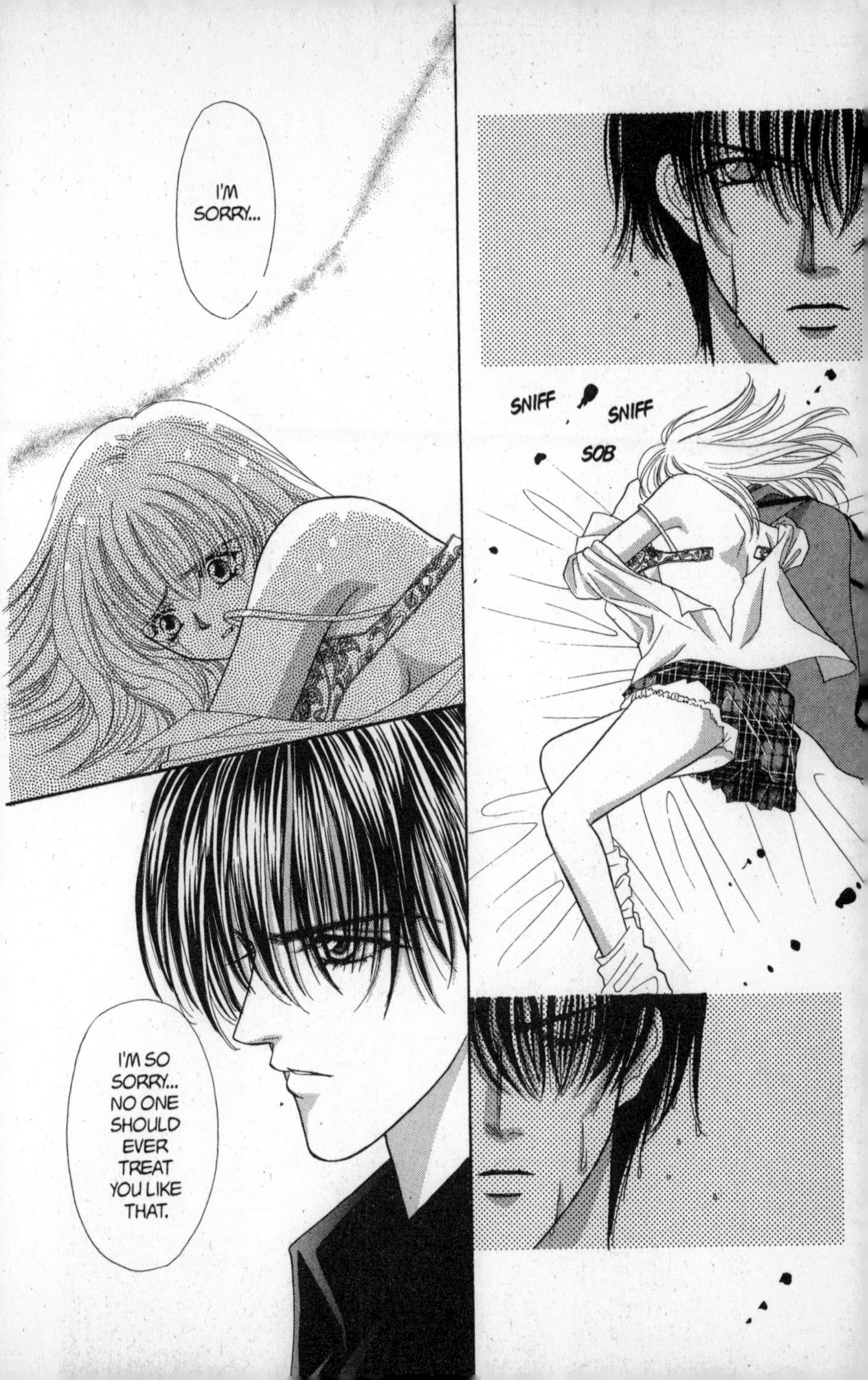
SNIFF
SNIFF
SOB
I'M SORRY...
I'M SO SORRY... NO ONE SHOULD EVER TREAT YOU LIKE THAT.

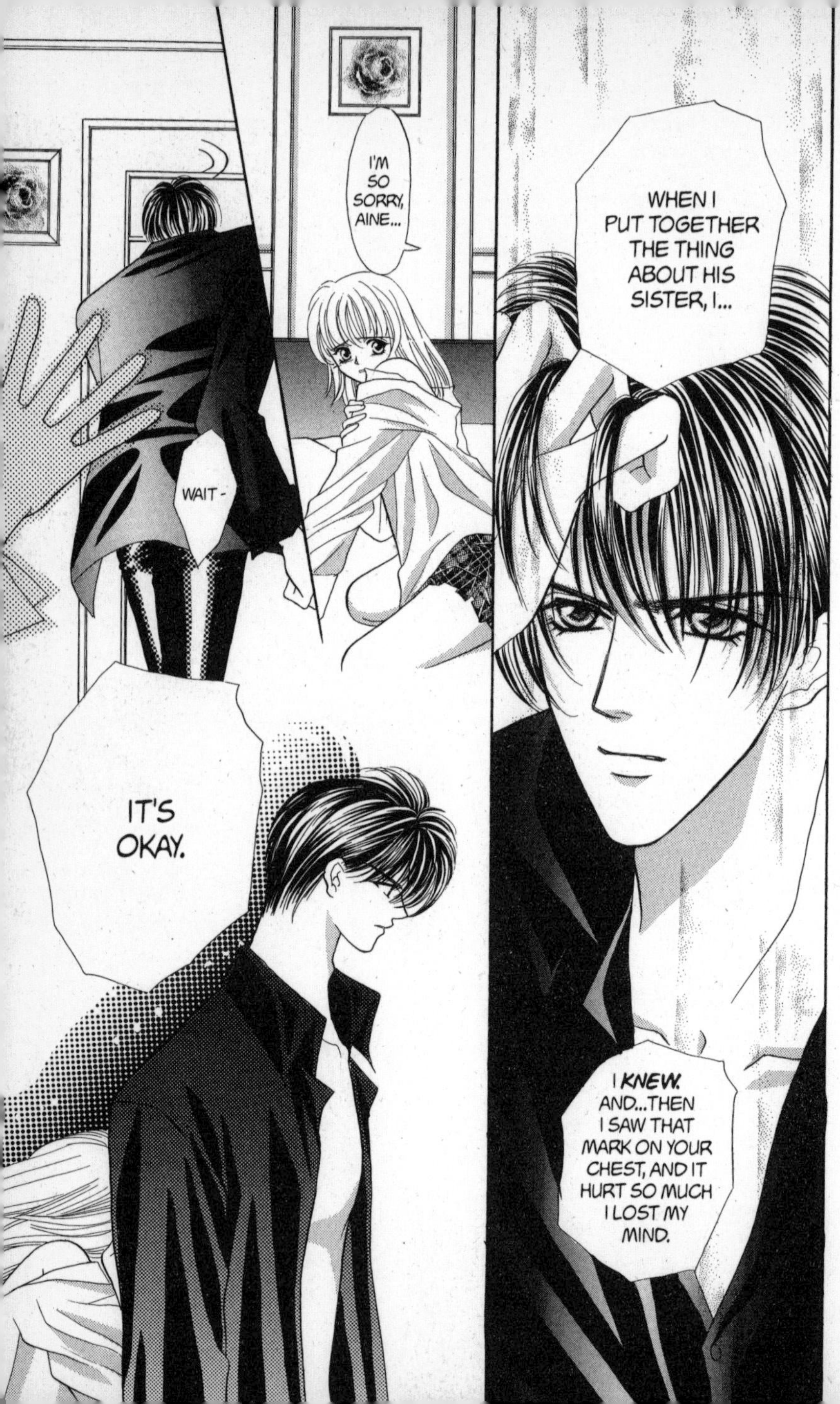
WHEN I PUT TOGETHER THE THING ABOUT HIS SISTER, I...
I KNEW. AND...THEN I SAW THAT MARK ON YOUR CHEST, AND IT HURT SO MUCH I LOST MY MIND.
I'M SO SORRY, AINE...
WAIT -
IT'S OKAY.

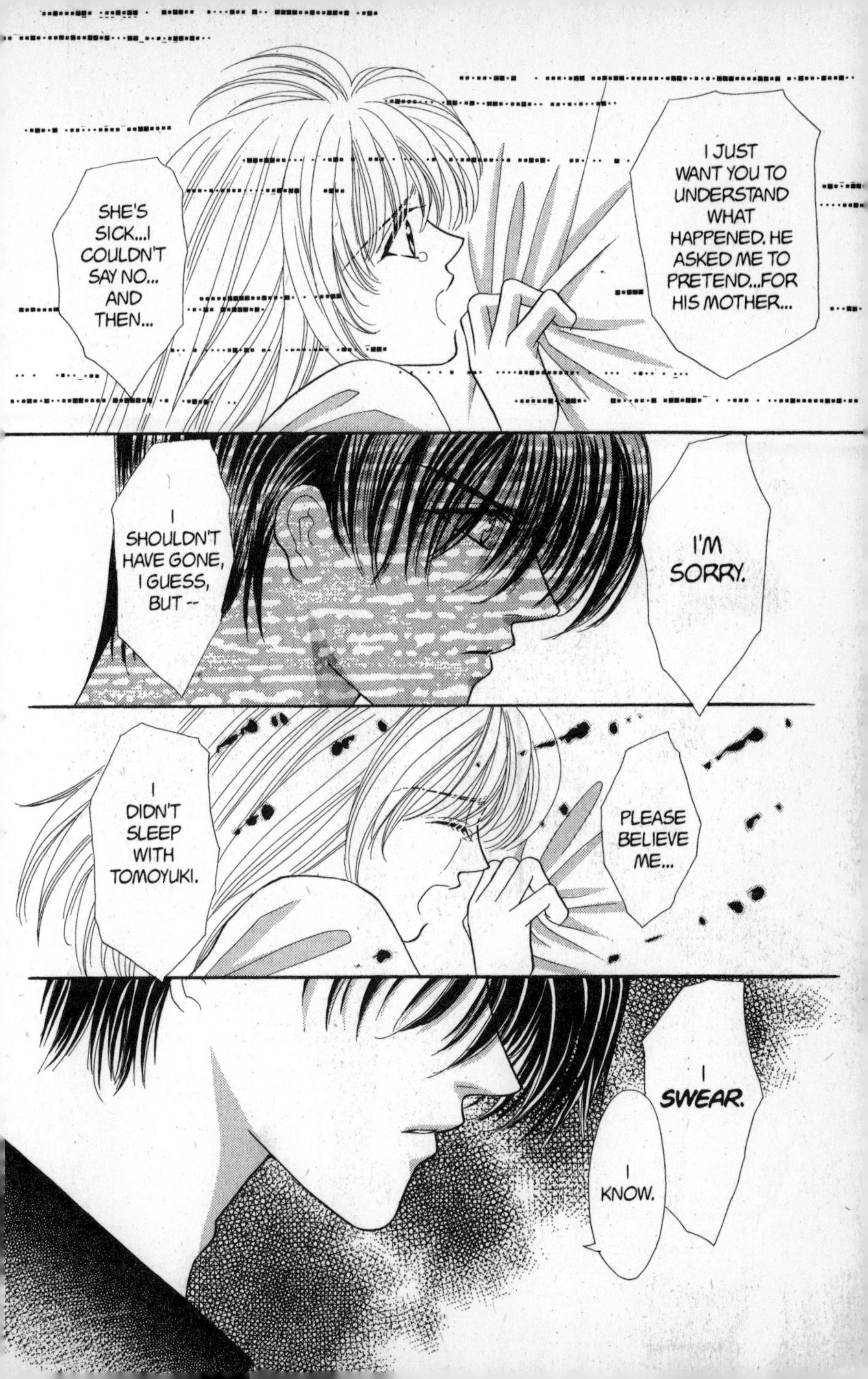
I JUST WANT YOU TO UNDERSTAND WHAT HAPPENED. HE ASKED ME TO PRETEND...FOR HIS MOTHER...
SHE'S SICK...I COULDN'T SAY NO... AND THEN...
I'M SORRY.
I SHOULDN'T HAVE GONE, I GUESS, BUT --
PLEASE BELIEVE ME...
I DIDN'T SLEEP WITH TOMOYUKI.
I **SWEAR.**
I KNOW.

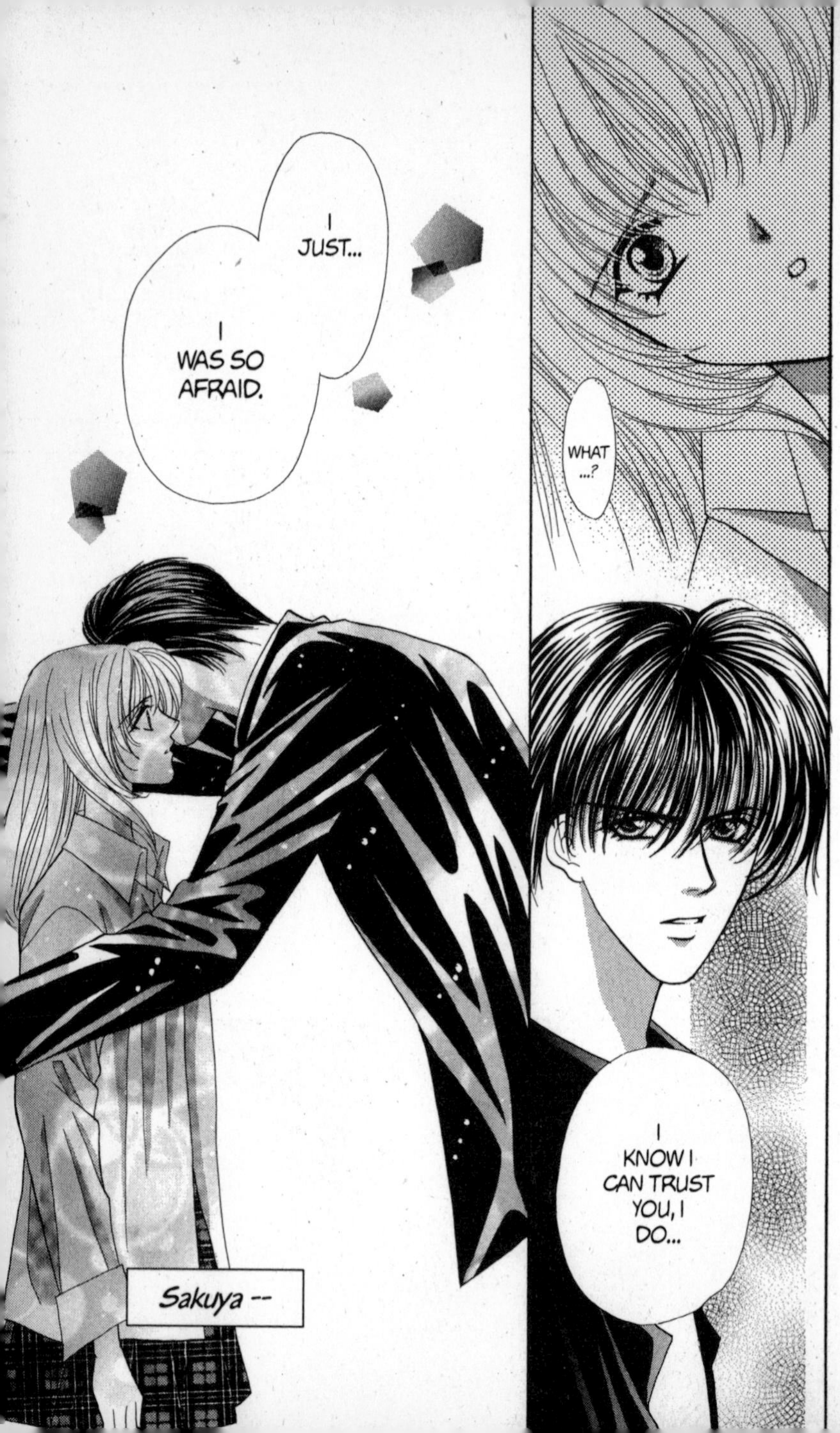
WHAT ...?
I KNOW I CAN TRUST YOU, I DO...
I JUST...
I WAS SO AFRAID.
Sakuya --

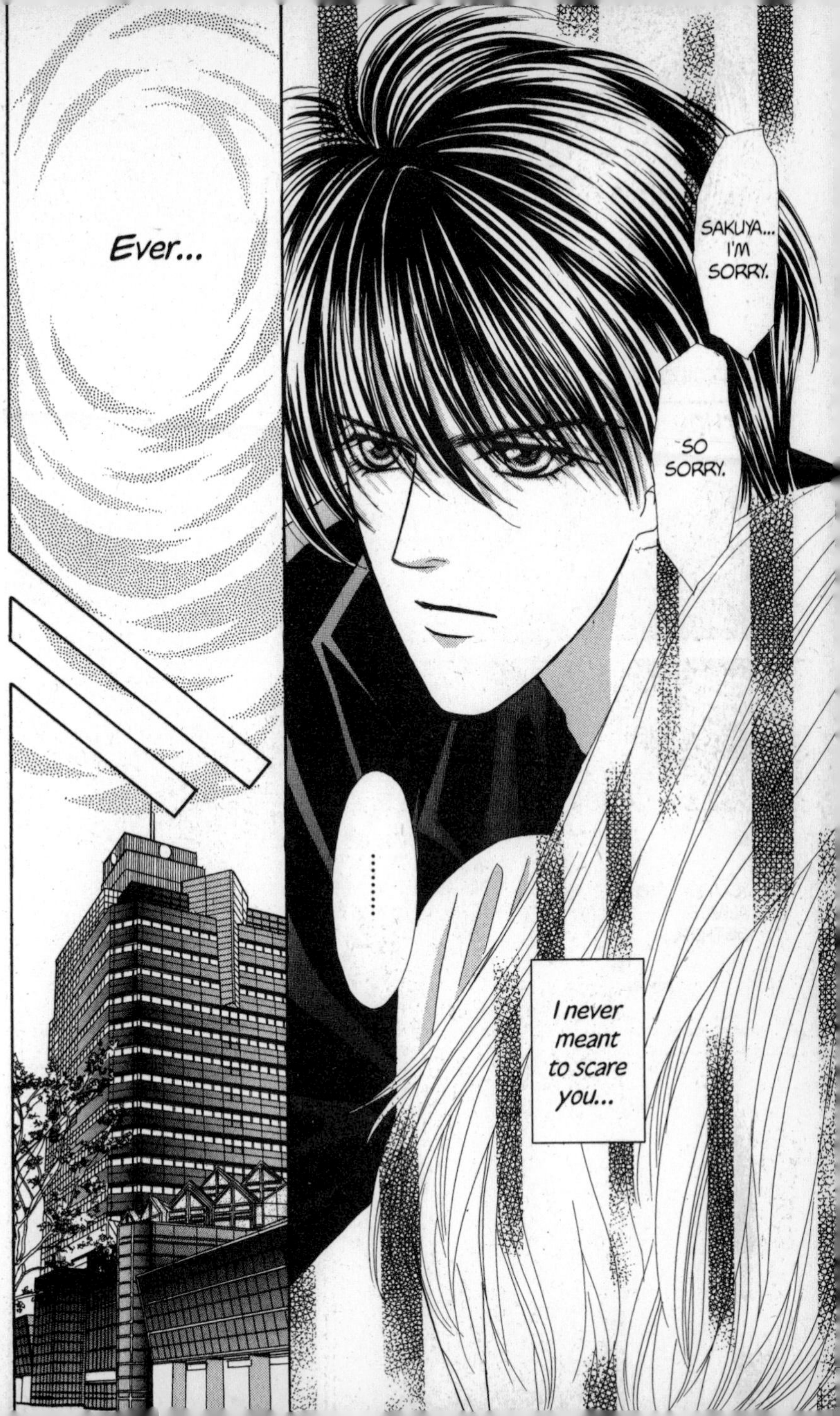
SAKUYA... I'M SORRY.
SO SORRY.
I never meant to scare you...
......
Ever...

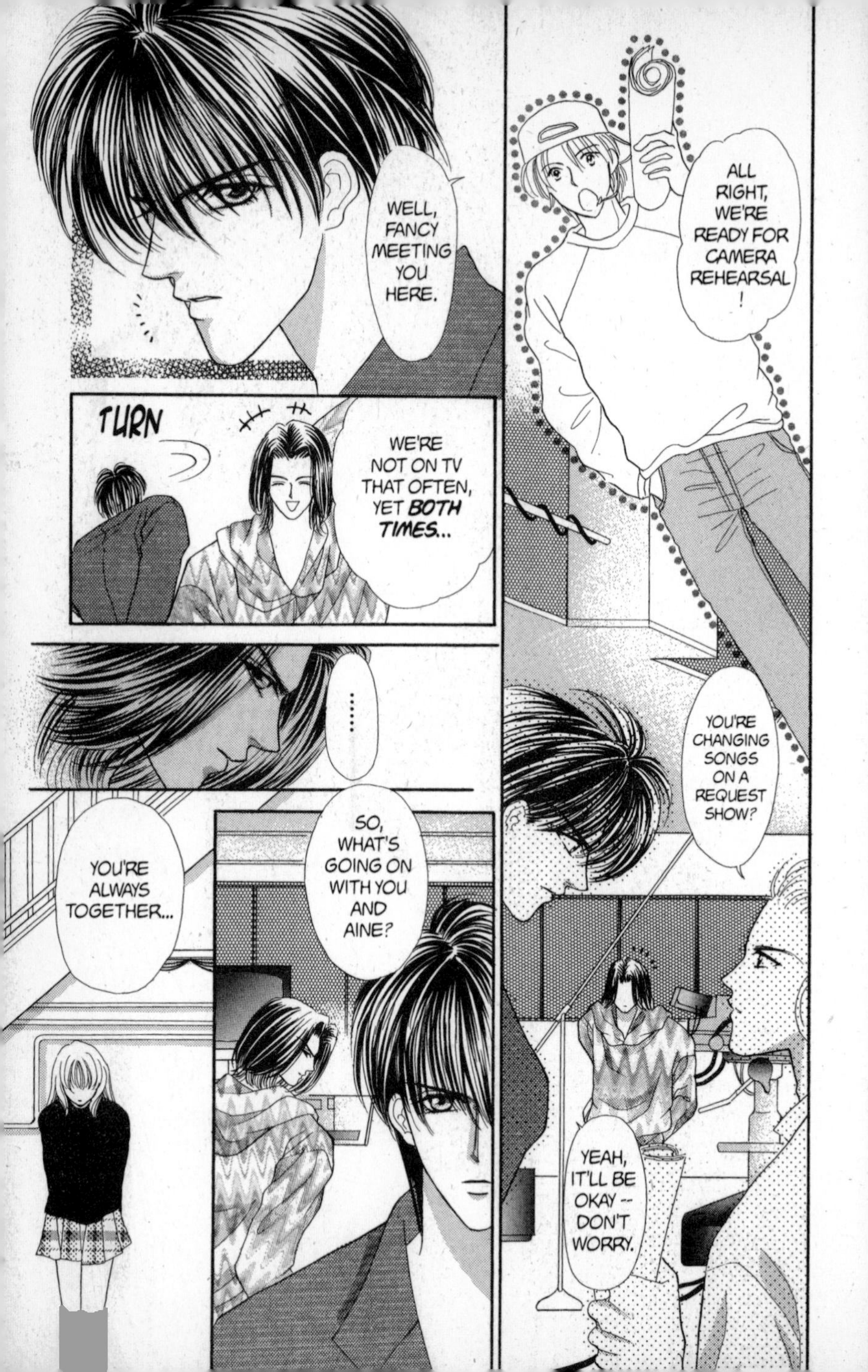
ALL RIGHT, WE'RE READY FOR CAMERA REHEARSAL!
YOU'RE CHANGING SONGS ON A REQUEST SHOW?
YEAH, IT'LL BE OKAY -- DON'T WORRY.
WELL, FANCY MEETING YOU HERE.
TURN
WE'RE NOT ON TV THAT OFTEN, YET **BOTH TIMES**...
......
SO, WHAT'S GOING ON WITH YOU AND AINE?
YOU'RE ALWAYS TOGETHER...

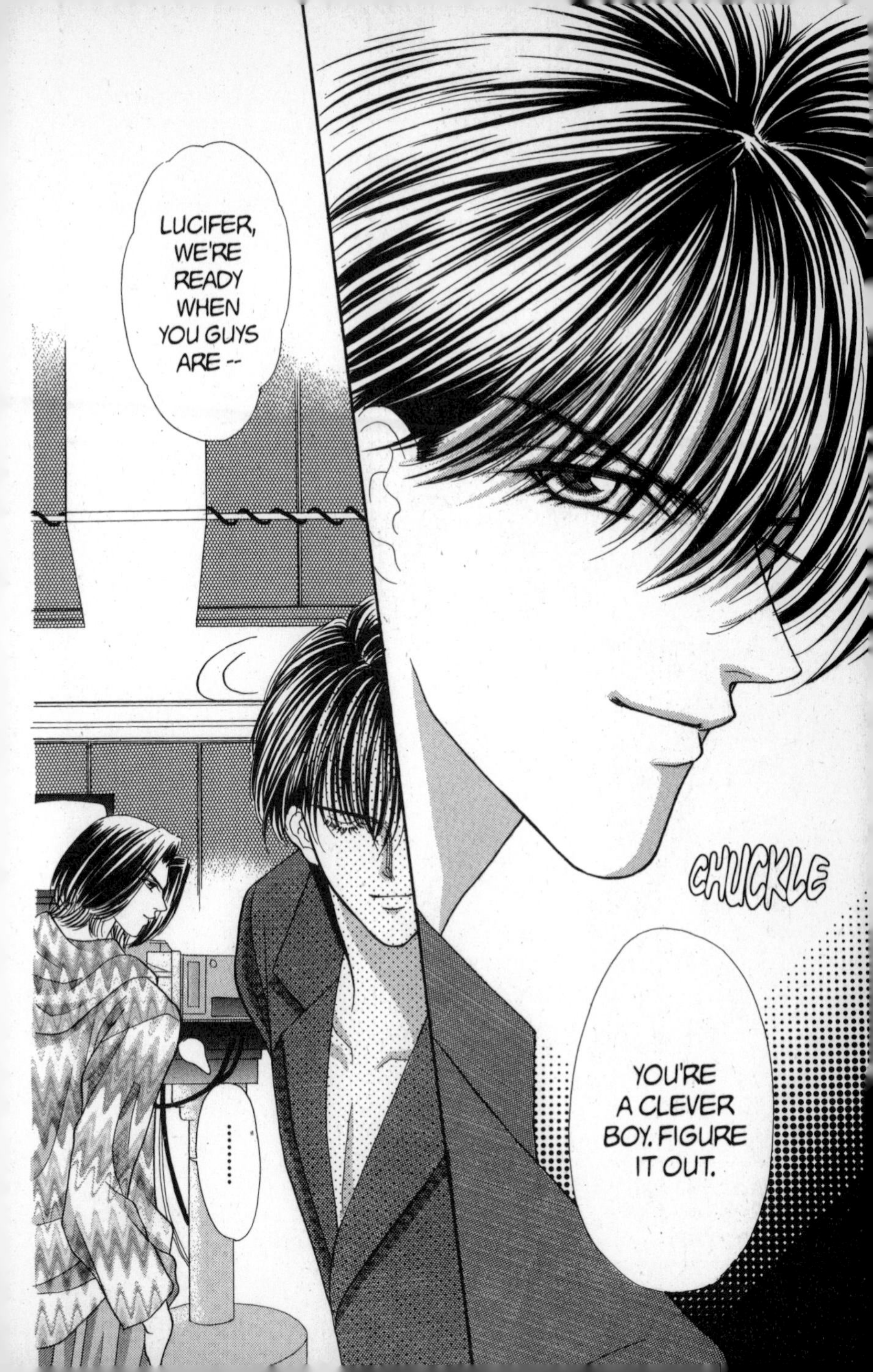
CHUCKLE
YOU'RE A CLEVER BOY. FIGURE IT OUT.
LUCIFER, WE'RE READY WHEN YOU GUYS ARE --
......

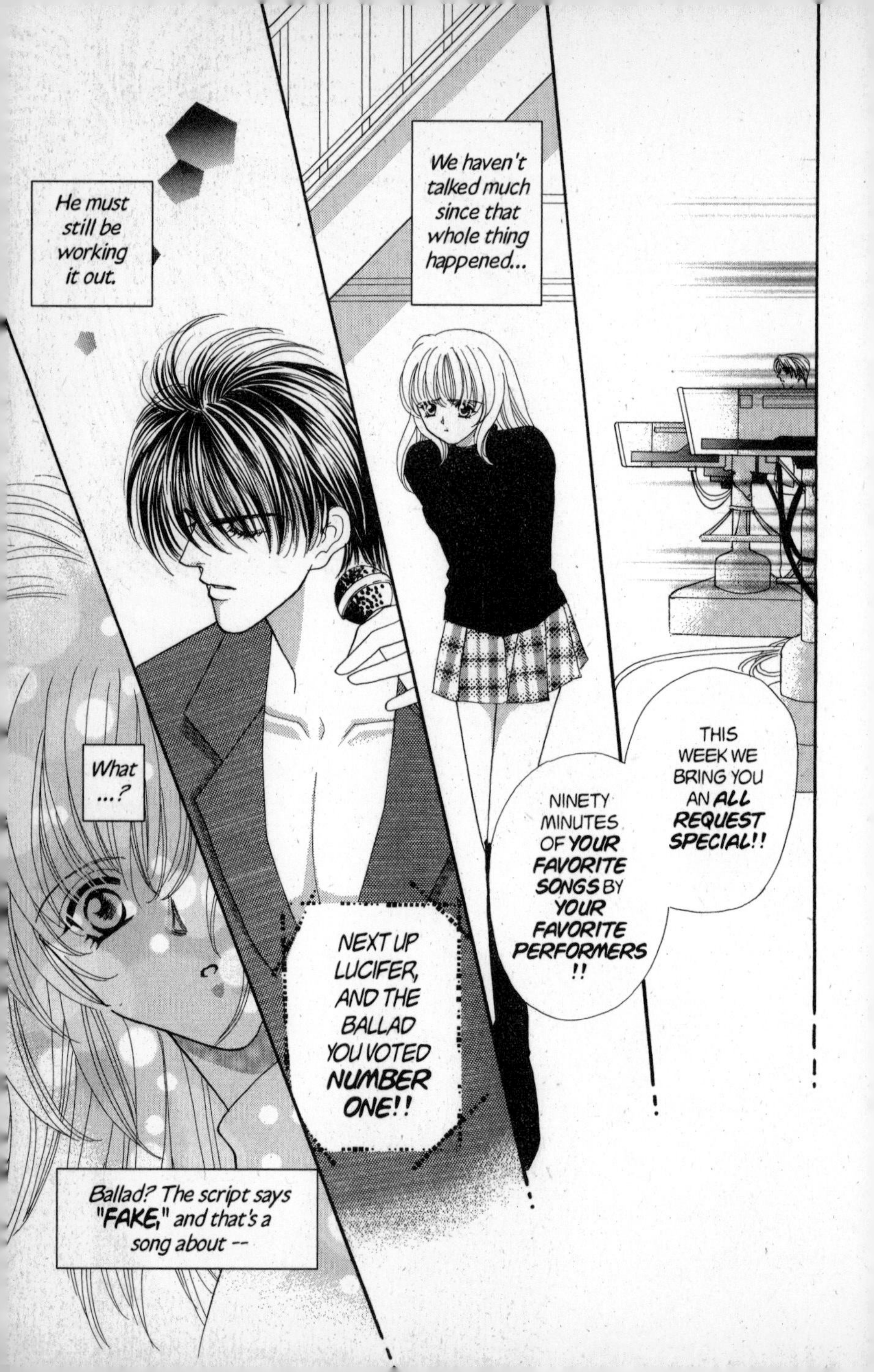

THIS WEEK WE BRING YOU AN **ALL REQUEST SPECIAL!!**
NINETY MINUTES OF **YOUR FAVORITE SONGS** BY **YOUR FAVORITE PERFORMERS** !!
We haven't talked much since that whole thing happened...
He must still be working it out.
NEXT UP LUCIFER, AND THE BALLAD YOU VOTED **NUMBER ONE!!**
What ...?
Ballad? The script says "**FAKE**," and that's a song about --

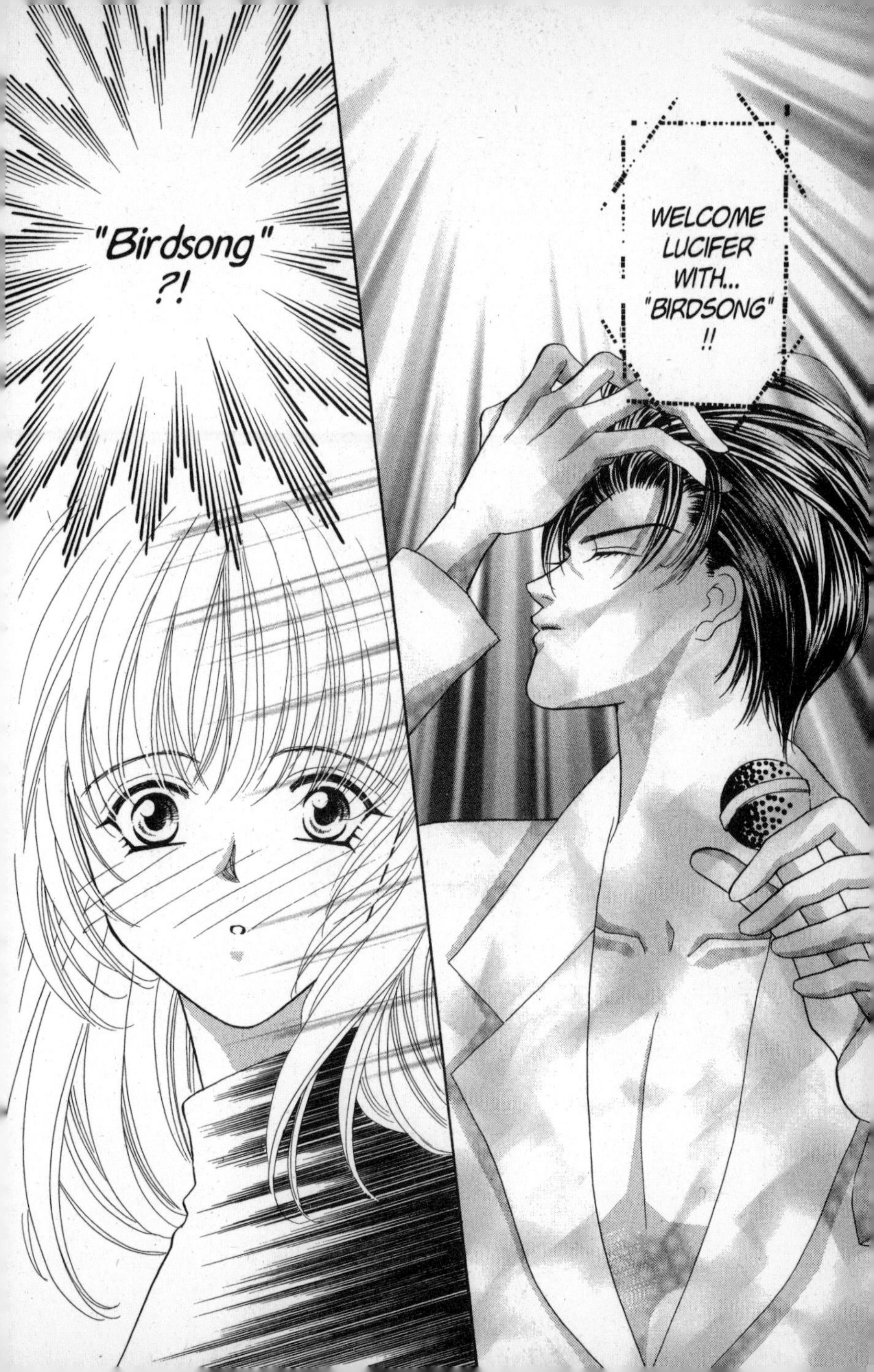
WELCOME LUCIFER WITH... "BIRDSONG" !!
"Birdsong" ?!

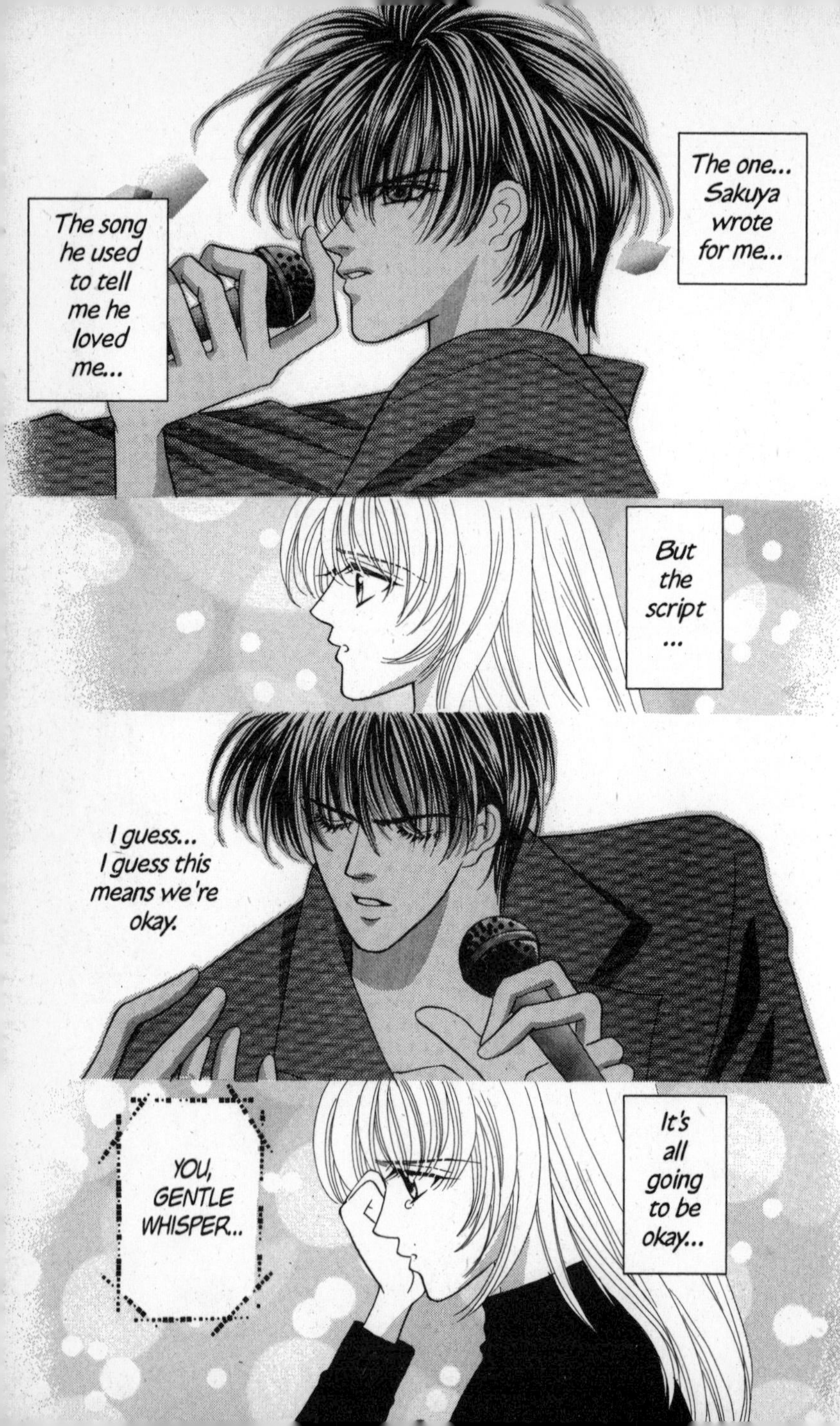
The one... Sakuya wrote for me...
The song he used to tell me he loved me...
But the script ...
I guess... I guess this means we're okay.
It's all going to be okay...
YOU, GENTLE WHISPER...

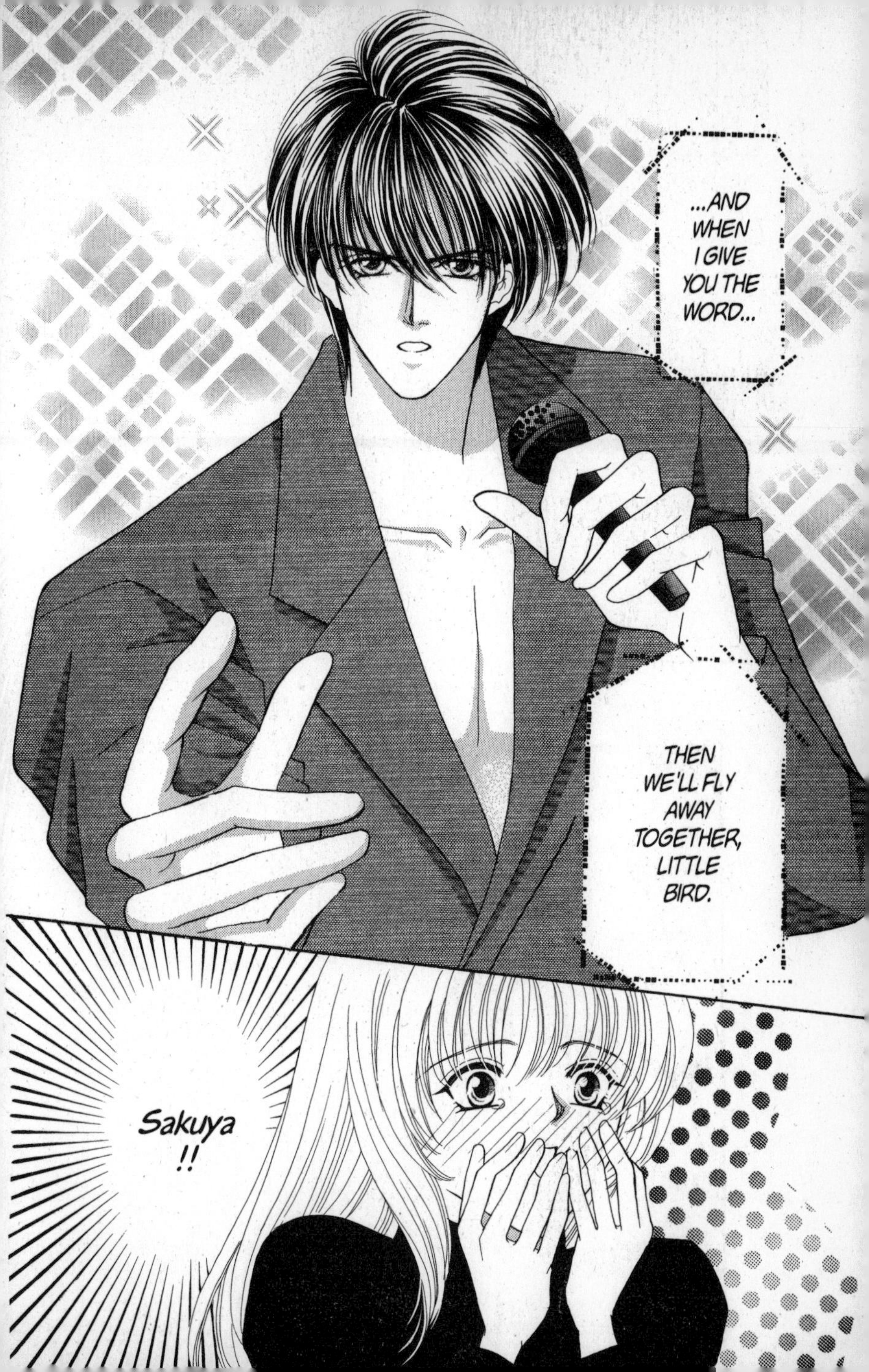
...AND WHEN I GIVE YOU THE WORD...
THEN WE'LL FLY AWAY TOGETHER, LITTLE BIRD.
Sakuya !!

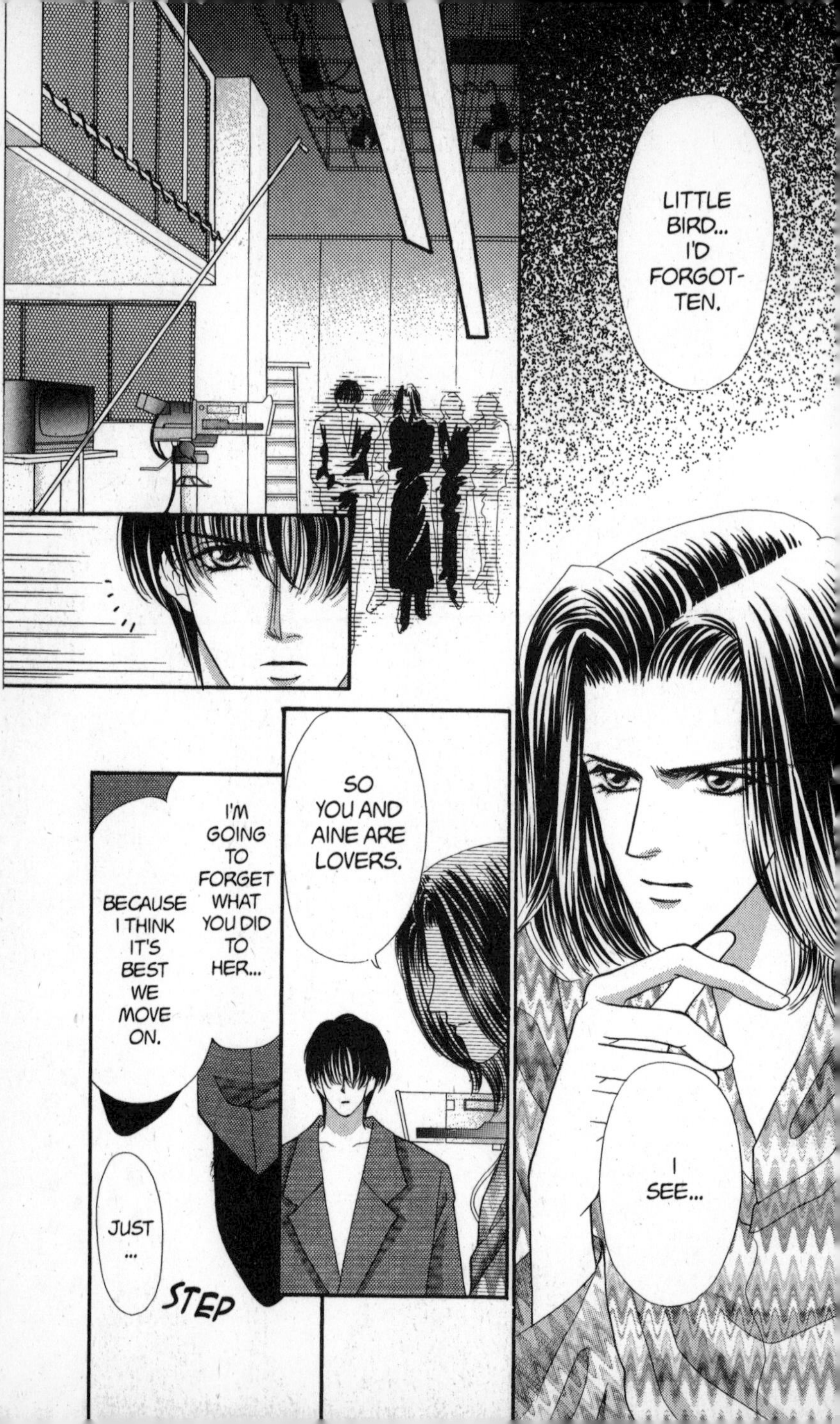
LITTLE BIRD... I'D FORGOT-TEN.
I SEE...
SO YOU AND AINE ARE LOVERS.
I'M GOING TO FORGET WHAT YOU DID TO HER...
BECAUSE I THINK IT'S BEST WE MOVE ON.
JUST ...
STEP

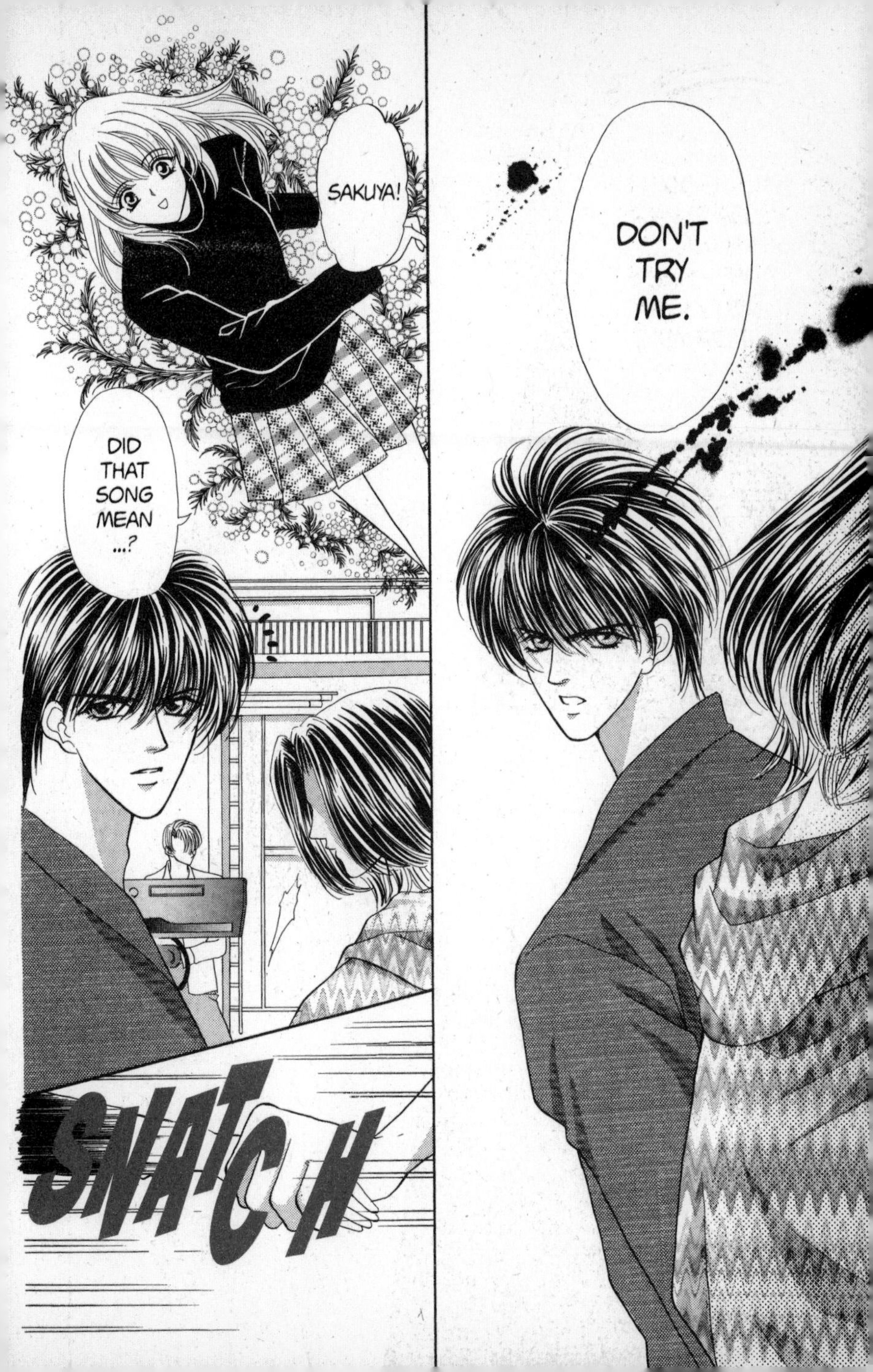
DON'T TRY ME.
SAKUYA!
DID THAT SONG MEAN ...?
SNATCH

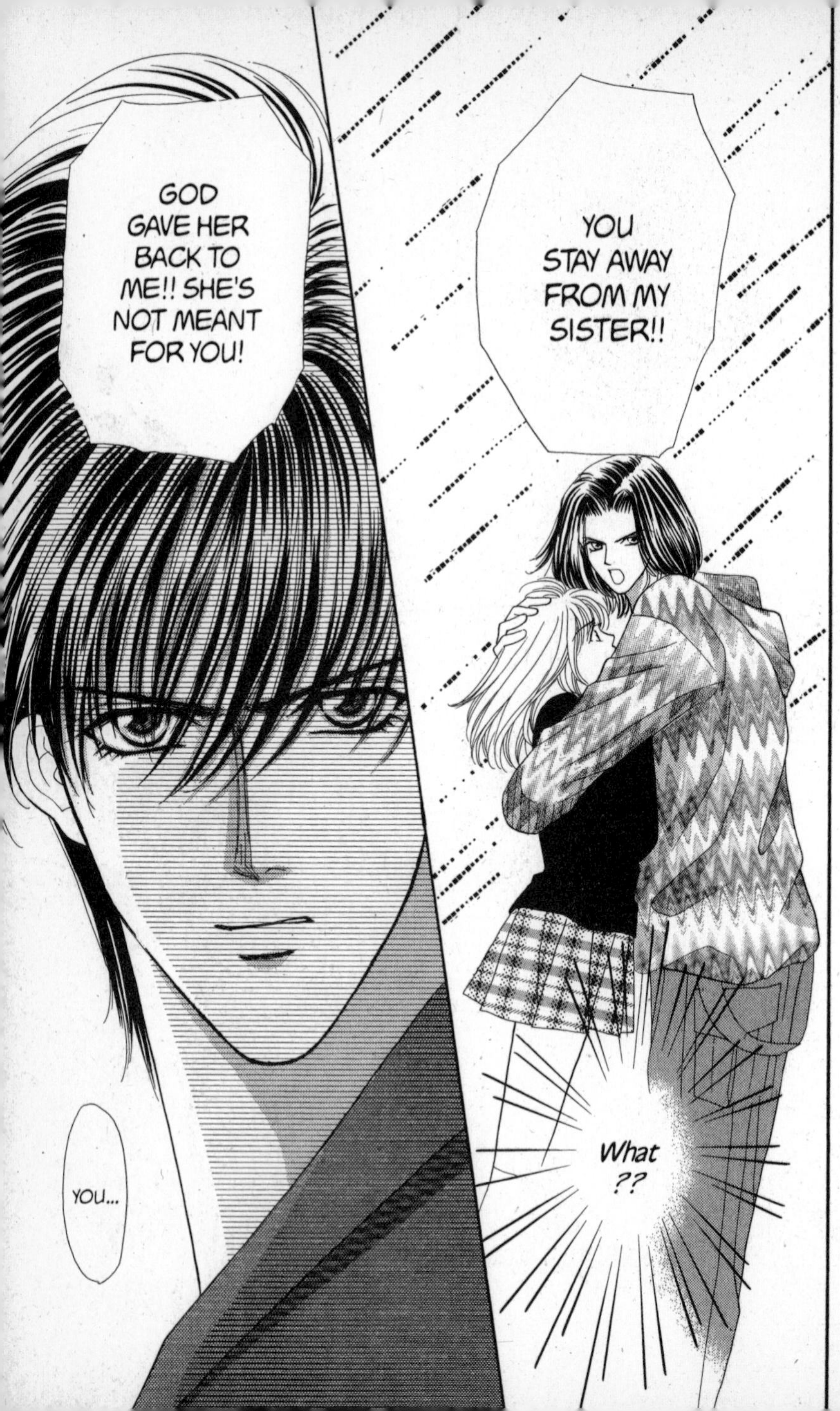
YOU STAY AWAY FROM MY SISTER!!
What ??
GOD GAVE HER BACK TO ME!! SHE'S NOT MEANT FOR YOU!
YOU...

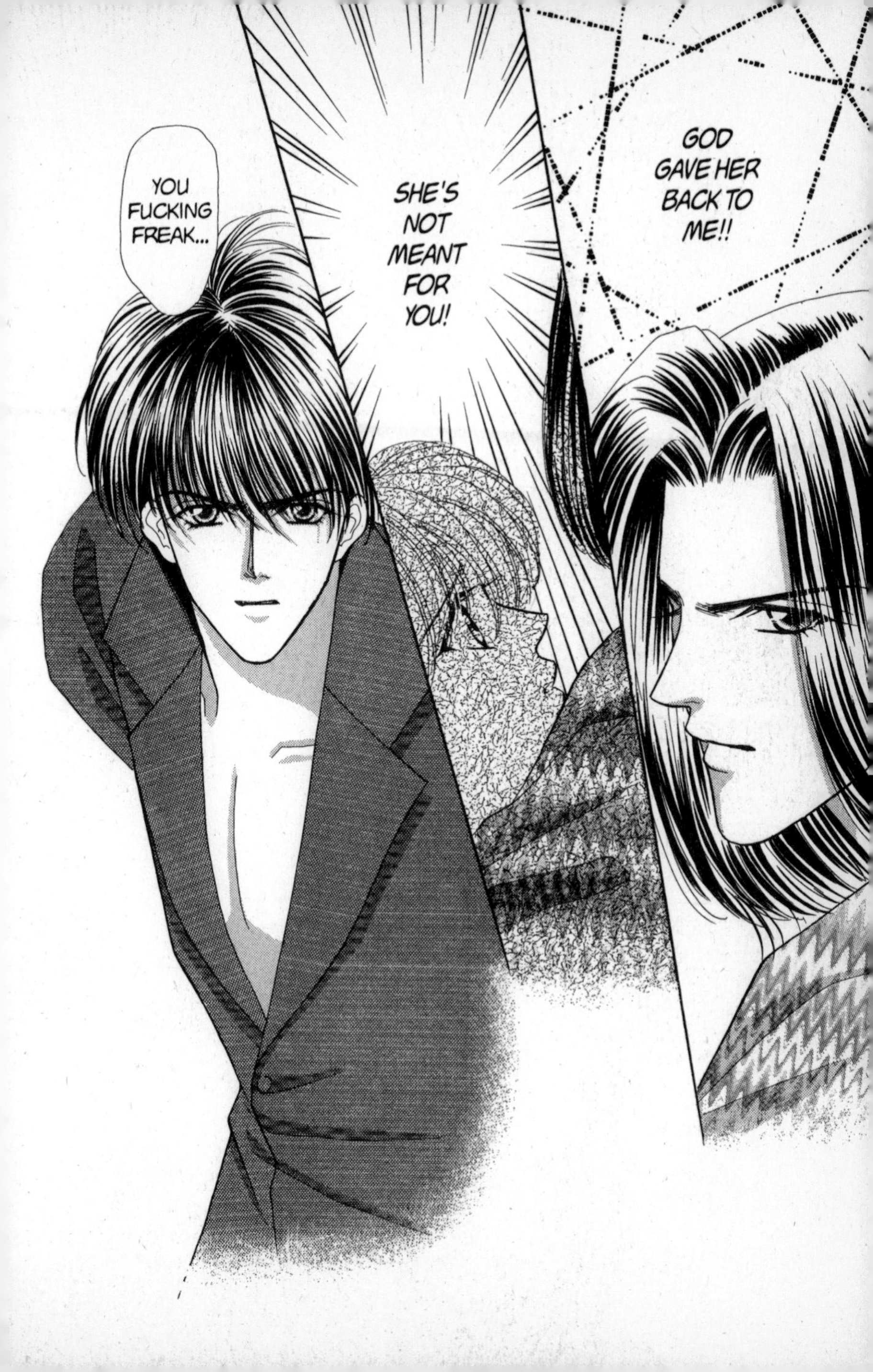
GOD GAVE HER BACK TO ME!!
SHE'S NOT MEANT FOR YOU!
YOU FUCKING FREAK...

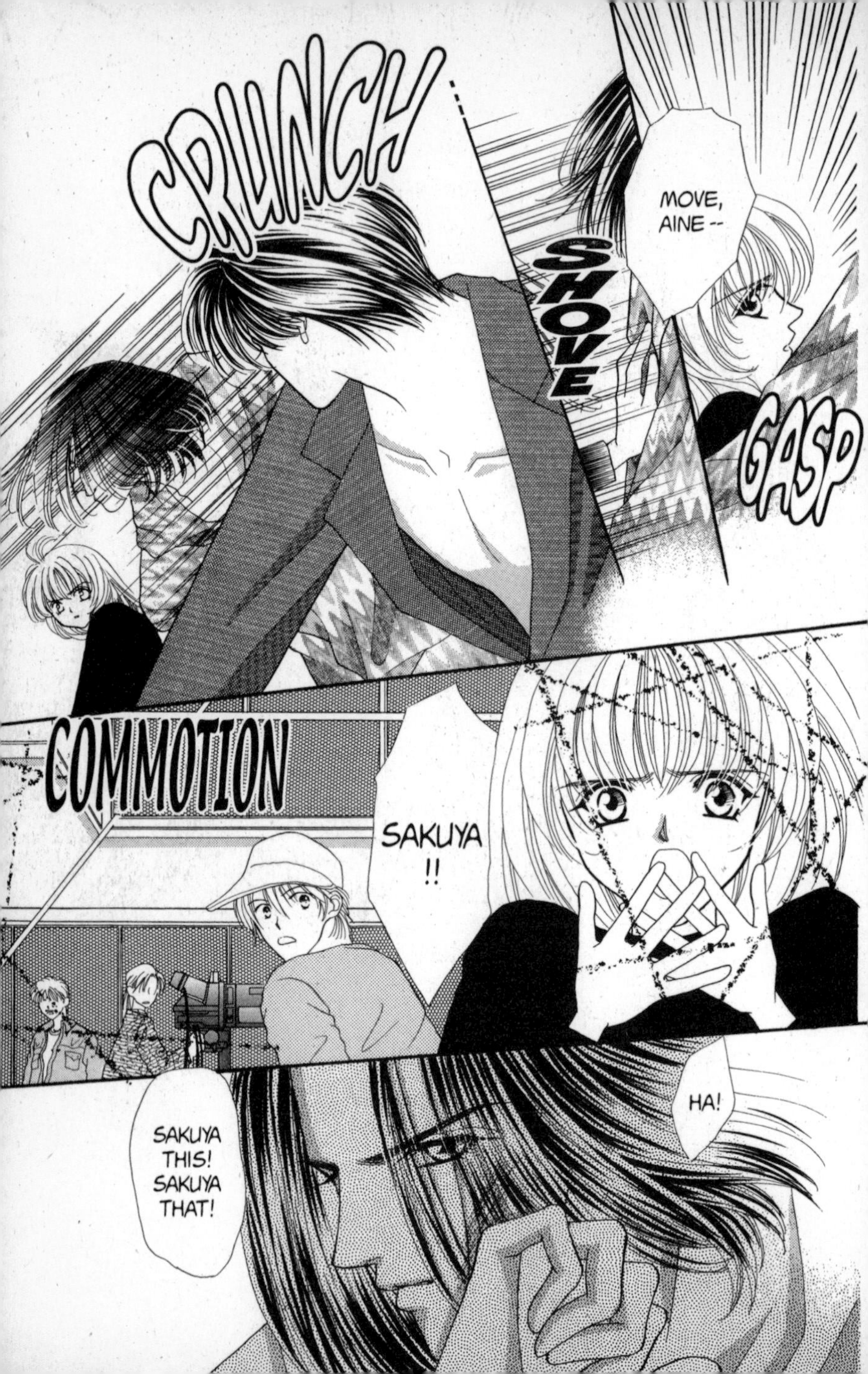
MOVE, AINE --
SHOVE
GASP
CRUNCH
SAKUYA !!
COMMOTION
HA!
SAKUYA THIS! SAKUYA THAT!

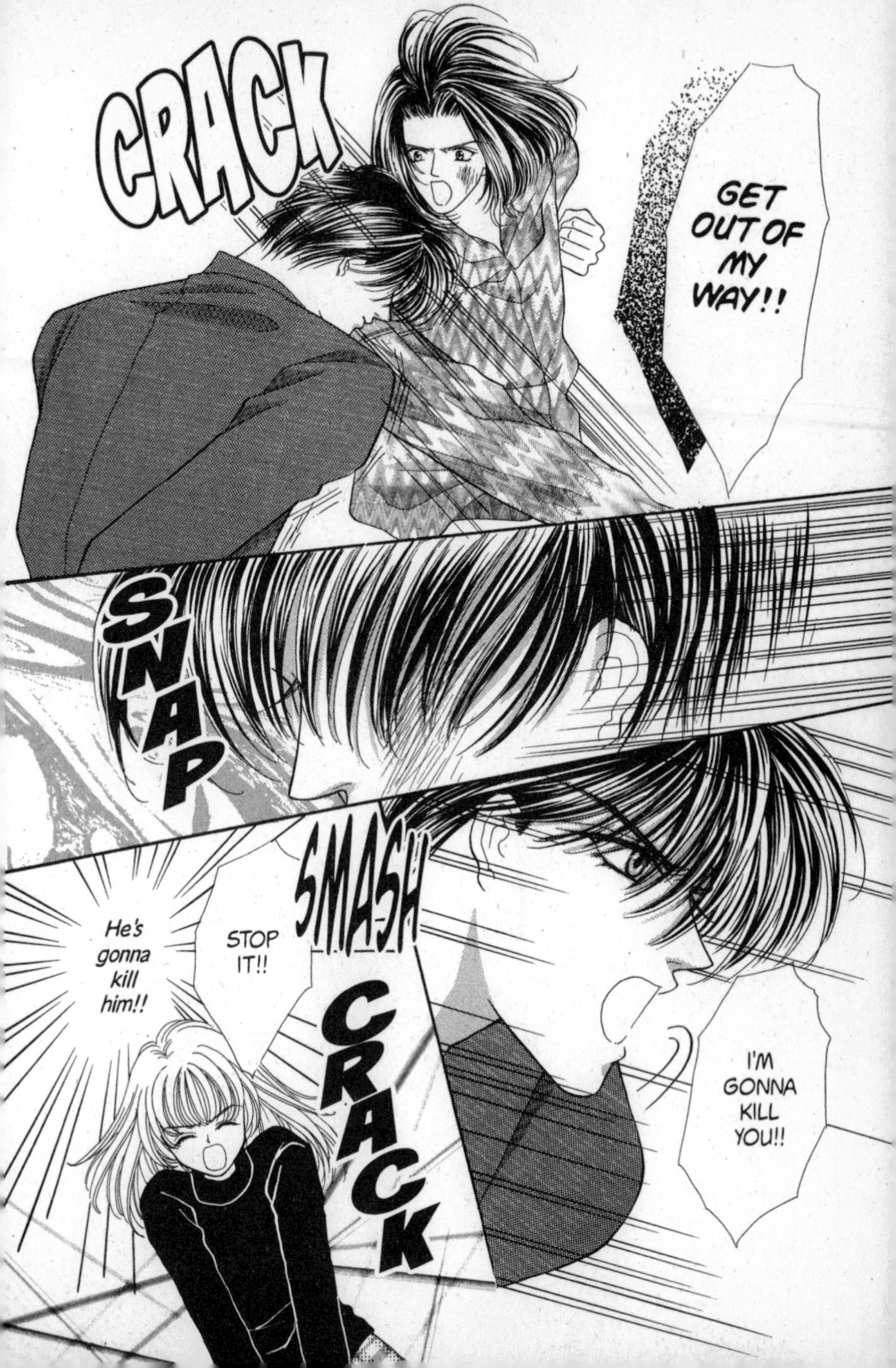
GET OUT OF MY WAY!!
CRACK
SNAP
I'M GONNA KILL YOU!!
SMASH
CRACK
STOP IT!!
He's gonna kill him!!

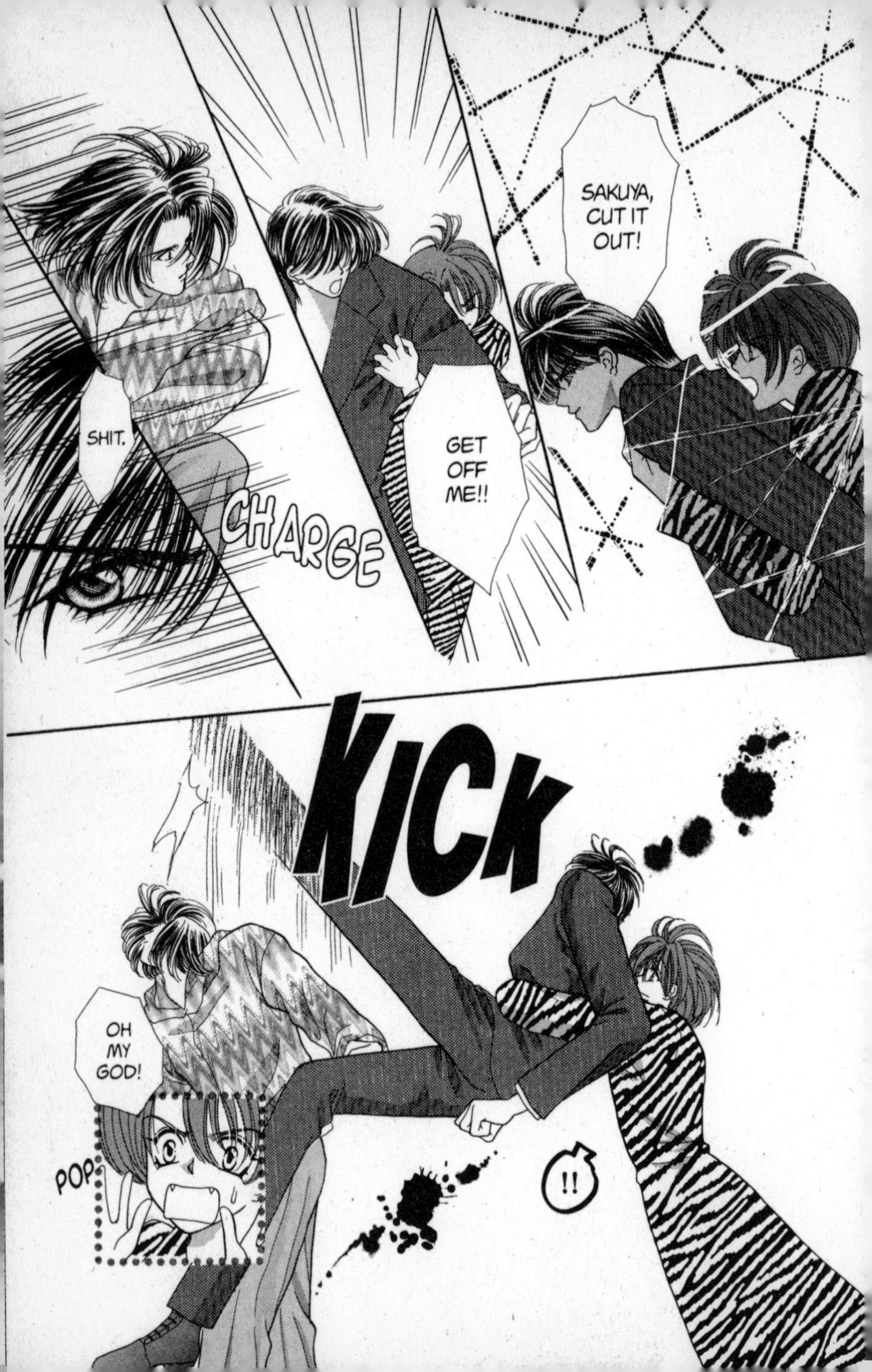
SAKUYA, CUT IT OUT!
GET OFF ME!!
SHIT.
CHARGE
KICK
OH MY GOD!
!!
POP

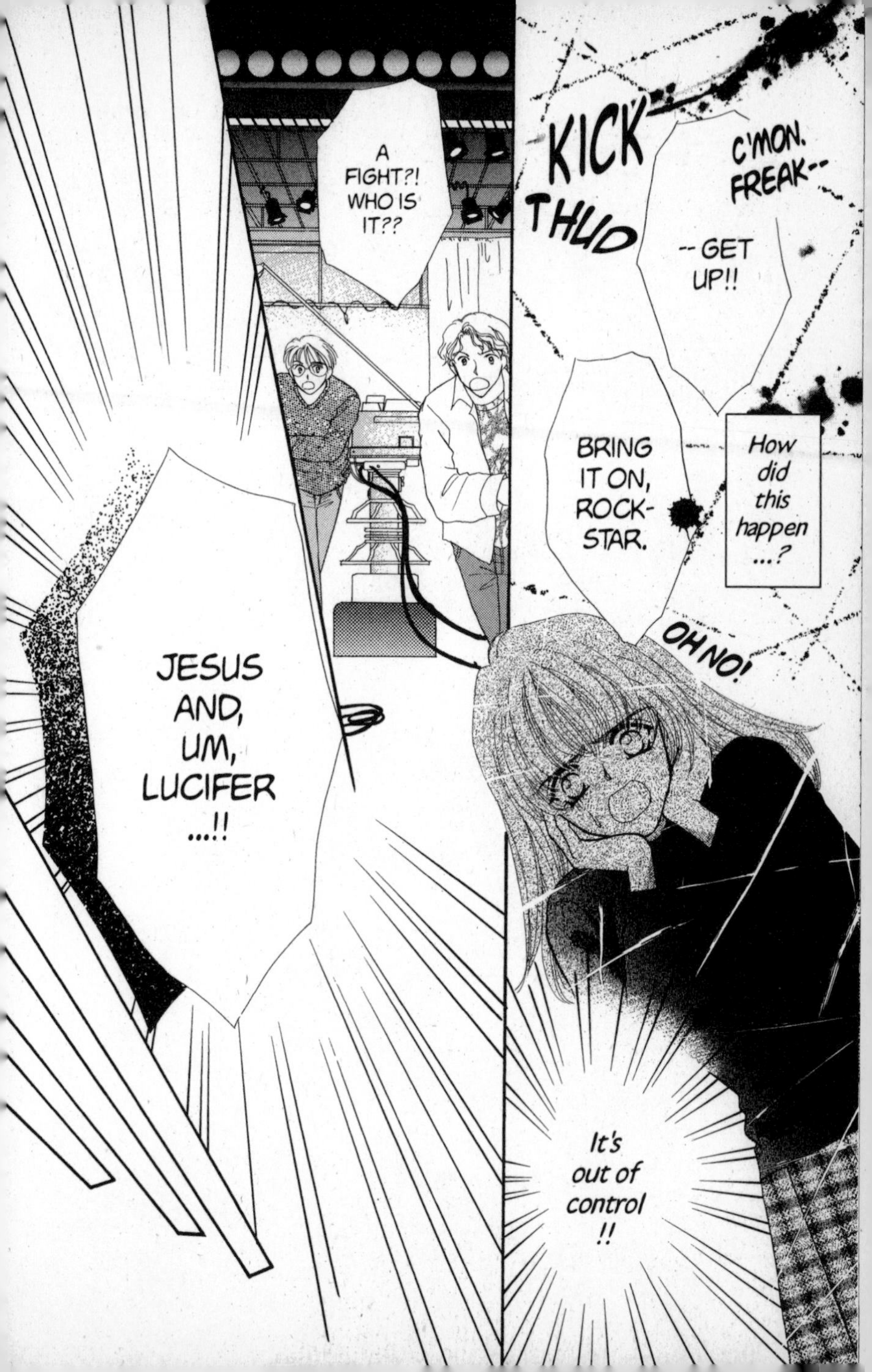
KICK
THUD
C'MON. FREAK--
--GET UP!!
BRING IT ON, ROCK-STAR.
How did this happen ...?
OH NO!
It's out of control !!
A FIGHT?! WHO IS IT??
JESUS AND, UM, LUCIFER ...!!

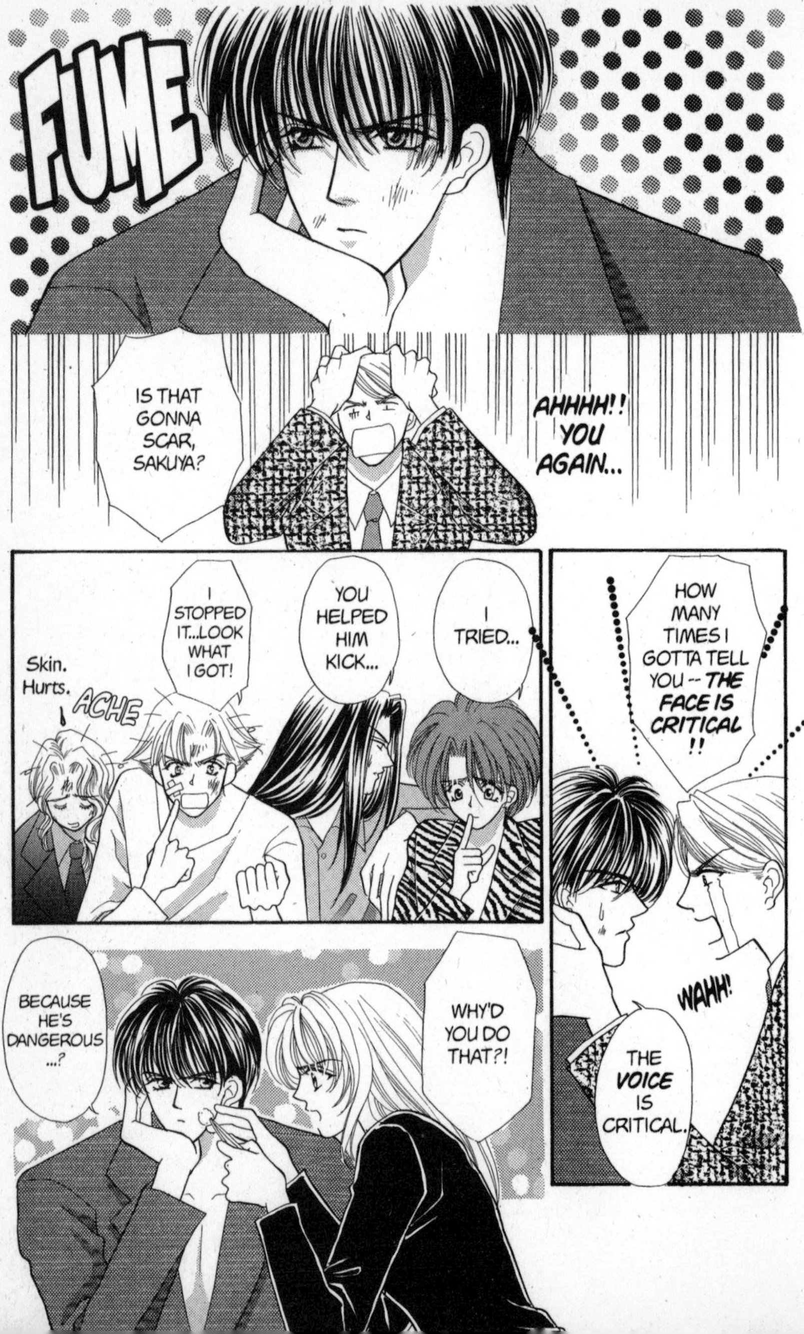
FUME
IS THAT GONNA SCAR, SAKUYA?
AHHHH!! YOU AGAIN...
HOW MANY TIMES I GOTTA TELL YOU -- THE FACE IS CRITICAL!!
WAHH!
THE VOICE IS CRITICAL.
I TRIED...
YOU HELPED HIM KICK...
I STOPPED IT...LOOK WHAT I GOT!
ACHE
Skin. Hurts.
WHY'D YOU DO THAT?!
BECAUSE HE'S DANGEROUS ...?

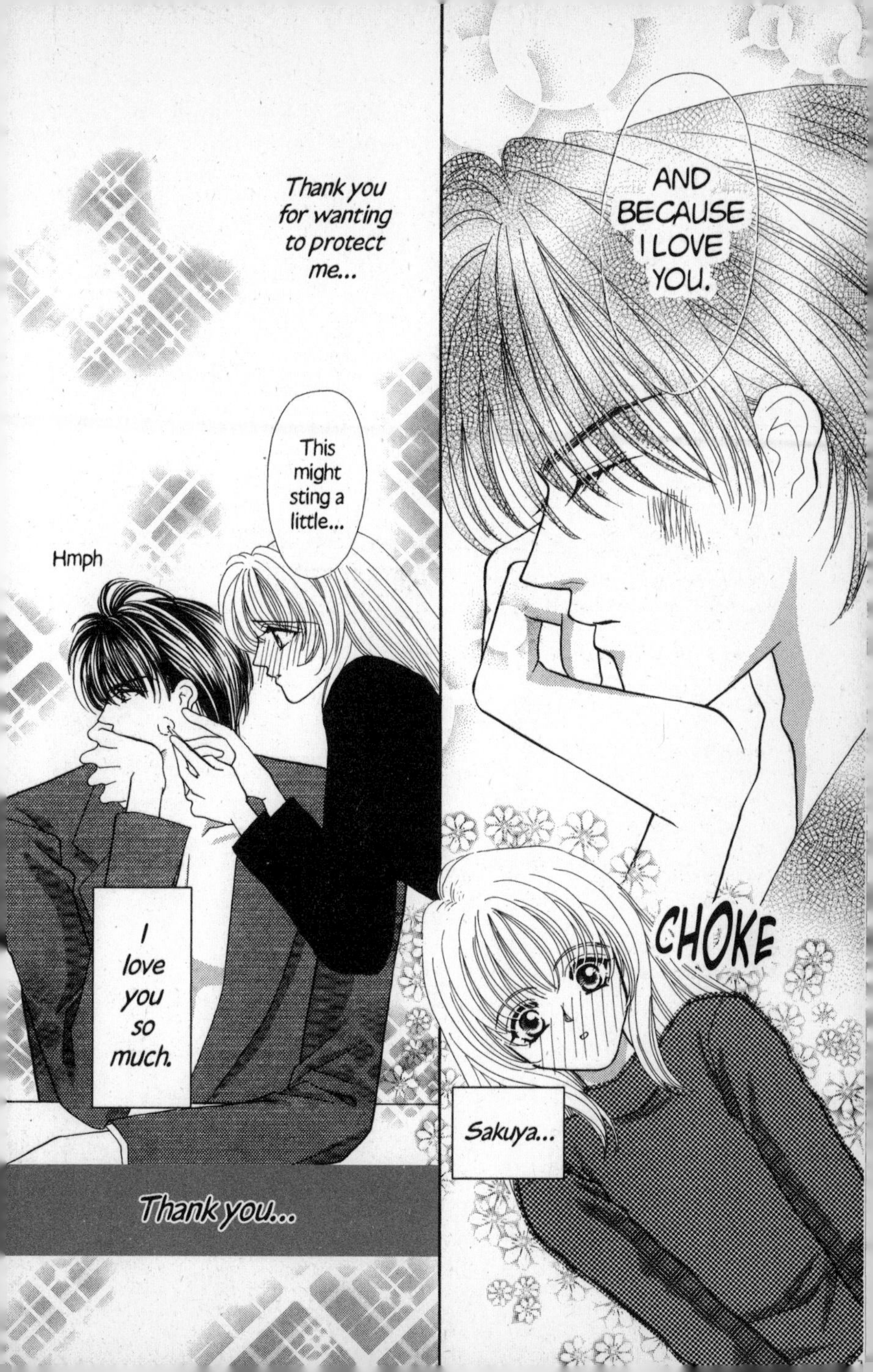
AND BECAUSE I LOVE YOU.
CHOKE
Sakuya...
Thank you for wanting to protect me...
This might sting a little...
Hmph
I love you so much.
Thank you...

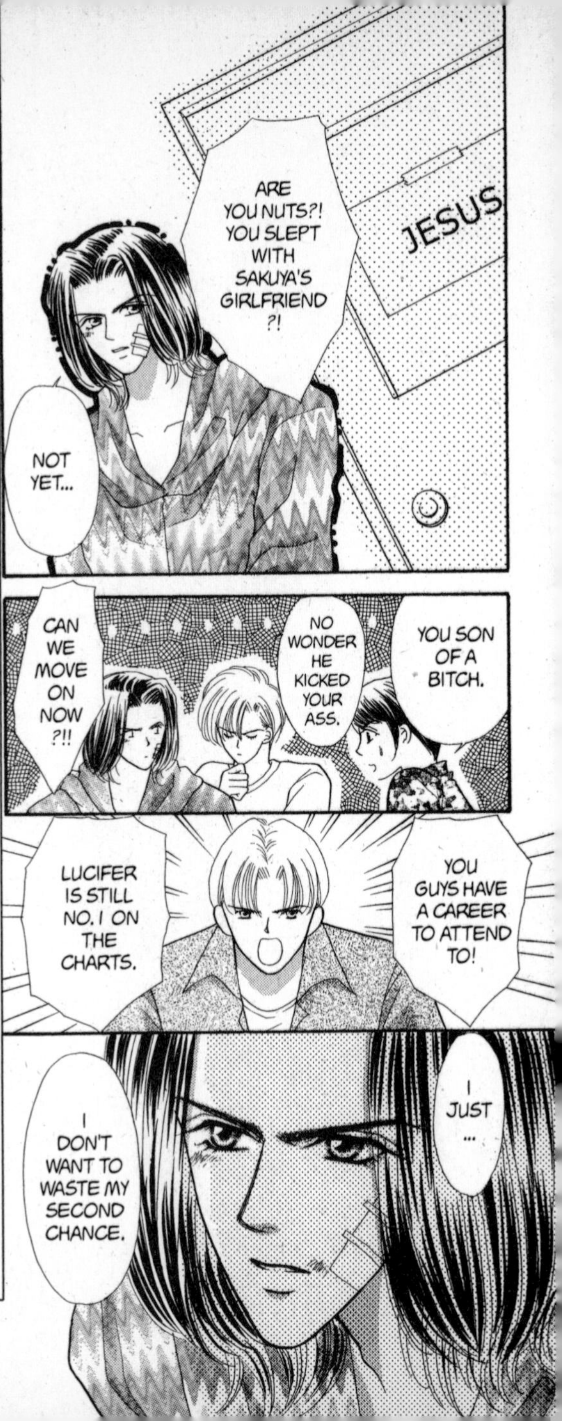
JESUS
ARE YOU NUTS?! YOU SLEPT WITH SAKUYA'S GIRLFRIEND ?!
NOT YET...
YOU SON OF A BITCH.
NO WONDER HE KICKED YOUR ASS.
CAN WE MOVE ON NOW ?!!
YOU GUYS HAVE A CAREER TO ATTEND TO!
LUCIFER IS STILL NO. 1 ON THE CHARTS.
I JUST ...
I DON'T WANT TO WASTE MY SECOND CHANCE.

Ta da! Here we are at the final third. What do you think so far? I'm doing an interview with Nishikawa of T.M. Revolution later today. I'm so excited I can't concentrate.

By the time you can read this, I will be in Hawaii for the Glay show. I couldn't get tickets to see B'z on their spring tour, but this summer, I'm going to every show!!

OUCH --!! Great. My interview is moments away and my cat just scratched my face!! Lovely.

I have to go put a Band-Aid on my nose...see you in Volume 5!!

Special thanks to:

Assistants
Sanae Yamazaki
Migiwa Nakahara
Satome Naruke
Ikuko Abe

Send letters concerning Sensual Phrase to:

Mayu Shinjo
c/o VIZ, LLC
P.O. BOX 77010
San Francisco, CA 94107

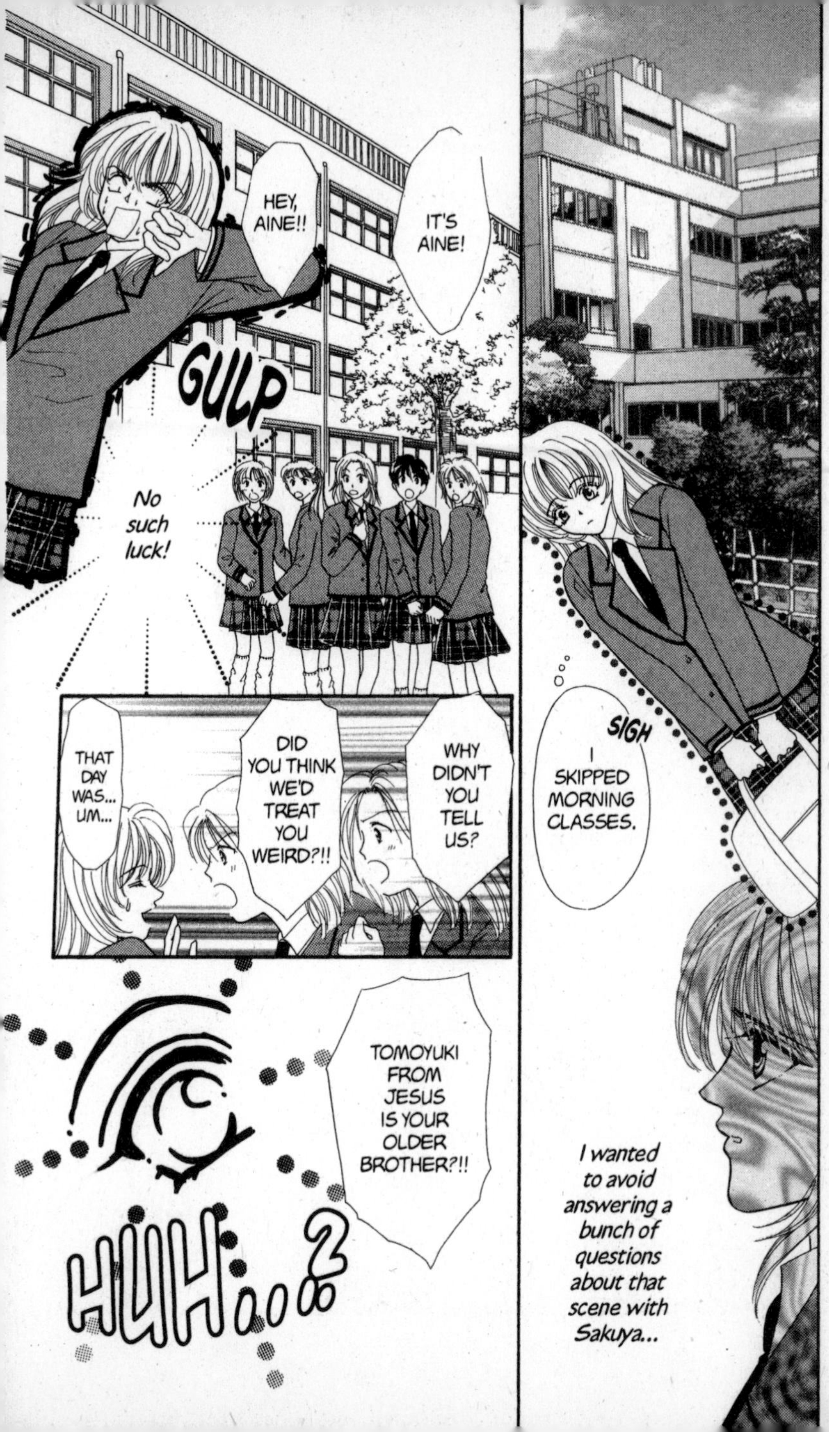
SIGH
I SKIPPED MORNING CLASSES.
I wanted to avoid answering a bunch of questions about that scene with Sakuya...
IT'S AINE!
HEY, AINE!!
GULP
No such luck!
WHY DIDN'T YOU TELL US?
DID YOU THINK WE'D TREAT YOU WEIRD?!!
THAT DAY WAS... UM...
TOMOYUKI FROM JESUS IS YOUR OLDER BROTHER?!!
HUH...?

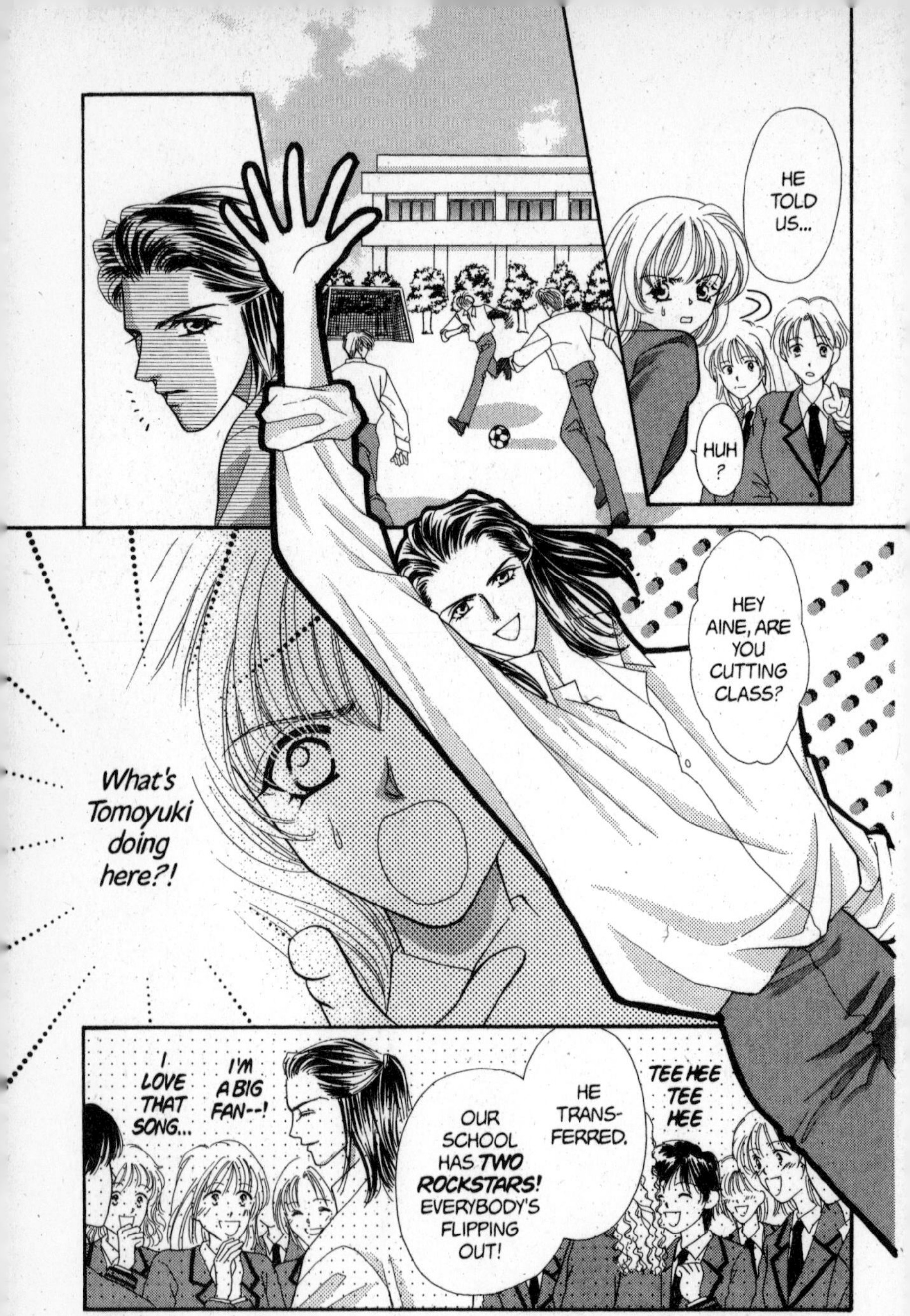
HE TOLD US...
HUH ?
HEY AINE, ARE YOU CUTTING CLASS?
What's Tomoyuki doing here?!
TEE HEE TEE HEE
HE TRANS-FERRED.
OUR SCHOOL HAS TWO ROCKSTARS! EVERYBODY'S FLIPPING OUT!
I'M A BIG FAN--!
I LOVE THAT SONG...

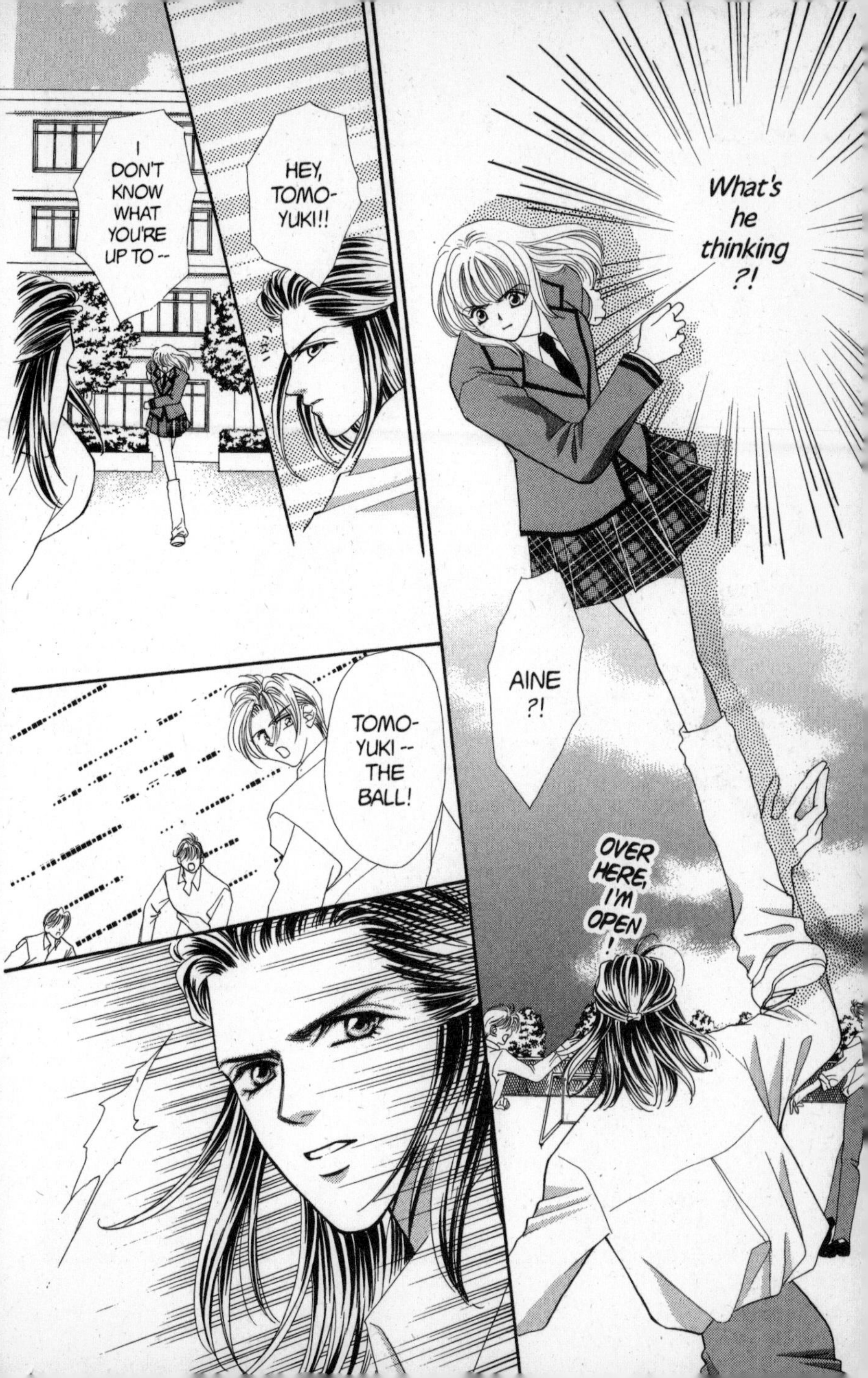
What's he thinking ?!
AINE ?!
OVER HERE, I'M OPEN !
HEY, TOMO-YUKI!!
I DON'T KNOW WHAT YOU'RE UP TO --
TOMO-YUKI -- THE BALL!

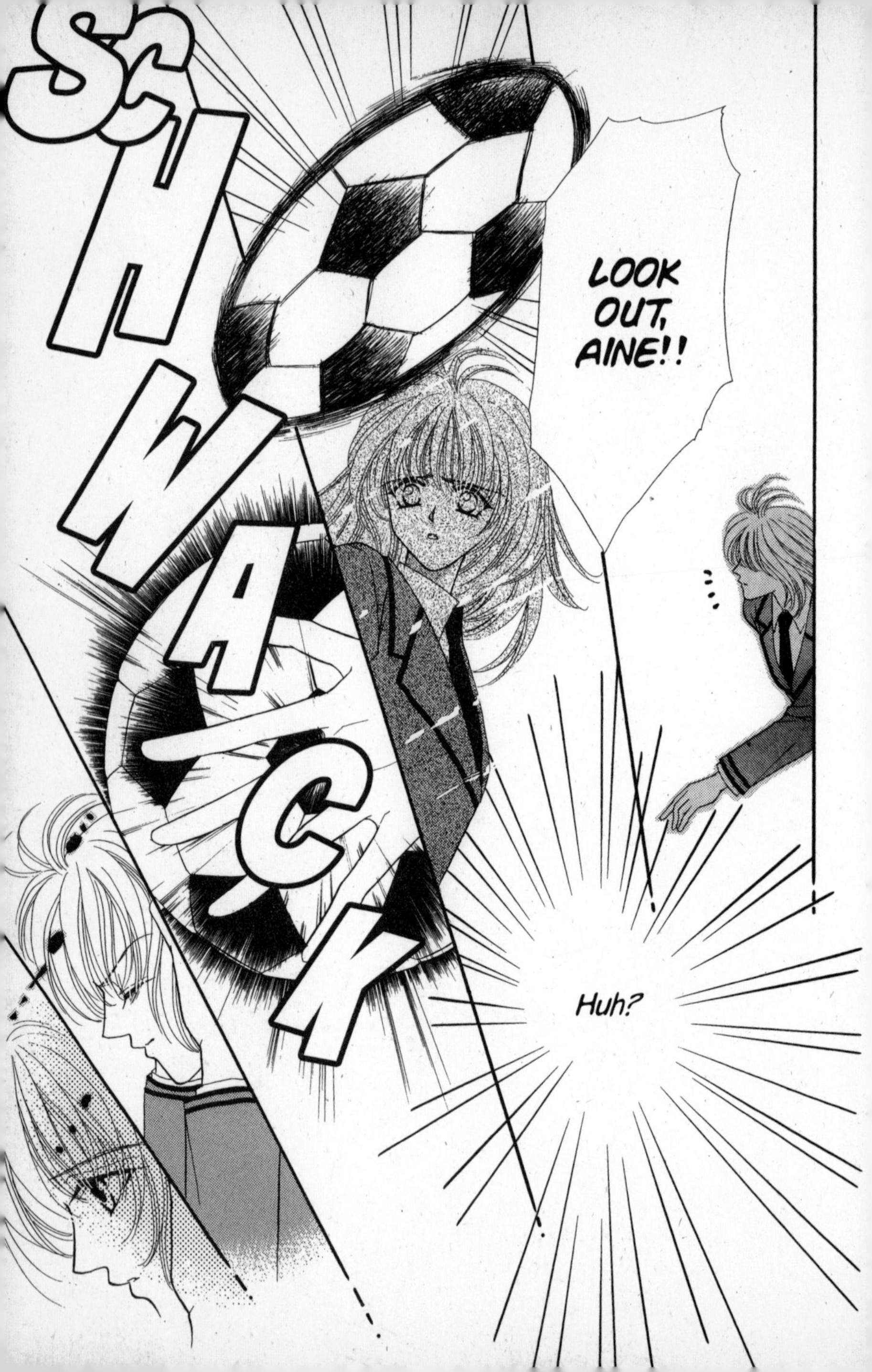
LOOK OUT, AINE!!
SCHWACK
Huh?

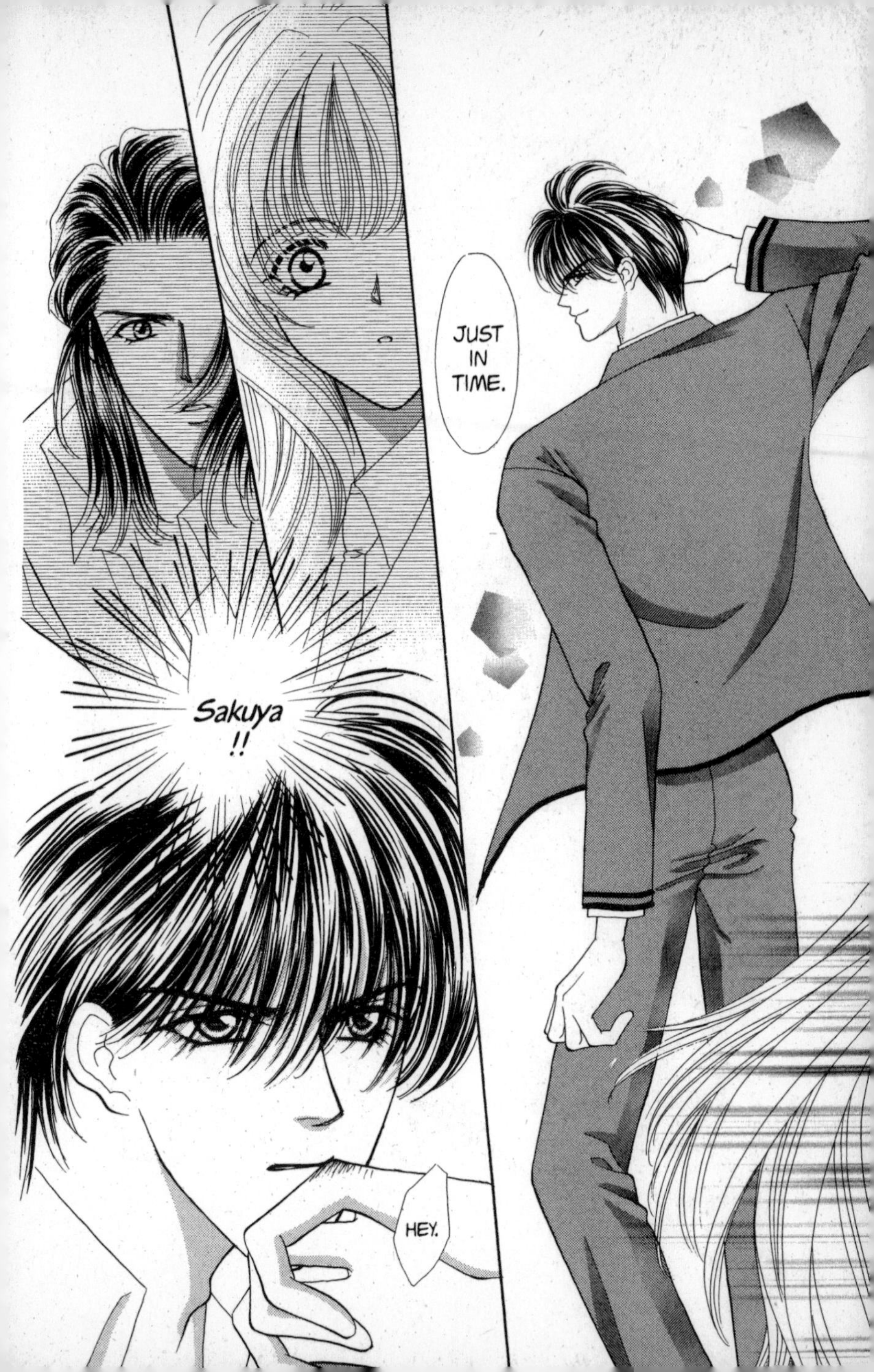
JUST IN TIME.
Sakuya !!
HEY.

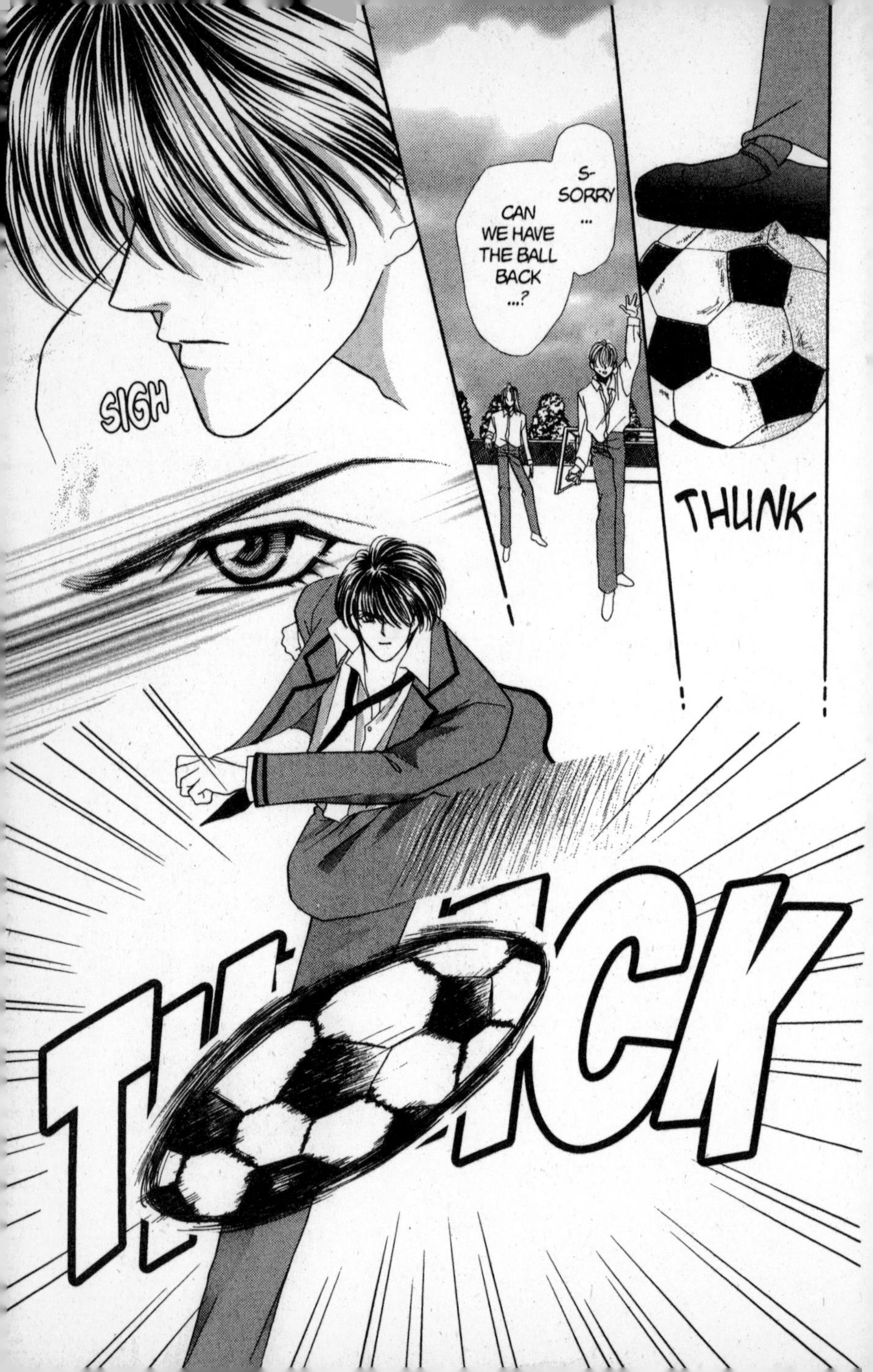
THUNK
S-SORRY ...
CAN WE HAVE THE BALL BACK ...?
SIGH

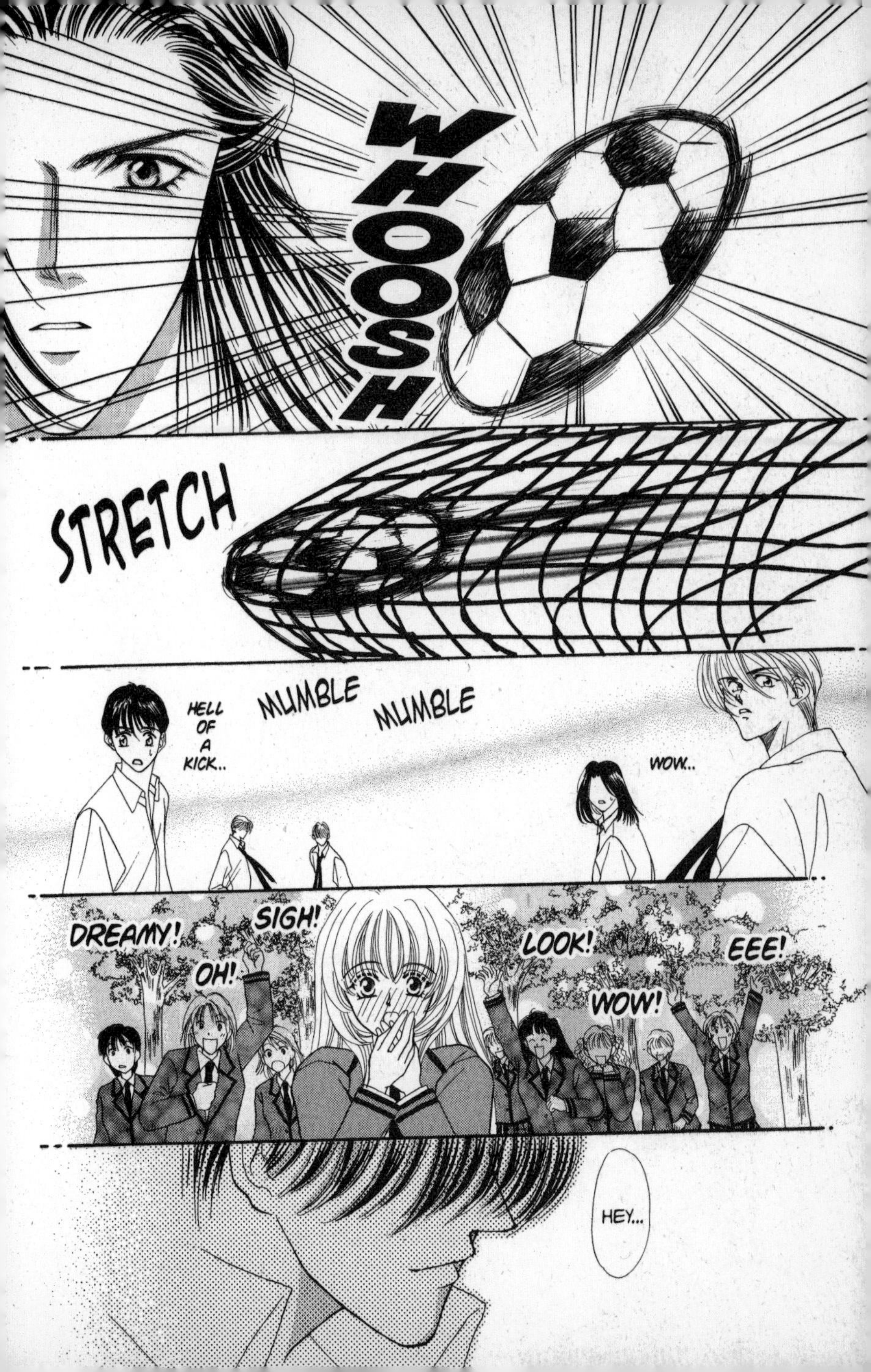
WHOOSH
STRETCH
WOW..
MUMBLE
MUMBLE
HELL OF A KICK..
EEE!
WOW!
LOOK!
SIGH!
OH!
DREAMY!
HEY...

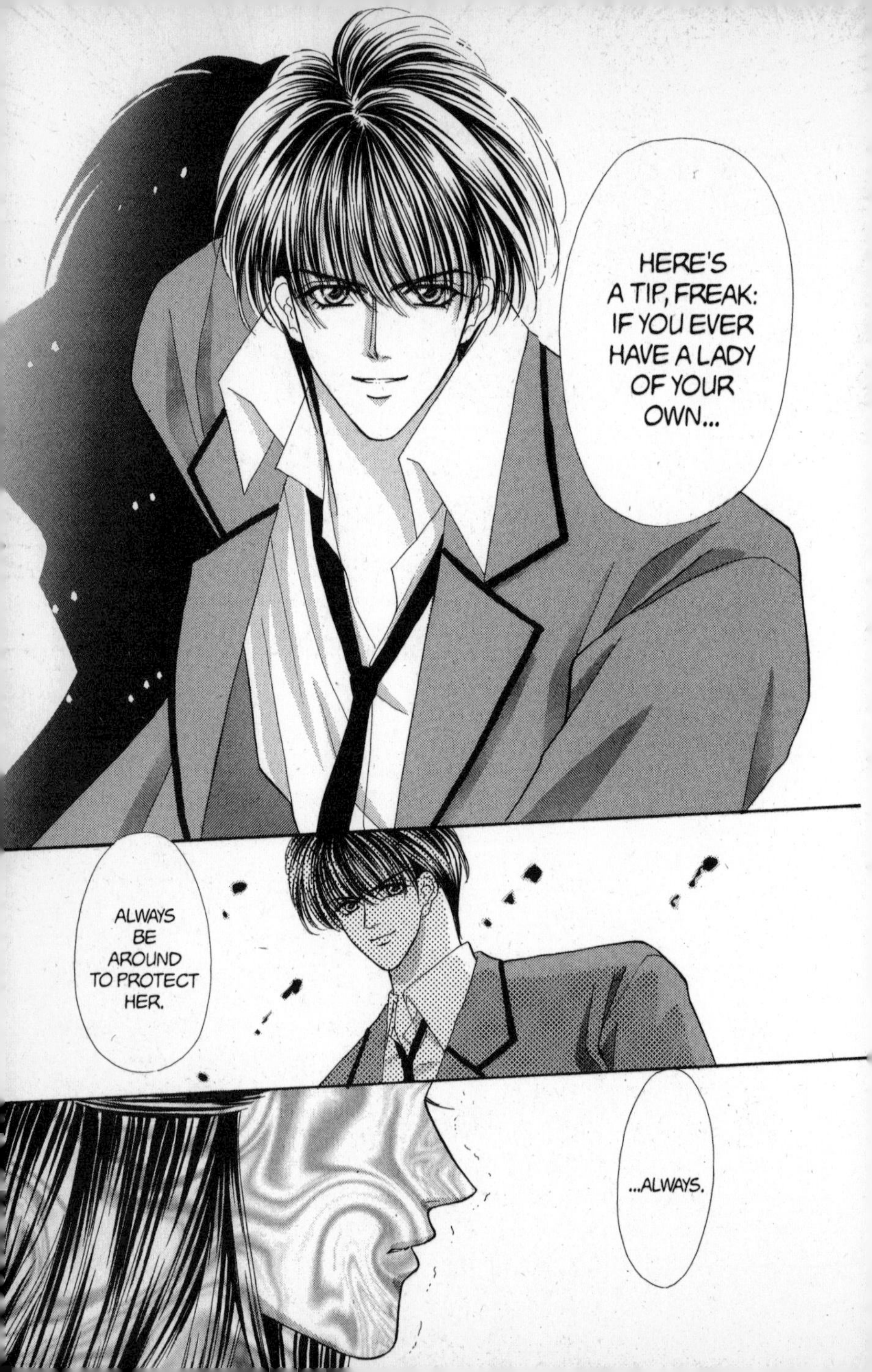
HERE'S A TIP, FREAK: IF YOU EVER HAVE A LADY OF YOUR OWN...
ALWAYS BE AROUND TO PROTECT HER.
...ALWAYS.

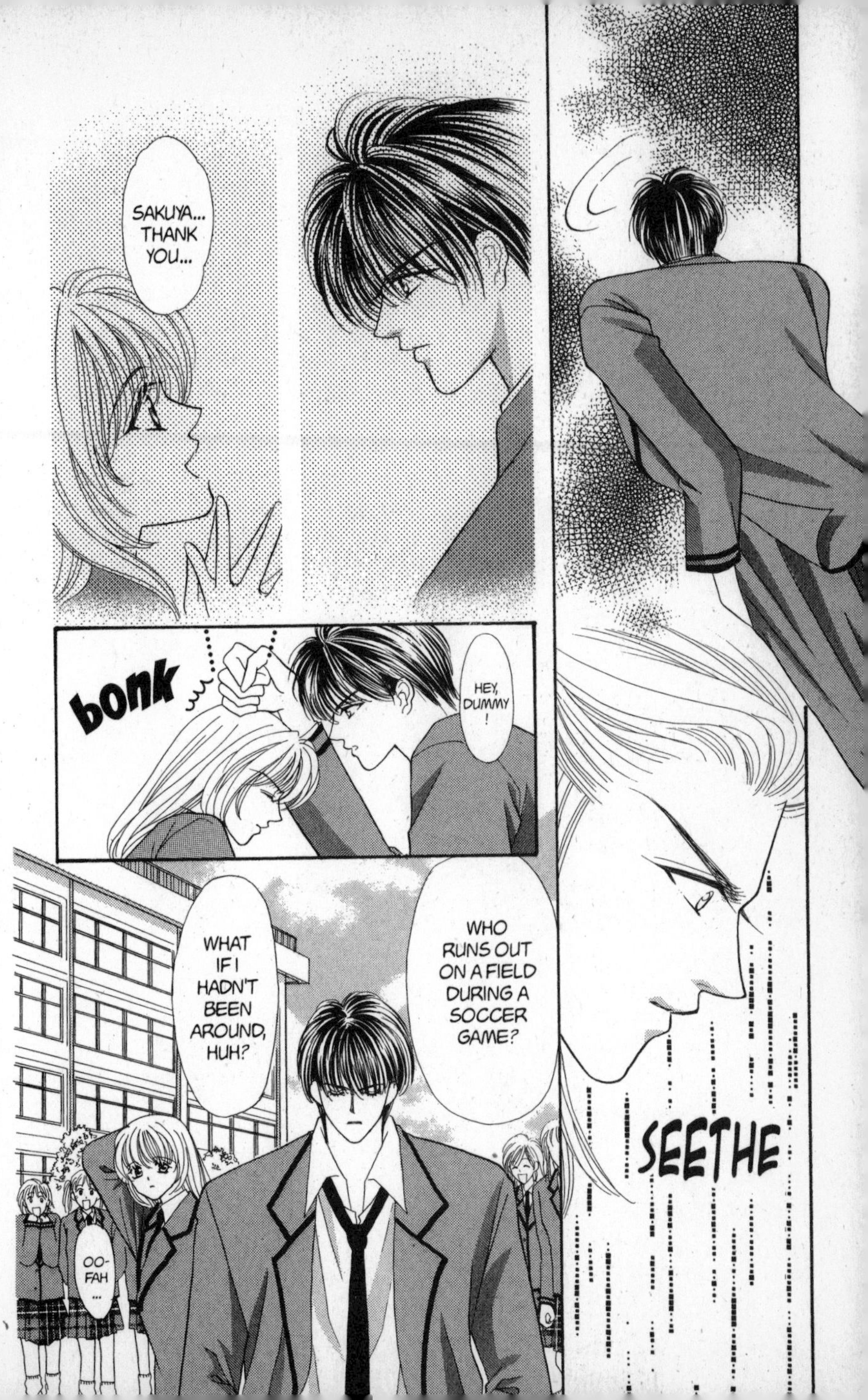
SEETHE
SAKUYA... THANK YOU...
HEY, DUMMY!
bonk
WHO RUNS OUT ON A FIELD DURING A SOCCER GAME?
WHAT IF I HADN'T BEEN AROUND, HUH?
OO-FAH...

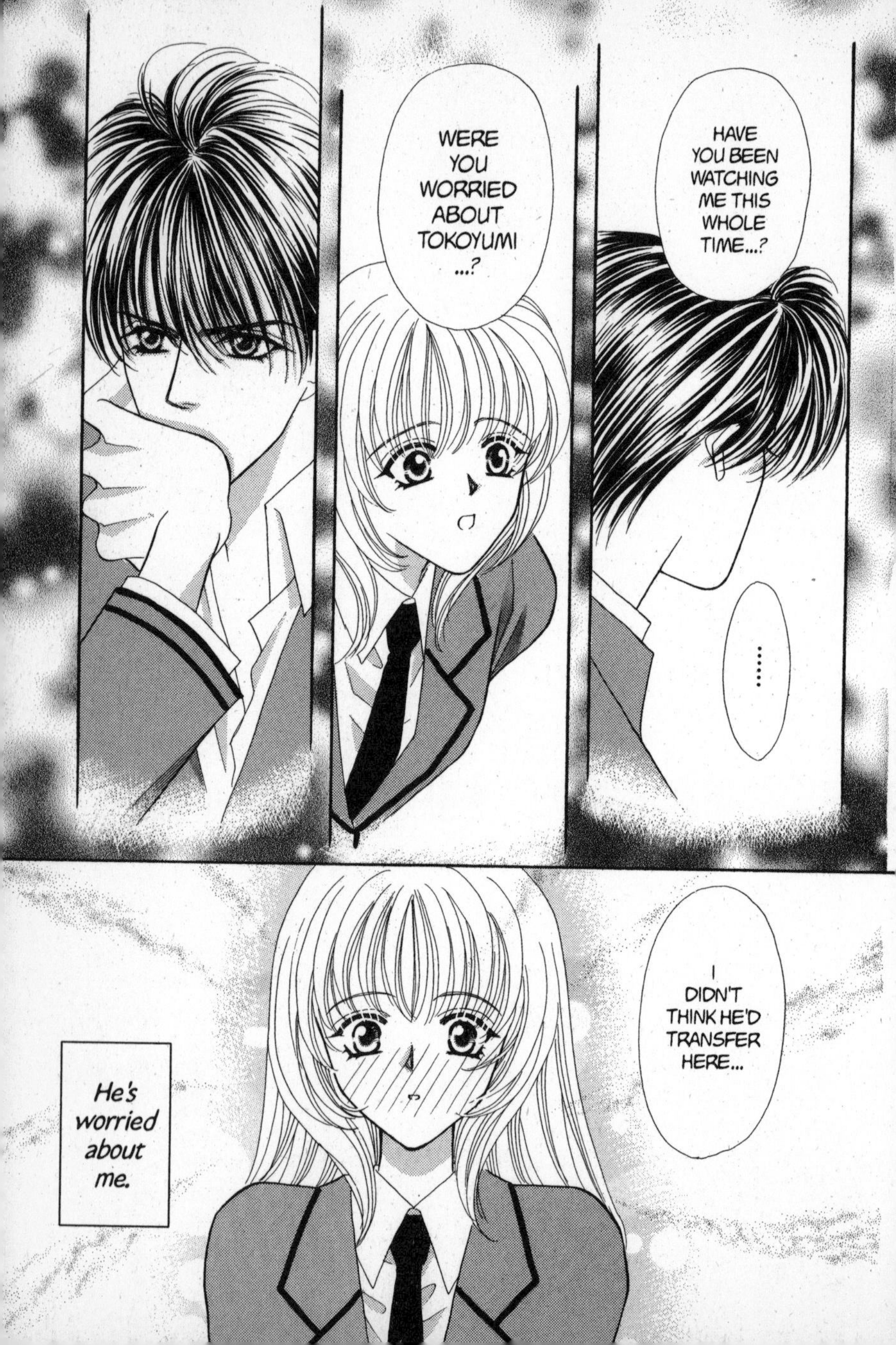
HAVE YOU BEEN WATCHING ME THIS WHOLE TIME...?
......
WERE YOU WORRIED ABOUT TOKOYUMI ...?
I DIDN'T THINK HE'D TRANSFER HERE...
He's worried about me.

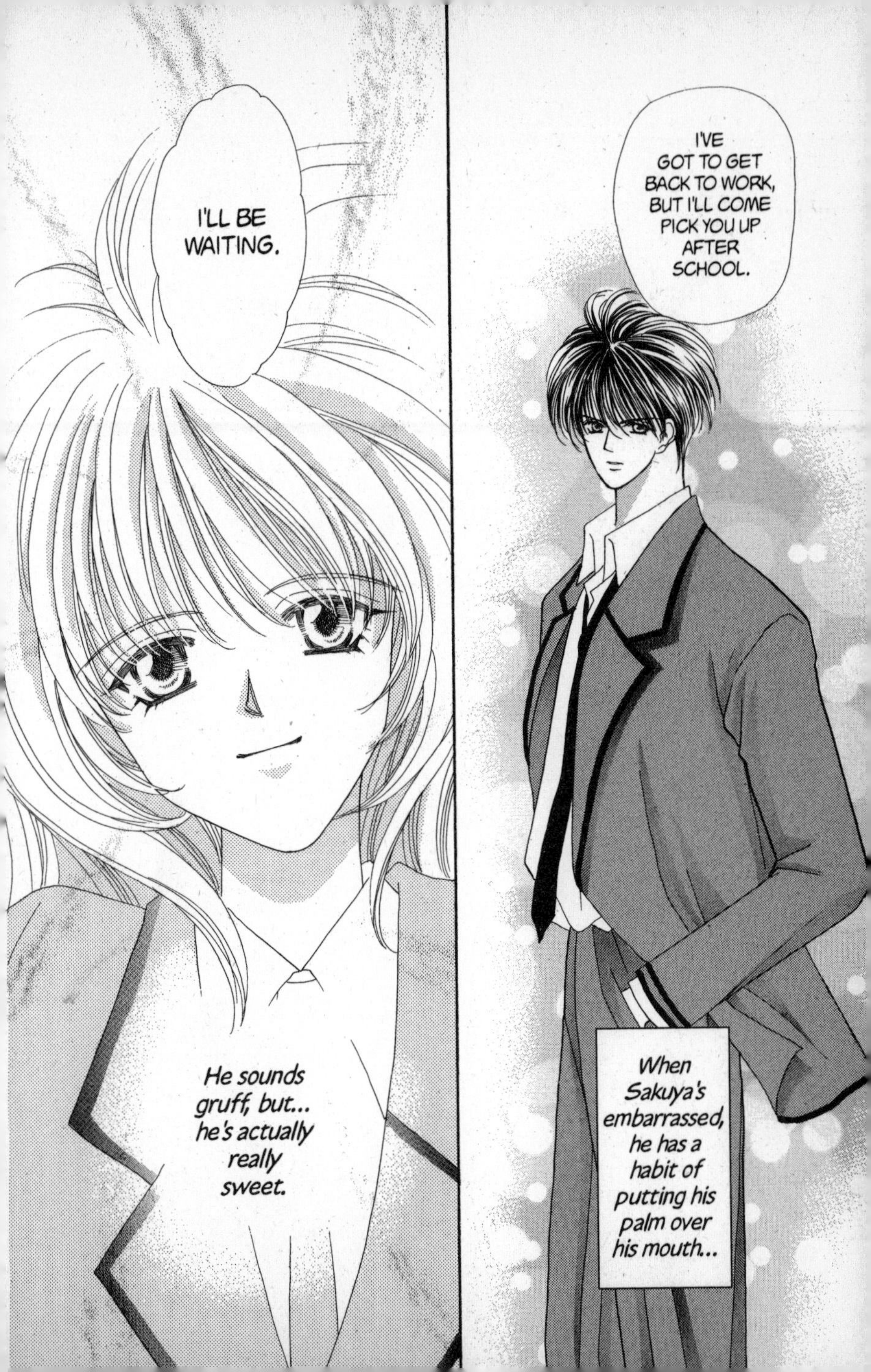
I'VE GOT TO GET BACK TO WORK, BUT I'LL COME PICK YOU UP AFTER SCHOOL.
When Sakuya's embarrassed, he has a habit of putting his palm over his mouth...
I'LL BE WAITING.
He sounds gruff, but... he's actually really sweet.

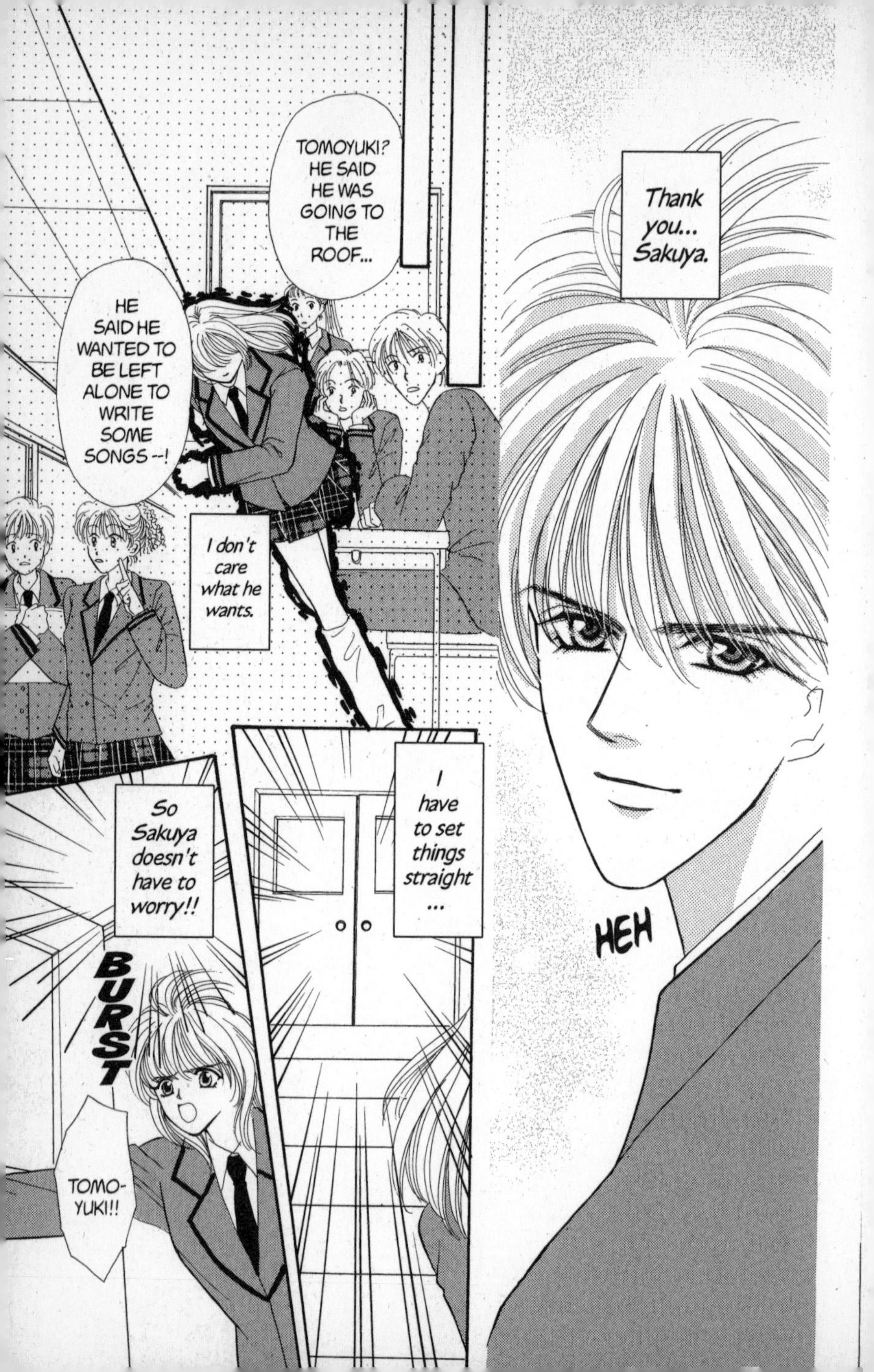
Thank you... Sakuya.
HEH
TOMOYUKI? HE SAID HE WAS GOING TO THE ROOF...
HE SAID HE WANTED TO BE LEFT ALONE TO WRITE SOME SONGS --!
I don't care what he wants.
I have to set things straight ...
So Sakuya doesn't have to worry!!
BURST
TOMO-YUKI!!

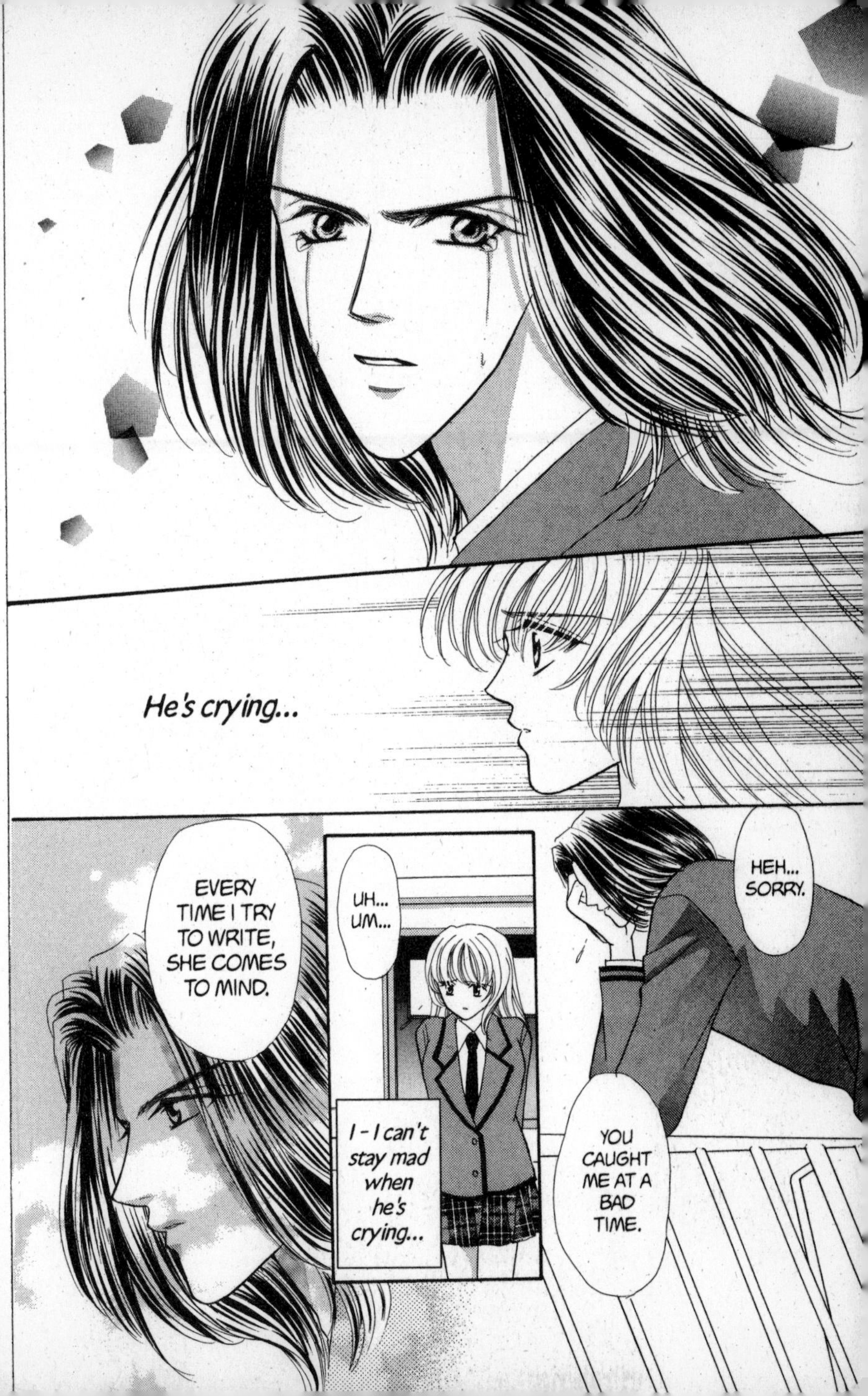
He's crying...
HEH... SORRY.
YOU CAUGHT ME AT A BAD TIME.
UH... UM...
I - I can't stay mad when he's crying...
EVERY TIME I TRY TO WRITE, SHE COMES TO MIND.

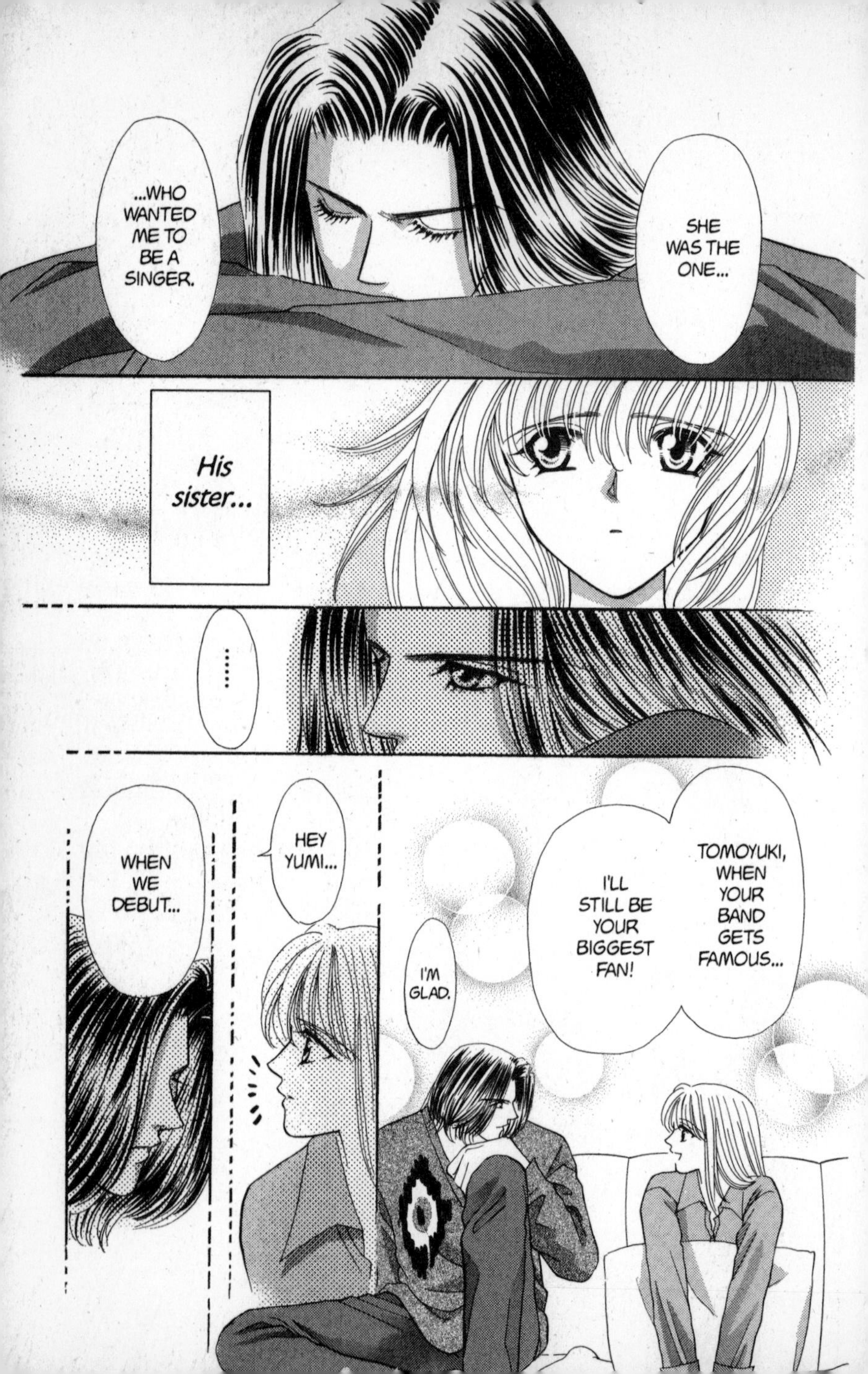
SHE WAS THE ONE...
...WHO WANTED ME TO BE A SINGER.
His sister...
......
TOMOYUKI, WHEN YOUR BAND GETS FAMOUS...
I'LL STILL BE YOUR BIGGEST FAN!
I'M GLAD.
HEY YUMI...
WHEN WE DEBUT...

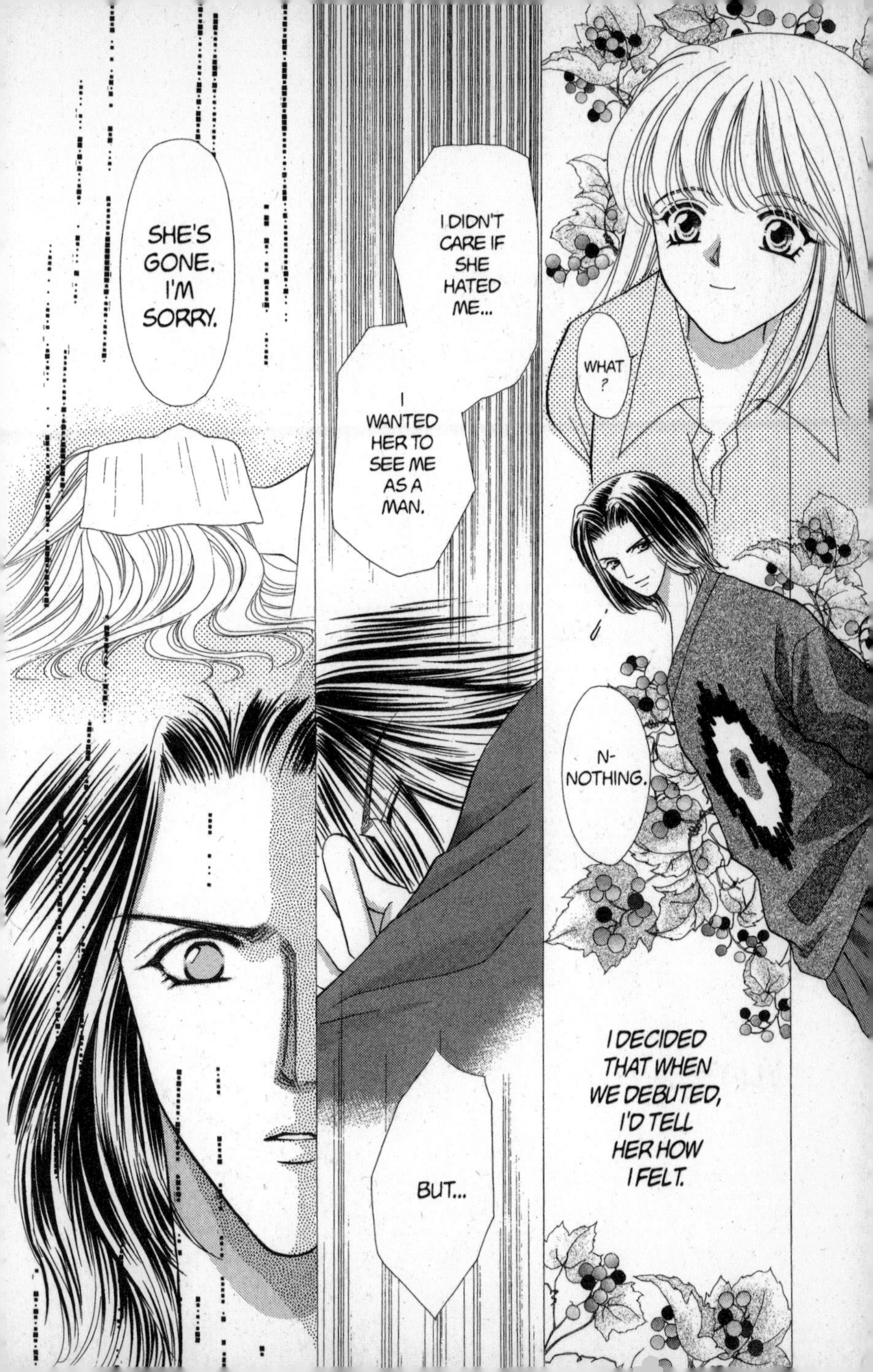
WHAT?
N-NOTHING.
I DECIDED THAT WHEN WE DEBUTED, I'D TELL HER HOW I FELT.
I DIDN'T CARE IF SHE HATED ME...
I WANTED HER TO SEE ME AS A MAN.
BUT...
SHE'S GONE. I'M SORRY.

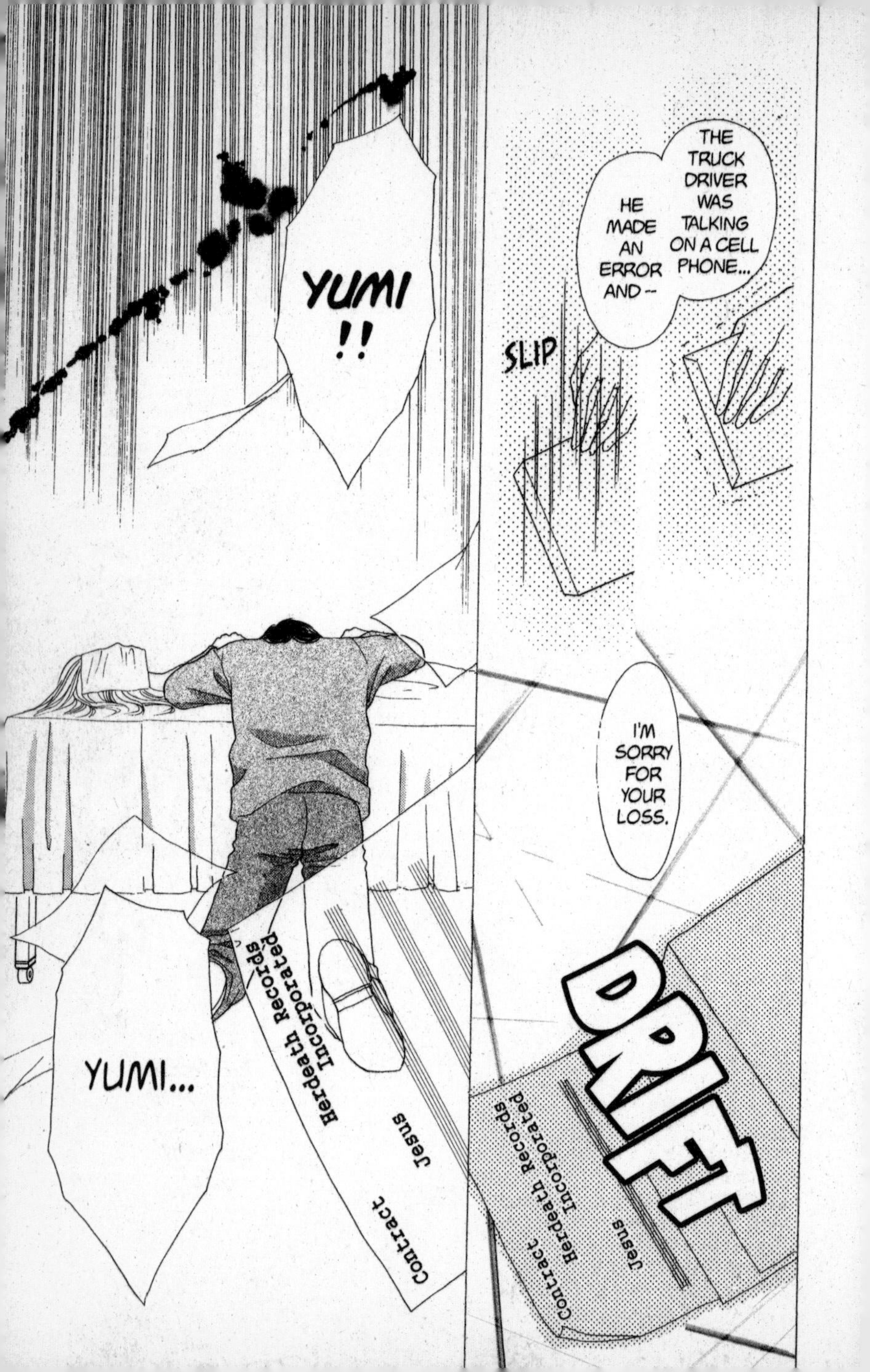
THE TRUCK DRIVER WAS TALKING ON A CELL PHONE...
HE MADE AN ERROR AND --
SLIP
I'M SORRY FOR YOUR LOSS.
DRIFT
Contract
Herdeath Records Incorporated
Jesus
YUMI !!
Herdeath Records Incorporated
Jesus
Contract
YUMI...

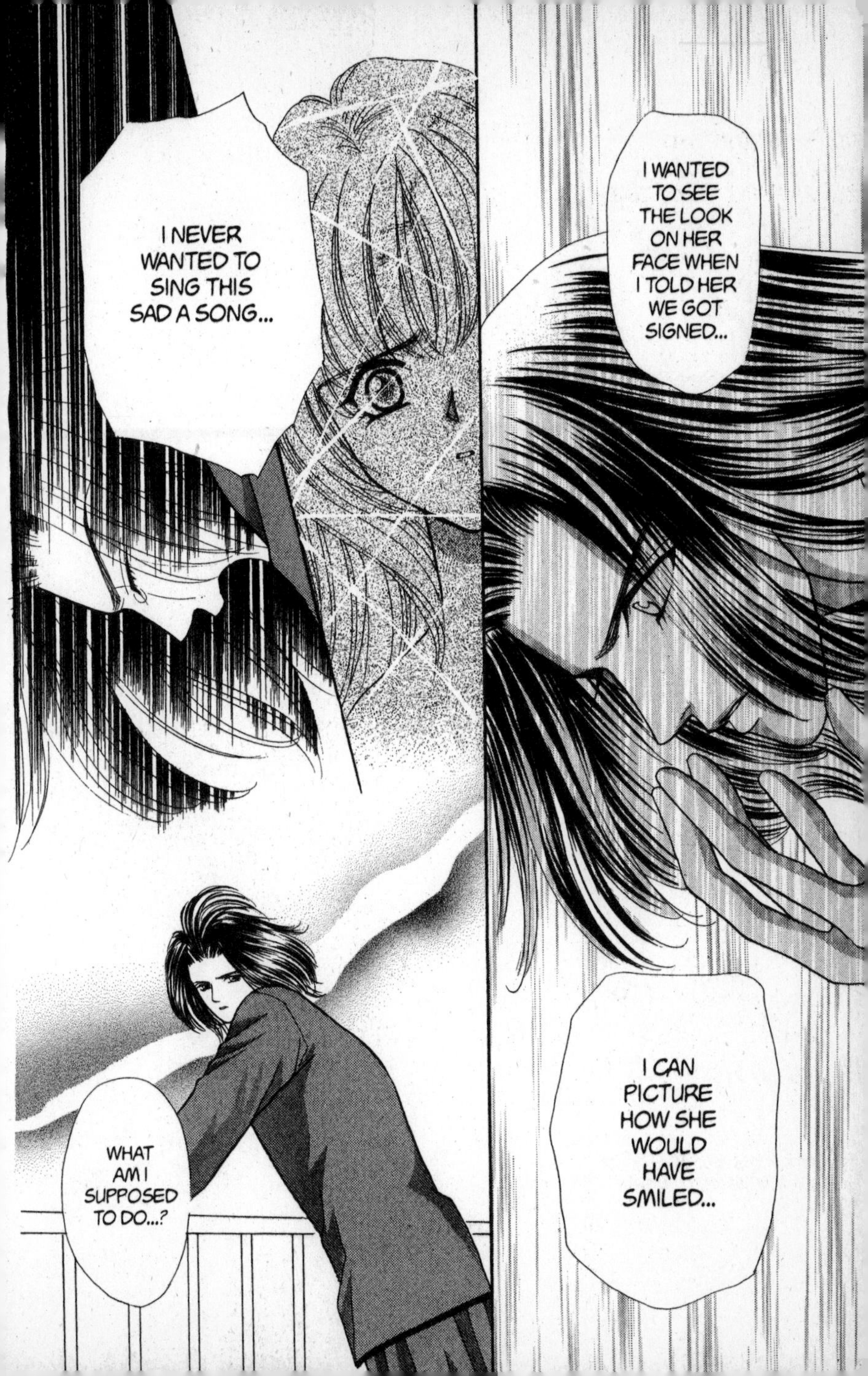
I WANTED TO SEE THE LOOK ON HER FACE WHEN I TOLD HER WE GOT SIGNED...
I CAN PICTURE HOW SHE WOULD HAVE SMILED...
I NEVER WANTED TO SING THIS SAD A SONG...
WHAT AM I SUPPOSED TO DO...?

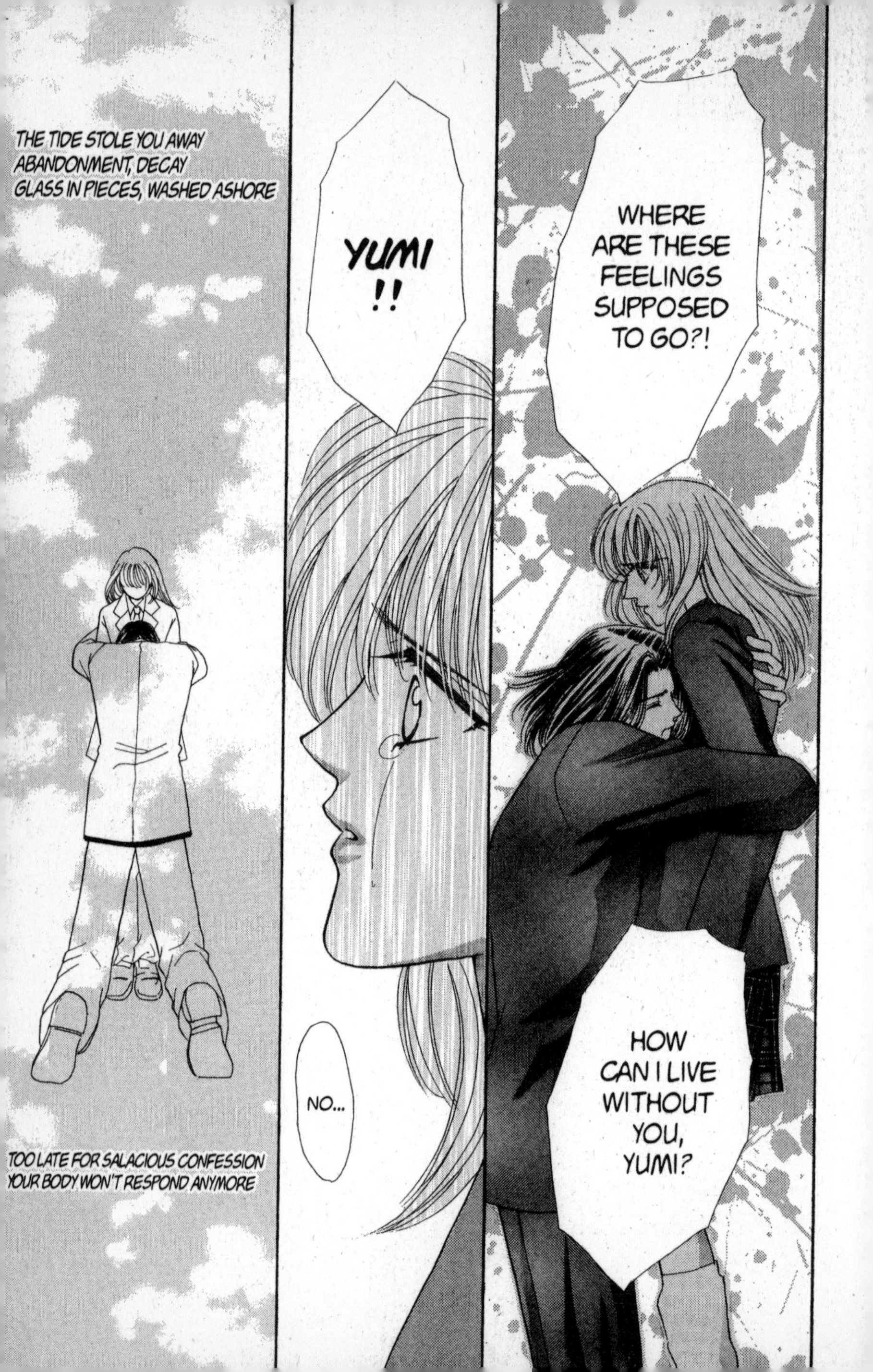
WHERE ARE THESE FEELINGS SUPPOSED TO GO?!
HOW CAN I LIVE WITHOUT YOU, YUMI?
YUMI !!
NO...
THE TIDE STOLE YOU AWAY
ABANDONMENT, DECAY
GLASS IN PIECES, WASHED ASHORE
TOO LATE FOR SALACIOUS CONFESSION
YOUR BODY WON'T RESPOND ANYMORE

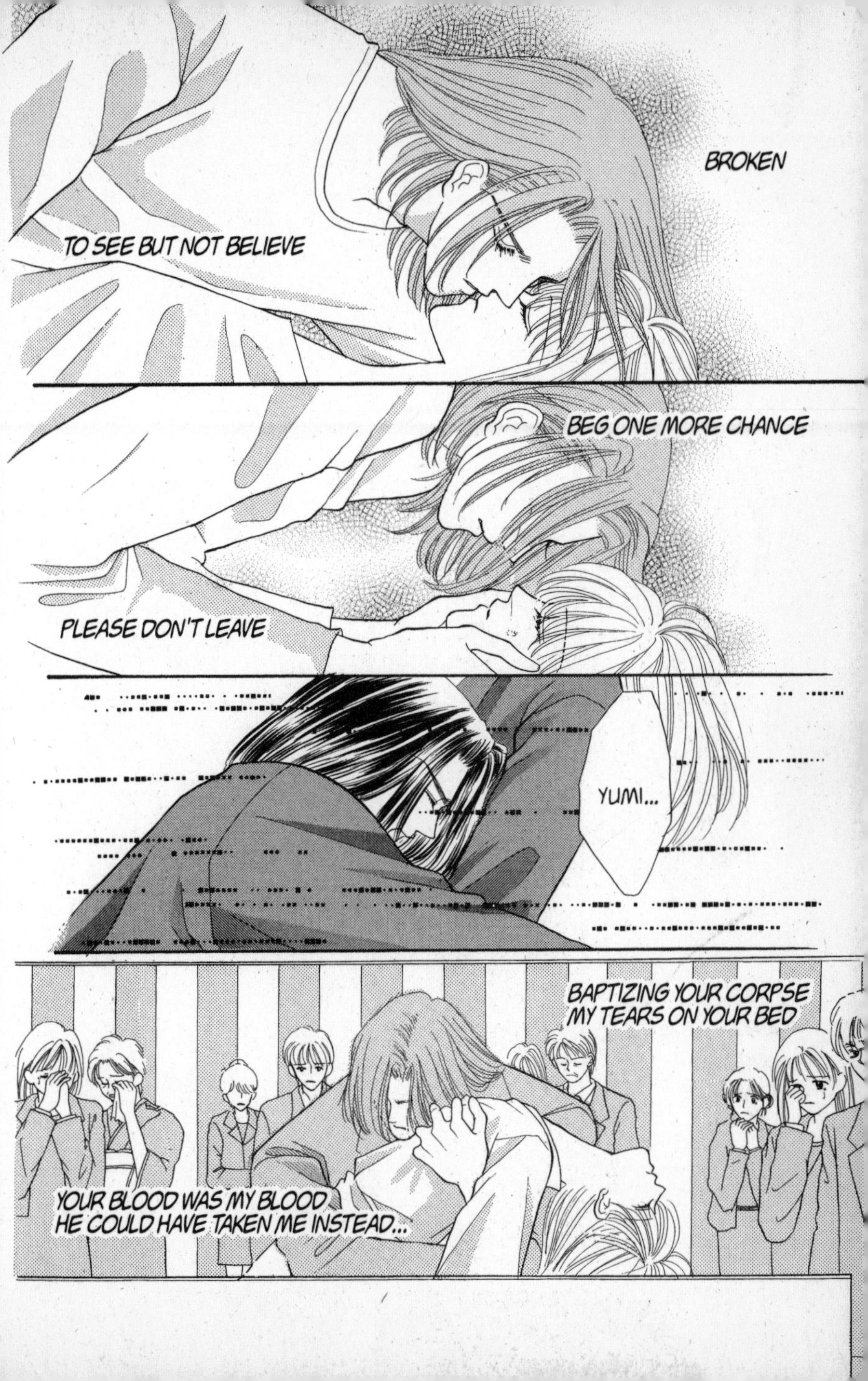
BROKEN
TO SEE BUT NOT BELIEVE
BEG ONE MORE CHANCE
PLEASE DON'T LEAVE
YUMI...
BAPTIZING YOUR CORPSE
MY TEARS ON YOUR BED
YOUR BLOOD WAS MY BLOOD
HE COULD HAVE TAKEN ME INSTEAD...

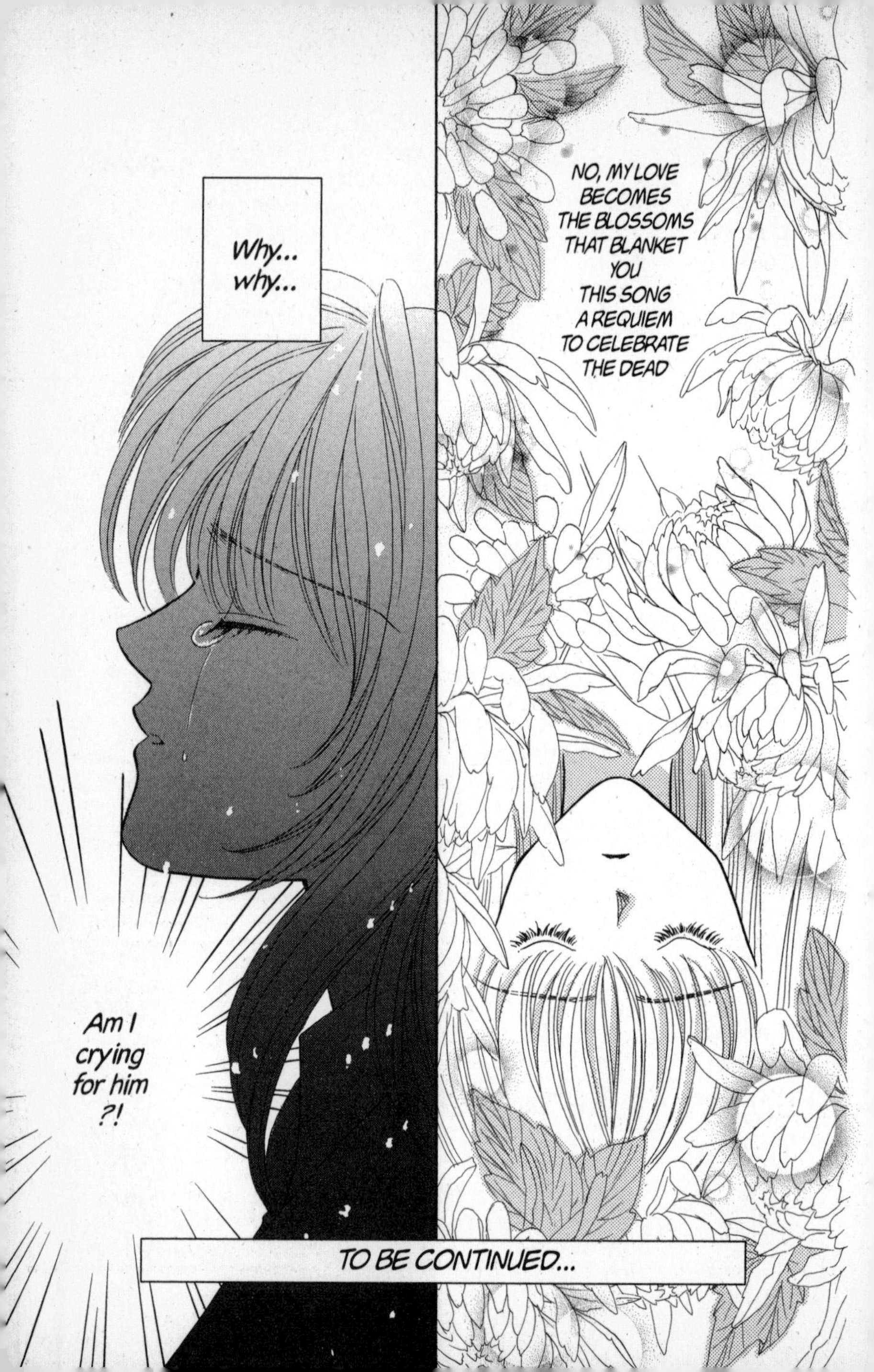
NO, MY LOVE BECOMES THE BLOSSOMS THAT BLANKET YOU THIS SONG A REQUIEM TO CELEBRATE THE DEAD
Why... why...
Am I crying for him ?!
TO BE CONTINUED...

YOSHIHIKO NAGAI (22) - SANTA -

(Likes)
Color: Yellow.
Season: Summer.
Cigarette: Lucky Strike.
Food: Chinese, Ramen.
Drink: Beer.
Movie: Tarantino flicks.
Phrase: "Pain is temporary, glory is forever, and chicks dig scars."
Town: Sangenjaya, Shimokitazawa.
I'm happiest: When I'm napping.
Designers: None in particular.
Bands: Aerosmith, Metallica, Pearl Jam.
Sports: Swimming.
Favorite Feature: My eyes.

(Dislikes)
Food: Fish eggs (ikura, caviar, etc..).
People: Gloomy people, people who take themselves too seriously.

(Personality)
Grand, but unrefined. Spontaneous and clumsy. Likes to make people laugh. Happy.
Hobby: Driving.
Weakness: Tear-jerkers.
Born: Christmas day.

Favorite Subject: P.E.
Least Favorite Subject: English.
Fave Place to Relax: A Bar.
How you spend time off: Outdoors with friends.
What you want most: Time.
Gift you like receiving: CDs.
Habits: I have a nervous habit of scratching my head.
How long does it take you to get ready in the morning: Twenty minutes.
Girls you like: Happy women.
Girls you hate: Gloomy Gerties.
Thoughts on marriage: If it's the right person, right away.
Ideal family: One filled with laughter. I want lots of kids.
What are you like when you're drunk?: Unintelligible.

(Thoughts on your band-mates)
Atsuro: Cute and honest. He's actually quite manly (ha!) but sometimes - since I'm a perv - I wish he was a girl.
Sakuya: Born to sing and womanize. Why does he get all the girls??
Yuki: Completely my opposite. Clean, sensitive, classy and quiet.
Towa: His bass is powerful. I don't quite get 'im.

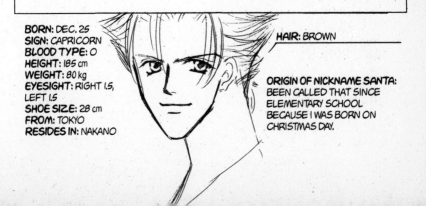

BORN: DEC. 25
SIGN: CAPRICORN
BLOOD TYPE: O
HEIGHT: 185 cm
WEIGHT: 80 kg
EYESIGHT: RIGHT 1.5, LEFT 1.5
SHOE SIZE: 28 cm
FROM: TOKYO
RESIDES IN: NAKANO

HAIR: BROWN

ORIGIN OF NICKNAME SANTA: BEEN CALLED THAT SINCE ELEMENTARY SCHOOL BECAUSE I WAS BORN ON CHRISTMAS DAY.

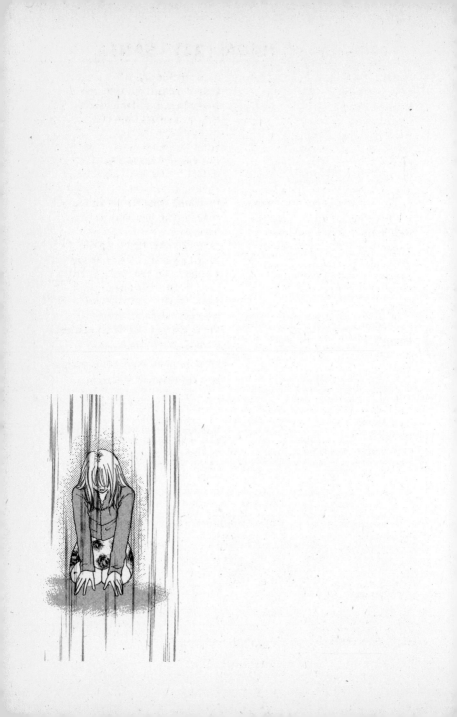

Satanic Verses
Kelly Sue DeConnick

Hello. My name is Kelly Sue DeConnick. I am 33 years old and I have a picture of Sakuya on my desktop. Please kill me.

It was never supposed to be like this. I openly mock other people for things *just like this*. I enjoy the mocking. I am good at it. It is one of my many talents.

As a professional in the comics industry, I am required to attend conventions. At said conventions, there are a great many opportunities for me to exercise my special gift for derision. I see grown women discuss important matters such as What Is Life Like For A Furry Klingon? And Which X-Man Would Be Better in Bed? And I think: YOU GIANT NERD. I whisper snarky comments to my compatriots. I whisper because I am very, very afraid of the furry Klingons and I do not want them to beat me up. Because I do not own a green velvet cloak and because every die in my house has a mere six sides, I am convinced I am in some way superior. I am cute, and I am cool, and I am right.

Or I was. And then *this*.

This book that you now hold in your hand has been my undoing. It has led me down that shame-paved highway of humiliation. Somewhere between volume one and volume six (which I'm currently adapting) my husband started referring to Sakuya as "your boyfriend." I developed a crush on a cartoon. I installed Sakuya wallpaper and I became my own enemy. Damn you, Mayu Shinjo! You insidious panderer!

I know you know what I'm talking about, so don't even *try* to play me. You know how I know? Because this book you're holding in your hand is volume four. And you bought it. At the very least, you borrowed it. And I'd lay money that you bought or borrowed volumes one, two and three, too. And if you've come this far, baby, then you feel my pain. You're reading the end essay! You know what that means? That means you finished the book and you still wanted more! If you haven't already, at some point soon you too will seek out Sensual Phrase wallpaper for *your* desktop. You'll start to think maybe Aine isn't such a ridiculous caricature after all. You'll tell your friends, "Okay, I know it's goofy, but it's really, really fun. And it's addictive." And you'll be right. It is goofy. And it is really, really fun. And dammit – it's *hot*.

So what am I saying here? I was wrong to mock the furry Klingons. I mean, okay – they're kind of creepy, sure. But hey, everybody has an Achilles Heel of Nerd-dom. Maybe you shake your booty to your collection of ABBA b-sides? Maybe that guy's into X-Men? Me? I apparently like fictional, vaguely misogynistic Japanese rock stars. Who knew?

Hello. My name is Kelly Sue DeConnick. I am 33 years old and I have a picture of Sakuya on my desktop. And soon? I hope you will, too.

Kelly Sue DeConnick is responsible for the English adaptation of *Sensual Phrase*. She also works on the titles *Descendants of Darkness*, *Kare First Love* and *Blue Spring*. She lives in Kansas City and can be contacted c/o VIZ.

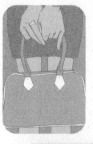
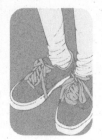
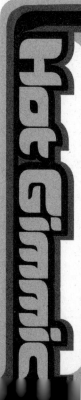
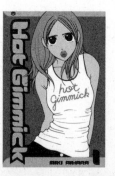

Collection

Complete your Angel Sanctuary collection—
buy the manga and art book today
at store.viz.com!

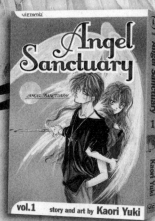

**Read the epic saga
of forbidden love from the start—
the 20-volume manga series
now available.**

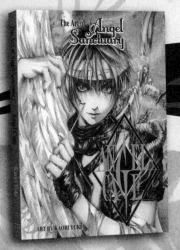

**A hardcover collection of illustrations
from manga volumes 1-8,
plus character info and an exclusive
interview with creator Kaori Yuki.**

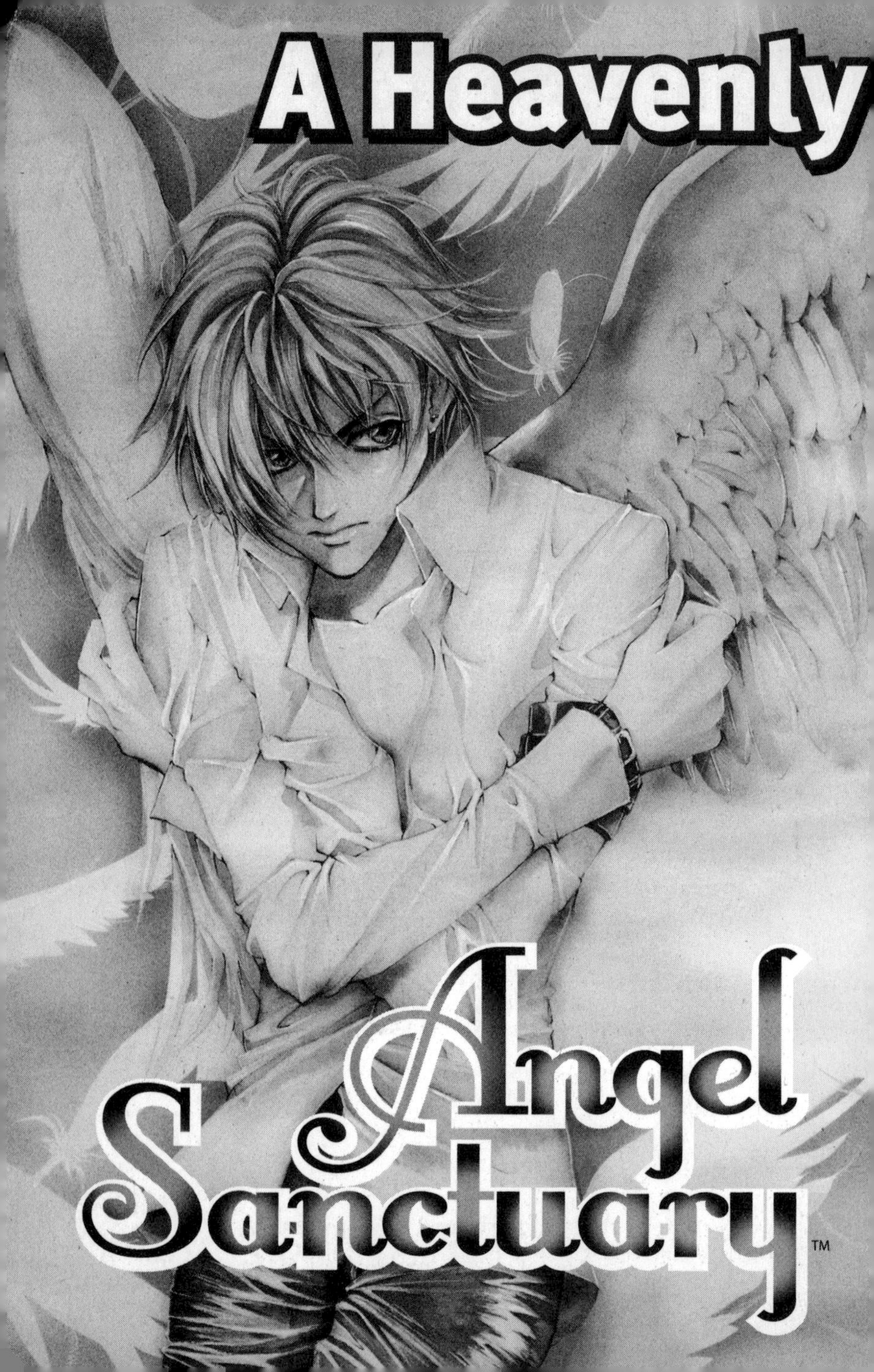
A Heavenly
Angel
Sanctuary™

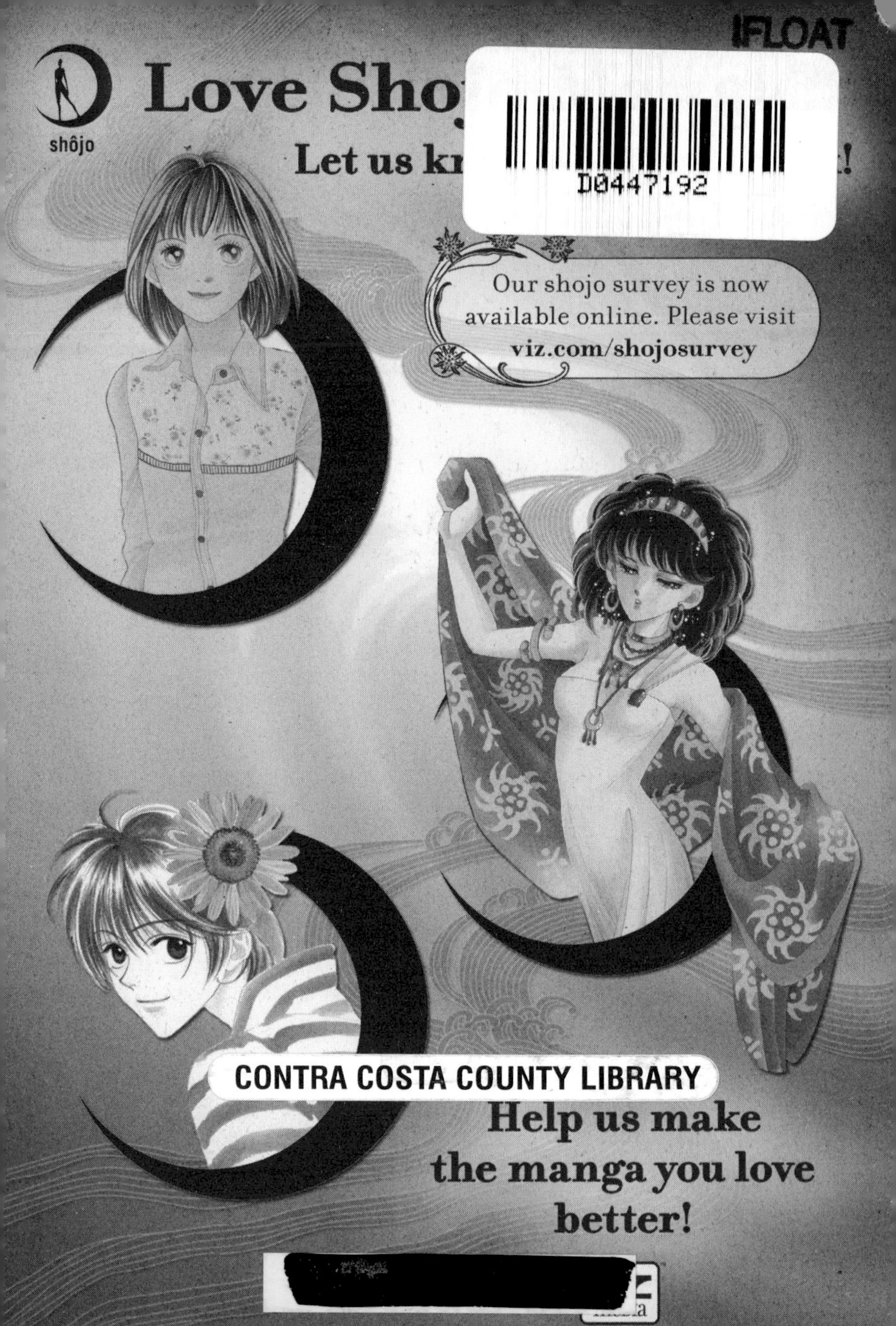

IFLOAT
shôjo
Love Sho
Let us kn
!
D0447192
Our shojo survey is now available online. Please visit viz.com/shojosurvey
CONTRA COSTA COUNTY LIBRARY
Help us make the manga you love better!
[redacted]